Once a Dancer . . .

University Press of Florida

Florida A&M University, Tallahassee
Florida Atlantic University, Boca Raton
Florida Gulf Coast University, Ft. Myers
Florida International University, Miami
Florida State University, Tallahassee
New College of Florida, Sarasota
University of Central Florida, Orlando
University of Florida, Gainesville
University of North Florida, Jacksonville
University of South Florida, Tampa
University of West Florida, Pensacola

Once a Dancer . . .

AN AUTOBIOGRAPHY

ALLEGRA KENT

UNIVERSITY PRESS OF FLORIDA
Gainesville · Tallahassee · Tampa · Boca Raton
Pensacola · Orlando · Miami · Jacksonville · Ft. Myers · Sarasota

14   13   12   11   10   09   6   5   4   3   2   1

Stars and Stripes, Bugaku, The Seven Deadly Sins, Diamonds, A Midsummer Night's Dream, Agon, Serenade, Episodes, La Sonnambula, Swan Lake, Brahms-Schoenberg Quartet, Jeux d'Enfants, and *Gounod Symphony*, choreography by George Balanchine © The George Balanchine Trust

Balanchine is a trademark of The George Balanchine Trust

Ivesiana, choreography by George Balanchine, courtesy of Edward Bigelow

Symphony in C, choreography by George Balanchine, courtesy of John Taras

The author wishes to thank all the photographers who have generously allowed their work to be reprinted: Richard Avedon, Radford Bascome, Lansing Brown, Gayle Corkery, Fred Fehl, Steve Maguire, Hank O'Neal, Gordon Parks, Bert Stern, Martha Swope.

Title page: photo by Bert Stern
Book design by Pei Loi Koay
Photo insert by Charles Rue Woods

A record of cataloging-in-publication data is available from the Library of Congress.
ISBN 978-0-8130-3440-9

The University Press of Florida is the scholarly publishing agency for the State University System of Florida, comprising Florida A&M University, Florida Atlantic University, Florida Gulf Coast University, Florida International University, Florida State University, New College of Florida, University of Central Florida, University of Florida, University of North Florida, University of South Florida, and University of West Florida.

University Press of Florida
15 Northwest 15th Street
Gainesville, FL 32611-2079
http://www.upf.com

For my dearest children, Trista, Susannah, and Bret,
and grandchildren, Miranda and Georgia,
and
in loving memory of my parents,
Shirley and Harry

Contents

CONTENTS

# Acknowledgments

I wish to thank Mindy Aloff, Nancy Bielski, Nina and Marshall Brickman, Nancy Conroy, Henley Haslam, Kristina Lindbergh, Clinton Luckett, Rosalie O'Connor, Carol Paumgarten, Wendy Perron, and Suzy Pilarre for their friendship and encouragement. Graceful sprays of larkspur to Linda Keep Atkins, who believed in this project and thought I could do it. Bending bows to Susan Sutliff Brown, who taught me how to tell my story. Gratitude to Sandra McCormick, who acquired the first edition of this book, and to Meredith Babb, who was enthusiastic about re-publishing it. My thanks to Bert Stern for his photographs and his generous and artistic support. Deepest appreciation to Faith Hamlin, my dynamic and gracious agent, who loved my dancing and encouraged me to write my story. And special thanks to Bob Gottlieb, a true master of the sentence, whose inspiring insights, guidance and expertise have meant so much for me.

As a child, I knew I had one great possession: my body. It was little and quick. I lived within it. I looked out of it with my eyes, my irises, and that was also my name, Iris—like the flower, like the rainbow, and like my eyes. I'd wake up in the morning, excited, ready to go out and look at the world. Breakfast would only slow me down. I wanted to leap into the empty lots outside our windows just as soon as I could and see what had happened overnight. I'd say to my mother, "I love life!" As an adult, I met people who talked passionately about their new Rolls-Royce. But that isn't a real possession. All we actually have is our body and its muscles that allow us to be under our own power, to glide in the water, to roll down a hill, and to jump into someone's arms.

PART ONE

1 9 3 7 – 1 9 4 7

From Iris to Allegra

Clockwise from top left: Harry Cohen, father; Shirley, mother, with Barbara, Gary, and Iris; Gary and Iris; Iris.

CHAPTER ONE

I suppose we are what we are because of our parents.

—RUMER GODDEN,
A TIME TO DANCE, NO TIME TO WEEP

O**ne** day my father introduced my brother and me to a tall stranger wearing a flannel shirt and straw hat. He was lean and lanky and seemed to be Daddy's long-lost friend.

"Iris and Gary, come over here and meet Buddy. He's going to drive you and your mother to Miami Beach, the land of palm trees." As usual, Daddy wasn't coming with us.

Gary and I didn't say hello, but Gary managed to shake hands; we were shy and very young. I was almost three and Gary was four.

Buddy gave us a bright smile. "Hello, kids. Now I don't want you to worry. This trip won't be boring, and it won't take too long."

Buddy didn't lie. We streaked across America without stopping. No overnight rests, just continuous driving by a madman. While Mother leaned over from the front seat to quiet us, from the backseat of our old brown jalopy Gary and I cheered Buddy on, yelling, "Let's go faster!" We weren't afraid of passing a slow car or falling off the side of a mountain. In our family, imagined dangers held more reality. Looking out the window, I had terrible thoughts when it got dark. Daddy wasn't with us. There were unknown perils. Who was going to protect me at night? I tapped my brother's arm. Gary was one and a half years older, my big brother. "Gary, do you think there are tigers out there?"

Gary paused, carefully thinking. He looked concerned. "No. There're no tigers in America. But there could be wolves and bears."

This was not the first time Daddy had hired a stranger to drive us across the country. These drivers usually liked to speed, probably because Daddy had invariably met them at the racetrack over the previous few days. Speed was a family characteristic.

While thousands of little girls were moving in and out of the five dance positions, having their hair fetchingly pinned up, and looking in the mirror while putting on miniature pieces of glitter, ruffles, and tulle for recitals, I was either zooming across America in the backseat of a car, collecting shells on the beach wearing a boy's bathing suit, or roaming through vacant lots. I yearned for a girl's bathing suit, but my pleas were ignored. I hadn't been civilized, and, when I did begin dance lessons, little in my life had prepared me for formal training. My brother and I weren't brought up. We haphazardly grew a little taller and a little older in California, Texas, and Florida.

My mother was a wanderer, and her restlessness and discontent kept us moving. For her, relocation was like a new love affair: it was much better to imagine than to know. We traveled through the South and Southwest in search of what she called "better living conditions." We had very few possessions—no furniture, books, or winter coats. Everything we had could easily be thrown into one footlocker and shipped ahead. We could outdistance the problems of a particular geographic location by getting in an automobile or boarding a train and quickly building up a barrier of miles. Thousands of miles were best. We would exchange one expanse of great ocean for another. A beach became our new living room, the crashing surf our radio, and old problems would be solved—at least for a while. We could buy bathing suits and get library cards anywhere.

Although my parents didn't officially divorce until I was five, they rarely lived together. When we did live near Daddy, or even with him, it never lasted. To Mother, Harry was like one of her journeys— a fresh start and a trap. Soon my maritime mother would decide it was time to leave, usually for another coast and the allure of a new sea.

When we weren't speeding to a new home in a car driven by Daddy or a stranger, we took a train. Once, during World War II when rail reservations were impossible to get, we boarded a train that was ready to split off into a smaller version of itself. Naturally, we were in the wrong half, the part that wouldn't take us to our destination. There was no room in the correct half. Mother started to beg, cry, and plead with the conductor. Couldn't he somehow squeeze us into a little space? He finally did find one upper berth, and Gary, Mother, and I dashed out of the wrong part of the train to wedge ourselves into one cramped upper berth seconds before the train divided. We were on our way to a new home. Mother was convinced that we might latch on to some special happiness if we could only be in the right location at the right moment.

An unfamiliar location might present an unusual challenge, but Mother lived by her wits. One time, as we entered a newly rented apartment, Mother gave us special instructions. The manager did not allow Jews in his building. Being Jewish was our secret, and we must not talk about it. Mother's message was taken to heart. Gary and I knew how to be very, very quiet when necessary, because a place to live was of the utmost importance.

I was born Iris Margo Cohen, the daughter of Harry Herschel Cohen of Texas (who liked to substitute "Cowboy" for Herschel) and Shirley Weissman, originally of the shtetl of Wisznice, Poland. When I was two, after we had been turned away by a landlord yet again, my mother dropped our last name and replaced it with one of her own choosing. Our new name was Kent. I was too young to notice that there had been a change, but when I was a little older I was taught that there was some enormous disgrace attached to my father's last name and we must be silent about it.

Even as children, both of my parents had searched for ways to escape their pasts. Daddy's family had bought land just outside of Dallas, but Dallas fooled them and moved the town the wrong way. They were brokenhearted. At fourteen, Harry ran away from home and began traveling throughout the Southwest transported by fantasies of fortunes and fame. Wearing a wide-brimmed cowboy hat to go with the name "Harry Cowboy Cohen," he wildcatted in the Texas oil fields and dabbled in amateur boxing. By twenty-five, he had formed a business and started to manufacture caps, making nearly a quarter of a million dollars that he then lost in the Crash of '29. But he was certain he would make it back.

Daddy had extraordinary posture. When walking, he pulled himself upward and broadened his shoulders. His gait could be called a swagger. During Prohibition, Harry and his cousin set up a scam with prescriptions, filling them with alcohol. They were caught, and the judge said one of them had to go to jail for eight months. Harry volunteered, for he was the younger. In jail, one of the inmates, a lifer, painted Daddy's portrait as a strikingly handsome man with olive skin and hazel eyes. The painting is still hanging in my brother's San

Fernando Valley home. Dearest Daddy would soon get out—the lifer never would. Harry looks proudly out of his picture, but this was a sobering moment for him. Life could very easily go very wrong.

Mother hated her family's first tenement dwelling on New York's Lower East Side. Because her mother and father hadn't learned English, Mother felt neither European nor American; she was ashamed of her parents. At one point, her family moved over a funeral parlor. The sight of tiny padded coffins for children haunted my mother for years. Dreaming of ways to escape, she borrowed a neighbor's working papers and took a job at twelve. By fourteen, she was teaching ballroom dancing at night in someone's private home, mostly to Japanese men. When Philip Leavitt asked her to marry him—and threatened to commit suicide if she refused—she said yes. It was 1927. The marriage faltered from the start. Nevertheless, Shirley had a baby right away, my sister Barbara. After five years, Mother temporarily moved to Chicago, worked six weeks to pay for a divorce, and was introduced to Harry Cohen, my father, at a party.

There was something about my mother that captivated my father, and, soon after their first meeting, Daddy sent Shirley train tickets for her and Barbara. He was waiting for them at the station in Shreveport, Louisiana, with a car full of toys. My sister and mother were entranced and rhapsodic. This man knew how to touch a child's heart, and in a letter to Mother he had written, "U are the most beautiful person in the whole world." At last she was loved and appreciated, she thought—although she didn't like the way Harry spelled "you."

Harry proposed, and Mother agreed. She said it was the most thrillingly wonderful day in her life. It was 1934, and Mother didn't know who Harry really was, but the externals looked perfectly lovely. Harry had a dress business and was living in a large house on the best street in Dallas. There were separate servants' quarters, four hundred fruit trees, and a horse. Now there would be a superabundance of everything, even the nonessentials.

Although one of Harry's relatives told Mother that Harry was "unstable," Mother preferred to disregard this alarming message. At the end of a week, Shirley became Mrs. Cohen and met the real Harry, the restless man who would wake her up in the middle of the night so they could drive to no particular place and back again. He had absolutely no tolerance for everyday frustration even at its lowest level; when life at home became too difficult or boring for him, Harry would leave for the track. Mother became pregnant immediately, and, during the pregnancy, she had to flee with Harry in the middle of the night because of an unpaid gambling debt. She threw up every mile on the way to Corpus Christi. They had to wait for weeks until it was safe to return to Dallas.

The reality of a family was not something Harry could visualize. He had a gambler's soul and a restless nature. After a year of marriage to Harry, Mother was living in an attic apartment in a poor section of town, and her baby was nearly due. Harry said he had an important business meeting in Los Angeles, and to make things easier for Shirley, he would take Barbara with him. What drew him to Los Angeles was the Rose Bowl game of 1936. When he arrived, he deposited her with my mother's relatives and went to the game, picking her up only as he was about to return to Dallas. While he was away, Mother had fallen down the stairs. Nevertheless, Gary arrived on February 7, 1936, and nine months later, another baby was started. After the first missed period Mother took something strong, but it didn't work. I was on my way.

Harry stayed in Texas and sent Mother to her family in California for my birth. I was born on August 11, 1937, on the very day Edith Wharton died, but in a different time zone. Daddy came to see me ten months later. By then, the oil fields had proved to be a complete and total loss, and Harry was deeply in debt. Perhaps the new infant would save the family. However, I wasn't a smiling baby. Mother was profoundly depressed, and I must have sensed that.

As the dislocation and desperation that filled my mother's life quickly filtered down to me, I became very sick. At this time it was the style to teach babies discipline and get them in touch early with a schedule. The theory was that if you held a baby too much, you could spoil her. Mom brought me to Shirley Temple's doctor because I had pus on the kidneys. He said there was nothing he could do; things looked hopeless. As a last resort I could be taken to a clinic where they would experiment. While he was giving this gloomy opinion, Mom started to pat my back. The doctor looked at my mother, startled. "Stop being so nice to that baby. You'll spoil her!" Could you be too nice to a dying baby? Apparently you could.

Through a new friend, Mother heard of Christian Science, and I was saved through the prayer of a Christian Science practitioner. Mother had found our new religion.

In the meantime Harry was still seeking his fortune in the oil fields, and, when a landlord put us out, Mother relocated us with two cribs and a footlocker, pawning what she could and giving the rest away. Travel light, keep nothing, deny the importance of possessions because they have no life, no truth, no substance; they're only matter. She adapted this Christian Science teaching to her packing. As we left one location for another, she discarded the excess, particularly any objects that took up space. A doll had to be given away because there was no room in the trunk; however, the tiny ones could stay, the storybook dolls, the ones that came to life and action in fairy tales and books. These were the ones I really loved.

In 1939, after we had to leave what Mother called "a dump" on a dead-end street in Santa Monica, Harry found an inexpensive hovel way out somewhere in rural California. He was leaving town immediately for a deal in Chicago, so he asked Mother's brother, Ben, to drive us there. The place had a dirt floor, two burners on an egg crate, and almost nothing else. When Ben started to set up the cribs, Mother began to sob. At the insistence of his new wife, Ben dismantled the beds and found us another place near Lake Elsinore, a lake with a high sulfur content and dead fish floating on the surface. We would sneak into a country club to partake of the green grass and pool. Mother wondered what was over the mountains and was told that it was Laguna Beach. The vowels had a magical ring. She loved the sound of it, and eventually we moved out of Elsinore and hitched a ride over the mountains to the seashore. The beach and ocean would sustain us.

The place Mother found in Laguna Beach was a cheap, rat-infested apartment over a grocery store. We had to vacate when the place was sold, and Mother wired Harry, who was in Dallas, to come fetch us. The appointed day arrived, but Harry didn't. Mother finally asked the lifeguard to help disassemble the cribs, and while this was taking place, Harry walked in. He greeted the lifeguard with warmth, appreciation, and no suspicion, and we all piled into a brown jalopy, the vehicle that took us everywhere before it finally failed inspection. This time we were off to Texas, living again on a dead-end street.

Months later, back in California, my family was hoping that its youngest member would become the breadwinner. Daddy had learned there was a search going on for a toddler to play an important role in a film. The irises in Daddy's eyes lit up. I was brought to a casting agent, who approved of my looks, and a screen test was scheduled. The infant was going to be sent to work.

Daddy took me to the studio. Up to this time he had barely been able to acknowledge me, my birth, or my development. But now we were together on a little jaunt. Jubilantly, Daddy realized that his Iris could be an ace in the hole. Once on the set I pursed my lips, looked sullen, and boldly stared everyone down. I was acting, all right, but with overt hostility to the grown-up world. I was frightened to death. And I was mad at my parents. The baby wanted to be a baby. They gave me toys, ice cream, and candy, but I couldn't be bribed. I knew grown-ups gave only when they wanted something back. Dejectedly, my father brought me home. Clearly I was a failure in his eyes, and in Mother's too. Life looked a little bleak.

The next day, Mother took us out for an ice cream, a great treat not often affordable. I refused. I pointed to a crimson bloom in the florist shop next door. I wanted a flower I hadn't seen before, and I cried until my mother bought it for me. I clutched it until it died.

Right from the beginning, there was a conflict of interest about what the family wanted for me and what I wanted for myself.

CHAPTER TWO

For a salesman, there is no rock bottom to the life. . . .
He's a man way out there in the blue, riding on a smile
and a shoeshine. . . . A salesman is got to dream. . . . It
comes with the territory.

—ARTHUR MILLER,
DEATH OF A SALESMAN

Every year my schoolroom was at a different end of America—
Miami, then Los Angeles, then back to Florida. My first touch with
formal education occurred in Miami Beach when I was four. My
mother sent me to a small private school where I was the only person
in my grade. Actually, my grade didn't exist; the school was just baby-
sitting for my mother. There was absolutely no chance to make friends
in my class of one person, and I would sit at a picnic table by myself
and copy words into a notebook. After a long while the teacher would
return and look at my pages. There was nothing to see in it except a
young child's lack of interest. I did not want to copy my teacher's
words.

What did interest me was creating dolls and tiny toys. I presented
my mother with two nails and a long length of string, tools for knitting, and I was a little hurt when she rejected my equipment. In
revenge, I never did learn to knit, but I became a furious crocheter,
making yarn dolls with tufted heads and fringy feet. Mother taught
me to sew, adding an alarming warning. She said if you left a needle
in the bed, it could puncture your skin, enter your bloodstream, and
eventually pierce your heart. The death Mother described terrified
me. I visualized every step of it and was sure that you wouldn't feel
the needle at first. When alone, I used to think that if I could only
ask God one question, it would be, "Is there a needle traveling around
in my body right at this moment?" I needed to know because I hadn't
been careful enough with the needles. At bedtime Mother used to
shake out the bed to allay my fears, but it wasn't enough. Nothing

was enough. Perhaps there was a needle in the mattress, left there accidentally in the factory. In the dark, the needle would start to travel up to me through the mattress and enter my skin. I was four years old, and night and darkness became a terror. This was the first of a variety of phobias—including stage fright—that I would develop over the years.

The days, however, were filled with exploring my surroundings with Gary. For years, the closest relationship I had in the world was with him. He was very mature, I thought, because he crossed streets so beautifully and always saw things before I did. We discovered the purple orchid and the dancing string bean tree in Florida, the huge cactus in Texas, and the avocado in California. There was nothing so beautiful to me as red roses—they were exotic in Florida, and their vivid, velvet beauty was perfection itself—and occasionally Gary stole one from someone's backyard. He understood my love. At the beach he had a keen eye for the unusual shell. Then I'd find one like it, but always smaller. I liked to wake up and look outside my window; soft morning light would be falling on the vacant lot next door. A fort my brother had built out of wood scraps, with some friends, was nestled under two tall trees with thick trunks.

I would run down three floors using the back steps, and there I was in my special backyard. Some little white flowers grew near the door, with five petals and a red center, but these did not interest me; they were too ordinary. I was looking for something unusual, a flower I'd never seen before or a beautiful "lost" object. Then I'd create a toy from whatever was there—a feather and a piece of leaf tied in tight embrace onto a stick. Vacant lots were my first thrift shop.

As we walked along Washington Avenue to the library, the palms made a wooden sound as their huge fronds hit each other. It was a warm night. There were many people out for a walk, and I could hear bits of their conversations. Mother was wearing a white sharkskin dress and talking to her best friend, Dorothy, about an officer she had met who was a writer. She seemed to know his whole life story. My mother would learn something and then discuss and discuss it with Dorothy. Everything she knew about someone was the topic of a conversation. I listened to some of it off and on. I never wanted to be discussed in this way. When we reached the library, some friends of Gary's were having a race on the wide sidewalk. I wanted to join them.

"Ready, on your mark, get set, go."

In the free dark expanse in front of me, I tried to move as quickly as I could, sending messages down to my legs—faster, faster. I felt a warm wind on my face and heard the rhythmic sound of my feet against the pavement. With more speed, I felt more air on my face and arms. I didn't come in first, but I wasn't last either. This was unimportant. I felt wonderful. I had done this alone, on my own, and I'd left my mother's conversations behind. I had traveled through the wind.

A boy came up to me and said, "Hello, little fast runner." Instantly, I fell in love.

By the time I was six, we were living out our childhoods at a rapid pace, racing through our young years. When Barbara was only twelve, she was playing the part of a twenty-two-year-old with the army's entertainment division in Miami Beach. We went to the park and sat outside to see her act in *The Eve of St. Mark.* Then, after an intermission, Barbara stuffed her bra with bust pads for the skit *Don't Put Your Daughter on the Stage, Mrs. Worthington,* which was also on the bill. I thought this was very funny.

Before the summer's heat arrived, we moved back to California and saw Daddy again. My parents were divorced now, but divorce meant nothing to Harry. His feelings for us were unchanged. Gary and I didn't notice a difference. We had no concept of divorce. How could we? We'd never formed a clear concept of marriage.

In the process of crisscrossing the country many times between 1941 and 1945, I missed first grade. Mother entered me in second grade. This was the beginning of a pattern. When I began to study ballet, Mother enrolled me in the intermediate classes. Without the beginning lessons, the basics eluded me.

Now I was finally in school, but not everything I learned was useful. In assembly, we were shown a lurid film on malaria in which mosquitoes slipped under doors and bit people during the night. I left school before dismissal and ran home.

At this time, we lived on another dead-end street in a rented house that had an oval bed of roses in the garden. The roses were the most wonderful thing, because it meant that Gary and I didn't have to steal flowers anymore. I could pick them whenever I wanted to and fall under their power and fragrance. However, I had developed a phobia about mosquitoes. I was afraid of dying at night. There was moment-by-moment danger in the world.

At the end of that school year, when we had to vacate our house and our next location had not yet been arranged, Mother sent me to live with a family near Azusa. After I ran away, Mother took me back home. Gary had been sent to a camp for asthmatics in Monrovia, although he may not have had asthma. Daddy drove all of us out one day to visit him. Gary was standing behind two fences with a six-foot space in between us. We could wave and talk but not touch; it was like a zoo cage for extremely wild animals. A few weeks later Gary came home, and for the first time, he liked vegetables. He was going to be good. We were both very desirous of pleasing Mother. She was all we had.

By the time I was ready for third and fourth grades, we had moved back to Florida. One sunny day, my mother picked Gary and me up from a movie at the Cameo Theater. Her triumphant look meant that she had done the impossible—found a one-bedroom apartment in Miami Beach in 1944. It was wartime, and no new buildings were going up. The three of us had arrived that morning. Barbara, fifteen, had stayed behind in California to study acting at the Pasadena Playhouse. As always, we had traveled light, without furniture or anything extraneous, but even with few clothes, we were always ready for the beach.

The furnished apartment was on the third floor at the end of a very long hall. I ran to the window and looked out at the vacant lot next door. I recognized it. My brother and I had built a fort there when we lived on the other side of it a year earlier.

Living in Miami this time, I was very aware of the war. The soldiers were stationed in waterfront hotels, and they conducted drills by singing. Newsreels in the theaters showed the devastation in Europe. The death and hunger of people far away made me understand that the world was enveloped in a terrifying battle.

As usual, at school I was an outsider. Quite early on, Mother had taught me to speak of Daddy in a disparaging way, so during my first day at Central Beach Elementary School when the other children asked me what my father did, I said, "I don't know, but he's a fool." My schoolmates were astonished to hear anyone not brag about her father.

Mother also encouraged letter-writing to Daddy, but mainly as a form of request. She bombarded Harry with mail, always keeping him informed of our whereabouts and our problems, asking for food, clothes, shoes, and little luxuries. She was fearful that he would forget us. Although Gary and I could write what we wanted, Mother always suggested that we include at least one sentence telling Daddy we were desperate for money. And also to send chocolates. We were low on our sugar coupons. Daddy responded to our requests. This was wonderful. Letters were miracles; I could send one anywhere.

Because of Mother's belief in Christian Science, we didn't go to doctors, but when I was eight, Mother took me to one in Miami Beach. I was terrified. He looked at my feet and made footprints. I had absolutely flat feet. He said that I needed a little arch support, and we put some in my shoes. The wedges bent my feet in an unusual way and they hurt, but it was necessary. In one month my arches had lifted. My footprints had a new shape, somewhat like a banana with five grapes on top, which meant a high instep. Coincidentally, I took my first ballet class.

I looked at them, and they looked at me, and then I shifted my gaze. The class consisted of girls about my age, all in identical uniforms except me. They were wearing white satin tunics with the initials G. M. embroidered in red on their chests. I was wearing shorts and a halter top and felt out of place. This would never work. Toward the end of the war when Harry had begun to prosper, Mother had searched out a Russian ballet school in Miami and enrolled me late in an already-formed intermediate class with George Milenoff. The training was traditional. I was sandwiched between two girls at the barre and tried to copy their movements. When Mr. Milenoff said, "Turn out in fifth position," I turned in, which to my mind created the same look. My body had the limberness to do this. What I did was very logical to me and still is—my toes were turning out. I had never seen ballet dancing before, and it struck me as pointless. In addition to disliking the rigidity of the movements and the pounding of Mr. Milenoff's stick to indicate tempo, I felt it unreasonable to twist my body into awkward positions. This peculiar study, at least as I understood it, held no interest for me. I asked to stop.

So while other little girls were learning to turn out, I was turning in different directions. Films were very important in my world. They were an escape from a hot afternoon. After seeing *Jane Eyre,* my tears would not stop for an hour and no one could console me. I saw the injustices in a world of terrible possibilities. A little girl had died in boarding school because her punishment was so cruel. I had been furious at the adults in the movie. They did horrible things. When Gary and I were older, we could choose our own movies. We saw them together during the afternoon at prices of nine to fourteen cents—*The Pirate, Leave Her to Heaven, Gilda, Spellbound, Sentimental Journey,* and *For Whom the Bell Tolls.*

In 1945, the war was over, and, like the soldiers, we were no longer to be stationed in Florida. My mother had a new plan. She would send Gary and me to boarding school in California so she could move to New York and help Barbara, who was lonely, with her acting career. My mother had always looked to California for new ways to heal the body, new religions, and new philosophies. She had studied the Bates eye exercises for improving her vision because it was the method followed by California intellectuals of poor eyesight, including Aldous Huxley, who was spending the war years there. At the same time, Mother had become fascinated with Krishnamurti, a popular guru who recently had found a second home in California. She became interested in a school based on his philosophy that was located in Ojai, California, but forgot its name, so she picked a different one at random in the same secluded valley seventy-two miles northwest of Los Angeles. The place Mother found was Ojai Valley School, a progressive boarding school for children in the third to ninth grades. Daddy would pay for it.

Out of the blue, or so it seemed to us, Mother took Gary and me back to California, where we saw my father again for the first time in a long while. "Well, hello there, little pretty girl." He didn't even call me by my name; he addressed me as if I were a stranger. Nevertheless, I fell in love with his gaiety.

Daddy had given up the more adventurous ways of earning a living and had become a traveling salesman. His home base was the Biltmore Hotel in downtown Los Angeles. Everyone there knew him and greeted him warmly, and he was all big smiles. Like a king in his own palace, he introduced us to elevator men, cleaning women, and some buyers. The Biltmore was now Harry's ranch. Here he could stay a cowboy and wear his wide-brimmed signature hats without criticism.

"Hi, Joe. I'd like you to meet my children, Iris and Gary," Daddy said to the elevator man on our way to Daddy's room.

"They are lovely children, Harry."

"Thank you. They are very smart kids." Mother was staying with her family for the night, and we were to stay with Harry.

His suite was a huge room with two double beds and three long racks filled with dresses hung very close together. This was his line of sportswear, Nardis of Dallas.

"It's like a store," I said gleefully, walking over to the dresses. The point of great interest to me were the swatches, the little booklets of different-colored fabrics that every dress had attached to a sleeve.

When he opened another door, a wave of fog came floating out of the gleaming white bathroom. When the mist cleared, I saw more dresses hanging on the shower-curtain rod. Daddy had steamed their wrinkles out. To save money he often traveled with the line in his car. Arriving from the road, he would take the clothes into the bathroom of his hotel room, steam the dresses straight, and show the new designs to a buyer in the hotel room. Mother told us his new profession was a job and entertainment all in one. He owned a hundred hats and changed them six times a day.

The next morning, Gary and I had breakfast alone, sitting in a huge booth in the dining room. The big booth and heavy hotel silver felt luxurious to us. It took us an hour to eat, because we picked over our food, carefully separating the egg whites from the yolks in our soft-boiled eggs. Maybe boarding school would be like this.

As we pulled into the curved driveway, I realized Ojai Valley School was not the magical place my mother had described but a group of buildings and schoolrooms built around a large square of dirt. The landscape looked dull and parched compared to the lush East. For the first time I was aware that the glamour could quickly rub off of Mother's tales. A photograph of me taken by my father, dressed like a mountain girl and leaning against a tree with one foot balanced on a rock, reveals an unhappy child, sulky and alone. I was nine, Gary, ten. Mother, whom I loved so much, was far away.

But this was not the moment to cry. Survival came first. After a few weeks, I built a secret fort from long wands of plant clippings and shrubs where I could stash food, because we weren't allowed to keep it in our rooms. I hated the food at the school and ate only small amounts, so I was always hungry. But to buy food, I needed money, and my weekly allowance was only thirty-five cents. Parents were told not to send money, and my mother obeyed the rules to the letter, even though the other parents didn't. I also wanted to help Gary buy more cars for his electric train set. I needed a business. But there were few career avenues open to little girls, particularly to those isolated in boarding schools.

Finally, I arrived at a plan. Mother had taught me how to crochet in Florida and had included in my footlocker four skeins of wool and a book on afghan making, which was rather complex. Nevertheless, I taught myself to make granny squares from line drawings and considered it a wonderful achievement. Daddy had also given me a present to take to school, the color swatches hanging from the garments in his dress line. I sold the swatches and my crocheted granny squares as tiny horse blankets for the tiny bronze horse statues that nearly every girl had on her bureau. These girls were passionate about horses, and my miniature blankets were an immediate success in color schemes to order.

With the horse blankets, I became a salesman like Daddy. My imagination had succeeded, and money was rolling in. I bought crackers, sardines, and jars of baby food. I had created a little place where I could be completely alone and where I could baby myself when necessary. I kept my money in a little wooden box inside my secret fort and covered it with a clean white Biltmore Hotel face towel. All of my sheets for school had been stolen from the St. Francis and the Biltmore hotels. My housemother always pretended not to notice the connection between my name tape and the hotel's insignia, even though they were only inches apart.

Despite my success in sales, I was intensely homesick. I realized I was going to be left in this strange place where I first saw a pomegranate and learned to make fish flies to my own design in the barnyard where pampas grass grew. Gary had his own schedule and we rarely met. Once I saw him alone on the school grounds. No one was in sight, and I asked him to give me a kiss. It took me a long time to make friends because I was shy and self-conscious. I even had the wrong kind of jeans. Mother, the most important person in the world to me, was in New York with Barbara. I wrote her:

Dear Mother,

I cann't wait to come home. The day seem like years, and week like centreys. I love you moor than ever darling.

Love and xxxx Iris

One afternoon Daddy arrived on a nonvisiting day in a white convertible, red shirt, and strangely bashed-in hat. His clothes looked especially joyous that day. It was lunchtime, and all the grades were gathered in the dining room. The students looked out of the window, fascinated with this man's getup, wondering who he was—exactly the response my father wanted.

I spoke up proudly. "That's my daddy." The other children expressed surprise and disbelief. They couldn't pair us off: I was a shy child, and outside the window was a person who was obviously an expert at capturing attention, a genuine show-off. I ran out to see him, and he swept me up high into the air. He was just passing through, he said. When he remarked that the scenery in this valley was magnificent, I immediately looked at my surroundings with new eyes.

On another visit, Daddy introduced me to orchids when he took me to the Boyle Orchid Farm in Ojai Valley. Maybe, I thought, he's an orchid lover, and I'm going to become one too. I felt respect in their presence. They were so wonderfully specialized in their configuration. One petal was always different, and that one was called the lip. To the eye there appear to be six petals, but actually the orchid has three petals and three sepals. I took this information on trust. Some orchids are so sexy and enticing in their configurations that they lure insects to pseudocopulate in their floral cup and ensure pollination. I was a voyeur when it came to plants; their natural history was titillating.

On our Christmas break during the second year at Ojai Valley, Daddy was called into service for his special style of baby-sitting while Mother stayed in New York. After Gary and I opened one present each—all that we had—Daddy said, "It's time to go, let's hit the road." Our trip was a choreography with cars, a ballet and a boxing match. First we went to the Grand Canyon. When we arrived, we jumped out of the car, and Daddy said, "Iris and Gary, it took Mother Nature two million years to make this place, and we have just seen it in one minute flat. Let's go to Boulder Dam! Everybody in the car!"

After Boulder Dam, the next stop was Las Vegas, then Sequoia National Park. Daddy drove the foggy mountain roads with hairpin turns at amazing speeds. I said nothing. Gary threw up. Driving was a test, an athletic contest. My father pitted himself against oncoming cars and narrowly twisted roads. Daddy loved to be the fastest car on the highway. We came out alive. Daddy had won. After this vacation, it was a relief to go back to school. We had driven one thousand miles.

I continued plotting a way to get my mother to take me out of Ojai to live with her. I needed a far-reaching plan, a way to get her involved with me the same way she was with Barbara. I promised myself that absolutely without fail I would grow up to be world famous and thereby receive lots of attention, love, and praise. I would figure out what my mother wanted, and I'd regain her love. Barbara was an actress. What would my profession be? What were my special gifts?

The things I enjoyed best at school were physical. I loved running fast at night as the world changed colors. I could travel through a monotone of darkness at high velocity on the spacious grounds. And I could leap over poles.

The fifth grade had assembled for sports on the back field. It was spring, and a flowering plum tree was in bloom on the edge of the playing field. It was so beautiful. I'd never seen this kind of a tree before.

Having had sessions of soccer, baseball, basketball, and broad jumping, today we were going to do high jumping. Our sports and shop teacher, Tom (he wanted to be called by his first name), started to explain it to our small class of seven boys and girls. It wasn't like jumping rope or hopping over a low ledge. You approached the pole from the side at an angle. When you were very close, you lifted one leg, then the other, taking your entire body, up and, over with the second kick. You couldn't start too close or too far from the pole; timing must be perfect.

Our class formed a line. We were going to make the jump. At first, the pole was placed very low so we all could do it easily and work on the scissor technique of the jump. But after ten minutes, Tom placed the pole very high, at four feet. I watched as some of my classmates tried and failed. The pole was loosely placed on two supporting poles creating an **H** shape, like my father's middle initial. The beautiful simplicity of the three poles delighted me. Two girls in front of me were gossiping, but I wasn't interested in their talk. I wanted to clear the pole perfectly and cleanly. I wanted to make that leap, do that scissor movement, and get over the pole. It seemed like a fantastic thing to do. To clear the bar. No one else had been able to do it.

I looked at the spot on the ground, the exact point where I would take off. The two girls ahead of me missed. Why did the teacher put it so high? I would have to be in possession of my body every moment of the run and jump. But I wanted to do this. I gathered speed on my short run and said to myself, "Now." I kicked one leg very high, then the other, taking my body up, over, and around. I was on the other side, and the pole was still there. Some of the other students cried out, "Yeah!" Something inside me was thrilled. It was a transforming moment. I had done what I wanted to do.

The teacher came over to me. "Iris, you are just a little taller than that pole. You did a great job." My jump was spectacular. Another teacher called me "Mighty Mouse." What would he have said if he knew Mighty Mouse was secretly eating baby food to sustain her strength?

I smiled. That leap was now mine forever and ever; it was my achievement. I would never forget that I could do something very difficult.

The experience with the high jump reinforced my belief in learning correct technique and incorporating it along with desire and coordination. I had listened carefully to the instructions, followed them, and they worked. I had made the jump on the first try with no practice.

Although I didn't trust most adults, I responded to maternal feelings with complete obedience. From a young age, I had extended that to teachers I perceived as generous and warm. But instructions had to be presented correctly.

Another teacher I trusted, Mrs. Dugger, also gave me direction. The school was having a Red Cross drive, and we were asked to "give till it hurts." I thought about it and at first I considered giving a portion of my earnings. But Mrs. Dugger had said "till it hurts." Well, that would be the whole thing, the last penny. I desperately wanted to have principles to live by, and I embraced my mother's fervently. I needed to have total faith in her. Now a teacher I trusted was telling me the same thing my mother had preached—give it all away, travel light, material objects mean nothing. I contributed all my horse blanket earnings, exactly $3.71. Of course, I knew I could make it back. Business was good.

On Friday nights, a teacher came in from the village to teach folk dancing, bringing with him a collection of his records. I loved the "Beer Barrel Polka," but I put my own stamp on the steps he taught us. I discovered that I loved to dance. It was all of the things that were best in life—leaping, running, jumping—in combination with music and sparkling rhythms.

The only music I had heard before Ojai Valley School were snatches of popular tunes and occasional symphonies on the radio and children's songs. We hadn't had a record player. The dorm living room had a phonograph, but the school owned only three records: the "Notre Dame Fighting Song," the Minuet in G, and the *Grand Canyon Suite*. Hearing the Minuet in G transported me. I did enormous leaps around the room. I immediately wrote my mother: "Yesterday in bed I dreamt I was a great balareany. I almost went flying off my bed out of the windows and dance in the air."

I had found my way to freedom. It was of the utmost importance to me never to return to this school. I practiced in the evenings during the free time before study hall. We gathered in the living room and played one of the three records. I loved to soar through the air. Enormous jumps were what I felt dancing was really all about. The music was my director. It told me what to do.

When I told my roommate, "I've decided I want to be a ballerina when I grow up," she told me I was "too skinny." She had seen ballet in London.

I had never seen a ballet dancer, and I immediately stuck out my stomach as far as it would go, turning red with the effort. "How's that?" I asked, laughing.

"It's not supposed to all be in one place."

"Well, I'm going to do it anyhow."

I wrote Mother another letter. By return mail, I received a reply. My bid for ballet had worked. Gary would stay on at Ojai, but I would go to New York to be with her. It was going to be just the three of us, Mother and two daughters. At seven and eight years old, I had felt that I was a little girl who was ordinary in all ways, with no special abilities. At ten, I discovered I could dance.

At the school's closing play I was the witch in *Hansel and Gretel*. I played the part so well that everyone thought I was leaving school to become an actress. But I had found something that was even better than acting. When I chose ballet, I had found the perfect way to win Mother back. Years later, I learned from Harry's sister that my mother had wanted to go dancing every night when she was living in Texas, she loved it so. Now, through me, Mother could still dance. She would participate in my career, and we could both be ballerinas.

I wrote her another letter. She was to get me a little kitten and a monkey. She was to have the ballet class already lined up so I could start right away. Also, I wanted Daddy to be with us.

I pushed the tweed-covered rocker and the yellow chair against the wall. Then I twirled the volume button until the sound was up very high. Carefully placing the needle in the groove, I stood perfectly still so that I'd be ready when the music started. With four distinctive notes, the music and my dance to it began. Instead of short segments as in boarding school, I now had a whole symphony to dance out.

The living room was not quite big enough for my leaps, but I could incorporate part of the dining room for a long run of sheer freedom. The music seemed to have two parts, the upper level and the lower level, so I split my body, keeping a rhythm with my legs and a legato with my arms. Then I moved in big jumps, big steps, or a series of runs and pauses. This was Beethoven's Fifth, music I had never heard before this summer, and I did a different dance to it every day, pushing myself when exhausted. During my intermission, I listened to *Madama Butterfly*.

Unsurprisingly, our plans had changed during the course of the year. Instead of being in New York with my sister, Mother, Gary, and I were living in an apartment house my father had purchased on Burton Way in Los Angeles. Of course, he lived somewhere else. Harry was doing well buying real estate, and for the first time that I can remember, we owned our own furniture. Mother had even bought a phonograph and three albums of classical music.

I couldn't start my ballet classes yet because Capezio didn't have shoes in my size and width. So, waiting for my ballet slippers, I was spending another afternoon dancing across my living room, doing what I loved to do—listen, invent, and move, as the music suggested.

During the middle of the first movement, my sister, Barbara, walked in with Harry. She had just crossed the country to spend some of the summer with us.

Wildly happy, I galloped over to kiss her as Mother ran out of the kitchen for a kiss and embrace.

I hadn't seen my sister in a year. She looked so grown-up and so beautifully dressed. I admired her style. "Barbara, I love your dress."

"Iris, I'm not Barbara."

"Victoria?"

"Not anymore. I have a new name now. It's Wendy, like Wendy in *Peter Pan*. Wendy Drew." The Drew was from Nancy Drew mysteries. My sister had been changing her name since she was sixteen.

"Hello, Wendy," I said, as she moved with me to my room to unpack.

"Iris, I have something for you." She quickly opened her suitcase. Her favorite colors had changed with her name. Everything was in neat order, in tones of oatmeal. Her gift to me was a book, a flower fantasy tale. It was beautiful. I also liked looking at her clothes. The shades were champagne, beige, and butterscotch. My darling sister, who used to twirl me around the living room when I was little, loved to play with color.

As she unpacked, a small piece of paper fell out. It was the list of choices Wendy had drawn up when she was selecting her new name. On the list were Francesca, Rebecca, Rachel, Candace, Amanda, and Allegra. She explained that for two years she had been considering names before selecting Wendy.

I paused and thought I'd change my name too. I'd take this one because I loved it. I'd become Allegra. I would be transformed into a new creature. It was very immediate, very un–thought out. But I would be just as serious about changing my name as I was about dancing. I liked the name Iris because it was an emblem of the wild iris that was always alive in me. Yet the music of Allegra was hypnotic. I knew where the name had come from. It was Longfellow's daughter, laughing Allegra, in "The Children's Hour."

Thus, my name changed in stages, but it was not a stage name. Mother had chosen Kent when I was two, and I became Allegra when I was eleven, the summer before I took my first ballet class.

At first, my family didn't take me seriously, but at my new school I introduced myself as Allegra, and soon the rest of my family adjusted. This fit our tradition of not keeping the status quo. Keep changing the exterior. Changing houses. Cities. Coasts. In our family it seemed to be the name that made the person, not the other way around. As Iris, I had been sent away; I didn't seem to interest my mother. But as Allegra, with a would-be career, I was definitely visible.

Gary remained Gary and went back to Ojai Valley School. He did not remold himself for Mother's needs, although later he would try. My life, however, was deluxe. My shoes arrived, I would begin dance lessons soon, and I had Mother all to myself.

This arrangement was fortunate, for it takes two people to launch a dancer. There must be a second person in the family who wants it too. Or a whole nation. The entire Navajo nation or one Jewish mother. The Imperial School of Russia or Shirley Kent.

PART TWO

1948 – 1953

From Los Angeles to La Scala

Left: Carmelita Maracci. Photo by Lansing Brown. Right: Felia Doubrovska. Photo by Martha Swope © Time Inc.

CHAPTER THREE

They danced by day as well as at night as people did just after the war.

—COLETTE, THE LAST OF CHERI

My mother and I stood in the open doorway watching. A thin girl was practicing fantastic pirouettes that I remember to this day. I was awed by the beautiful bodies and their clean and smooth movements. A secretary pointed out Belita, the ice-skater, and Vera-Ellen, the movie star. The names meant nothing to me except that they were famous people who wanted the best training. I was in the right place. I was surprised, however, by the number of grown men in the class. They were former GIs, all doing complex steps and combinations. The GI bill covered the study of ballet as well as college.

The Yellow Pages had helped us locate the studios of Bronislava Nijinska, the sister of the illustrious dancer with the extraordinary leaps, Vaslav Nijinsky. Madame, as she was called, a plump, nice-looking woman in black lounging pajamas with a long cigarette holder (an outfit that never varied), stood off in a corner with a pianist. She was counting in Russian; I would hear *"ras, va, tri"* from all my Russian teachers for the next thirty years. Her husband was simultaneously translating everything she said into English. She had great authority and was single-minded about what was going on in that room. The world began and ended right there at that moment. Extraneous aspects of life didn't exist for her. I was impressed.

Even though I didn't know what ballet dancing looked like, let alone how to do it, Mother had again enrolled me in an intermediate class. For her, it was never necessary to start at the beginning. Once again she was exercising her reckless courage through me, but I was in a state of dazed happiness. At last I was where I wanted to be.

I changed into my two-piece sleeveless sunsuit and met Irina, Madame's daughter, who would be my first teacher. She also was in black lounging pajama pants but with a flowered top. Mother told her how little I knew about ballet, but that didn't seem to matter, and I joined the large class of perhaps forty people. I looked at the ex-GIs who were so big next to the young girls in the class. These men had been through a war and all that that meant, and I was an extra-small eleven-year-old, but strangely that didn't make me uncomfortable or self-conscious. My yearnings had brought me here, and eleven is a receptive age for a child, no longer a baby and not yet a teenager. I assumed that the mixed group was typical.

From my experience in Florida, I knew that a ballet class started at the barre, so I took a place near a window and waited for the class to begin. This time I understood that a turnout was not a turn-in. Mother was sitting on a long bench at the back of the studio already engaged in earnest conversation with another mother. Was their gossip about me? No, not yet. Today Mother was my investigative reporter.

Class began with pliés. These I could do, but as we progressed to more complex steps, I felt discouraged. I tried to imitate the steps the others were doing, but the movements were too advanced. The obvious became a reality: I hadn't had the basics. I threw all of my energy into concentrating. My body had to do what the other bodies could do. But I was about two years behind everyone else, and my athletic abilities didn't help me as much as I had thought they would. I also couldn't understand the instructions, because Irina spoke rapid-fire English with a heavy Russian accent, and she indicated only vaguely, impressionistically, what she wanted. I looked at Mother. She was now talking to a mother seated on her other side.

Still, I wasn't going to give up as I had in Florida. I had the utmost faith in my ability to dance, and I was convinced I would catch up. In some ways, I'm glad I didn't start at the beginning. The pace might have been too slow, and dry technique might have dampened my spirit. This was top-of-the-line training. Had it been less than that, I might have wasted years and been ignorant of what the best can give.

At the end of the class, Irina gave a repeated pattern of step, step, leap—or as she called it, jeté—in a circle around the large room. I immediately did this combination with a free, powerful style, jumping high. This was the athletic side of dance I understood. What I had been doing on my own was already in the dance vocabulary. Then I looked around. For my size, I was jumping higher than anyone else. Although I was unable to do some of the more basic steps, the most difficult moves came easily. And I knew I could learn the rest, it was merely a matter of time. I had the beginning and end of class in place; I would have to learn what needed to be done during the middle. But the moment I made my mighty jump and flew higher than anyone else, I knew this world would be my life.

So that I could learn to leap in a more balletic way, Mother arranged for a few thirty-minute private lessons with Irina. Mother and I believed years could be compressed into a half hour. During these sessions, Irina told me that her uncle Nijinsky used to crouch slightly in his preparation and then spring to full height at the peak of a jump. This enhanced the elevated look of his grand jetés. I understood that dance is partly based on illusions and magical effects.

I worked ferociously, embarking in all innocence on a systematic and accelerated crash course. I increased the number of regular classes I took and copied the imagery as best I could.

Because Irina's English was almost incomprehensible, I took out books from the public library to learn the names of the steps. I read an illustrated book on the fundamentals of ballet, a biography of Pavlova, and books on dance history. I read about Fokine and Massine. There was very little space given to the name George Balanchine. I also read a softcover pamphlet called *The ABC's of Ballet* by Lincoln Kirstein. (I never told him about this.)

Apparently I caught up, because Irina told me I was ready to begin pointe work some six months after starting her class. Most young dancers cannot wait to get on pointe, but I contradicted her. I had read that two years of training were necessary first. As a compromise, I said I needed another month. After a total of seven months of hard work, I began lessons on pointe.

By the second year, I took classes from Bronislava Nijinska herself. She used a set barre, which meant that the same exercises were done every day to the same music. One piece by Burgmüller was played for grand battement, and when I hear the piece today I think of Mme. Nijinska, the woman who told us "arms cannot be like spaghetti." One day in class, she asked me to try to push her arms around. I exerted great effort, but they wouldn't budge. She wanted me to see her underlying strength and power, which ballet requires in order to project its airy look. She wanted me to understand that the light look of dance was merely the surface of the sculpture—there was a mixture of steel and quicksilver at the heart. Madame herself was on the heavy side, but, in a demonstration of how to hold the body, the men who lifted her were amazed at how easy she was to raise from the floor.

This was the dichotomy—the achievement of fragility and delicacy meant a core of strength. Butterflies are not weak.

Madame couldn't stand anyone chewing gum in her class, but she never directly confronted the person who was doing it. Instead, in a surprising move, she would deflect her anger toward another target. In flight, with feathers extended and her black lounging pajamas flapping against her legs, she would rush over to an innocent spectator and accuse him or her. I think she always chose a timid soul to point out how upset the real offender should be. The accused visitor never understood what was happening. After class, Madame would explain her tactics to the bewildered onlooker; it seemed this was some variation on Russian etiquette or some law of the steppes. Another forbidden action was whistling, which Madame considered bad luck in the studio or theater. I would remember these things thirteen years later when I danced in her native country.

After class we grouped around her, and she hugged and kissed us with great emotion and warmth. We had tried to be dancers, but that was over, and now we were once again human beings who needed affection. She told us that when she was young she had never fussed over pointe shoes—she'd wear anybody's if they were the right size. To dance was all; the equipment was incidental and shouldn't be overemphasized.

From her, I also learned not to fear competing with men. Toward the end of class one day, Madame took my hand. The men had just done a big jumping step across the floor and covered an enormous amount of space. Now the two of us, an old woman and a child, were going to do the same. I looked in Madame's face. She was gloriously ready. She signaled for the pianist to start. We would not be outdone by the male dancers—or anyone, for that matter. I looked at the corner of the room. That's where I was going. And so we were off and flying. We did it. "Very good," Madame said in Russian, smiling wildly. For her, life was really only a series of moment-by-moment triumphs in dance. She was absolutely her brother's sister.

When I saw her years later in Paris, Madame was, as always, Madame—savoring the joy of being herself and wearing lounging pajamas with her fingers producing a narrow V for victory. This pose produced a resting place for her long cigarette holder and was also an emblem of her outlook on life. At other times she raised the holder like a baton; she was always the conductor. Ever the emotional Russian, she hugged me warmly. Then, becoming my teacher once more, she felt my "wings" to see if I had developed more back strength.

In 1981, when I was trying out for a job as a spokeswoman for Lycra, the agency people asked me what I'd wear if I had only one outfit. "Pj's?" I ventured. I said it uncertainly but meant it definitely.

The correct answer was offered with a certain disapproval: "A blazer, shirt, and Lycra stockings."

I didn't get the job, but I remembered Nijinska's lessons. We don't all have to look alike. "We are born originals, we die copies."

My first glimpse of Carmelita Maracci was through a peephole, a small circle scraped free of paint on her classroom door. She was a tiny woman, about my height, with dark hair pulled back and twisted into a low coil. Wearing little girl's rompers and pointe shoes, she was demonstrating how the tip of a beautifully pointed instep placed on the floor becomes the support structure for an arabesque, and she was describing the process in flawless English. We arrived while a class was in progress, and Mother and I took turns spying. Carmelita was dressed for the playground, but her face and head had the look of a Latin visionary.

This was what I wanted. She was actually demonstrating how to dance, explaining clearly what she was doing, and offering the training I had not yet had. At the Nijinska studios, the regular class was so large that I was missing the basic foundation—how to gain strength, flexibility, agility, and form. After half a year into my classes at Nijinska's studio, I joined Carmelita's advanced class and alternated between the two schools, keeping carefully silent about my divided love.

When I shook hands with Carmelita that first day, I stared at her beautiful hands and unusually long fingernails. For her part, she sized me up the way all dance teachers do, by looking at the equipment, the body. However, from the way she taught I also understood that she loved children. Her greeting was genuine and warm.

For me, Carmelita's class was the beginning of an adventure. Up until then, dance lessons had been my recess, monkey bars, and jungle gym; now I was out of the backyard and in the study hall. In contrast to the crowded classes at Nijinska's, I was in small classes with a teacher who broke down the steps and did them in slow motion, pointing out what was important: how to coordinate legs and head, where the snap or spark should be. Jumping up in an energetic way, she showed us the tiny, swift movements of the Italian school, or perfect pirouettes on pointe—two slow revolutions in high, proud passé followed by six more in a low *sur le coup de pied* at twice the speed. The woman was a dervish. It was exciting to contemplate. She demonstrated her way of balancing in an arabesque; it was not a wobbly, unsure thing, but a movement that branched and grew like a tree, fingertips like tendrils. She stayed as long as she wished. "Not bad," she'd say matter-of-factly. At other times she demonstrated from her chair, leaning back and lifting her leg with an extravagant gesture. She was up and down for the whole class. Sometimes her fingers curled over the castanets and produced nightingales in flight, the whisper of their wings, and the hum of hummingbirds. She never tired.

One day Carmelita told us that La Argentina, the great Spanish dancer, thought the best castanets were made from pomegranate wood. This news thrilled me; the magical pomegranate had a practical use!

In Carmelita's classes, we explored physical possibilities. She broke the bounds of what I thought technique could be. Watching her, I learned physically and metaphysically how a dance step was to be done. She could do eight pirouettes on pointe in a high passé. One day I did that too. She had provided the visual proof that it was possible. We did steps in great quantity, almost until the breaking point. That's how strength was developed. Carmelita's two late-afternoon children's classes were composed entirely of girls, and she didn't spare us. She told stories of how she had practiced alone for hours on end, doing circles and circles of chaîné turns. She told us about the romantic ballerinas of the distant past: Marie Taglioni, Carlotta Grisi, and Fanny Cerrito, the women in the old prints whose costumes were like clouds, mist, and dew. These dancers caught the elusive and intangible when they portrayed sylphs, elemental creatures, and undines. Their beauty was ethereal and unearthly, but their technique was achieved by endless work. Carmelita was an extremist. The leg could never be too high, there were never too many turns, and there was no limitation on beauty or expressiveness either.

Carmelita believed that even if you never had done a step correctly before, if you got excited enough you might just do it in her class. Something might connect; a firecracker would go off; flashes of color would sparkle in the sky.

One day, a student brought in a favorite record, and, as the first sounds of Offenbach's *Gaîté Parisienne* swept over me and invaded my funny bones, I took off. I couldn't do the steps that some of the girls could, but, finally, on this day of improvisation, I had my first chance to spring into the kind of jump I excelled in—the big expansive leap of a mountain goat happy within its skin. The music threw itself out as startling little bursts of staccato presentations followed by a teasing rhythm, then four distinct sounds seeming to imply four questioning attitudes. Sometimes the music languidly zigzagged in an upward path with the strings leading the way, ending with a ripple of joyous cool, high tones. There were stories told and surprise responses. So, let the drums roll. We will have fun and fun alone. Sadness should not be considered today. At other times there was an impending storm about to break loose, and then a quietude. Afterward, a waltz with a heartbreakingly beautiful melody was followed by little quivers and squeezes to extricate the water from the laundry. This musical story was liquid. In a final rush of deepest exuberance, the topsy-turvy clowns entered like bouncing balls with a Ping-Ponging beat. The music colored the room, crawled under the piano, plunked, tiptoed, and galloped.

Offenbach had made me an entertainer. I was crazy with delight and reverted to my primitive, pre-ballet style, just as I had done at Ojai and in the living room at home. I did nothing I had learned in any class.

After a while, I was aware that Carmelita was struck dumb. Her attention was riveted on me. I danced with abandon but secretly took note that my teacher was looking at me in a different way. Her expression revealed that she was having a great time. She began to point me out. "Good, Allegra!" To hear this was enough. I looked at her. She was like a scientist watching a primate. And I was the monkey. I was proud of my monkey-mad self. I could swing from the treetops when necessary or bound to a branch just for the thrill of taking off. She would later describe me as "demonic" in a letter of introduction for the School of American Ballet. I loved the effect I caused.

This was the turning point in my relationship with Carmelita. I was no longer just a girl studying ballet and working hard. I was a potential "original" whom she could direct, raw material in the hands of a great teacher. I thrived on the attention, and I filed away everything Carmelita said. She told us what the first pointe shoes looked like and what the inventor felt when she first rose on the tip. Carmelita spoke about people I had never heard of before: Carmen Amaya, Harald Kreutzberg, and Miguel de Unamuno. Unamuno's name had a poetic rhythm to it; it was fun to chant like a catchy tune. Years later I read some of his books. I was interested in what interested her. She liked to quote Oswald Spengler: "Not the brow, but the experience, not the eyes, but the look, not the lips, but the sensuousness." Carmelita taught creativity, courage, and humanity—then ballet.

One day I wore a hat I had made to her class, a hat I had created from palm leaves with flowers and fake plums. Carmelita was wild about it and asked me to make her one. I had to climb into the heart of a palm tree to get the unborn, pale, yellow-green leaves—the raw material of the hat—that I then wove for her. Upon completing it, I presented it to her, and she spoke about it for the next thirty-five years. I felt she understood something about me because of that hat. I was her student and my father's daughter.

But I was also my mother's daughter. At times, Mother's sense of fun transformed her, and she became a joyous playmate my age. Once, while we were walking down a steep hill in Los Angeles, the momentum pressed us forward, and we broke into a run, which felt easy and natural. Mother and I exchanged glances and laughed. With tight fists, we began sprinting in long strides, the happiness of downhill gravitation hurling us ahead. This was its own delight; there was no effort in our run. Mother had told me she always wished that she had had a sister, an understanding flesh-and-blood friend who would ease her loneliness, a small, adorable creature who at first would be like a just-born butterfly and then would be a lifelong ally. As her daughters grew up, she saw that they could fit that special place. Running down the hill that day, I saw it too.

All was high spirits and swiftness until Mother fell, scraping her knee. I knew that my wildness had led her into the stumble, and I felt guilty, but she was an amazing sport. Her knee was skinned, but she picked herself up, grimaced, and then defiantly smiled. She was in pain, but the preceding moments were wonderful. Only our forward flight would be remembered. We were sisters in exhilaration.

Mother was not only my companion in fun during this year but also the person who believed in me and made possible the other thing I loved—my ballet classes. Nothing could prevent me from attending, not fever, floods, or fog. During the first summer after I started studying ballet, when I was twelve, without blinking an uncertain eye I created a program for myself. During the winter I had been taking four classes a week; now I decided on nine. I alternated classes between Mme. Nijinska and Carmelita, adding a punishing three-hour Saturday pointe lesson with Maria Bekefi. An indefatigable Kirov-trained Russian, Bekefi was a perfectionist. There were so few students in her pointe class that it was, in effect, a private lesson. Mothers were banned from the classroom. Three hours on my toes coaxed them toward strength. Then with Nijinska and Carmelita, I tried for the most expansive movements. I was always happy when I finished class. I could go home and drink lots of orange juice and enjoy an afterglow of well-being. I was going to make a profession of this joyous romp. I would bypass real work and do this child's play all through my adult life. What could be better?

Mother, without a job or career or husband, had made herself a partner in my aspirations—something that, at least for that moment, held no complications. She freed me of all chores and of anything that caused strain. She cooked while I did homework. She did all of the assignments that I didn't like to do—her favorite was writing my compositions. On weekends, when I wasn't in ballet class, I took a three-hour art class, during which time I often was so caught up with looking that I fell off my chair. Still lifes and flowers, with their subtle variety of shapes, enthralled me. In my mind, a fruit stand was very closely related to an art museum. I had no friends, so I spent my free time crocheting two afghans in green, blue, and navy. Mother was the chauffeur. When Gary quit Ojai Valley School, he became the family cook.

Family sacrifices are often involved to subsidize a career. The story goes that the mother of one aspiring ballerina ordered the girl's sister to give up the piano and go to work to help defray the family's expenses. One child's talent is often sacrificed for another's. Our weekly routine revolved around me and my schedule. And our religion.

At this point in her life, Mother had plunged fanatically back into Christian Science. I had been able to do the four-foot-high jump on the first try because of my belief in the teacher's instructions. Now my mother, the person I trusted most in the world, was my teacher. She was an irresistible propagandist, and I became a fanatic too. It was easy, because Christian Science diminished the force of many of my childhood fears that a needle had the power to kill me or that mosquitoes were lethal, particularly at night. Now, nothing in the material world could hurt me.

I joined Sunday school and went to church faithfully twice a week. Mother enrolled me in a private Christian Science school, Berkley Hall, a few streets from where we lived. I was immersed.

From Mother and my teachers I learned that everything we see— the externals—is unreal. When my afghans were completed, my mother had them lined and gave them away. We, her children, were extensions of her, so she gave away our things too. She gave away the pictures I painted and the dolls I made. I was sad to see them go, but, as I understood clearly from our religion, these were only physical objects, unimportant stuff of the external world. There is only the divine idea behind everything. I was a very literal child, too literal. Just because a parent or teacher gives instructions doesn't mean you have to follow them exactly. Unless you're a born-again Iris, now called Allegra.

As I grew older, I often found myself trapped by principles that I took literally. I took Mother's teachings to heart and became so fanatical about not holding on to physical things that I was impractical. I never kept even essentials, and many times I found myself with nothing, stripped down to my underwear and a couch. That's what would happen to my character in *The Seven Deadly Sins,* although, fortunately, the underwear would be black lace. By my thirties, I would have nothing and three children to raise.

However, this philosophy had a positive effect on my dancing when I was a child. According to Christian Science, not only does the physical body have no substance but pain and pleasure are not real. In a fanatical mood, I stopped celebrating my birthday but then missed it. No cake, no candles, and no gifts. It was a deliberate choice; after all, we didn't recognize birth or death. If I drove myself hard in ballet class and my muscles felt tired and the exhaustion hurt, I'd keep going. Why not? I told myself the pain was not real. I pushed myself. That is something that an athlete needs to do. For most people drive comes from the outside. For me, it was intrinsic and metaphysical.

In addition to my success in dance, at my new Christian Science school I enjoyed my only brush with popularity, even though I was shorter, thinner, and younger than anyone else in my grade. In addition to Allegra, I created a descriptive nickname for myself. "Little Joe" proved to be an instantaneous success. "Her name is Little Joe," my new friends said in wonder. "Hello, Little Joe!" At Berkley Hall we had to wear dresses or skirts and blouses. By way of protest I wore brown shoes and socks, a ragged T-shirt, an inside-out vest that was really a lining, and a skirt. It was as near to a mountain man's outfit as the school would allow, and I also walked like a mountain man. My idol was Jedediah Strong Smith, the first non-native man to cross the Sierra Nevadas. Then, at our first school party, I stunned my principal and classmates by walking over to the boys and asking the partner I wanted for a dance. When he said yes, I was nearly swooning with happiness. I was finally going to have a social life. It began with a waltz. Even then I wanted great partners; the boy I asked to dance had run like a giraffe when he crossed the schoolyard, and he moved like a dream at the fortnightly. He alone was the one I wanted to ask for every dance. In 1985, I wrote in a publicity bio, "I've danced with Mikhail Baryshnikov, Erik Bruhn, Edward Villella, Peter Martins, Jacques d'Amboise, and David McCrea." David McCrea was the boy who ran like a giraffe.

Seventh grade continued to be glorious. I was the most popular girl in my school, and in ballet I was bounding ahead, pirouetting on pointe and able to do a series of beautifully executed entrechat-sixes.

During this period, we saw Daddy on Sundays for a family drive, if he was in town. This was usually the only time we saw him, but when Mother decided it was time to have our new name legalized, in a surprising move Harry joined us in the change from Cohen to Kent. He didn't want to be left behind. Yet once the matter was accomplished, he continued to use Cohen—a source of irritation to my mother. As I understood it, she thought my father was unsophisticated. When *Death of a Salesman* came to town, Mother said I couldn't see it because that was Daddy's job. I knew that if I couldn't see it, it must show something horrible about his kind of work. For years, I maintained a steady hostility toward Arthur Miller. How could he write that play without knowing the quintessential salesman of all time, Harry Cohen? The man who loved to wear cowboy hats and had the calling early?

My love for Daddy inspired a little green costume I created that year. I invented it from a light green suede tie Daddy had discarded in our apartment. My father's color was red, the most obvious of shades, the first color chosen by ancient flowers; mine was green, red's complement and the color of the rain forest, probably the most important one in nature. I bought long pants, a long-sleeved turtleneck shirt, and a beret, all in slightly different tones of green and all from the little boys' department, something not done in those days. I was a verdant creature of the woods, Peter Pan, a little boy-girl. The outfit made from Daddy's tie was in his honor—what he was and what he wasn't.

At the same time, my mother decided that my portrait should be painted in a ballet costume, and we bought some hideous chartreuse satin and tulle, which was on sale, and the artist William Schulgold, with whom I took my Saturday art class, started in. But I hated posing, and I hated the finished product. I wish someone had taken a photo of me in my greenish gamine splendor, my creation, the outfit that reflected my feelings for my father.

Although I had been a social success my first year at Berkley Hall, by the next year I reverted to my usual role as shy outcast. In eighth grade, I was still a year younger and still smaller than all my friends, and I was left behind socially. The girls were thirteen, and I was twelve—a young twelve. They were thinking of boys, and my thoughts were of ballet. I was out of step and knew it.

At Mother's request, I also dropped out of school sports—the easiest time to talk to friends—to save myself for ballet. Mother felt that I would be exhausted by too much physical activity. But I had plenty of energy, and I loved sports. I could have done it all. Yet I didn't question Mother about any of her decisions. I was still a child and could see that life ran more smoothly without constant dispute. Our religion also made me feel there was no place for a difference of opinion. Mother liked to soliloquize, and I kept silent. With dance I could bypass words; exquisite and correct sentences weren't required. At times, Mother had corrected and replaced my words immediately after I said them. "You have used the wrong word!" In ballet I could avoid all these corrections. Ballet wasn't about words, but movements.

Dancing, I was out there on my own, dangling in the air. I didn't have to modify my behavior or repress my feelings in the studio; there I was, a four-star general. Crossing the floor in big jumps felt like victory over the enemy. I was so powerful that I could mow down the opposition—without bloodshed. Carmelita was right to use the word "demonic." My muscles were my tour de force, and dancing was the way I chose to fight with my mother. It was not very effective. She would express her feelings, and instead of responding immediately, I would go to class and pour out my emotions into dance, putting enormous quantities of energy—much more than was required—into a movement or a jump. This was an inconclusive way to argue.

It was at this point that I developed a new phobia—shrunken heads. In *Under Capricorn,* a film I saw with Mother, a woman is being driven crazy, and the object that does it is the appearance of a shrunken head. At one point in the movie, when the audience is shown the little withered face, I screamed in terror. That image became seared in my brain, and I couldn't dislodge it, particularly at night in bed. It haunted me throughout eighth grade. I didn't tell anyone and became more exhausted and prone to sickness, thus causing my mother to become worried about my health and my output of physical energy. There was some residue of an old wives' tale in this. My mother's brother was shocked by the intense exertion of ballet training. He thought it would break down my health and that exercising once a week was more than enough.

Christian Science taught sexual abstinence, as did Mother, and I felt that to have or display any emotions at all would make me vulnerable to her scrutiny. It would change the delicate balance between us. At this moment, I was her most important focus. I wanted to keep my emotional life private. I'd always had a secretive side, which was not part of my mother's style. She was accustomed to talking everything out—the talking cure. I wished to speak in a different way, soundlessly—the dancing cure. With ballet, I had finally found a way to express myself but not reveal my thoughts. I was happy I had captured my mother's interest and had her all for myself, but I also needed something she couldn't touch. No one can touch silence.

Mother and I traveled downtown by bus to see the Ballet Russe de Monte-Carlo at the Philharmonic Hall. From deluxe seats in the first balcony, I was finally going to have a first view of the dances and dancers I had read about: Alexandra Danilova, Frederic Franklin, Mary Ellen Moylan, and Ruthanna Boris. Michel Fokine, Léonide Massine, and George Balanchine were listed among the choreographers. At long last, I was going to see a professional ballet performance.

What was on stage, however, couldn't match what I had imagined in my head. *Gaîté Parisienne* seemed too contrived, somewhat empty, perhaps silly and overacted. I disliked it. I saw more in *Swan Lake,* but it wasn't wild enough for me; *Schéhérazade* seemed to resemble a silent movie. The only ballet that interested me was *Night Shadow,* a mysterious fairy tale choreographed by Balanchine. Alexandra Danilova danced her part exquisitely, with Frederic Franklin as the poet. The sleepwalker's exit astonished me, but it happened so quickly. Did a woman with a candle carry a man offstage? I wondered, *Did I really see what I saw?* I wanted to quietly dwell on this haunting vision—the imagery and painting I had just seen—but Mother wanted to talk. I didn't want my thoughts interrupted with words. I snapped at her, and we argued.

I was nearing my teens and beginning to question my mother's teachings. One issue of *Life* magazine contained a chart of taste, including lists of what was highbrow, upper class, and middle class, down to vulgar. American Indian jewelry was relegated to a very low place, and lamps with a porcelain Chinese lady were somewhere near the top. My mother was critical of another ballet mother who wore what is now called Native American jewelry from Arizona, silver with turquoise. Mother loved gold antique jewelry but regarded silver as a secondary metal. And hadn't my mother implied that my father's profession was low class? I read the article carefully and understood that Mother had passionate likes and dislikes. It would take me decades to understand that things in her "dislike" category were quite all right.

In just another year, I would meet someone who wore a silver bracelet with a flourish, a man considered a genius, a man who would eventually re-create *Night Shadow* for me, the first ballet I had ever adored. And George Balanchine loved his solid cuff of silver and turquoise.

CHAPTER FOUR

*It's not the lessons that you take but the ones that you
don't miss that make you a ballerina.*

—SHIRLEY KENT

In the middle of a typical afternoon class at the School of American
Ballet, a thin, nicely dressed man opened the blue door of the studio
and walked right past me, only inches away, to the front of the room,
where he sat down on a long, low bench. I followed his entrance with
my eyes. The day I was to be judged had finally arrived. Mr. Balanchine would decide if I would receive a scholarship and move to an
advanced class.

It was the fall of 1951, and I was fourteen years old with three years
of ballet training behind me. Mother had decided that all the women
in the family should unite in the East. As Wendy pursued acting, I
would pursue dance. Gary, not wanting to be in New York, was sent
to Principia, a boarding school for Christian Scientists in St. Louis.

New York was the place for my ballet career to blossom, particularly at the School of American Ballet. My mother absolutely understood this, and she had done all the talking, coming on strong with
charm and salesmanship as she explained to the executive secretary of
the school who we were and where we came from. Mother was very
nicely dressed. I didn't have to talk, and that suited me; I may have
said three words. Our first visit at the school was probably very similar
to those of many others—a silent child with a classic ballet mother,
sparkling with wit, goodwill, and high hopes.

We had been sent to the School of American Ballet by Carmelita
with the letter of introduction in which she described me as "demonic." The letter was addressed to one of the teachers, her friend

Muriel Stuart, who had been a member of Pavlova's company. Carmelita respected Muriel tremendously, even though Carmelita didn't like Balanchine's choreography. Carmelita did mostly personal solo dances, and Balanchine did complicated constructions, where the intricate heart of great musical compositions was revealed through movement. When Carmelita decided to send me somewhere, however, she sent me to Balanchine's school, generously casting aside her personal prejudices. Mme. Nijinska, of course, would never have written such a letter or sent me to this school. Balanchine and she were both from Russia, and she considered him a rival.

Every student who was not in the working group turned to look at this man. He was good-looking and, for his age—forty-eight—very trim; his cheekbones elegantly defined his handsome face. He had been a dancer himself and, I suspected, a great dancer. He spoke briefly to Pierre Vladimirov, my teacher that day, and Vladimirov pointed to me, a serious teenager, leaning against the barre. I had been placed in this intermediate class until Balanchine could watch me dance and make his decision.

When my group's turn came, I took my place and did the combination. Moving to the advanced class was very important. I wanted to be in a room with wonderful dancers, people to watch, be inspired by, and compete with, people who would let me see by demonstration what was easy for them.

With a thoughtful look that gave nothing away, Balanchine studied my small jetés, my glissades, and perhaps the proportions of my figure. Almost involuntarily I mirrored his face with mine. I gave nothing away, either, not my eagerness to gain the distinction of a scholarship or my understanding of how important this moment was to my future. How could this man fail to see my raw talent and my potential? Carmelita and Nijinska saw it. The combination was basic and easy, and already within the two weeks I had studied at this school, my new teachers had shown their interest. My confidence was unbounded.

Mr. Balanchine stayed for four minutes or so and then walked out. He had not seen my proud high jumps and my exciting turns. I looked at the round clock on the wall; there was still a full twenty-five minutes of class to go.

Today, when thinking about this, I am amazed at my confidence. If Mr. B. had rejected me, I might have had some sort of breakdown. This was a metaphysically all-or-nothing moment. But I wasn't suffering with anxiety. His presence didn't intimidate me, because I had no real sense of who this man was. He wasn't highlighted in the dance books I had checked out of the Beverly Hills Library. They did not feature Mr. B. but emphasized the eras a little before and a little after him in Russia and Paris. I knew much more about Fokine, Massine, and Nijinsky.

At last, class was over. Rushing out, I found Mother smiling. I had won a scholarship and could go into C class immediately. I had done it. I had vaulted over the pole. Mr. Vladimirov was just as excited and happy as I was and offered me a butter-rum Life Saver to celebrate the occasion. The word "rum" made the Life Saver festive to him, and he pointed to the word on the package. I knew that the secret ingredient in the Life Saver was vinegar, not rum, but I decided this was not the occasion to act like a smart-aleck. The gift was symbolic; it was like sharing a shot of vodka as a toast to success. The two of us were in cahoots. Vladimirov's sweetness and generosity touched me.

All my lessons would now be free of charge, but the honor and vote of confidence from Balanchine were the most important part of this audition. I knew he had founded this school with Lincoln Kirstein as the kindergarten for the New York City Ballet Company. A great dance company needs an incubator to turn raw embryos into the polished material of dance. In the transforming warmth of the School of American Ballet, translucent whites and golden yolks hatched as swans, firebirds, enchanted fauns, and furies, indeed, Fabergé eggs— the New York City Ballet Company's foreground and background, the body of the corps, and the soul of the ballerinas.

The C division was exactly where I wanted to be, and I studied with a variety of teachers, including Mr. Oboukhov, who gave a completely exhausting class. His ways were strange. He held the *"s'il"* in his *"s'il vous plaît"* very long and in a singing tone. Had he seen a mouse, or was he a bit eccentric? No. He had developed this style to overcome a stutter. He used these words to request the new group to assemble and begin the combination. I liked what these Russians did with language. It was stylized and theatrical. He would say things such as, "Small miss, come forward," and, with very narrowed eyes, point at me. His barre was so fast it was almost impossible to do, an exercise in not giving in. During it, Mr. Oboukhov would walk up to the chosen person, look him or her in the eye from a distance of only two inches, then, squinting and frowning, he would snap his fingers in tempo to the music, saying "chug-a-chug-a-chug." Perhaps he was impersonating a steamboat on the Mississippi? What was the point of this? Endurance and concentration. No matter what he did, we had to disregard his antics and dance.

All of the teachers were wonderful, but Madame Felia Doubrovska had a special place in my heart. She had graduated from the Imperial School in St. Petersburg, had made a dramatic escape out of Russia, and had been teaching at the school for only three years. She was married to Vladimirov, the man who had offered me the Life Saver. Madame had been the original Siren of Mr. B.'s early masterpiece *The Prodigal Son,* and she still embodied beauty and elegance.

I got on the right footing with Madame immediately, and I was lucky to have her before she could become discouraged by decades of recalcitrant students. Many times I felt she did the entire class for me and what my body needed that day—more stretching, or more adagio, or an exercise freshly invented to help with fouettés. She saw everything because, as she announced in her low, richly accented voice, "I have eyes in the back of my head." (The mirror helped with this magic trick.) Only later would I understand how difficult it is to teach, saying the same thing every day and hoping it will be absorbed and appreciated. When she gave me corrections, she'd blink her dark lovely eyes with the magnificent lids. Many years later Jerome Robbins suggested her image for an entrance in *The Concert:* He said to think of the way Doubrovska entered the classroom. I thought of this and also of a spring morning on the top of Topa Topa, a mountain in the Ojai Valley. In terms of hard technique, her explanations were a little sketchy—probably because she was such a natural dancer herself—but I was relieved that her English was better than that of my earlier Russian teachers. Her classes had more to do with artistry, and I loved them. Madame Doubrovska's pointe class was a twice-weekly masterpiece, a marathon of steps. There was charm, wit, and femininity in her combinations. Even for me, the former mountain man, this was what ballet was all about.

Class, a special occasion for Doubrovska, required special dancing dresses that had sweetheart necklines and fluid knee-length skirts. A color-coordinated scarf at her waist wafted after her as she floated around the room. Sometimes she seductively tucked her skirt up to show us how unbroken and extended the ballet line should be. Then I could see that her long legs were perfectly shaped and that they would always be, no matter what her age. Her arches had an exciting, extreme curve to them, like a swan's head, gorgeous finials on the sculptured configurations she created. Her pas de chat were two fleeting, distinctive triangles flashing in the air, moving through space, a combination of shapes that pass and also linger in the memory.

One day Doubrovska told a story of a wonderful balance she did long ago in *Les Sylphides*. She had been angry with Mr. B. because a favorite part had been taken away from her. She went out and balanced forever in an arabesque. Caught in an endless suspension, she was thrilled with the experience. Then Mr. B. came back and complained that by lingering too long, she had been off the music. Telling us the story, she grinned in fun. Was there no satisfying this man? This genius taskmaster? Even with perfection? Years later, I held a balance in the second movement of *Bourrée Fantasque*. I went up and stayed. A part of me realized I was going to stay, and I let the music roll past me. Everything came together. I smiled happily, thinking of the teacher I loved. I wished those balances would occur all the time. They were mystical, and so were pirouettes.

Melissa Hayden and Jillana were almost always in Mme. Doubrovska's class. Although she was a star, Melissa did not have the proportions that we had heard Balanchine favored. She had wide shoulders, narrow hips, and not particularly long legs, but elegant insteps. Nevertheless, her line was long because it was an extension of her dramatic persona. You saw what she wanted you to see. She looked stunning in *The Duel* and was openly sexual as Profane Love in *Illuminations*. While I expected warmth and love from my teachers, from the principal dancers I expected complete self-absorption. Instead, Melissa was very friendly in the dressing room, and I was surprised to find a ballet star who was not aloof. Melissa walked in a turned-out position that broadcast the word "ballerina" when you saw her on the street. I resolved to have a completely straightforward gait—like a Tennessee walker—without a trace of turnout. I believed that your profession should not be advertised or appear in your stride.

Jillana, with her dark hair and pale skin, was absolutely beautiful. She had a gracious manner but not a strong technique. The rumor was that Mr. B. liked her very much. I liked to watch her, and I marveled over her graceful arms. She was only eighteen, but she seemed mature and womanly to me. She wasn't awkward at all, and her elbows weren't pointy like mine.

Class consisted not only of doing combinations but also of incessant watching. I could have patterned myself after Jillana or Melissa, but I wanted raw wildness too. I didn't want to forget Carmelita, Nijinska, or Jedediah Smith when I danced.

I also first saw Eddie Villella in a regular C ballet class. The students were all girls except for one skinny little boy with enormous dark brown eyes, a boy with whom I would one day dance one of the most sensual of Balanchine's ballets. He was dressed just like a good School of American Ballet (S.A.B.) student, with black tights and white shirt. Class stopped for some reason, and Eddie was up in a leap—not a ballet leap but a very spontaneous high jump. Gravitational pull lost its power when he soared into his pronging springbok elevation, and the image stayed in my head. He was way, way up and idled in the air for a brief moment. I liked this boy who could fly.

While I took class, my mother and Mrs. Zimmermann, Jillana's mother, would speak at length. Mr. B. was topic number one. His past, his views on everything, and his ballerinas were fascinating subjects, and the mothers were experts and founts of knowledge about every recorded piece of information and any hearsay. What else did they have to do?

From these conversations my mother learned that Mr. B.'s real romantic interest was the tall, long-legged, limber ballerina, Tanaquil Le Clercq. An only child, Tanny was eleven when Mr. B. discovered her, and she began her professional career very early. With her poetic face, she had a new and different ballet look. Like a lean Giacometti, she reflected modern art. Her chaîné turns in *The Concert* were ones that a Georgian folk dancer would be proud of—they had speed and character—but in *Swan Lake* they were slower because she felt the swan ballet was sacred ground; her usual freedom was tinged with fear. At other times, she could show poetic and mysterious depth with her exquisite acting ability, or she could be an elegant clown. She was magnificent in the ballet called *Metamorphoses*. She went through the stages of larva and pupa in the dressing room before the curtain went up. Onstage, she ruled as Queen of the Invertebrates, a bug wearing a bikini, antennae quivering delicately. Finally, she flew in as a winged creature with turquoise plumage as the entire cast took to the air with long, translucent wings of many colors.

Tanny could turn the strange geometric shapes her willowy body made into romance or the darker emotions. One day she came in with a bandage on her nose. She had kicked too high in front, or as they say in ballet, in her grand battement. She had karate-kicked herself. I was very impressed. We communicated very little, however. While some of the older ballerinas like Maria Tallchief broke the ice and did their best with me, the impossible youngster, it wasn't in Tanny's temperament to do so. She was too close to my age to play a motherly role with me.

It was Mme. Doubrovska who babied me. She didn't want me to

overwork. If I took two classes in a row, she'd tell me not to. She shouldn't have worried. S.A.B. was not a professional school the way it is today. I think she was wrong, actually. I needed to work harder, and I would have done better with more competition. Madame also noticed my everyday movements. She told me to walk with my legs together, not apart with my weight shifting from side to side in a roll, like a Boston bull terrier. This made me happy. Her interest in me did not end when class was over.

We were told not to buy presents for the teachers at Christmas, but I ran after Madame with a tiny wrapped box, a purple glass heart. When I handed her the present, she said, "You're breaking the rules."

"I don't care. Merry Christmas, and thank you for your wonderful classes."

"Thank you, darling."

Ballet was the magic and exhilarating force in my life. Natural laws were held in abeyance. The floating laws of clouds and the gyroscopic laws of tops took over, stretching the limits. The body could do wonderful things. Some of these marvels were achieved by technique, but there was something else. How I wanted to have the untiring, springing, elastic muscles of a grasshopper for my leaps, and the pneumatic knees of a swamp mangrove. Jumping was a wonderful part of dancing. Look at my leap. Was there ever such a leap? I couldn't believe how wonderful my leap looked and felt! The first leap ever done on earth felt that way. Some might leap higher, but they must feel less about it. My leap was nothing less than fantastic.

Although I loved my ballet classes, I wasn't adjusting to my new life in New York City. I needed hills and hiking. I missed nature all around me, and the windowsill at the apartment I shared with Mother and Wendy on East Thirty-sixth Street soon became crowded with plants, pots, dirt, and miniature implements. Daily, I overfertilized in my effort to see a fast-growing jungle within my grasp. Instead my garden wilted and died from the too-rich diet. I wrote:

Dear Daddy Darling,
My plants are growing nicely. The pansies are only little tiny seedlings but someday they will be real plants.

Mother dictated a portion of the letter: "Why aren't you using the name Kent instead of Cohen? Because if you aren't, we can't use your name as a reference and even worse, we can't introduce you to our friends." Not being able to introduce Daddy to my friends was sad news indeed. I liked to think of Harry Cohen as a grand name, and I liked to dream of the legions of men who are and have been Harry Cohen, multitudes of them on the march in heaven and hell—a special species. But Mother didn't want Daddy to use the name even ten years after their divorce. Even though he lived three thousand miles away from us, the name revealed too much.

Mother and I were sleeping in a tiny bedroom and Wendy in the living room of our small apartment. Wendy had a passion for what she called black raspberry walls, a particular tone that could never be realized by our painters. We made attempts at black raspberry in three successive living rooms, and usually it came out a bright, hideous, glaring purple, though we kept patiently trying for the muted color of Wendy's imagination, opening cartons and cartons of ice cream so the painters could see the color as done by Howard Johnson's, Schrafft's, and Louis Sherry.

While I had been waiting for Mr. B. to decide on the S.A.B. scholarship, I auditioned for the High School of Performing Arts and was accepted. Robert Joffrey was my ballet teacher there. Years later, he generously recalled my entrechat-sixes as "entrechat-dixes." Once I received the scholarship from Mr. B., the combined schedules of both schools added up to three classes every day. That was too much, and I became sick. Sad to leave Joffrey's great lessons, I quit Performing Arts and entered tenth grade at the Professional Children's School, which took only one-half of the day. Professional Children's was located on Broadway in an office building. I arrived for my earliest class by elevator. My first question was about the playground—there wasn't any. How could I even start to like a school that didn't have any trees? On other school grounds, I had encountered palms, pomegranates, and sycamores.

The one person I liked in my new school was Edward Preble, my science teacher. He had an unusual approach to his subject. One day he looked out the window and renamed an atom particle an "alcazar." It was the name of a bar across the street. I looked out the window. Men were going in and out of the bar at eleven in the morning. I understood that I too could rename scientific terms. I invented a pseudoscientific name for a small nucleus by adding a Winnie-the-Pooh ending. There was Piglet. Why not nucleilet? The word wasn't graceful, but it was imaginative. Mr. Preble liked the idea, and we became attuned to each other. I would be surprised twenty-five years later to meet him again.

The next year Mother and I decided that I would go to Rhodes High School, just a deep breath away from our new apartment on East Fifty-eighth Street. Change, as always, was in our blood, but this time it was practical. Our new home, the School of American Ballet, and my high school were all within a six-block radius. No buses were necessary. Rhodes, a small private school in a beautiful brownstone on West Fifty-fourth Street, also had an abbreviated school day so that students could act or dance. The girls were zaftig teenagers. I was fifteen but looked more like ten. The other students thought of me as a toddler, so no social life there was possible.

I was surprised to see Eddie Villella in my English class at Rhodes. I hadn't noticed him because he was in regular clothes and there were lots of other boys in my class, but he came up to me and told me he had been in my ballet class at the American School. He wasn't a skinny little boy anymore; at sixteen, he had grown four inches and filled out a bit. I thought he was terrific looking and very nice. Another boy there called me "skinny idiot"; that was the kind of attention I got. But Eddie would never have said that.

I didn't get a chance to talk to Eddie often, however, because I left Rhodes early each day for a mad dash to Mme. Doubrovska's pointe class with a bare minute to spare for changing clothes. I'd run, skip, and gallop over to S.A.B., crossing from west to east on Fifth Avenue near Tiffany's. The School of American Ballet was in those days at Fifty-ninth and Madison.

Despite the move, I wasn't adjusting completely to my new life. With my heavy schedule balancing school and dance, my sleeping patterns were becoming odd. I wanted absolute silence, but instead I heard the "subtle" symphony of steam heat. The invisible pipes jangled at midnight, playing a percussive tune, thumping and reverberating, Ping-Pong balls hitting a table faster and faster, then a celery-chewing sound as they lost momentum, and a delicate *ting* from a triangle. I was developing into a crank, and Mother began giving in to me on strange things. She was still doing my homework. Wendy warned her she was spoiling me, but I knew I was being saved for ballet alone. I could almost sing it as a refrain: I was being saved for ballet alone. And it was working.

In the fall of 1952, several of the ballerinas—Maria Tallchief, Melissa Hayden, and Janet Reed—started asking me questions about myself. How long had I studied? Where did I start? Whom had I studied with? They were surprised to learn I had been taking ballet classes for only four years. This interest contained a message. I had been a student at the school for a little over a year, but this attention meant I had been noticed. I was being singled out. I wasn't ordinary in every way.

I came into the dressing room three hours early to get ready. The girls had cleared a space for me, and I arranged the items I had acquired in the past few days: Max Factor greasepaint, medium brown hairnets, and Dippity-Do hair gel. I also had dark brown pencils to help me etch delicate and bold lines, bright red lipstick, pale powder, rouge, and a small mirror to reflect the back of my head.

It was December 12, 1952, the night of my first stage performance. One year and four months after entering the School of American Ballet, I had been made an apprentice so I could dance in the corps de ballet of the New York City Ballet Company. The invitation had come from Mr. B., but we learned of it through a secretary who called my mother. Although I had yet to take a class with him, this was a clear message of Mr. B.'s interest in me. The School of American Ballet did not put on performances at that time, and Mr. B. wanted me to have some stage experience. I'd never been in a recital. I'd never put on a tutu, snapped rhinestones on my ears, or powdered a shiny face. In fact, I'd never put on a real dance costume, only my mountain-man garb. Performing was important, and Balanchine recognized that. In Russia, the children from the Imperial School were incorporated in this ritual at a young age, as Balanchine himself had been, so they would have stage experience.

I was intensely delighted to be made an apprentice. This was suddenly professional and real. Now I could freely watch the ballet backstage or from an empty seat in the audience and see any program I wished. Stage technique seemed to me very different from class technique. But watching the performances had brought out new fears. I would have to be as skilled as these girls on stage. Was this possible for someone who once thought she had no special abilities and was average in all ways?

Vida Brown taught me the steps for the corps de ballet part to the second movement of Bizet's *Symphony in C,* a piece of music that Mr. B. had, in effect, discovered. The symphony was exquisite, and the section I was learning was wistful and romantic. It caught me with its beauty. I was unbearably nervous but proceeded to learn. As Balanchine ballets go, this part was particularly easy; it is somewhat of a tradition for beginners to start out in *Symphony in C,* but I didn't know that at the time. The company girls had amazing heads full of millions of steps. Would my brain ever be able to absorb all of them? I was worried about what lay ahead. It kept me up at night. Nevertheless, I learned the part in three rehearsals, with an additional one onstage for spacing, but there had been no costume or orchestra rehearsal.

I stared at the tubes and powders in front of me. I knew nothing about the ABCs of makeup, let alone "stage" makeup, or the hairdo termed "classical," with the hair pulled first back over the ears and then into a low bun on the neck.

I parted my hair in the center and draped some strands in soft locks over my ears, anchoring the gentle curve in place with hairpins. Several willful tufts could not be caught, so I glued them into submission with Dippity-Do. The cold, moist aqua gel dried stiff and dark. My bun felt as if it would come apart during turns, so I added more pins, stabbing myself and making the back of my head too heavy. Finally, I arranged a hairnet over the entire nineteenth-century nightmare.

That part was easy compared to my fake eyelashes. I nearly glued one of my eyes closed with the liquid adhesive, so Basia Walcyak, my friend in the corps, suggested her beading—jet-black wax heated and melted in a teaspoon over a candle and applied to the eyelashes.

The rest of the corps girls, most of them in their early twenties, were advanced at makeup. Professionals for years, they'd been playing with lipstick and experimenting with colors and perfecting their stage faces for hundreds of performances. Their sophistication impressed me. I looked at the girl to my right and did what she did. Then I surreptitiously glanced at the girl on my left for additional ideas. She did this, I'll do this. She does that, I'll do that. The two sides of my face were different. I created a split personality, an accidental Picasso. Another dancer had put on white eye shadow, and I copied her. The effect was Egyptian, and I looked terrible. I stared in the mirror. My bright red lips ran slightly over the boundaries. I felt dismay in my heart; when I began the evening, I had been a cleanly scrubbed fifteen.

Next, Dunya, the wardrobe mistress, gave me a pair of silk stockings that I had to split evenly at the seams, put a little diamond of material in the middle, and sew into tights that would become a well-fitting second skin. This was the tradition in ballet. I didn't split my silk stockings evenly, and the legs were not the same length; one side stretched on its own. I was too nervous to thread the needle. Time was edging up on me.

At last, I was in the wings. The ballet was underway. I would soon be out there on the strange territory of the stage of the City Center, much of me encased in the confining artifices of the ballet craft and decades of tradition. I was wearing a strangulating corset of shiny fabric with a flying saucer attached—a platter of white tulle extending from my hips. I had to dance in it and be graceful, but the tutu had a life of its own. I couldn't see my feet. I tipped it. There they were, the shoes and ill-fitting tights. I had sewn ribbons on my pointe shoes and then broke them in. Were the ribbons tucked in or had they escaped? If they had, this signified sloppiness and was not excusable. The details were numerous. Should I review the choreography in my mind? That was probably a good idea. I didn't know that the dancers warmed up again before going on stage. The first movement was almost over. There was the applause, and then there I was, part of a line of six girls doing the entrance step of bourrées, a trembling motion of the legs— tiny shimmers of dance, that resembled nothing in real life. No one does this step to board a subway—a trill of the toes that propelled the body forward with a magical motion.

The music for the second movement reached me through the acoustical barrier of my Victorian helmet. I was terrified. This was the first time I ever danced on a professional level to orchestra music and not the piano. The symphony sounded as if it were coming through water. And the lights. It was very foggy out there—a moonstone mist flowed from the beams. In the parallelogram of space known as the stage, things were different. The reflective mirror of the classroom was now the huge darker area of the audience. I could no longer see myself but had to feel and relate to the other dancers of the corps. Somehow I managed to stay in line and on my counts. With so much fear, the fun and joy were lost. It was possible that my great career idea was a mistake.

Muriel Stuart and Mme. Doubrovska both sent bouquets backstage. Madame's was a nosegay of violets with one pink rose in the middle. This small piece of perfection took my breath away. Her card read: "Dear little Allegra! My wish is that these violets may bring you luck for the first of many, many successes. Love, Felia Doubrovska." I was in love with the bouquet and the card. The charm of this woman enchanted me, and when I thanked her profusely, she told me that Mme. Pavlova had given her a bouquet like that for *her* first performance. I was completely awed; I knew I would never forget it. I had been studying for four years and four months toward this night.

Even though my new status as apprentice meant that Mr. B. was interested in my dancing, he had his new muse. Just a week and one day after my first performance, Mr. B. married Tanaquil Le Clercq.

It was from Mrs. Zimmermann, Jillana's mother, that my mother heard the talk about me going around the New York City Ballet. I would soon be asked to join the company as a real member. Perhaps Mr. B. had told Maria Tallchief who told Bobby Barnett who told Irene Larsson who told Jillana, who told her mother. So my mother and I were warned.

We had accomplished this goal very quickly, almost too easily. For a moment, Mother thought perhaps we should reconsider. She didn't want my childhood to disappear overnight. I would become a professional at fifteen, a regular working girl. Maybe we had been too successful. Mother seemed to treat this news like a pregnancy; maybe this wasn't appropriate for a teenager. She was frightened and reassessed the direction of my life, so I did too.

Did I really want to be a professional at this age? I wasn't sure. Joining a ballet company when I was so young could only ensure the loss of my teenage years. Mrs. Dugger, a favorite teacher at Ojai, had said that when we got certain things too early we didn't appreciate them. She had been thinking of cars and formal gowns, but this was something bigger. I sent my doubts cross-country to Daddy:

September 11, 1952
Dearest Daddy,
    It looks like I may be in the ballet company any minute. Don't let it happen. I'm too young. I want to go back to golden California and lead a normal life.

When official word finally seeped down to us, filtered through Mr. B.'s staff, I had even more qualms. Did the company just need more girls to replace some who had left? In 1953, it wasn't so difficult to get into the New York City Ballet corps. Was I just filling a hole? There was no glory in that.

But, in the end, the invitation was irresistible. It was couched in exactly the right terms for Mother. She was told that Mr. B. was "very interested" in my potential. I wouldn't simply be one of the rank and file. Despite her earlier reservations, my mother accepted for me, and I was jubilant.

I had become a real dancing girl. As a member, not only would I draw a weekly salary instead of the fifteen dollars a performance I made as an apprentice, but I would tour with the company through the United States ending in California for the summer and in Europe during the fall.

As usual, I had learned about my rise in status from someone in the ballet office, not from Mr. B. himself. It was always indirect. Perhaps this was some form of Russian etiquette, like Mme. Nijinksa's attacking the wrong people for chewing gum. Balanchine once promoted a soloist to principal dancer, but the news never seeped down to her. She didn't know. Finally, she realized that her salary had gone up.

As a company member, my schedule became more difficult. I was dancing at night, going to school during the day, and, at times, being an understudy. Even though I still received good grades, I began devoting less time to school and more to ballet. I accelerated my studies so I would be graduating in June at fifteen.

It was dance alone that I wanted to study. At this time the New York City Ballet had nineteen principal dancers and a relatively small corps de ballet of thirty. Some of the corps women were very serious about dancing, but to others it was just a job. They didn't attend class or even warm up for performances. They were not obsessed with ballet as I was.

This was my university, and I was a student. One of my joys was watching Maria Tallchief. She had a way of dancing so musically that it was a thrilling experience. Her foot curled as the music curled, and then it extended as the sounds elongated. She moved quickly and then slowed down so that the endings matched perfectly, the movement and the music finishing together. I used to watch every pas de deux she did. She didn't seem to be frightened of the stage, like some of the others. She had an iron will inside, and I never worried when I watched her dance. She phrased her curls and extensions as delicately or as strongly as the music itself. She was a silent song.

When I wasn't onstage myself, I attended performances. I liked the way Jacques d'Amboise did his multiple turns in *Filling Station,* a ballet that had been revived just for him. As his turns became slower and slower, my heart beat faster and faster; when he finished, he stepped aside with an insouciant grin, and the audience showed their delight. I was thrilled when Jacques asked me to join an adagio class with him. Janet Reed—tiny, with flaming red hair—portrayed the drunk rich girl in *Filling Station* in a hilarious way, with mimed hiccups and makeup that looked plastered. Her intoxication ended at the waist; from that point on down she was sober. The part combined a mix of sophistication, comedy, and the sun coming up over the Rockies. I watched everything. I would be touring the United States and Europe with these dancers.

Things were going awfully well in this fairy tale that was also my life, but oftimes, in these same stories, terrible years follow a success too easily accomplished. Could that happen to me? I was now a professional. But, at fifteen, I was also the youngest member of the company, the baby.

CHAPTER FIVE

Physical Training—Cannot be overdone; exhausting for children.

—GUSTAVE FLAUBERT,
DICTIONARY OF ACCEPTED IDEAS

We were seven thousand feet above sea level, and the stage was tilted to one side, so most of the swans veered toward the base of the hill. It was a lopsided performance, the girls done in by gravity. Our train had taken us to the first stop on our tour, Boulder, Colorado. By the end of the evening, I was sick from the altitude, but not before going out front to watch the closing ballet, *La Valse,* Mr. B.'s eerie fable of danger and death to Ravel's music. The setting against the dark pines set off the flashes of brilliant magenta, cherry, lavender, red, and flame from the underskirts. I was deliriously happy.

I was learning new corps de ballet parts every day. The monster role in *Firebird* excited me, and I threw my heart, soul, and entrechatsixes into it. The other corps girls thought it a nuisance; we were all just rank-and-file monsters in the Chagall costumes. The part was tiring, not classical, and we were hardly seen in the dim lights. Nevertheless, I loved it. Nora Kaye said she made a special point to watch me as a monster. This was the Halloween party I had missed when I was nine. It had finally arrived, in grand style and with music by Stravinsky.

However, by the morning after our first performance in L.A.'s Greek Theatre two weeks later, my body felt awful. The stage floor was hard. The difference lay in the stucco that was embedded half an inch under a thin covering of wood, just a tiny distance from the tips of my toes. The cement had crawled into my body and crept into my calves and thighs, making them bulge out. The strain continued upward, and my head sat fatigued and inflexible on my stiff neck. I barely recognized my muscles. So there was discomfort in this business. I thought it would be more abstract, like the pain in the movies that had a heroic ring to it. This pain did not.

I soon learned that Mr. B.'s classes were conducted to explore his own creativity; not designed to warm us up in a careful manner. The main function of a ballet company is to get the performance on. Mr. B. wanted us programmed for reliability, like sharpshooters. We must hit the mark every time, and that's the way he gave his barre—without frills. Onstage I could be a willow tree and bend to the right and to the left, but not in class. In 1953, the New York City Ballet was still a small company, not the institution it is today. For a young dancer, it was catch-as-catch-can, and progress and remaining injury-free could be haphazard. Mr. B. was like a god who touched us occasionally.

Many details of my first class with Mr. B. don't come back to me; I remember only that it took place in a high school gym in Colorado. My important childhood teachers—Doubrovska, Nijinska, and Carmelita—still teach and move in my memory, returning fully dressed in the colors they favored. In their distinctive styles, they still pirouette and pas de chat in my dreams, while specifics about my first classes with Balanchine remain in a haze. The difference: he was a man and they were women. I was allowed to love them safely and with complete sanction from my mother. A great male teacher was not within this realm. A man was automatically grouped in the Harry Cohen category, the group to be dismissed. And so these early classes stay in the shadows. In my letters home to mother, I didn't quote Balanchine, I quoted my roommate, Dido Sayers, her sayings and her personal idiosyncrasies. "That's for sure," as she used to say.

But the essence of these first classes remains. There was the wonderful energy that traveled back and forth from teacher to pupil; it was freely expanded and expected. I remember the architectural precision that Mr. B. wanted and the importance of the exact center. We were building arabesques. I saw that repetition opened the channels to possible perfection. He was Russian, like Nijinska, and so, of course, he used imagery to explain what he wanted. From him I understood that greed in ballet is all right; it's akin to desire. Mr. B. threw this out to surprise and confuse us. Another day he told us to create an arabesque that, in its reach and desire, was "gold and ice cream."

• • •

One night after the company had arrived in California, a dancer from the corps, Janie Mason, mentioned the fact that when she was very young she lived away from home with older girls, "the type that destroy you." She said that she would rather not have any friends at all if she had to have that kind.

"Do you think I'm going to destroy you?" I asked Janie, trying to give my voice a mischievous tone.

Janie laughed. She was having dinner with me and my roommate, Dido. I was making my first girlfriends. In high school, no one even bothered to talk to me because I was smaller and younger than the others. Since I had accelerated and graduated high school at fifteen, my classmates were two and three years older. Even though I was also the youngest member of the company, I felt accepted. Late at night on the train, I listened as the girls in the corps told stories of near-mythological happenings, a ballerina who fell out of bed doing an entrechat-six. I think this particular story about Marie Jeanne meant that her technique did not disappear overnight.

Certainly Janie was the most unusual of this odd cast of characters in my new family. She possessed a full-blown individualistic streak for dressing. The company girls didn't approve of the giant-size hatboxes she stuffed her clothes into and piled on the train platform as we left New York City for Denver; they wanted her to have suitcases like everyone else. With her black stockings, black high heels, and strawberry blond hair, she could have stepped right out of a Toulouse-Lautrec drawing. In Denver Janie bought a black velvet wide-brim hat with a string of pearls around the crown and a very alluring veil. The day we arrived in Los Angeles she wore the hat with a tight black sheath at high noon on Hollywood Boulevard. A group of men swarmed around her. In a few months, I would see this repeated on train platforms all over Europe as men crowded around Janie to help her with her baggage. No one else in the company went to these extremes. Janie was years ahead of her time, and I thought her courageous. This was true of her approach to life as well. On the train she played chess with Dido, and I overheard her say, as we crossed Colorado toward Denver, "Oh, please, don't move that horse." She had instantly brought the Wild West into her chess game, and I smiled about it in my upper berth.

One of the things I liked best about my other friend, Dido, was that she talked in her sleep. She spoke in the same softly accented voice that was hers by day, and I listened in fascination. It was as if she were acting a part of great intensity in a horizontal position, and she knew her lines perfectly. Perhaps dreams are our first acting lessons. We use the right emotions in the right scenes, and our subconscious writes the script.

I smiled happily at my two new friends. Janie had been lonely, and we had invited her to join us. Now she was ready to create a little sisterhood. "Why don't we three promise to always be together and give each other friendly criticism?" she asked.

"That's fine with me," I responded, but I was wondering if any criticism I'd ever received had been friendly. And I knew right away that I'd never mention her dress or hat to her.

"I can never have children," Janie confided. Dido didn't catch this piece of information.

"I'm sorry," I said, but I wondered how she knew. I didn't know if I could have children or not.

"Let's link pinkies in a pact of friendship," she said. So Janie, Dido, and I hooked our fingers together and swore friendship and eternal helpfulness. Janie then went on to tell us about the sexual relations of some famous ballerinas.

I loved Janie and her uniqueness, but when I wrote home I adopted some of Mother's judgmental attitudes. On paper pulled from the dresser drawers in my hotel room I printed in pencil:

> While we were discussing such subjects as marriage and the sexual relations that such ballerinas as M. Hayden and M. Fontaine have had (wow!), Janie mentioned the fact that she could not have any children. (Dido didn't even catch this bit of information.) I am telling you this just as it happened without my personal opinion, although I guess you can gather it. She wants to get married when she is about 35 and to a good friend only. The way she dresses, all the men on Hollywood Blv. tried to pick her up. On many subjects if you draw it out of Janie, she is truely very intelligent and has interesting opinions.
>
> Love to you, Allegra

I had adopted a self-righteous attitude for my mother's benefit. No matter how many of the so-called rules Janie broke, I liked her a lot.

The company not only had brought me friends, but the tour had also brought me back to California, the place I had been dreaming about for two years. All the familiar plants were there for me to see again. The succulents were magnificent and the Washingtonian palm trunks high, shaggy, and comic. At fifteen, I still favored tomboy outfits that saleswomen allowed me to buy only when I said they were for my brother. I felt that they would blend in nicely with the pepper and eucalyptus trees.

Although I couldn't reach Daddy at first when we arrived in Los Angeles, I hadn't been forgotten. He sent some Biltmore Hotel flower-shop roses to the Greek Theatre for me. A salesman sends a small traveling flower garden to the stage door to offer encouragement for his daughter's ethereal strivings. To the others, it looked like a bouquet.

I was excited and happy to be in the company and to work with Mr. B. I knew that I had his vote of confidence. During class one day he said to me, "You can do anything," and I understood that he meant it. Everything was working out beautifully. The next stop was Europe.

As I entered the famous La Scala opera house with my roommates, Dido and Barbara Bocher, we heard the distant muted metal clang of cymbals. Somewhere deep in the theater, behind the heavy stage curtains, the orchestra was rehearsing *La Valse*. The dry smell of plaster dust mingled with the sweet perfume of tuberose. Several Italian ladies dressed all in black handed us each a nosegay of the fragrant blossoms. They inspected us and our clothes with friendly curiosity. *"Grazie molto,"* I said, lifting the little bunch of flowers to my face. No one had ever welcomed us like this in an American theater, and I loved this gesture. I was out of my mind with happiness.

On my first European tour with the company, we would be visiting nine cities in Italy, then on to Belgium and Germany. Milan was our first stop.

Because the interior of La Scala had received a few direct hits during World War II and was still under reconstruction, the place was alive with workmen pushing wheelbarrows full of cement; there were many unfinished areas and detours. The backstage area was confusing, but the ladies in black were fantastic at sign language, so eventually our little group headed toward the dressing rooms.

As we progressed along the complicated route, we met one of the Italian dancers wearing a bathrobe over practice clothes who again gave directions with charming descriptive curves of her hands and fingers. We marched upstairs hoping to find our dressing rooms, theater cases, and rehearsal hall so we wouldn't miss class. On the next landing, the fourth floor, there it was. Adjacent to the costume room,

Dunya, our ancient wardrobe mistress, was bustling about. We also had our very own Italian little old lady dressed in black who would shortly offer to cook hard-boiled eggs for me. I had arrived in a country with great cuisine, but I still preferred to have my food utterly simple. I hadn't changed much since breakfast at the Biltmore.

On our way, we had stopped to look at the stage. The downward slope of the old boards shocked me. The floor of La Scala is raked—tilted so that the front of the stage is lower than the back. I would have to dance on this Italian hillside in a few days. Jacques d'Amboise had told me about the slanted floors of European opera houses and assured me that once I was used to it, the rake would help me dance.

Changing quickly into our practice clothes, we met Jacques in the corridor and followed him to the main rehearsal hall. This was a startling sight. Encased in the huge studio was a duplicate of the same foothill of the Italian Alps that had been on the stage. It was a room with a rake. A long mirrored panel was at the base, and at the top, windows overlooked the roofs of Milan. I tried out various positions at the barre, one where I would look uphill on the right side and downhill on the left as I used alternate legs. Finally I decided on a position where my body would work in a more even way. This was at the top, shallow end of the room, near the windows and near the ceiling. While waiting for class to begin I did some stretches.

Mr. B. walked in looking very pleased and, with a clap of his hands, said, "Let's begin."

I tried to act like a plant and stand upward no matter what the ground level was, but my position felt precarious. Over a period of a few days, however, my body did find a new balance, all by itself. Moving upstage was a struggle, mountain climbing and dancing at the same time, but jumping downstage was wonderful.

Jacques, Barbara, and I started taking classes with the Italians at nine in the morning. Mme. Bulness, who taught the La Scala company, was an excellent teacher, and I liked to take her class and then Mr. B.'s afterward. Throughout the tour, I never missed one of Mr. Balanchine's lessons. I was striving to find myself as a dancer and a performer. Very often, the majority of the company went off sightseeing, and sometimes only nine people showed up, sometimes only four. I was glad; the fewer the better. Some of these classes were like private lessons but not meticulously technical. Tanny was always there, and usually Maria. She would get close to the mirror to study her mannerisms.

It was all thrilling. And I was doing it by myself.

When I heard that Edith Le Clercq, Tanny's mother, was going to Europe with the company and would share a suite of rooms with her daughter and Mr. B., I had hoped this information would not be used against me by my own mother, because I knew she would want to join the tour once she heard. This arrangement would not do for me. As a new member of the corps de ballet, I felt I had to prove how grown up I was. The company was like my college, and mothers didn't go to college with their children (although John Ruskin's mother did, and look what happened to him).

One of the older girls of the corps had brought her mother, and I observed them during plane and train trips. They seemed too close. I would never display my need for my mother in front of the entire company in such a way. There was something wrong and very sad here. The thought occurred to me: What did this mother do all day? Yes, I did believe in appearances. As the youngest member of the company, I couldn't appear so needy. On the summer trip to California, I had learned how much fun it was to travel with the other girls in the corps, so when Mother asked to go, I said no. I usually followed her lead and obeyed her wishes, but on this issue I was adamant. I had to shed my "baby" status alone.

When I arrived at the theaters in the different cities throughout Europe, however—even those that were difficult to find—my mother was already a presence there. Waiting backstage at the guard's quarters would be several letters from her. In Venice, there were five. Mother wrote me in detail about Wendy's boyfriends. I wrote by return mail, "You must realize Wendy is twenty-four." Mother wrote that Harry had come to New York and looked terrible, very overweight. She said his friends were all laughing at him now because traveling salesmen were out of date. His ten-gallon hats looked ridiculous, and business wasn't good. I wrote Daddy a note to try to comfort him. My poor daddy was going through a bad time.

Mother wanted to accompany me on the next tour. She worried about me. What could I do from so far away but reassure her that I was using the time to mature?

Although I did not invite my mother along, I did take her adopted religion with me. When Mother felt alone in the world, she drew closer to Christian Science. Modeling myself after her, I packed two "important" books in my luggage, *Science and Health* by Mary Baker Eddy, and the Bible. There was a daily lesson with readings from both books in an alternating pattern. Searching for the page and reading the prescribed lines was boring, but if I didn't do it guilt loomed over me. Some of the subjects of the week were Atonement or At-one-ment, Spirit, Mind, Truth, and Life. I often fell asleep reading. But my mother wanted me to study these lessons and so I did, and I wrote home to report my faithfulness, hoping somehow it would make a better person out of me. I knew Mother had moments when obscure passages were illuminated with intense insight, so I didn't give up. I was just as religious about avoiding medicine. I left Mother, Wendy, and New York City without taking any pills with me, not even a small bottle of aspirin for a headache. If I developed a soft corn, I had to pray my way out of it. All I took were a few bandages for bruised toes and blisters, and my spiritual books. For leisure, Wendy had given me *Flowering Judas* and a biography of Henry VIII.

At the airport Mr. B. had told Mother that he would look after me. But this was untrue. During our first weeks in Milan, my older roommates left me behind as they ran off on dates or for elaborate dinners while I stayed alone eating boiled eggs. I was socially un-graceful and too shy to ask a group if I could join them. Sometimes members of the company included me in their activities, but I was also often left on my own, finding places to eat, locating the theater, washing my tights every night—sometimes in cold water—getting adequate sleep, seeing a discreet portion of the sights, sewing my shoes, and never missing Mr. B.'s classes. There was always learning my whereabouts in a new city and trying not to let a deep-rooted shyness prevent me from functioning.

I also had to learn to perform like a professional. Even though I desired to grow up, sometimes I behaved like the sixteen-year-old kid I was. Balanchine's *Orpheus* was on one of the programs, and Maria Tallchief was our Eurydice. I was one of many Furies, dressed in a gray bodysuit with long pointed tails sticking out all over. At a certain moment in the ballet, a group of us circled around Maria and froze with our hands held high and our tails at rest. During an actual per-formance of this section, something made me feel as if I were taking part in a Jerry Lewis movie. I started to giggle and struggled to contain my laughter as well as the slight reverberations in my body, but then I gave in and the giggles spread contagiously to the others. Soon the Furies were undulating gently, trying to stifle the comic moment. Maria came up to me after the performance. "I know who started that," she said in her authoritative voice. I apologized. My intent was not to ruin her performance; my spontaneous mirth had a life of its own and had simply surfaced at the wrong moment. But I knew it was wrong. I had behaved unprofessionally.

Maria was very generous, however. Even though I had behaved immaturely, she forgave me and treated me protectively. Maria's husband at that time was Elmazar Natirboff, whom I liked very much. I played canasta with him on our train trips, and he would stage the game. It would seem as if he was winning by overwhelming odds, and suddenly, through a master stroke, I would win. I would scream in delight and he would look chagrined. This happened too many times for me to consider it an accident. Was Maria in on this game?

I imagined that she may have instructed him how to behave toward me: "Elmazar, Allegra may be lonely at times. She's the youngest person on this tour. Let her win at canasta, but make it appear as if she won't. Create an event for her. She's such a hardworking child of the ballet and a religious fanatic too. Oh, these ballet girls are so complex. Now, Elmazar, look humiliated when you let her win, then we will wink at each other as she laughs with delight." These moments made me feel safe and happy, but during a lot of the early weeks of the tour, I felt alone.

I was not about to let my mother know that I was lonely, however. This was my new family and my first big separation from her since boarding school. I wrote: "My days have been absolutely cluttered with important work. Our room is about $2.00 a day, which is quite expensive for Italy."

I was determined to grow up on this tour—as a dancer, as a performer, and as a person.

The sad crisp smell of fall was in the air, and every breath had a cool freshness, a vibrancy, and a small message: summer was over. Our next stop after Milan was Lake Como, and my roommates had taken off without me. I had written down the instructions, so I knew what to do, although I hadn't anticipated doing this alone. After the performance there would be no problem because the entire company was taking the train back to Milan where we had kept our hotel rooms. We were commuting. The management was taking up our terpsichorean theater suitcases filled with what we needed to dance—practice clothes, makeup, and hair paraphernalia. We were responsible just for ourselves.

It was a great trial for me to get to the theater alone. I went to the North station and asked in faulty Italian, all by myself, for a third-class ticket to "Il Lago di Como." But I did it, suffering agonies of nameless fear just to speak some words not in my native language to an unknown person. I understood that this was what I had to go through to grow up. I had to have some ridiculous fights with myself over my absurd sense of shyness. It must have been in my family's genes; my sister had it too. It made me too reliant on my mother.

Finally, ticket in hand, I boarded the train, intoxicated with my own bravery.

As I disembarked from the train, I noticed a watery smell in the air. It was the famous nearby lake. The air of fall against my face made me feel sensitive to perfume, the perfume of change. Like a dog, I knew something was different. It was the coolness. The season of secondary colors had arrived—burnt orange, burnt sienna, and burnt umber. In the shops, brown pears and brown lipsticks were on display. The world was changing in the slanted light of a new season. I walked alone on an Italian street trying to act unself-conscious. All this trouble just to try to appear as a natural person. I had turned sixteen only two months earlier. The youngest and least sophisticated member of the New York City Ballet was walking alone in a small Italian city.

A small drizzle led me to quickly find the theater and the stage door. Although the stage was a slanted arrangement of old splintery boards, the inside of the opera house was beautiful, a small sparkling gem. The boxes were almost on the stage. I could reach out and shake a hand or read a program during a lull in the choreography. Perhaps this place was some contessa's toy theater. The gilt of gold and dark red velvet told a story of the opulent past—not a story, hundreds of stories. This was a jewel box with five tiers of parallel rings close to the stage, right on top of the action.

With my new secret feelings of a small private triumph, I felt I could really dance here. *Symphony in C* was scheduled that night. I was only in the corps, but that didn't matter. The mysteriously sad music of the second movement reflected my mood of the moment, my wistful, unknown yearnings. Like a tree, I was growing a little higher in the forest.

I was not even discouraged by the dressing room and the whole backstage area, which were dank and damp. The slightly older members considered themselves world travelers and joked about mushrooms and fungi growing on the wall. One naked, low-powered lightbulb in the center of a large room did not have enough power to illuminate our faces. We guessed at our makeup. But I didn't care. I was getting ready for the ballet I loved most in the entire world.

It was at Lake Como that I felt free and safe for the first time with what I did onstage. In that toylike theater of exquisite beauty, my natural expressiveness welled up, came to the surface, and spilled over. I changed my style dramatically and started dancing rather than just doing the steps. The tour so far had been my homework, but now those days were receding. I understood something new about a performance. A transformation could happen that was exhilarating while, at the same time, the choreography could be meticulously observed and executed. During that performance, I was no longer Allegra the academic classroom dancer. Pulled deeper into the spell of music and motion and lifted by magic, I changed form while staying the same— like water into mist. This would enable me to emerge from the corps and become a real dancer.

Once I had learned a little bit more about my profession and my shyness with people was abating, I noticed that there were foods I liked to eat in this country. In Rome, Ambassador Clare Booth Luce and her husband invited the entire company to an afternoon party at their villa. When I saw that the dessert was chocolate ice cream cake, I developed a plan. Acting as if it was my first piece each time, I ate three portions with three different groups of people.

One night Jacques invited Barbara Bocher and me to go with him after a performance to a small, offbeat restaurant that he said was his discovery alone; no one else knew anything about it. We were all in the last ballet, and after removing our makeup and changing our clothes, we followed Jacques conspiratorially through street after street until we reached the restaurant. When we entered, our mood changed to surprise. There, already seated and being served, were Maria Tallchief and her husband, Elmazar; at another table André and Leda Eglevsky; and at a third table, Mr. Balanchine, Tanny, and Edith Le Clercq—not a single person in the corps de ballet or even in a high middle level, but only the biggest wheels themselves. There was a moment of silence while uncomfortable stares went back and forth. Then Mr. B. said, "You know, Jacques, when I was your age I did the same thing. I always took out two girls at the same time." I smiled and thought this an odd comment, because at that very moment Mr. B. was still with two girls.

We felt exuberant. We had joined the stars in their game and at their special place. Perhaps no one could stop our progress, onstage or off.

I had lost much of my stage fright and was losing more and more of my life fright. In Brussels, Barbara's cousin took us to an American restaurant where I had a banana split: three scoops of ice cream, chocolate, strawberry and vanilla, with pineapple, fudge, nuts, whipped cream, and a banana. After that I had a chocolate soda and was about to have something else when the snack bar closed. "Too bad," I wrote home.

By the trip's end, I felt proud of myself. Although my shyness was not in total retreat, I was more confident. And I was pleased that I had done my job. I had taken every one of Mr. B.'s classes. I had impressed him with my constancy and faithfulness; when we returned he told my mother that I was "very conscientious." The corps de ballet of the early 1950s was not the serious group that it is today.

Mr. B. had noticed the radical change in my style. His secretary, my friend Barbara Horgan, told me he had observed that I danced differently at Lake Como and that he had been watching me since then. He liked what I was doing "very much." I had found a home and would fit in. I might like this profession after all.

When we returned to the United States, Mr. B. started to choreograph Nutcracker with Maria as the Sugar Plum Fairy. I liked the way she jumped up to Nicky Magallanes's shoulder with unwavering determination and an about-face leap. I was only a mouse and a shepherdess. I longed to be Dewdrop and do some jumping. And I knew it would happen. I hoped soon.

I should have worn two sweaters. The summer night in Seattle had a chill in it. It felt good to come inside. The theater was dark, warm, and dry. It was our first class in three days. Only that morning we had arrived by train. These were my last few days of being sweet sixteen, and I think an idea came to Mr. B. about my future during this evening of our summer tour.

Class was to be onstage. Many members of the company had already found something to hang on to—ladders or poles of lights, anything substantial and easy to grasp. I found a place in the wings where I would have to walk out to see Mr. B. after each combination.

This evening, there was no choreography in Mr. B.'s barre, just the unadorned warm-up steps, given quite straightforwardly. We finished in the usual way with grand battement. Most of us were not visible, so there were very few corrections in the first half of class. The backstage lights were dim; the theater was waiting for us to give it life.

This evening, my body felt good, my muscles felt long and loose.

The difference was with my feet. On the train I had done foot-strengthening exercises in my small shared compartment. With naked feet, I tried to grab the rug on the floor and then stretch out my toes, first right, then left, passionately trying to form a fist, using my feet like fingers. This was one exercise in a whole series of movements designed for toe and instep power. My feet felt exceptionally strong.

When we left the barre, I had trouble with the adagio. The semi-dark theater threw my balance off. We exercised in two groups. The principal ballerinas stood in front of the first group. Mr. B. looked at them with pleasure. These were the ladies who daily tried to jump over metaphysical moons and lifted their legs in extension reaching to the top of the rainbow.

The ballerinas excelled in a turn step done on the diagonal. I wondered if this beautiful combination would find its way into one of Mr. B.'s ballets. These special girls were eight to eleven years older than I was. Maybe I had a little more time to become like them.

My muscles were stretched from rest, but my feet were strong. When I soared so easily in the jumping steps, I knew again why I loved to dance. It was for this feeling.

Mr. B., chin uplifted, was standing near the footlights, facing his dancers, looking, giving a few instructions, encouraging. The theater had a dry smell of dusty comfort. I felt joyous; the strong rhythm of the piano washed over me. When I did my leaping sissonne forward, I suddenly felt his eyes on me. Like the little cowboy who became the palace gardener in "The Twelve Dancing Princesses," his eye was on the youngest one. I wondered when he'd call upon me for a dance.

When the next season opened, Mr. B. answered my question with "The Unanswered Question," and my charmed life turned to gold sparks. It was like seven lilies blooming on one stem, a candelabrum of yucca burst into bloom.

PART THREE

1954–1958

*From the Unanswered Question
to the Unanswered Letter*

George Balanchine choreographing on Allegra, with Todd Bolender. Photo by Radford Bascome.

CHAPTER SIX

Measure ten times, cut once.

—RUSSIAN PROVERB

"Allegra, take your slippers off. You'll be in bare feet for this ballet." Mr. B. walked over to where I was sitting and watched me remove my ballet shoes. Then he turned to the four men in the room and said, "Everyone come to this corner."

Mr. B. took my hand and led me over. The four men met us there. I looked eagerly into Mr. B.'s face, waiting for further instructions. He knew he was surprising me.

Mr. B. tapped the top of the barre with his hand. "Allegra, climb up here and face the room." While I was perched in the corner three and a half feet above the floor, Mr. B. positioned the four men in two tight rows of two facing away from me. He took my hand again. "Good. Now, Allegra, step on the men's shoulders." Mr. B. pointed to where I should put each foot, then turned to the men. "Lower, demiplié, so Allegra can climb on." Still holding my hand, he guided me as I stepped aboard and told the men, "Hold her legs."

I winced as I felt eight hands clutch my ankles, calves, and knees rather too tightly. Mr. B. gave the men further instructions. "Support her a little, but not too much. Don't forget she's a monkey."

I was to have no contact at all with the floor. At first I felt as if I would tumble, but then I got used to this way of transport and gained equilibrium. It was fall 1954 and the opening rehearsal of the first major role created for me by George Balanchine. I had just turned seventeen and had been in the corps de ballet for two years.

As the rehearsal began, I had no time to ponder my excitement about receiving this part. Just the night before, I had gathered with the other members of the company around the rehearsal sheet to find out my schedule for the next day. That's how I learned I had been singled out for a major role in an experimental new ballet called *Ives-iana* with music by Charles Ives. "The Unanswered Question," one of the episodes, was mine. Todd Bolender, a principal, four men of the corps, and I were Mr. B.'s choice for this unusual section. Now we waited for our next instruction.

Mr. B. clapped his hands. "Good. When the music begins, walk very slowly forward. Don't count." The pianist started to play. Moving in slow motion, we followed Mr. B.'s directive.

"Did you hear that?" Mr. B. imitated a trumpet and repeated a voice we just heard in the piano score.

I nodded my head.

"Allegra, when that starts, open your arms slowly and start to sit." Now the men received their instructions. "Make a chair for her with your hands." Mr. B. continued to surprise us.

I was to be like an elastic icon, ever unattainable, standing on the shoulders of two of the men who were to be my floor. The two others braced me while Todd, arms outstretched, was in front of me walking backward. That is how the dance began. The four men were my spaceship, constantly manipulating me in a slow rhythm around and above their bodies, through their legs, lifting, turning, supporting, sometimes pulling me around as though they were hauling rope.

Mr. B. never explained the story, only how to work out his ideas mechanically to achieve the effect he wanted.

"Now hold her up above your heads," he instructed. As I curved myself into a small shape like a lima bean, he directed four pairs of arms to hold me aloft. From this seed position, I was to extend one leg downward and, as my body uncurled, stretch the other leg into an arabesque. He told the men that they could talk quietly among themselves—even during the performance—to coordinate their effort. "So everyone will be ready to move simultaneously." In this way, beginnings and endings became seamless and transitions liquid.

While I was standing high on the shoulders of two of the men, Mr. B. told me, "I want you to lean backward very slowly until you fall. Don't do it yet." He walked in back of me to instruct the other two men on how to catch me. "Okay, Allegra, let's try it."

My backward fall, which started almost imperceptibly, gained momentum until my body disappeared from sight. This was so startling that I later heard gasps of terror from the audience during performances. I trusted my men, but nevertheless in that first rehearsal I had to look back to make sure that they were ready. Mr. B. was there also to make sure of my safety.

By the end of the first day, I loved this moment when I fell over backward from a great height, slowly inching my way into a grand swoon and toppling over. It's fun to fall if you know you'll be caught.

Singing the trumpet part again, Mr. B. told us what musical clues to listen for along the way. This dance was like a hike in the mountains. A certain sound was a big white boulder or a tree bridge over a stream.

With this solo role, Mr. B. gave me a thrilling message. Something about me interested him. Perhaps I would become one of his favorites. He knew how to send his ballerinas up like rockets, one after another, higher and higher. He knew how to ignite spirits and careers and send his chosen girls into ballerina space. I was aware that I had a chance of joining that very special group of dancers like Alexandra Danilova, Marie-Jeanne, Tanaquil Le Clercq, Mary Ellen Moylan, Vera Zorina, and Maria Tallchief.

On one level, Mr. B.'s interest in me was as a choreographer and the head of a company. Even though he had a young wife whom he was developing as a dancer, he never stopped looking for new talent. His eyes were always on the next generation, the lifeblood of a ballet company. And for a while I was the new one. The baby.

This was a position I loved being in. Mr. B. believed in my instincts, and he was willing to accept me as I was and work with my raw material. I knew that he gave his dancers a lot of freedom if he trusted them—that he would visualize a ballet ahead of time and try to put the right person in it. He thought I was the right person for this role, and I didn't want to disappoint him. A smile from Mr. B. after a rehearsal was an enchanting gift, particularly if he was wearing a cowboy shirt and the turquoise cuff given to him by Maria Tallchief.

This role was not technically difficult. "The Unanswered Question" had more to do with creating an atmosphere than with dance technique. My costume was simple: a white leotard and nothing else—no tights, no shoes, not even hairpins—bare legs, bare feet, long hair. A bare body with a white costume. The color white was symbolic in a Balanchine ballet. This piece was the latest version of his constant recasting of the enigmatic "girl in white." The spiritual. The otherworldly. Not only was the bareness of the costume related more to theater than ballet, so was the choreography. Unlike what happened in classical partnering, where contact was mainly on the waist and arms and involved lifts and sustained moments on pointe, in this ballet

I was definitely "manhandled" by my four supporters. (Brooks Jackson, one of the men, asked me at the second day's rehearsal if my body was sore, and when I said no, wondering why he asked, he said, "*Ah, la jeunesse.*") In this role I was manipulated—threaded under legs and pulled into splits—all the time remaining passive and inaccessible. The woman in this ballet ultimately represents the unattainable. She attracts and eludes the man who tries to grasp her. The mystery is never solved, the question never answered.

Arlene Croce said of me in this role, "Allegra Kent does not seem to belong to herself, yet she doesn't belong to her manipulators either—they're her mystery." Later, I would learn that the artist Joseph Cornell obtained a rehearsal photo of *Ivesiana*. It shows me held aloft by four men, with Mr. B. looking on and Todd Bolender on the floor. Cornell used this image or a close-up of it in many collages and several of his boxes, including *L'Apothéose* and *Villa Allegra*. He coupled the photo with the themes he associated with me—a shell, a coffeepot, and the Madonna with the long neck.

One of the other dancers, Ruth Sobotka, was dating Stanley Kubrick at the time, and he watched this dance opening night from backstage. His interest in movement and music would eventually show in his films. He had been very complimentary when he saw me in "The Unanswered Question," and I was always sure there was a connection to *2001* and its space ballet. In the movie, flight attendants move to the tempo of the "Blue Danube." Mr. B. might have suggested that they move against the rhythm. There are times to go for the obvious—and times not to.

Why had Balanchine chosen me for this unusual role? As I came to understand it, the ballets Mr. B. did for me evolved from my suppressed inner life as much as from my dancing talent. He saw in me the psychological raw material that could be molded and remolded into images of sensuality—unrealized and restrained, but there, just under the surface. The star inside the sapphire.

He was a casting genius who knew what I could project and what I could do long before I did. He was a lie detector who could see right into my soul. Onstage in my bare leotard, I felt exposed, and I was to feel this same level of physical and psychic exposure in many of the roles Balanchine created for me. Perhaps he intuited that I had decided to become a dancer in part because I believed it would be a continuation of my childhood forever. I would never have to grow up and come to terms with the other parts of myself—my emotional and sexual natures—the parts denied by my mother and my religion. I had decided to become Peter Pan. My version. My sister had chosen to be Wendy, but I wanted to be Peter, a girl playing a boy who doesn't want to grow up.

It was a safe thing to do. At seventeen, I had never had a boyfriend. I had never even had a date. For me, dancing was a way to experience physical and emotional freedom. It was the only way. And I didn't have to be shy about it. All the manhandling took place in the ballet. It was part of the job—a rehearsal or a performance, but not real life.

There was, of course, always the question of what Mr. B. ultimately wanted from me. I believe that neither of us really knew, but when he was creating this part, I felt he was in love with me, because it was such a gift. Different kinds of love were bound together in him, and I realized that, although I may not have wished to say it to anybody. Many of Mr. B.'s dancing loves did not become his wives or lovers. But I also heard the rumors. My mother was still gossiping with the other dance mothers on the sidelines while their daughters were working. Mr. B.'s life with his five ballerina wives was very entertaining for these women who did nothing. While the ballet was in rehearsal, they might have said to my mother, "Look out."

Mother decided that she needed to watch over me, and she began a subtle campaign to undermine Balanchine's influence. But this was unnecessary, because I had already formulated my own impression of Mr. B.'s pattern. Through observation and calculation, I had decided there was a time limit to Mr. B.'s love. It usually lasted seven years. He married his dancing girls when they were between the ages of fifteen to twenty-three. Tamara Geva was fifteen; Alexandra Danilova, twenty-one; Vera Zorina, twenty-one; Maria Tallchief, twenty-one; and Tanaquil Le Clercq, twenty-three. The ages of his wives stayed roughly the same while Mr. B. grew older. He had married Tanaquil just two years earlier. He was now fifty, and I had just turned seventeen.

What existed between Balanchine and me was never acknowledged. Although we were working closely together, Balanchine and I never had a truly personal conversation when I was young. Once when I was fifteen he watched me backstage eating a big tomato. "What's that?" he asked. He seemed to think this was a strange thing to be eating. I looked at it closely. I had been struck by its beauty. "It's a beautiful, perfect tomato." Another time he asked me about a bag of Siamese-twin cherries I was eating for lunch. My brother and

I had loved them. I told him they were very cheap in California because they were seconds, only fifteen cents a pound.

The way Mr. B. communicated with me was almost the way a human relates to wildlife. Some people are good with untamed animals. They don't startle the creatures.

In "The Unanswered Question," I was held aloft, a sensual and spiritual object sought by a man who could never possess her. The object of a quest. Writing years later, dance critic Anna Kisselgoff said of the kinds of ballets Balanchine made for me: "Allegra Kent was always herself, and there was never anyone like her. This is what Balanchine recognized when he took her at fifteen into the company and a year later began to create for her the enigmatic roles he never did for anyone else." As I look back, I feel that most of the dances Balanchine created for me were based on this dynamic and the many unanswered questions between us.

What if you paint a picture and you're told you can use no red, only blue? Then you must use blue in a way that suggests red.

"Allegra, if you had a little more chin and a little less nose, you would be so much prettier." Mother had begun to look at me differently since "The Unanswered Question."

"Mom, my face is okay. It's good enough for the ballet."

"Aren't you interested in a face that would be closer to perfect proportions? Then you would be beautiful."

Mother was observing me carefully as I ate a baked potato. It was not the first time this topic had come up. This obsessive idea had been growing in my mother since my success in *Ivesiana*. My face was in flux, and Mother perceived an awkwardness in my looks that made her unhappy. But this was a problem that could be solved. With each new day, her campaign for a change of my face picked up momentum. She could not look at me without thinking about it. Being Jewish remained a problem for her. She had eradicated it from our names and now she wanted to remove it from my face.

"Mom, I don't want to do it. Everyone will know. They'll think I'm vain. I don't want people discussing me. Also, I don't want to be an actress. My face looks all right for a dancer."

My sister had already had both her nose and chin altered, but she had wanted to do it. With quick, rapid determination at a young age, I had changed my name and chosen a theatrical career just as my sister had done, so Mother expected me to follow Wendy's lead without resistance. She was surprised by my reaction.

Mother, dressed in a housecoat, was sitting with me at the kitchen table. "No one will ever know. We could do it now, between seasons. Just a little off here and a little added there." She touched the two spots on her own face. She had said "*we* could do it." It was a joint venture.

"No." I had pushed aside my potato. "I don't want people laughing at me behind my back."

"You know, Allegra, when you smile, your nose drops and widens. It ruins your expression. A little surgery could fix that." Mother rose, came around the table, faced me, and delicately molded the two points of dispute on my face with the tips of her fingers as she visualized their improvement.

I lightly pushed her hand away. "Look, Mom, I'll stop smiling." I'd always heard that a smile lights up a face, *any* face. Apparently I was the single exception. It revealed too much. A happy look did nothing for me; it only announced that I might be Jewish. Clearly, the Weissman quality in my nose and the Cohen in my name could ruin my life.

"If your looks improved, you'd start to date. I know you haven't been very happy."

Mother was wrong. I was happy. I finally had a personal life—it was on stage and on tours when I was away from home. Perhaps, after I'd achieved a success in such a short time in ballet, Mother was hoping for bigger things. Did she suddenly think she might be stage mother to a movie star, not just a ballerina?

I asked how she reconciled an operation with our religion. "We don't believe in doctors, only the operation of Divine Mind. If all matter, including my face, isn't real, then why should we be so concerned with it?"

"We most definitely should be concerned. And there are times when doctors are necessary. Mary Baker Eddy says so."

Mother believed in conventional beauty. She didn't realize that the very things she disliked in my face could possibly have been assets. The image that Joseph Cornell saved in his files for twenty years and placed in his creations had my original features. But to Mother this portion of me was like an apartment that could always be improved.

Eventually Mother accused me of listening to my mortal mind and my own feelings instead of following her inspired directive. As far as she was concerned, we had a partnership, and I wasn't doing my share. "*We* bought this coat in Europe," she had told someone once. She hadn't been with me on the tour in Europe, but she wouldn't let me leave her behind, ever. Five thousand miles was reduced to nothing by her use of the pronoun "We."

Now, however, I was doing something on my own. I wasn't yielding. Yet it made me nervous. Maybe I was in "error," as a Christian Scientist would say. Mother had impressed me deeply with her perceptive insights. My unease began to show. During a rehearsal, one of the male principals asked me why I never smiled anymore. What was right for me was mired in the quirky concepts of Christian Science.

As she went on discussing her plans for my face, I grew tired of the daily harangues and quarrels. I also began to look in the mirror questioningly and became convinced that Mother was right. My face must be altered; it's not beautiful as it is. Mother promised that I would look the same, only better, and that no one would notice the difference. I knew this was a lie, because Wendy's face had changed noticeably. But I couldn't stand the turmoil, so finally I submitted. If I was ever going to have peace, there was only one place to go: to the operating table.

This was the beginning of another pattern in my life. An advance in my dancing career was followed by something disastrous in my personal life. At barely seventeen years old, I had risen to the top of the Ferris wheel of fortune and remained poised on high for a few minutes listening to the calliope and watching the tiny starry lights before the seat suddenly tipped. This time when I fell, I wasn't caught.

No one in the company knew my mother's plans, nor did the teachers at school. I never asked Mr. B. for his opinion. I just disappeared one day.

Coming out of the anesthetic, I pushed the bandages around and fought the nurse. I dislodged the addition to my chin, and it became set at an angle. When I finally woke up, Mother seemed guilty. She hadn't picked a very good doctor. She said, "What I went through was horrible. I lost ten years of my life last night."

My new face was grotesque. It was shockingly distorted. It was not me. The doctor had done a bad job, and I recuperated slowly. My mother's obsession with externals and what could be done about them had been played out on me. This was the first irreversible event of my life. After the operation, I felt physically and spiritually destroyed. We had gambled, and it was a failure. I lost face—literally.

• • •

Jacques d'Amboise looked at me in horror. "What happened to you? What did you do to yourself?"

I had forced myself to appear for the first day of rehearsal for the new season. It was agony. I felt humiliated. My face was still swollen, and my eyes were dark. I looked as if I'd been through a war.

I told Jacques, "My mother wanted me to change my face." I should have replied, "I allowed my mother to change my face." Everyone stared at me. I heard that Maria Tallchief and Janet Reed were discussing my operation. I had opened up my life, and now the company knew about my secret weakness, vanity. I had no safe place to hide. No one seemed to respect my mother or me. Typical of our relationship, Mr. B. didn't say anything in the rehearsal hall that day, but I read disapproval on his face, and proved to be right. All my corps de ballet parts were in place, but I stopped receiving solo parts. Mr. B.'s plans for me were suspended.

How could I reconcile this with my mother's guarantee that there would be no difference? I had let myself be beguiled.

I fell into a deep depression and rarely left the new apartment on East Fifty-eighth Street where I lived with Mother and Wendy. Even at the movies, I couldn't seem to get away from myself. I'd wake in the morning briefly feeling all right—until I looked in the mirror. In profile, my nose had been shortened and clipped. I possessed a false face.

An enveloping abstract shame became part of me, and I could not shake it loose. As my depression intensified, I developed new phobias, and I stopped going to regular class. How could someone who never wants to show her face have a career as a professional dancer? I didn't return to the School of American Ballet for lessons. Instead, I went to an obscure teacher who had only three students.

I had been a poor sleeper all my life, and now I slept less and less. As a child, fears of needles and insects kept me awake. Now it was depression. During these wakeful hours, I read incessantly. I began with Dostoyevsky and then went on to most of the other Russian writers. Poor sleeping habits are not good for a ballet dancer. Later, I compared notes with my friends in the company like Patty McBride, who was a fantastic sleeper. Somehow, she wasn't as disturbed a human being as I was, so she had the sleep necessary to function in her career.

During long intermissions in the middle of the night, I would eat to put myself back to sleep. It was during this period that I first had problems with weight. I began slowly and systematically overeating. Desserts—strawberry shortcake and ice cream. I had always eaten sweets, but I had never eaten more than my natural balance required. Now I went on eating long after the hunger was gone, and, in the throes of one of these eating episodes, it didn't matter what I ate. Maybe that bitter chocolate will be what I want. Maybe that apple pie. But it all tasted the same. The overt effects weren't dramatic; I didn't gain a lot of weight. But here were the seeds of a pattern—too much food and too little sleep, the two worst things for a ballet career. My awkward age had turned into an awkward life.

For thirty years after this, I struggled with depression and my inability to handle it. Usually, the end of every season was bad for me because there'd be a lull. I'd fall into the same trap over and over again. Raspberries, whipped cream, ice cream. Exercise would end. I would be embarrassed about my weight, so I'd stop going to class. Sleeping would become a problem. When dancing strenuously, I needed a lot of sleep, and after four ballets and rehearsals on weekends, rest was welcome. But on days off I couldn't rest or relax. This stretched on for weeks between seasons and became a pattern of depression, during which I would wake in the middle of the night and eat and read.

Dostoyevsky and Turgenev were a great comfort, but I was also becoming more and more fanatical about Christian Science. When I looked in the mirror, I'd close my eyelids tightly together and try to put my mind on some other plane of existence. I realize now that I was having a nervous breakdown. I tried to think about my face in spiritual terms: "There was no life or truth in it." *Science and Health* asserted that "Divine Love has met and always will meet every human need," and I hoped this was right. I wanted to find what was right and do it. When I looked to a Christian Science practitioner for help, she stressed that I had to lose my sense of "false ambition and selfishness." What was false ambition? I'm not sure even today. Was this woman telling me to stop striving, that I shouldn't try for too much success? I was confused. I had had my face changed for Mother and was dancing for both of us, but in the practitioner's appraisal I still had false ambition.

At a party given by this woman, she showed me off, introducing me as a ballerina and a guest of honor. She seemed very proud to be my friend. Her prayers and mental work had to be paid for, which I did for almost a year. But after the party I decided she was a bit caught up herself with my accomplishments or "false ambitions." There was a double standard that I didn't like.

Eventually, my brother would follow the family tradition and have his nose and chin fixed. Encouraged by Mother, he too would look at the world with a new face. Despite what had happened to me, Mother still felt that surgery would unlock the door to success and happiness. It would combat shyness and make subtle, positive changes. Fortunately, Gary did not have the adverse reaction to the procedure that I did.

"Mr. Balanchine, my mother wants me to go to college and leave the company. I want to make her happy." We were standing in the hall after a rehearsal. I stared at the floor.

Mr. B. said nothing.

It was the spring of 1955. I was finally beginning to look less freakish, and Mr. B. had again been giving me a few parts. I had learned the corps in *Concerto Barocco,* and Mr. B. told me that if I did a good job, he'd give me a dime. After the performance he had come up to me with the coin.

"Mr. Balanchine, I'm not happy in the company anymore. You have stopped giving me parts." My mother had scripted this conversation. She hadn't acknowledged that I'd actually overcome the problem of my face and that Mr. B. was giving me roles again. She was three months behind reality. I was afraid to speak above a whisper. "My mother wants me to go to the University of Utah."

"Utah? Don't you want to dance anymore?"

I could barely look at Mr. B. as I spoke, so I kept my eyes down. Mother's plan was that I go to the University of Utah and take ballet classes at the college. Her new doctrine was an ax to the heart of my career. Could a pure stage mother want her daughter to quit dancing professionally? Rather than have me compete in the dance centers of the world, she wanted me to go to the backwoods of ballet. I felt this was a mistake. I was already a professional. But I continued with Mother's dialogue, "I'm going to take ballet classes in Utah. I want a normal life, to date boys, and receive an education."

His voice was calm. "Don't do that. I have plans for you."

I looked up at him.

He was staring into my face. "First of all, I'd like you to learn Tanny's part in *Four Temperaments,* and I'd like you to demonstrate for me at a lecture I'm doing at the Ninety-second Street Y."

This was an honor. I knew he had appeared at the Y before with Maria Tallchief. He took only his wives and top dancers for demonstrations. He didn't want me to leave the company. He was luring me with lollipops.

"I'd love to go to the Y with you and learn *Four Temperaments*," I said.

"Good. Vida can teach you Tanny's part tomorrow. I'd like you to be ready in one week." He looked relieved. He thought everything was solved now, but it wasn't.

I bit my lower lip. Mother would not be pleased with the direction of this talk. She had anticipated a fight. She had carefully instructed me to complain about Mr. B.'s treatment of me, and now he had plans.

I tried again. "Mother thinks I won't be happy unless I have a normal life."

He placed one hand on my shoulder. "Allegra, don't go to Utah. Stay with the company."

As I headed home to see how Mother would react to Mr. B.'s ideas for me, I thought perhaps I wouldn't have to go to college after all. But Mother wasn't happy. She wanted me out of the company.

I set aside my anxiety over Mother's plans and focused on my immediate assignment from Mr. B. The next day, Vida, the ballet mistress, began showing me the steps for "Choleric," Tanny's part in *The Four Temperaments*. I found them very hard. The dance started with a series of intense, angry movements, kicks and flings, all followed by pauses. These small rounds of fiery dancing were strangely exhausting. Watching Tanny dance hadn't given me a clue as to the difficulty of the choreography. For my first performance, a terrible stage fright took over. I was nearly immobilized with exhaustion after the first short segment. I wasn't acting out anger, as the temperament indicated, but real desperation and panic. It was a nightmare.

Trying to live up to the Christian Science ideals, I was becoming weak in my work. One of the precepts of Christian Science is that only loving words should leave our lips. Other words as well as feelings should be barred. The human element in humans should be disregarded or buried. But I needed other feelings to fuel my energies for dancing—aggression, mischief, anger, crazy joy, and a little backbone. The kind it takes to fight injustice. The thing Carmelita had when she pounded her heels into the floor and did her Spanish dances fighting fascism. Now I had it, only in a suppressed form.

I also thought that anyone with a working mother was lucky.

Mother became more obsessed with her plan to diminish Mr. B.'s influence over me and get me out of the New York City Ballet. She again assumed the role of the protective stage mother to legitimize her plans to pull me offstage. "After all," she'd asked, "what has the company done for you in the two years you've been there?" Why, she wanted to know, wasn't I farther along? Didn't she realize that it was the surgery that had slowed my progress?

Mother finally suggested I give up dancing altogether. Quoting Christian Science, she made me feel that my need for dance was a weakness, the result of some deficiency in my personality.

Perhaps she simply looked at the ballet life and decided it wasn't good for me. She had watched me suffer after the surgery and was angry at Mr. B. Maybe she felt threatened. Originally, she was my partner in this career, but now I was leaving her behind. I had achieved more success than she had expected. Mother was forty-nine at the time and did not work, leaving her too much time for introspection. She must have felt that her future was very uncertain.

Mother's new wish for me was a college education, not a career. Her motives were unclear, even to herself, and they were certainly complex. Just any university would not do. It had to be in Utah— she wanted me miles and miles away from the New York City Ballet and Mr. B. Thousands of miles were best. She may have seen herself and Mr. B. as rivals for me. My mother's explanation of Balanchine was that his talent was in one area alone, choreography. He had a narrow band of genius, but as a man he couldn't stand up because of his pattern with women. Although she was concerned about the physical and emotional pain I'd just gone through, in my mother's mind there was only one type of pain that could be truly serious. And that would occur if Balanchine got me. Giving up dancing, leaving the company, having my face changed, my breakdown —none of these was as terrible as his making me another Lolita in his ballerina gallery.

But she never said these things to me directly. She said, "You must go to college," and I listened to her. She told me that I had to withdraw from my dance career, and I didn't rebel. I let Mother have divine rights over me. I traded what I loved for her love. I agreed to leave the company after the summer tour of 1955.

Finally, I had to tell Mr. B., "My mother is putting a lot of pressure on me. I have to leave the company by the fall." I hung my head so that I didn't have to look at him. To leave the company could be a very dangerous thing, because Mr. B. might not want you back. Disloyalty really hurt him. He encouraged personal allegiance, and, although he didn't overtly encourage awe or worship, in a subtle way he used the idolatry of the corps to keep the company together.

I could not continue my dance career without my mother's support. Mr. B. understood this. He gave me a warm hug. He had certainly encountered close mother-daughter ballet relationships before—he had the example of Tanny and her mother. In a few years, he would bring Violette Verdy into the company, a dancer very close to her mother. Violette's father had died before she was born, and when Violette was twelve or so, her mother could have remarried but turned down that chance: Violette's career required the dedication of both women, and Violette's mother opted for a partnership with her daughter and not a man. Tamara Toumanova was another ballerina who was extraordinarily close to her mother. Her mother used to break in her shoes for her. Mr. B. told me, "If you have to leave, remember we are here when you come back. And, Allegra, your pointe work is getting stronger."

I later learned through a member of Mr. B.'s staff that the company would be doing *Ivesiana* again, but Mr. B. had decided to remove my movement because he couldn't think of anyone to replace me in it. I was touched beyond belief. He had not replaced me with a young star. Mr. B. was loyal.

But I was not. A letter I wrote home to Mother during my final weeks with the company illustrates how determined I was to adopt her thinking:

This week has been one of discovery. The joys from dancing are very fleeting. I sound like I'm leaving with sour grapes; actually, I feel grateful that these things have happened and I don't feel disappointed in not obtaining important parts because I have lost interest in company ballet, but never, never in dancing.

Grandma and Grandpa are getting me War and Peace for my birthday. I'm getting them a dining room set. It's not so generous of me. Money is the easiest thing for me to give. Like Harry! Giving of myself is more difficult or being generous in kindness and sweetness. Well, at least I recognize my faults so I can correct them. And I shall. Every last one of them. But I musn't make a reality of them or else they won't disappear.

Before I could leave the company, I had to do an about-face and dislike everyone and their dancing. This was the only way I could cope with the coming separation. I had to believe I was doing the right thing, and, by the end of the summer, I had accomplished this. I wished my mother had given me *Tom Sawyer* instead of Mary Baker Eddy's *Science and Health* to read as a child.

Mother's plan was that I divorce Mr. Balanchine by letter, *her* letter. During the final week of the tour, I received from her a manuscript which, she instructed, I was to copy over and give to Mr. B. as my own. My brain could stay suspended in limbo; all I had to do was supply paper, penmanship, and my usual willingness to do whatever she asked.

In the letter, Mother rehashed her grievances and dramatized what she saw as the terrible things he had done to me. In my role as ven- triloquist's dummy, I was to tell him that the dancing life was not for me, that I wanted to see what a normal life was like, that he had not done all he could to develop my talent, and that I was unhappy with his treatment of me. This was to be my farewell message.

I managed to follow her instructions, but with an important vari- ation. I sent the letter out, but not to Mr. B. My solution was to reroute it, three paragraphs to Muriel Stuart and two to Mme. Doub- rovska. Deep in my heart, I knew I didn't mean these things. Mr. B. never saw the letter. He knew the truth anyway. It takes two people to launch a dancer. There must be a second person in the family who wants it too, and Shirley Kent had abandoned me.

Even though Mother was still insisting I go to Utah, I decided to enroll in UCLA for a term, and I moved to Los Angeles with Daddy and Gary. I attended some university classes, but mainly I devoted my days to taking ballet lessons with Carmelita and Tatiana Riabouch- inska.

Away from the company and Mr. B., I had decided never to let my emotions show on my face while dancing—absolutely nothing. If I did something well, I'd show no joy; if I did something poorly, there would be no sign of disappointment. I wanted the safety of an empty, blank face. At this time, my features had almost normalized, and I looked all right, although my shame was still very strong.

While he was in California, Jacques d'Amboise set up an audition for me for the movie version of *Carousel*. Jacques was signed, but Bambi Lynn's part was still uncast. I didn't want to be put on the screen, and my deepest fear was that I'd get the part. My face might be up for discussion and there might be widespread gossip about its having been changed so totally. My life would be washed through and through with humiliation and shame. Everyone would smirk and sneer at my weakness. I had succumbed to vanity, and that was laughable. A character in William Saroyan's *The Human Comedy* says, "The nose has always been a source of embarrassment to the human race." I knew what he meant. I thought of the way Anna Pavlova had looked into the camera, without embarrassment or self-doubt. I longed to do that, but I felt I could not.

I told Gary my fears, and he became very angry with me for planning to pass up such a grand opportunity. His anger made me cry. Jacques arranged for me to go to the set with an agent. When told that the director wanted a tomboy, I acted in the opposite manner and didn't get the part.

Gary and Daddy were disappointed, but my father had another plan. "Allegra, I have a great idea. Why don't you and Gary go in for politics?"

"Daddy, I'm good at dancing, and I'm not particularly diplomatic, as you may have observed."

"Allegra, it doesn't matter." Daddy was off on a distant cloud.

When Mother moved back across the country to California and discovered that my day revolved around dance and not my college courses, she was adamant that I follow her plan and enroll in the University of Utah. She started corresponding with administrators at the school and was promised a scholarship. This was a step toward the elusive "normal life." I left for Salt Lake City on New Year's Day at age eighteen. The facial surgery had taken place thirteen months earlier. This trip to Utah was my mother's last effort to counteract the negative effects of the operation.

As soon as I arrived in Utah, I organized an informal class to see the level of the local dancers. It was not very high, and this depressed me. I wanted to watch Maria and Tanny dance. Why was I here?

Even the news that Tanny was to do both my part and her own in *Ivesiana* didn't hurt so much. I wasn't competing with Tanny. I was wild about the way she did *In the Inn*. Her lighthearted jazzy antics and courageous good-bye were addictive. The handshake with Todd Bolender was straightforward as the music turned wistful. It made me think, *Will they see each other again?* Tanny was hopeful, but the music implied uncertainty. She had a sublime touch. No wonder that moment appealed to me: I was an expert in good-byes.

After four days of listening to the Brandenburg Concertos over and over again and writing fourteen letters to Mother, I reconsidered. No plan had ever been made to pay for Utah. The scholarship was only a partial one, and I had arrived with two hundred dollars. As I saw the money disappearing, I panicked. I might be stranded in the middle of America. I bought a plane ticket and returned to New York City and the company.

I ran into the main room of the School of American Ballet and was greeted by Mme. Doubrovska. She thought I was in town only for the Christmas vacation. I said, "No, I'm through with college. I'm back for good." And I was.

Once Mother realized that she couldn't keep me away from the company and Mr. B., she wanted to return to New York to pick up the life she'd forced both of us to leave five months earlier. I had moved in with Wendy again, and Mother's plan was to live with us— a mother and two daughters with no men involved. I emphatically refused.

My dance personality emerged once more, and I began attending Mme. Doubrovska's class with the goal of a stage performance. Every day in class for the next week, Madame asked me if I was happy. My behavior the last year had mystified her and everyone else. Her concern moved me deeply. For some of us it wasn't easy to be a teenager with a professional dance career. For the first of many times, Mr. B. also welcomed me back. As usual, he expressed his feelings symbolically, not verbally. He gave me new demisoloist parts immediately and I was an understudy for *Serenade* and the third movements in *Symphony in C* and *Western Symphony*. I would be included in the year's schedule and a fall tour to Europe.

CHAPTER SEVEN

With what eagerness she danced! . . . she swept by like a whirlwind. Her cheeks flushed, her eyes sparkled, and it was plain that she loved dancing better than anything else.
—"THE TWELVE DANCING PRINCESSES,"
THE RED FAIRY BOOK

I first met Joseph Cornell in 1956, about a month before the European tour. It was a bright summer afternoon, and I was just nineteen, living alone with my sister in a one-room apartment on East Sixty-first Street. Cornell entered Wendy's apartment and looked around. The living room had whimsical touches—a carousel giraffe and billowing yellow silk curtains that were always moving, always flowing.

I found out only much later that he had been following my career for two years. He appeared without an introduction, and I immediately sensed his interest in me and felt self-conscious. He was gaunt and intense. I may have had an inkling that he was a famous artist, but I had no idea that around this time Joseph was making shadowboxes based on my dancing. I studied him. His hands in particular frightened me. They were stained the color of tobacco leaves. I was used to Mr. B., who always was quite reserved. He made no sudden moves and gave few encouraging smiles. I feared that this strange artist might be an obsessed fan who would haunt me, and when he asked me to appear in a movie, I immediately said no. It was too dangerous. I was uncomfortable with men.

My connection with Cornell might have ended after this meeting, but ever since boarding school I had understood that love could travel in an envelope, and I wanted words and entertainment in my mailbox. When letters from Joseph started to arrive, I was enchanted with them. We became pen pals. Since I couldn't spell, I always tried to distract the reader with paste-ons, embroidery, or anything at hand. I delighted in sending him odd presents, weirdly wrapped. My preference has always been to send a letter of things rather than words. I love individual words but find it difficult to put them together. Joseph certainly could. He always responded when I wrote. His letters were mysterious and beautifully poetic. Often they arrived at special times, a collage carried by a mailman. I had an enormous letter collection from him until, years later, Hilda, my housekeeper, threw most of them away. She weeded out and discarded the ones she didn't like.

Cornell sometimes addressed his letters to "Miss Allegretta Kent," because I often signed my name that way. Allegretto is a slower musical tempo than allegro and seemed to have a little regret built into it. I don't trust people who say they have no regrets.

On the European tour, I received all the jumping roles that had previously been done by Carolyn George, who had married Jacques d'Amboise and was now pregnant—third movement Bizet, third movement *Western Symphony,* and *Serenade.* I wrote Mother: "As you know my schedule is harder than most anyone else's. I certainly have more new ballets, more ballets per evening, and more substituting for people who were out than any other dancer. I love every moment of it." The truth was that I was overworked and thrown into too many ballets. I also danced with an injury, but luckily it wasn't serious enough to harm me.

One day, while I was eating a Coupe Jacques in a German café, Barbara Horgan, Mr. B.'s secretary, smiled at me and said, "Allegra, Mr. B. is going to make you a principal next season." We were rooming together in Frankfurt because I was exhausted and wanted to stay in a hotel with hot water for two nights. It was Sunday, the end of a long weekend, and I had just completed eight ballets, four in the afternoon and four at night, dancing both corps de ballet and principal parts.

"Don't you mean a soloist?" I asked. That was the next level up from the corps. I looked at Barbara and continued to shovel in the ice cream, laced with hot chocolate. I was exhausted, hungry, and elated.

"No, I don't. You're going to skip ahead and become a principal." She paused. "Mr. B. is also thinking of reviving *The Seven Deadly Sins* with Lotte Lenya for you."

I stopped eating, wiped my mouth with the soft white napkin, and could not suppress a smile. "Is *The Seven Deadly Sins* a ballet? I've never heard about it."

Barbara, the historian, tilted her head as she ran her fingers quickly through her hair. "It's a Kurt Weill piece that Balanchine did in 1933 with the singing part played by Lotte Lenya. And I think he wants you to do it, but maybe he'll use Pat Wilde."

However, as Barbara said this, I knew it wasn't true. She was merely being cautious. Mr. B. was thinking of me alone for this part. Pat Wilde and I were two very different types: if he was thinking of me, he wasn't thinking of her.

I slowly put down my spoon. This news was gloriously exciting. I couldn't wait to write home about it. The genie had come out of the bottle for me. I silently speculated that this must be what it is like to go out in your backyard after a tornado and find moonstones instead of mayhem.

Again, Mr. B. did not tell me of the promotion himself but let his decision seep through the filter paper of his trusted staff. He must have told Maria Tallchief about his plans for me, however, because the next day she became very concerned with my makeup. She ran backstage to say my eyes looked "too round"; I must elongate them with lines and shading.

Because I had rejected Mother's plan to go to a university and begin meeting boys my own age, I still had never had a date. But I didn't care. I was not in Utah taking novice ballet classes. I was going to be a principal dancer. The New York City Ballet had been my junior high and high schools, and now it would be my college and graduate school.

I knew I'd have dates one day, but right now ballet was my life. And the one man in it was Mr. B.

As promised, when the company returned from Europe, I had been given principal billing, but I was to spend my first season with this status working with other choreographers, not Mr. B. Tragically, his young wife, Tanaquil, only twenty-seven, had been stricken with polio in Copenhagen. The company had been in shock and went off to Stockholm in deepest gloom without Mr. B. and Tanny. Despite the fact that Tanny had become desperately ill, I refused to take the polio shot being given to all the dancers. I had been thoroughly brainwashed by my mother and the Christian Science Sunday school teachers.

For my first performance as a principal dancer when we returned to New York, I worked with other choreographers, not Balanchine. Jerome Robbins told me, "It's a warm summer's afternoon, you have just washed your hair, and your shoes are brand-new. Move as if the air is heavy, or as thick as honey." The image was beautiful and fresh, but I felt that I couldn't please Jerry. He could see my nervousness and made personal corrections as I prepared for *Afternoon of a Faun*.

During rehearsals, Jerry worked very hard to make his dancers look good, ready, and polished. He wanted to see us execute exactly what he had in mind, with no extras motivated by fear, lack of concentration, or misconception. If a tiny frown appeared, it had to go. Jerry believed in creating tension between himself and a dancer. It was a way of stirring up feelings. Something exciting might happen. When a butterfly struggles to get out of its cocoon, it gains strength for life and flight; at times Jerry tried to bring out the fight in a dancer with his corrections. The right amount of criticism can create perfection, but too much can destroy. This was Tanny's part originally, and my idiosyncrasies did not exactly reflect my predecessor. Deeply upset by Jerry's adversarial style, I focused on my faults, and after some of the rehearsals I felt demolished. I was too insecure for this technique to work, and eventually he dropped this approach with me.

I never performed exactly the way I rehearsed. In *Faun,* the floor cloth was slippery, so the easy look of the steps was deceptive; it was hard to be firmly planted and not wobble. I was glad when my first performance was over and I could go on to the next ballet, *Symphony in C,* third movement. While dancing it, my shoe slipped off my heel. I was upset yet still relieved; *Faun* was over. I pulled myself up extra-straight into a perfectly balanced posture, and, when the diagonal throws occurred, I went up higher than ever before. These were miracles in the mind and body. Jerry came backstage, smiling. That was a good sign. "I could tell in *Symphony in C* how glad you were that *Faun* was over." I had said nothing, but Jerry had read my mind. He knew I had suffered during his rehearsals, but now he was pleased; the preparations were over.

Francisco Moncion, who did *Pastorale* for me, was my friend, a fellow dancer, and I was more relaxed while working with him. Too relaxed. During every rehearsal I fooled around with Tony Blum, treating the rehearsals as a toga party. Frank was so annoyed that he spoke to Maria about my antics. She spoke to me, and I listened to her. Overnight, I developed my characterization in time to take the premiere seriously.

It was with Mr. B. that I felt the most comfortable. While Jerry was from the school of adversity, Mr. B.'s corrections were professional and uncannily helpful, not personal. He gave me and everyone a lot of freedom. He showed us what he wanted and trusted his dancers and his casting instincts. Balanchine looked at what was present and evolving. Mr. B. was like Mother Nature working with the armadillo and ancient horses, helping them to be all they could be in ten thousand years or in the next performance. Some dancers had grown up with organized, formal training. I had a different kind of advantage: from Carmelita I had learned to dance with my instincts. Mr. B. gave me the freedom to do that. He chose me for certain roles because of it. I missed him. Even though he wasn't there, it was for him that I danced.

When Bert Stern opened his studio door, I was struck immediately by his uncanny resemblance to my father in face and coloring. A wave of recognition and attraction passed over me; it was strong and sudden, like a change of climate from calm to turbulent. Was I remeeting someone I had known and loved and who was inaccessible? I paused at the door for a second while these thoughts held me in confusion, happiness, and sadness all at once. To Bert it was boy meets girl, while the question in my mind was, Would I have a romance with my father's replica? I was infatuated. Bert, unaware of my range of feelings, invited me in and showed me his workplace.

I had arrived at Fortieth Street and Sixth Avenue, across the street from Bryant Park, wearing a demure dress borrowed from Wendy. Wearing my sister's clothes was a comfortable old ritual. I had all the joy of wearing her beautiful wardrobe, but none of the responsibility. These clothes revealed very little of my likes and dislikes.

After a brief conversation, Bert placed me in front of his camera. I had a horrible time trying to be at ease. This was a blind date and a photographic session all in one, a doubleheader of anxiety. My solution to this emotional and physical problem was to never stop moving. I did a very slow dance for the camera. Allegra became andante.

It was early 1957, and Bert had called after seeing me in *Shinbone Alley* with Jacques d'Amboise and Eartha Kitt, a Broadway show in which I played a mischievous kitten on a fire escape. The musical's subject was Archy and Mehitabel, the cockroach and the cat. The original choreographer told me, "In the first act you are a tomboy cat. I'm putting you on a fire escape with a lot of other dancers. Do everything you can to attract attention to yourself." I liked the instructions. It was up to me. During rehearsals I hadn't done anything too extreme, and I could see that the choreographer was beginning to worry about my improvisational abilities. But the minute we started to perform onstage, I adhered literally to his instructions. Eartha Kitt had a tantrum because I was upstaging her, but they couldn't stop me, because there was no one in authority whom I respected. If Mr. B., Jerry, or Maria Tallchief had told me to tone something down, I would have, but I just didn't regard Broadway as serious. It was also in my nature to be true to original instructions. I did my spider-monkey suspensions without a tactile tail; after all, I had spent a lot of my childhood in trees. One evening, after a lot of frantic fire-escape antics, I calmed down, hung upside down by my heels, took out the evening papers, which I had tucked under my belt in back, and read it upside down. The show's understudies, Chita Rivera and Tom Poston, were enthusiastic about my irrepressibly bad behavior. After all, they had to be in the theater night after night and they craved diversion. I wanted to make them happy.

Apparently Bert had been attracted to what he saw on stage. I knew his name as the photographer for the Smirnoff vodka ads in *The New Yorker* that I had admired. Surprisingly, the ballet office had given him my home number. When he had introduced himself over the phone, I liked the sound of his voice. He had been to one of the last performances of *Shinbone Alley* and said he liked the way I danced and read newspapers wrong side up. From our conversation I saw that he understood my humor and my rule-breaking boldness on stage. That was nice. What he could not know and what was not revealed was my almost pathological shyness in real life. Bert just wanted to take my picture.

I thought that this must be the way photographers make dates, but I couldn't be sure. I'd never really had one before.

After the photography session, we went to lunch at the 4-40 Club. I studied the menu.

"Don't worry about trying to find the cheapest thing," Bert said.

That was exactly what I was doing.

"Where were you brought up?"

"In California, Florida, and Texas, but not completely."

Bert laughed. As our lunch progressed, I could see that he was surprised I wasn't like my onstage character, flamboyant and ready to be carried off. I was a young nineteen. I had often wondered what the mysterious things were that men and women talked about together.

After that afternoon, I didn't hear from Bert again. I was interested in him but felt that he was moody. Nine months later, I called him with an invitation to see a Russian dance movie. Now I was twenty. After that date, Bert started to ask me out often. At a party at the photographer Eliot Erwitt's country house, he deliberately tried to make me jealous by ignoring me and flirting in an obvious way with Betsy von Furstenberg. I felt awful. If he didn't like something about me, I tried to change it. I was completely willing to try to mold myself into something he would like. If he didn't like a blouse or hat, I gave it away with no second thought. At Eastertime an enormous azalea plant arrived from him. Wendy and I smiled at the pink flowers in appreciation. It meant only that Bert was capable of a splashy gesture, but we read reams of other meanings into the shrub, and it calmed my doubts and fears like a Christian Science practitioner.

When Bert came to the ballet for the first time, I was dancing the girl in *Serenade* who does a large leap that travels forward and then backward through the air into Nicky Magallanes's arms. It was tricky timing, and I was jubilant when it went well. Bert loved that moment, and he also understood immediately the greatness of Balanchine and his ballets. He came to the theater often, and afterward we would go out.

I decided that Bert was someone who must have been popular in high school, and I imagined that I was going out with the most favored boy around, something I had missed. Our incompatibility only occasionally surfaced. I was making up for my dateless past. I was happy when Bert took me along on a working trip to Death Valley. We traveled there with four male models and an assistant for sunrise photos of men and vodka. This left the rest of the day for diversions of swimming in hot water springs and playing badminton. We had fun, and at night the soundless desert enveloped us with darkness, a near perfect setting for romance. Bert was at his best, because he had a special feeling for the sculptural quality of sand, and the trip had a purpose but was also a vacation. It gave me a chance to see a great craftsman at work. At last I had a boyfriend, and he had talent and ability.

Sometimes I felt engulfed or overwhelmed with love for Bert, but nothing could make me follow the feelings I had been told to deny. Our sensuous moments together went only so far, and Bert respected my chaste wishes.

Certainly he was surprised by my views on sex. According to my mother and Christian Science, sex before marriage was not allowed. It was most definitely an "error." Even though she was thousands of miles away, Mother still had a metaphysical hold over me. My fear was that if I gave in to the propensities, I would feel weak, the way I had after my surgery. And this fear enhanced my own religious fanaticism, which made me even more susceptible to this particular rule. But there was a lot in Christian Science that was baffling. Exactly what sensations *were* normal and real if all matter was unreal?

Mr. B. secured me with both hands, one on each shoulder. He had stopped me in flight. I was just leaving, and we were standing near the large front desk at the School of American Ballet. It was October 1957, and Mr. B. had returned from Europe. "I must talk to you, Allegra. Dr. Kiddon told me that you still won't take the polio shot. It's very important that you take it."

"But I can't. It's against my religion. I'm a Christian Scientist."

As I spoke, Mr. B. slowly released my shoulders. "Allegra, you can be a Christian Scientist and still take this shot."

I stooped slightly and placed my heavy practice clothes bag on the floor.

He continued. "Everyone in the company has taken it. It's so important. The shot is to make sure that you don't get sick." He opened one of his palms to punctuate the urgency of what he was saying. My resistance surprised him. His plan was so logical to him. "What if you get polio?"

"I believe that I could be cured if I got it."

Mr. B. frowned at me as I said this. I liked to make Mr. B. happy, but I couldn't on this issue.

A new company member walked through the reception area and waved a good night to us. Mr. B. acknowledged her with a small lift of his chin. Then, exhaling, he cast his eyes downward. It was evening and most of the rehearsals were over. Even though Mr. B. had been back from Europe for only a short time, he had already begun several new works. This talk with me must have been high on his list of priorities. I was the only one in the entire company not complying, the only one to be so abstract about life that I didn't understand real danger.

"Allegra." Mr. B. decided to start again. "I'm religious also. This shot should not interfere with your religion. You eat food every day to stay alive. This medicine is like food, like breakfast. Polio is a terrible disease, and the way to prevent it is now possible."

I could see the pain in Mr. B.'s eyes. If Tanny had had the shot, she would still be dancing. It was a horrible reality. A beautiful dancer was never to dance again, never to walk again.

But I had to live exactly by the rules as I received them and understood them. As a child, I seemed to be effective with headaches, but once into my teen years, I noticed that reciting passages from *Science and Health* did not free me from pain. Just the year before, at nineteen, I had somehow contracted chicken pox and had tried to pray my way out of that; it hadn't worked. I did not seek a doctor's help, however, and the chicken pox had run its full course. It was difficult. I wasn't spared the itching through any qualities, good or bad, in my intrinsic nature. However, chicken pox was nothing compared to what Mr. B. was talking about. My own personal vanity about this situation astonishes me today. Did I think God knew that I was a Christian Scientist, or did I refuse to recognize that I was not talented in the art of healing?

I gave Mr. B. a small, sad smile. I was sorry I couldn't comply with his wish, but the door to logical thinking had been closed. Christian Science had imprisoned me, and I could not drop my mantle of the zealot. I had directed all of my dancing energies toward pleasing him because I trusted him so, but in this area I was a brainwashed fanatic.

Mr. B. shook his head. "Please reconsider."

"I'll try to."

Mr. B. had put the full force of his charm and persuasive abilities into this conversation and had met with a seamless wall. He had made some ballet critics rethink their views on his works and do a total about-face, but I was more difficult.

"Allegra, I want Karinska to make you a secret costume." Mr. B. approached me five months later, before we were to leave on an extended tour. "You know, Maria is leaving after Japan, so in Australia only Diana will be doing *Swan Lake*. If anything happens to Diana, I want you to dance it." It was March of 1958, and the company was scheduled for a long dancing journey, one month in Japan and four in Australia. It was obvious that a third possible cast was necessary and practical.

"I'm thrilled you want me to do it," I told him.

Mr. B. was upset that I was still refusing to take the polio shot, but this day he didn't mention it, and his attitude was warm. "Karinska has the bodice ready. Go over for a fitting tomorrow. We will send the tutu along in a wardrobe trunk. This is a secret. If everyone knows they will complain and say"—Mr. B. gave a prima ballerina imitation, lifting his chin imperiously—"I am supposed to do it, not Allegra."

We both knew that he meant Melissa Hayden. I felt as if we were Peter Pan and Tinker Bell, or secret agents. This was how things must have been in the old Ballets Russes, where intrigues were rampant. I was excited. Perhaps I'd be doing another great part—the Swan Queen— in the next few months.

The next day I went over to Karinska's. Madame appeared in her blue-purple hair, her navy suit, and tons of silver jewelry. I wondered if my Swan Queen costume was really as secret as all that. Didn't the wardrobe mistress have to know, and the ballet mistress? How could I use the costume if the management didn't know about it? Mme. Karinska supervised the fitting in Russian. I tried lifting my legs. Some of her tutus seemed to prevent the legs from going up, and this concerned me. I knew the costume would be beautiful visually, but I wanted to be able to dance in it. Luckily, this one had a supple construction.

Whenever I was to dance something new, I had a way of tricking myself into calmness. I'd watch the other ballerinas in the role and assess their merits. If they were great, I was relieved and released; no one could top what they had done, and now I didn't have to compete. Their greatness was a fact, and now I could forget it and do what I wanted to do with the role. I planned to watch Maria and Diana closely as they danced *Swan Lake,* waiting for a transcendental performance.

It was going to be hard for me to leave Bert. He was my first boyfriend, and I was in love with him. For the previous month, he had been my constant companion. On March 9, 1956, he drove me to the airport and presented me with gifts, flowers, and a fruit basket. I kissed him good-bye and boarded the plane. Lincoln Kirstein had brought along *War and Peace* and was going to read it cover to cover on our long nonjet flight to Japan.

While we were still on the plane, I started in immediately on my first letter to Bert. When that was finished, I started on the second one. About three weeks into our stay in Tokyo, I began to expect a reply. Daily I searched the mail; as in boarding school, letters were the only way to communicate. But there was nothing. I was baffled. I had been rejected, and it hurt terribly.

Five weeks later when we left Japan, I'd still heard nothing from Bert. What had happened to this man who had acted so in love with me? Overnight he had stopped caring. I felt miserable and helpless.

Food began to look more delicious. I wrote more letters. He didn't respond. I gained seven pounds, which is a lot on my small frame. I got it down again, but my weight began to fluctuate.

Four months into the tour, I asked an Australian friend what she thought had happened with Bert. She said he had to be involved with someone else. Why couldn't I have figured that out? Was I such an innocent? Janie Mason had told me I was too idealistic, and she was right. I was idealistic to the point of stupidity. I did my best to suppress thoughts of Bert, but it was hopeless. We were like Napoleon and Josephine. I was Napoleon who wrote; Bert was like Josephine who didn't. With a feeling of sadness and disbelief, I finally gave up writing. I tossed my feelings into my dance steps, as I had learned to do as a child. Dance out frustration and anger. I was surprised to find that sadness worked well for comedy.

Melissa and I sat in tense silence in the principal women's dressing room in Sydney, Australia, making up our faces before the matinee. We were preparing for a performance of *Stars and Stripes* in which Melissa was to dance the pas de deux, the leading role she had created six months earlier. I was doing the first movement solo part I had originated. While I was dabbing touches of blue and coral on my face, the ballet mistress, Vida, walked in.

Melissa caught sight of her in the mirror, turned around, and said dramatically, "Vida, I'm not sure I can dance *Stars* today. You'd better teach it to someone."

Vida responded in alarm. "Oh, Melissa, are you sure? You were all right this morning. Who should learn it?"

"I guess Allegra should."

"Allegra, can you do it?"

"I'd have to learn it first. I have four ballets today, but I'll try. Don't forget that I'm already in *Stars and Stripes*. You'll have to replace me in my own role."

"Okay. Let's start right now." Vida led the way to the stage, lit by one naked bulb, and proceeded to show me the steps. Melissa stayed in the dressing room. I felt nervous. In a few hours I might really have to dance Melissa's part. It was an exhausting pas de deux and required more technique than I thought I had at that moment. Did I have enough shoes ready? Fear flooded me, and my mind was in two places at once—half of me on stage with Vida, learning, and the other half visualizing a poor performance. Luckily the steps were basic and the music Sousa, not Stravinsky. Jacques appeared in his bathrobe and offered a few suggestions. It didn't help to know that Melissa and Jacques usually brought the house down in this pas de deux. After an hour of this mild torture, Vida said, "Okay. Let's see how Melissa is doing." We both returned to the dressing room. I noticed that Melissa had completed her makeup.

Vida must have noticed too, but she still asked anxiously, "Melissa, how are you now? Are you feeling better? Do you think you can dance today?"

"I'm not sure yet. Does Allegra know it?"

"Yes, she knows it."

A sly smile appeared on Melissa's face. "Well, I think I can do it."

"Oh, good!" Vida said, patting Melissa on the shoulder. "That's good."

So Melissa was a quick-change artist. She had not been pleased that I and not she had been Mr. B.'s first choice to replace Diana in *Swan Lake*. This was her repayment.

As Mr. B. had anticipated, Diana had been out a week earlier and could not do a regularly scheduled performance of *Swan Lake*. My secret costume had been ready, but I didn't know all the steps and had needed to rehearse with the Prince, but there was no time for that. Although she had been upset to discover Mr. B.'s plan to use me, Melissa had stepped in and danced because she had done *Swan Lake* before. We were doing Balanchine's one-act version.

Although Melissa had been generous to save the ballet by dancing in an emergency situation, she had been slighted, and now, in the dressing room, she was reverting to old-school ballerina one-upmanship. I almost started to laugh, and when this scene was repeated the next week, with a different ballet, I did laugh.

If Melissa wanted to play the matinee game with me to even the score, I decided that I would play it with her even if it was at the crack of dawn. The executive director, Betty Cage, spoke to me about these now-predictable matinee mornings and suggested I not let Melissa use me in this manner. But my response was that I wanted to learn these parts anyway and wasn't going to be fussy about where or when.

I finally got to wear the no-longer-secret tutu during our four-week stay in Melbourne. I was given some rehearsals of *Swan Lake* with Nicky Magallanes and got on at last. *Swan Lake* was such a success that it was put on for an additional week, so I ended up doing ten in a row. This ballet—even the one-act version—always has audience magic and tremendous appeal, and I was glad for the chance to learn this wonderful role in which a woman's dancing evokes a swan's grace while she never for a moment looks like one.

I soon discovered that Melissa could be as generous as anyone and even offer help in a tactful way.

"May I say something?" Melissa asked most gently, one night after a performance of *The Cage*.

"Of course."

"I think if the soles of your pointe shoes were longer and placed nearer the tip, your shoes would give you much more support."

"What a good idea!" I looked at Melissa. She was thin, but the metatarsal areas of her feet were substantial and strong, like work machines. My feet were weak, thin, and delicate.

"I wish I had your insteps. They're great."

Melissa smiled. The game was over.

The game had served a purpose, however. By the end of the tour, I was stepping into new roles almost every day. For one matinee there was no one to do the first movement of *Symphony in C*. I learned it and did it, but then for that evening's performance I was put into my first second movement in the same ballet. Melissa had been moved out of something else and into first movement. The ballet mistress, Vida Brown, had a mad time juggling: If someone does this, someone else can do that, and then a third person can learn something else. In the theater each morning, I donned practice clothes and wondered what I'd be learning for that day—*The Cage* or *Serenade?*

Because there was little time to develop a role so quickly learned, these parts had an improvisational quality; my instinct was all I had. I think my dancing had a certain freshness and originality, along with a roughness and sometimes a desperation. Often I could learn in a wink, but at other times I'd turn my mind off. I was convinced that little surprises woven into the fabric were important. Some of my performances had too many surprises, though. I was also distracted. I wanted to go to the great coral reef, sip tea in the jungle, and drink passion fruit punch under a shady tree.

Five weeks before our return I received many sprays of cymbidium orchids. Before opening the card, I shook my head and guessed the sender. The card said only "B." Bert had surfaced. Obviously the day-to-day effort was not for him; his was the splashy way. He hadn't considered my feelings once. Actually, I was used to that kind of person. A bitter feeling lodged in the center of my body. Looking at the bouquet in my freezing flat, I knew those orchids would last a long time. I would leave Australia, and they would still be alive.

On our return to the United States, our plane crossed the international date line on my twenty-first birthday, and I turned twenty-one twice. We had been away five and a half months, and I had learned thirty new parts. Back in New York, I would dance *Swan Lake* under Mr. B.'s direction, and I would see Bert again.

PART FOUR
1 9 5 8 – 1 9 6 0

From Sinner to Somnambulist

Photo by Richard Avedon, *Harper's Bazaar*, June 1959.

CHAPTER EIGHT

Commit the oldest sins the newest kind of ways.

— WILLIAM SHAKESPEARE,

KING HENRY IV

It was midafternoon in September, but on the dark stage it could have been any season, place, or time. Standing in front of the unlit footlights, Mr. B. motioned with a downward nod to the pianist that we were ready to begin. At the right moment, as the music gained momentum, I flew on. I was rehearsing for my first *Swan Lake* in New York City. Mr. B. had time to oversee only this one rehearsal on the very day of my first performance. Jacques would be the Prince. My pure white pancake was ready. My body and arms would be pale when I emerged tonight from the dark recesses of the velvet wings, but would I be good enough? As always, the symbolic jumps that took place in my head were the impossible, tortured ones.

Company policy had changed since our return from Australia, and now all the principal women could do *Swan Lake*. The white feathers had been flying at Karinska's shop as she busily made each ballerina her own swan suit. This was my chance.

I tried hard to concentrate. This was the moment Mr. B. had planned for me nearly six months earlier. I didn't feel shy about working with Balanchine after such a long break. My reunion with my choreographer was turning out to be much more fruitful than the one I would have with my erstwhile suitor, Bert.

As I moved through the rehearsal, I only wished I had greater technical ability. When I was fifteen, Mr. Balanchine had told someone he'd never seen such raw talent. However, at twenty-one, I was still raw talent. I had watched Maria Tallchief as her *Swan Lake* deepened over the years and became more romantic. The moments of stillness were the way she moved the story forward—a pause really to see something and rest the eye. She had perfect pitch and always timed her entrance with a musical note. Vaguely I wondered if I'd live through my own career and never enjoy it because of the stage fright and stress. It was possible.

Almost immediately Mr. B. clapped his hands and stopped the pianist. He wanted to show me how to dance the opening, and he narrated each move with a running commentary. "She's surprised by man." His face froze in fear. "She is trying to get away." He ran from one side of the stage to the other and wrapped his arm around his head, eyes averted. As I studied his movements and his line of thought, he went on. "The Prince shows he will not hurt her." Mr. B. stared at the weapon as it is renounced by the Prince, and then he bowed in gratitude. "But she still has to get away. She thinks, *I'll go there*." Mr. B. looked around for a safe area. In his acting I read mistrust and fright. "No, the Prince is there!" In a quiet moment, Mr. B. looked at the Prince and fell in love. "Rothbart appears, she must protect man." Mr. B. stood in front of Jacques with his arms stretched out. "Oh no, he's moved." Jacques raised his crossbow. "No, don't shoot!" Mr. B. dashed over to Prince Jacques and placed one hand on the bow. "She's in love, but she must leave." Mr. B. took tiny fast steps and leaped off the stage.

He was wonderful. His eyes circled around their edges to locate the Prince, or to show how his thoughts took in the situation. In this giant-size chess game, he was prima ballerina, trapped animal, and mad Russian all in one. I lost some of my fear while marveling at his energy and his ability to cover space and to make a woman in love emerge from the swan creature's movements—an artificial evocation that rang true.

There was never enough time to rehearse, but luckily, a demonstration and a few words of encouragement from Mr. B. could transform a performance. Feeling his unqualified belief in my abilities helped me to do my best that day. He was also a patient man, and his goals were reachable through consistent work. Years later, I added a romantic touch to *Swan Lake* rehearsals: I'd practice the ballet's solo variation to "Love Walked In." The pianist Sonny de Soto and I really enjoyed these playful times together. Dancing the right steps to the wrong music diminished my stage fright by forty percent. Distract and conquer.

I was also glad Jacques was my partner. With enormous, almost superhuman strength, he would hurl me aloft in a gloriously high cast, a long-necked bird in flight. During these violent upheavals I'd knife my way upward, breathe the rarefied air, and hope that the costume would stay put. Jacques was very hard on tutus; sometimes the fragile elastic on the shoulder would rip open.

John Martin gave me an excellent review in *The New York Times*. But what was Mr. B.'s response? I later learned from Mme. Doubrovska that Mr. B. liked my second performance of *Swan Lake* even better than the first, but he was afraid to tell me. I had developed something off-putting about myself as a form of protection, and Mr. B. sensed it.

My life at work was going along swimmingly as I toiled with Mr. B. at the ballet craft in a rewarding way. Dance offered me a pseudo-participation in life without the threats posed by the real world. I could live in a fairy tale set to music. Of course, in fairy tales the punishments for mistakes are often very harsh, involving years of retribution. And offstage what was going on between Bert and myself still was unclear.

At our first meeting after my return from Australia, I questioned Bert about his not writing me. He finally admitted, "I didn't write because I was involved with someone."

"I figured that out." We were taking an afternoon walk. As we paused at a curb waiting for the light, I looked at Bert. The deep circles under his eyes had darkened.

"Well, it was terrible. She tried to kill me." He looked at me and smiled. His style on this walk was lightly flirtatious.

"I bet she did." I smiled back and thought, *What a wonderful thing to do to a difficult boyfriend.*

Bert's voice changed. "I'm not joking. It's over."

"It's over for me, too. I'm no longer interested." I was happy to be back in the United States, and this man had already broken my heart once. "Anyway, the orchids were nice. Did you know that orchids and bananas are related?" I said this as we passed through the East Sixties.

"Next time I'll send you a bunch of bananas."

"There's a piece missing in your brain, Bert. I baited you, and you fell in the trap. The hook had a piece of banana on it."

"Oh, Allegra, you're always talking about flowers."

"I'm still very mad at you for being so mean to me when I was away."

Bert stopped smiling when he realized that my voice had turned cool. I was bitter. Only when conditions changed and his love affair was over could he give me a thought. I couldn't depend on him.

My indifference worked miracles on Bert. All my letters and the infatuation they expressed from Japan and Australia had not moved him at all, but now that I wanted to turn the flame down from high to low, his interest rekindled. He began wooing me. Gorgeous flowers. Flashy presents. Dinner after performances—he loved going to the ballet. The thought came to me that at the moment there may have been a vacancy; the next girl had not been moved into place. I tried to push the relationship back to a less serious level, but I didn't want to break with him entirely either. I was twenty-one, Bert had been my only date, I had no other boyfriend, and this was the male attention I had missed for years as a teenager. However, I still had my misgivings.

Meanwhile, after two years in Los Angeles, Mother finally arrived back in New York. She returned in a frantic state. In the airport, she didn't recognize me. I wasn't that changed—only my hat was different—but she was in a panic, frightened that she was about to be cut out of her daughters' lives. Neither Wendy nor I wanted Mother to step back into her old role; her presence was too restrictive and critical. Mother sensed this, but she was determined to be back in New York with her girls and their exciting daily adventures. She had no life plan of her own, and she felt displaced. Her babies had grown up. She had no purpose. She had never really worked. Now she had lots of time to ponder and scrutinize every detail of our lives. Wendy and I finally realized we would have to absorb her back into our lives, but until we could figure out how to do it, Mother stayed at the Hotel 14.

From this closer range, Mother was now able to assess events and offer her insights. Mr. B.'s interest in me was still there, and, as always, she worried about that. She also had Wendy's boyfriends to contemplate. It was exhilarating for her to enter into a real-life soap opera played out in the exciting locale of the ballet world and New York City. Especially when the players were her very own daughters who inhabited two fascinating realms.

The newest leading man was Bert, who excited Mother. When she first met him, she touched his lapel with an unconscious nonchalance, feeling the texture of his jacket and smiling as she spoke to him. They played off each other. She was experiencing a surge of wild hope, the kind of feeling you have before your drill strikes oil. She, too, was struck with Bert's resemblance to Harry. All the old unresolved emotions of her original infatuation with my father came back into focus. She basked in Bert's charm and was excited by his success. Bert was well paid (years later, Truman Capote said "overpaid") for his work as a young, hot photographer who had also just shot a film on jazz. He was successful and good-looking, and Mother enjoyed his attention.

I was working closely with Mr. B. again—as I had four years earlier in "The Unanswered Question"—and I was to be the focal point of his new ballet.

Perhaps Mother was now more fearful than ever that I was going to fall under Balanchine's spell—even though he hadn't made a move, was married, and was always a perfect gentleman.

However, the threat was lessened because I had a suitor, and Mother would be my guide into the right relationship. She didn't want her life to repeat itself in mine. But, by being overzealous, she accomplished the exact opposite of what she wanted. Just as with her choice of Harry, Mother's appraisal of Bert was on the surface; she never looked deeper. By choosing Bert, I was about to repeat her life exactly.

But I hadn't quite chosen him yet. My important dates were with dance.

I wasn't thinking of Bert when I stood in a spotlight all alone in intimate apparel and nothing else. All my assets have been taken from me, and I am stripped bare except for black lace panties and bra. I look around me, trying to figure out what to do next. There are many doors—real ones—entrances and exits; all must be tried. As I approach one, it opens to reveal a white-faced figure. A harsh, tormenting musical sound throws me into a back bend of despair. I go on to the others, but marching out of these are masked men in trim tuxedos and bowlers or women in rhinestoned bikinis, padded bras, and high-heeled black boots. Their blank faces are uniformly cast from a mold. Identical wigs and long cigarette holders complete the outfit. As each door opens, I am thrown into another back bend, exposing the extreme arch of my naked ribs. There is no escape through these exits.

This occurs in "Envy," the final episode in *The Seven Deadly Sins*. As Barbara Horgan had told me earlier, Mr. B. had first done the choreography for this theater piece in Paris in 1933 with Lotte Lenya as Anna I and the dancer Tilly Losch as Anna II. My raw, primitive response to dance plus my unusual family configuration matched Balanchine's vision for the role of Anna II in his revival of this showcase ballet.

Mr. B. assigned no understudy for my part, just as he had not for "The Unanswered Question." This was meant as a compliment. Also, as in the earlier ballet, the type of role he created for me required a dramatic dimension, not just dancing talent. Although he didn't know the specific details of my life, his insight, as always, was unerring. If I were selecting a racehorse or choosing from an orphanage, I'd take Mr. B.; he'd tell me what I needed to know. With his extraordinary intuition, he cast me in a story that in some sense resembled my own. What he saw in me was my instinctive understanding of the character of Anna II.

As I understood the ballet, Anna I and Anna II were two people living as one unit. Anna I defines sin as she chooses, rather than conform to the world's definition. She forces Anna II—me—to obey her corrupt schemes. All that roving around from city to city and the deep dependency on another person seem like a variation on my own life story.

In the opening scene, Lenya and I walked together wrapped in one cape. We were wearing identical sweaters, skirts, berets, and pointy T-strap shoes. It was a crowded interior situation with a climate of claustrophobic closeness and intense jealousy. These Annas are detachable Siamese twins, but there are distinct divisions of power and areas of action as dictated by Anna I, the mother figure. The black cape turns out to be like a jail cell or a black sheet on a double bed, inviting an unhealthy closeness.

In the ballet, Anna I supplies the narrative, speaking, singing, and explaining everything in her terms. Lenya would ask me a question. A word would form on my lips, but before I could speak, she would answer the question herself. "Isn't that so, Anna?" "Yes, Anna." Mr. B. directed Lenya to cover my mouth. My vocal cords were superfluous: no one wanted to hear from me. My thoughts were never to gain a voice. My childhood use of silence could stay with me. My character, Anna II, had to find other modes of expression, and the only thing left for her to do was to act up, dance, and throw herself silently and passionately into what the older Anna willed.

Many of the costumes were shocking, pseudonude and minimal for this sexy tale of cardinal desires. I changed outfits at least once for each of the seven sections, sometimes more. Karinska executed designs created by Rouben Ter-Arutunian. I asked her to use certain stretchy fabrics that I could quickly pull off and on, and a tiny black tube of Lurex became my miniskirt. I lined up all my garments and props in the wings for changes that took seconds to do. I wore my white T-strap shoes a size larger in order to kick them off swiftly. Right, left, I'd launch them into the wings. One day, some blue velvet house slippers arrived backstage for me at the City Center without a card. They must have been from Mr. B., because I knew it upset him when I dashed upstairs to my dressing room with bare feet after a performance. This ballet of rapid changes and dramatic possibilities had dimensions to explore on stage, the best place for life in the abstract to be lived. Seven years could be compressed into forty-five minutes with an all-male quartet portraying the family. Mother had a mustache.

I loved Lenya's warm accented tones and the way she sang. I listened endlessly to her recording in German to prepare for my performance. And Lenya and I liked each other. She had intelligent eyes, orange hair, and curving crimson lips which, in photos, looked black. On the street she carried a lollipop. She loved ballet, and before we went on in *The Seven Deadly Sins,* she usually stood in the wings and watched other pieces on the program. She and Balanchine had known each other since the first Paris production in 1933, and I often thought about their long friendship. I was always amazed by the variety of people Mr. B. knew who came from many other worlds. He was the master of classical and neoclassical dance, while Lenya came from cabaret and theater.

Mr. B. choreographed this ballet at breakneck speed. In rehearsals, he would take everyone's part, girls' as well as boys'. He was expressive as an actor, and this was dance-acting, which means full-blown, carried to the last row, and eloquent. He was nimble, and his insight into music was lightning quick.

During one rehearsal, Balanchine demonstrated with great relish my part in the first episode, "Sloth." The two Annas desperately need money, and Lenya has a blackmailing scheme: I entice and entrap men, and she photographs us together. Mr. B. played me, Anna II, at that moment exhausted, sleeping on a park bench, mouth slightly ajar. Lenya roused him. An opportunity was at hand. His eyes flashed open, he sat up straight, and he took in the scene with a guttural gasp. The moment for making money must not be lost. He sprang into the arms of Billy Weslow. The lightbulb flashed. Extortion would follow contortion.

Balanchine envisioned much of the action before rehearsal—for example, in the "Pride" section my near-naked entrance on a platter with giant spoons and forks, being held aloft by waiters. In this I was an appetizer. He also wanted me to invent some of the movements for the "Gluttony" section. His choreography called for me to do some exercises on a mat to reduce Anna II's weight. Anna I, Lotte Lenya, is nearby, eating an ice-cream cone and pointing a gun at me. Lenya is my ever-present jailer, and everything I do, feel, and eat is measured, watched, and judged by her. Every bite I take is her decision alone, just as every word I try to form is suppressed on my lips. As Anna II, I look at my body after a series of sit-ups and recoil. I'm disgusted: my body is not as my ruthless other half wishes it to be. Perhaps a little stretching will help. I extend my left leg and hook it behind my head. I then twirl my foot twice to two ripples in the music for an obvious accent. In this contorted posture, I look at my foot in surprise, as if it has a life of its own. Mr. B. loved this absurd behavior, and it always got laughs.

Balanchine also wanted to experiment with a lot of sensational acrobatics. Much of the continuity came from what finally was proved possible in rehearsals. In the "Envy" section, for instance, Balanchine wanted me to be thrown a huge distance across the room into the arms of four corps de ballet men. Unfortunately, it didn't always work. After I had a few crash landings, Balanchine asked Billy Weslow to be my rehearsal substitute. Billy was a soloist who had done Broadway musicals and was favored by Mr. B. for his special abilities as a stunt man, great jumper, and turner. It worked with Billy but not with me. Balanchine ultimately didn't use this in the ballet, though I think we could have if I'd only had more circus training.

I was proud of my back bends in the final section, "Envy." John Martin in his *New York Times* review mentioned, among other things, Tilly Losch's famous back bends and said I reproduced them. Of course, I always thought they were my own. In another segment of this section, the men bent over, forming a dinosaur's giant-size spinal column, and offered me a path of their bodies. During rehearsal I'd yell, "Don't round your backs, keep them flat." Then I would run on them in my bare feet. I didn't know you could run on men's spinal columns, their dorsal fins. It was a great feeling to have these boys underfoot. However, at another moment in the choreography, they showed me they could give abuse as well as take it by tormenting me and being inhuman. Every tormentor looked alike, stamped out of the same mold. They hated me because I was different. I wore my own face, not a mask, and I wasn't part of any group, except the group that believes in black lace underwear.

While acting out this last sin, the ballet unfolds until everything becomes unbearable, and, as the young Anna II, I decide to end it all. Anna II is wild and uncivilized. Her raw physical power is her most important asset. She reacts and overreacts too quickly, and finally she dives through a closed window in a suicide leap. I had to run furiously to gain momentum to fly through, my fingertips piercing the aluminum foil covering the window, my whole body taut and following outstretched. Eddie Bigelow, Balanchine's assistant, stood behind a screen, unseen, to catch me on the other side. There was also a mattress under the foiled panel as extra protection. Another assistant would peek through a hole in the set to warn Eddie of my approach. "Get ready . . . here she comes!" Then I'd dive through in my black bra and panties and break the foil in an irregular pattern. If I began my dive from too far away, I'd hit a lower part of the set and my shins would scrape a wooden board near the floor. I had a strong leap, but this was a case of exact timing and true fearlessness. Some times went better than others. Scraping your shins is a little like falling off a horse. After it happened once, I understood that it was possible and should be avoided.

The sensational dive into the backdrop was one of the high points, among many unusual things. I could always feel tension from the audience, but I never got hurt. That mighty jump through the tinfoil would have enchanted the ten-year-old Iris who wanted to get out of Ojai and dance.

When Balanchine demonstrated for me, he often transposed himself into the feminine—sometimes exactly. Often, as he had a new thought, there would be a cry of *"Voilà!"* When doing women, he wisely became French. Brigitte Bardot was his model. When I tried to copy him and add a movement of my own, he loved it. This happened in the "Envy" section, where I walked backward in a deep back bend and recovered in a side bend. One movement led me to another. He didn't say anything, but I could tell he approved. He once told me I was a Bardot; he felt I communicated the same allure.

I think he was in love with me then.

Everyone outside the company assumed we were lovers. People who didn't know me or Balanchine and saw this ballet that he did for me said, "Oh, this is a relationship." Everyone in the company knew the truth, however. Balanchine was married to Tanny. His life could not conform to his past patterns at this time, and my sophistication in the role of a sinner was deceptive. I had never had a lover. Anna II has to have a childlike quality of innocence, and I believe that is one of the things that attracted him to me for this role. He knew I was unjaded. Anna II is an innocent who's accused of committing all the sins—lust, vanity, anger. The figure in the ballet does all kinds of things but remains baffled and innocent. On one level, her actions aren't sins. She's been corrupted by Anna I, who defines what the sins are.

He had also intuited an uncanny parallel between the ballet and my life. The Annas could be two sides of myself—what I would and would not allow myself to do. Mr. B. had already seen this in action when I wouldn't take the polio shot. I could feel and convey pure emotion and appear practically naked on stage, yet I still repressed my emotions and sexuality. I had not only taken an unspoken vow of chastity because of my religion, I had taken a vow to remain eleven years old for the rest of my life—Iris forever high jumping at Ojai.

When I was in my thirties, I had a dream that seemed to echo my *The Seven Deadly Sins* role. In the dream, secret agents were working against me and I was forced to submit to an operation. When I came to, I realized that in this one destructive move I'd lost three distinctive sides of myself. I had been sewn to someone and had become one half of a Siamese twin. I had been attached, in a reversal of the usual: Siamese twins are normally separated, not put together. My singular self was now plural, in more ways than one.

Also, I was painted black to match my other half, who was a young black boy. My sex and color were now uncertain. I hoped it would rain so that my own color would return and that the disparity would be very visible.

In despair, I realized that I must now go everywhere in company. I would never be totally alone. I would always be watched. However, when I started to talk to my twin, I became aware that he was not my adversary but an ally and partner, willing to help me. All was not quite lost. I had a friend, though our next move was uncertain.

The dream left me shaken.

Long after *The Seven Deadly Sins* was no longer in the repertory, the images and implications stayed with me. They were true.

The Seven Deadly Sins made me a star. It was my second major principal role with a dramatic story behind it, and it was a showcase.

top left, *Gounod Symphony*, with Jacques d'Amboise;
top right, *Jeux d'Enfants*, with Roy Tobias;
bottom, *Stars and Stripes*

Afternoon of a Faun

top and bottom left, with Jacques d'Amboise;
bottom right, with Mikhail Baryshnikov

A Midsummer Night's Dream

top, with Jacques d'Amboise;
bottom, with Peter Martins

Agon

top and bottom left, with
Arthur Mitchell; bottom right,
with Jean-Pierre Bonnefous

The Seven Deadly Sins

top right, with Lotte Lenya

Gordon Park

Martha Swope © Time Inc   Fred Fehl

Fred Fehl

Gordon Parks

The whole ballet was Lotte and me in an allegory come to life. Suddenly Tennessee Williams's agent called me and my picture was in *Life* magazine. *The Seven Deadly Sins* was considered one of the theatrical events of the season. I was photographed constantly. Richard Avedon wanted me to model for him, and eventually I would appear on four pages in *Harper's Bazaar* in fashionable outfits. I liked modeling for Avedon; he played music, and an improvisational dance for the camera ensued—a dance of self and sepia seersucker. Kenneth the hairdresser did my hair in a jungle style, transforming me into Tarzan's Jane doing Pilates.

At the end of this season, I decided to go away alone to St. John's in the Virgin Islands. I was exhausted. I was one of only three principal female dancers working that season, and, in addition to my role in *The Seven Deadly Sins,* I had been on stage continuously.

When Bert, who was still eager to step back in my life, asked where I was going, I told him, but added, "I want to be alone and rest. I need to get away from everyone. I want to hear the rhythmical sound of the waves and nothing else."

I had forgotten how dangerous vacations were for me. They represented an interruption of my routine. I looked forward to them, but the one I had planned was too sedentary. Later I would discover that, to ward off depression, there was a crucial medical reason why I needed the natural antidepressant the brain manufactures during exercise. Perhaps my father had a problem with these periods of gloom and sadness also. Often he had to make a trip to nowhere and back. You stay still. The car moves.

A few days after I reached St. John's, Bert sent a telegram that he was arriving—my mother had told him where I was. I met Bert at the airport—I was wearing a white sailor's suit. Bert rented a Volkswagen and we headed to the hotel to check in before dinner. In the car, Bert handed me a small blue box from Tiffany's. I opened it and took out a diamond heart on a chain. I started to put it around my neck and said, "Does this mean you want to marry me?"

Bert said, "Yes, I guess so."

After dinner, we sat on the veranda, watching the water reflecting the moonlight. Two violin players came up and serenaded us. Bert said, "I guess we're engaged." I agreed.

"So when do you want to get married?" Bert asked.

"Tomorrow," I said.

"Where?" he added.

"Puerto Rico," I answered.

The next morning we took a plane to San Juan.

Clearly, I was interested again. Maybe Bert would be kind to me if I should get sick. This was a peculiar thought, but it occurred to me. Perhaps I was thinking of Mr. B. and Tanny. The depression that had set in made me vulnerable and lonely. And I liked Bert's fearless gutsiness, particularly when he told me he had shot some of his movie, *Jazz on a Summer's Day,* hanging out the window of a Piper Cub.

But this trip did not have the quality of our Death Valley sojourn. Our days together felt too unstructured, and Bert acted like a different person. He seemed to have lost something.

When we couldn't easily arrange a blood test and other formalities in Puerto Rico, we gave up.

On the airplane home, Bert said, "We have three choices: get married, get engaged, break up."

I said, "Can you repeat those?"

When he repeated them, I thought a moment and then said, "Get engaged."

"Okay," Bert said. "Then when do you want to get married?"

"Next week," I said.

But then I decided we shouldn't get married after all. I was twenty-one. Except for Bert, I had never dated. Why was I getting married? Besides, Bert had shown me something about himself I didn't like at all. Bert had been deeply discontented the whole time in the islands. "I hate this place," he had said over and over. He needed real life to be like a movie—the dancing girls, the showgirls, the models, the scenic designers, the stylists, the choreographers, the ice cream swirlers, the bucks, and the power. Women seemed to fall all over him, and he enjoyed it. The women in his film and photos were lighthearted players, while there was more pain and sweat in my work. When an interviewer once asked me to define glamour, I replied, "*Glamour* is a magazine."

I knew my entrance into the spotlight was one of the reasons Bert wanted to marry me. He had completely neglected me for a while, but now that my career had leaped forward, he was pushing himself back into the picture. At the time, he said to Aram Avakian, a man with whom I would form one of my most serious relationships twenty-four years later, "She's playing over here at City Center and my movie is going to open just down the street from her. We should be married."

Aram said, "Bert, leave her alone. She's just a kid."

But Bert saw marriage to me as the joining of two celebrities. It was also spurred by one-upmanship. He was excited by the competition with Mr. B. Suddenly, I was a prize.

When I returned from the Caribbean, I found that Mother had moved from the Hotel 14 into the apartment with Wendy and me. I walked in and found her drinking her special beverage evolved from a poor childhood—hot water with a few raisins as chasers. On the table next to her cup was a bowl of pistachios. She was in a housedress because she loved loose comfortable clothes. Mother looked up, eager for news. She was ready to evaluate the situation.

I sat at the table across from her. "Bert has asked me to marry him. I think I shouldn't."

At that moment, I needed a solid piece of conventional advice about marriage. I wish Mother had said, "You're twenty-one. You should date for years before you marry. Besides, this man is dangerously like Harry." But what she said instead was, "I think you should."

I was stunned that she and I held opposing views on what step I should take next. But who had more wisdom and experience?

I stared at her. Perhaps she thought a husband could be chosen as quickly as a plastic surgeon, and with as little thought for the outcome; the important things were speed and action. At that time, Mother was worried about marriage prospects for Wendy. She may have felt that as a woman ages, her chances lessen. But this message didn't apply to either of us, and less to me at twenty-one.

"You know, Allegra, Bert's career is zooming upward. He's charming, and I see success ahead."

"Mom, don't forget to look at *my* career. I'm moving ahead too." Maybe she was worried that I wouldn't take advantage of the opportunities that now appeared. After *The Seven Deadly Sins,* David Begelman, vice president of MCA, had called. He had seen me dance and had a great idea for my future. I put him in touch with my mother. She'd arrived in New York without a role; now she could talk for me on the phone. Movies were her business; mine was ballet. Begelman had told Mother he thought I could be as charming in the movies as Leslie Caron, although he had no particular film in mind. But the fears of 1940, when I was three, had never left me, and I still didn't want to be in the movies. I apparently insulted him and Gene Kelly to their faces, although I have no idea of what I said. I had not wanted to subject myself to the scrutiny a film career would require. I felt I had too much shame in my life that had to be hidden. My name must be downplayed and my face not shown. Mother was still telling me at this time, "If anyone asks you your father's name, say it's Harry

Kent." So I didn't enjoy this attention. It frightened me. If it were ever printed somewhere that I'd had my face changed, it would show how weak and vain I was.

I had refused to capitalize on my publicity, and now my career was no longer Mother's priority. She took a sip of hot water. "I still think you should marry Bert. He's nicer than any of Wendy's dates. She's had a terrible time on her vacation. That miserable doctor went with her."

I knew Mother wasn't pushing for my marriage to Bert just because he was a success. She was becoming anxious about Balanchine's interest in me. Perhaps in her mind, Mr. B. was competition for control of my life, and Mother wanted to win.

"Allegra, you should do this."

I sighed. I knew this was not the moment to start complicating my life. Not only couldn't I manage a career or a marriage, I couldn't even get rid of a soft corn I'd developed in Australia. Not only was I not ready for marriage, I wasn't even ready for a chiropodist.

I leaned back in my chair and looked at my mother. At least marrying Bert would be a solution to sex. Even though the excitement I had felt in our kisses a year earlier was no longer there, marriage was still the only way I would allow myself to have a sexual experience. This decision was a mixture of Christian Science and my mother's dictates. She had said it was the only way possible, and it was what I allowed myself. I was the person who would not take the polio shot— I clung to principles for their own sake. I was stubborn in this, a fanatic. I had just stopped attending Christian Science Sunday school; the age limit forced my departure. Peter Pan liked to go to Sunday school.

Mother suddenly frowned. She had been reading my mind. Without shyness or reserve, she asked, "Allegra, have you slept with Bert?"

I hated her intrusions, and I hesitated. "No. Of course not. And it seems very important to him to marry a virgin."

"Oh, my God, I can't believe it! He's so conventionally middle-class, so bourgeois!" Her voice lifted in a crescendo of scorn.

I was confused. "I guess you're right." But what did she mean? I had thought that I had admirably abided by my mother's rules by remaining a virgin, yet now she was mocking Bert for observing these very rules when it came to choosing a wife. When Bert's friends realized that I didn't know anything about him, some of them suggested that we should try living together before we married. But I wouldn't deviate from my mother's teachings and the dictates of Christian Science.

Now even my mother was suggesting that maybe I should sleep with Bert.

If Mother had said to me, "I'm sorry, you don't have to live by those rules anymore. That was for then. I did that to protect you. But those don't apply anymore," I would have said, "You're changing the rules now? What does that mean? You were so adamant. I did all of this because I loved you. I'm sorry, but those were the rules you told me, and those are the rules I've accepted, and that's it."

I was so anxious to have consistent principles that when Mother suggested I not follow them exactly, I could not accept a relaxed interpretation. *How is that possible?* I wanted to know. *I thought we were supposed to abstain from sex and alcohol. We're Christian Scientists. Isn't this hypocritical? All this time you've been lying to me?* I was very upset.

She kept repeating her belief that I should marry Bert. She was frantic, her speech rapid and disconnected.

I stared at her. Maybe living with Bert would be easier than living with Mother. But something dishonest was happening. Mother would bend rules for her convenience. It was not my good that was being considered. Perhaps all of these truths my mother imparted were merely self-serving devices. Also, Mother spent too much time thinking about every detail of my life, and that scrutiny made me uncomfortable. But Bert had been on his best behavior and she was advising that I do it. I either had to be married to her or to Bert. I thought about them both, and he seemed a little more placid.

"You think I should marry him?" I said. "You know what? I'll do it. I'm going to schedule the marriage right away and get it over with."

I always went to extremes. Many of the bad things that happened to me in my life occurred because I was trying to follow the exact letter of my religion's dictates rather than questioning or thinking for myself. I didn't have teenage dating behind me. I didn't know anything about men, and there I was marrying the very first of that unique species who offered a proposal. Lotte Lenya wondered why I married so quickly. She said later about Bert, "Who does he think he is?"

"A red dress?" Bert's mouth assumed an ugly shape as his voice rose. "That's a horrible idea."

"But I have a Paris original duplicated in Japan and it's red." I wanted to wear that dress and have a chocolate wedding cake. I shifted my legs on the corner of the couch and recrossed them. "Well, what would you like to see me in?"

"A white dress, of course." Bert was motionless, frozen as he said this. He was visualizing the horrors of a red dress.

With a knuckle pressed against my front teeth, I mentally ran through my entire wardrobe and my sister's in their respective closets. "But we don't have one. What's wrong with red?"

"Because that's not what you are supposed to wear. It's not traditional." Bert glanced down at my wide-wale corduroy pants, the one thing in my wardrobe he liked.

"Is the color really so important? It's just a small gathering of friends and family."

"Allegra, why do you always have to break the rules? Anyway, you're a virgin."

I relayed this conversation to Mother and Wendy. The dress and the color had to be right.

"How bourgeois," my mother said, smiling. She was already one up on this ordinary man. At this point, I no longer cared what color the dress was. The weeks before my wedding were turning out to be joyless.

Wendy thought for a moment. "I remember seeing a white lace dress on East Fiftieth. There's a small shop there." We piled into a taxi and the garment was obtained—a lace shirtwaist that was not fantastic but serviceable and mildly festive.

When we returned, Mother announced that she wanted to take a bath and left the living room. I opened the box for a second look at my purchase. It would do.

Wendy watched me for a moment, then said, "Allegra, what are you going to do about birth control? Are you planning to use a contraceptive?" She frowned lightly. Wendy was uncomfortable in this role.

Jolted, I stared at my sister. As soon as Wendy said this, I knew this idea had been on her mind for a long time. She must have realized that Mother hadn't prepared me for marriage. Now Mother was taking a bath. From being too intrusive, my mother had stepped back and not said the things that should have been said to me. I also realized that my sister and mother must have been having talks about this, and I was uncomfortable knowing I had been the subject of discussion.

Finally, I said, "Nothing. I'll just see what happens." This was actually my plan.

In a controlled voice Wendy continued. "You can't do that, Allegra. You'll get pregnant right away and have a baby in nine months. You have to get a diaphragm."

Wendy had just rolled a bowling ball in my direction, and I was going to topple over. Quietly, I tried to figure out what I needed to do. This kind of a visit to a doctor was not to cure a disease, so it did not conflict with Christian Science. I was furiously thinking.

While waiting for me to respond, Wendy neatened up a pile of books and looked at the titles. She was letting her words sink in.

"I guess you're right, Wendy, but the wedding is so close."

"Call my doctor. He can probably squeeze in an appointment before the wedding." Wendy and I had avoided talks like this during our two years of living together, but I had no friends my age in or out of the ballet company. My roommate on tour, Ruth Sobotka, was eighteen years older.

Now, all at once, I was going on a crash course to experience all that teenagers did. What most girls figured out during the course of six to seven years, I needed to learn in a few days.

What Wendy had said to me was important and I had to do it. Two days before my wedding, I had the appointment with Wendy's doctor. My equipment for the wedding was ready, but I was not.

The ceremony took place on February 28, three months after the opening of *The Seven Deadly Sins*, at our apartment on East Sixty-fourth Street. We decided on a maximum of seventeen people. The guests included Bert's brother and sister with respective wife and husband, his parents, and some of his good friends. There was also my mother, Wendy, and three of my friends. Where was Harry? I had invited no one from the dance world—none of the dancers or my teachers, not even Mr. B. Perhaps I was hoping I could keep my two lives separate.

Before the ceremony, the Unitarian minister took us into the bedroom. "It's still not too late to change your minds."

"I'll go ahead," I said despondently. My interest in Bert had diminished drastically.

During the ceremony, the minister asked me to repeat after him: "I pledge my truth." I replied, "I pledge my *truth?*" My voice rose, and I looked quizzically at him, wondering if the word wasn't "troth." Evidently, he had taken it upon himself to change the wording. Everyone laughed at my joking around, but Bert was upset. He didn't think I was taking the vows seriously enough. What I did take seriously were my rules. I refused to toast my marriage with a sip of champagne.

After the ceremony, Bert and I went to his apartment in Sniffen Court. We didn't have a honeymoon, and our first evening of marriage was not particularly wonderful. Bert was annoyed that I was completely inexperienced. Once again, I hadn't gotten the basics. I'd enrolled in an advanced class without ever having been to first grade or high school. This was on-the-job training.

I immediately knew the marriage was wrong. Bert and I weren't right for each other. He was moody, and I had no practice in relationships of any kind. I didn't even trust Mr. B., particularly when he was complimentary. To me all men had a crazy side: I equated some of Mr. B.'s greatest ideas with my father's wild schemes. Now anything Bert suggested I immediately placed in the crazy category. And I was a disappointment to Bert. The day after the wedding, I had trouble getting myself together for a party a friend was throwing for us. I hadn't taken any of Wendy's clothes with me, and I had very few things of my own. When we arrived at the party, Bert said to Wendy, "Take her into the bathroom and do something with her." My hair had been done for the wedding; now it was as always. Bert was used to models and disappointed that at this moment I couldn't be more like one. *Glamour* was a magazine.

From the first day, my life with Bert consisted of arguments. He teased me constantly, but his teasing had a cruel edge. It wasn't in fun. He attacked me for not having my own wardrobe. We also argued about my ballet career, and he began to compete with Mr. B. Early in our marriage, Bert asked me to skip class so he could carry out a photographic idea with me. I felt I was in a scene from a corny movie: choosing between ballet for myself or posing for Bert. After seeing me hanging by my heels in *Shinbone Alley,* Bert had pictured me as a sophisticated theatrical type experienced with men. Of course, at the same time he knew I was a virgin, and that had been very important to him.

Twenty-one is young for anyone to marry, and I was the youngest twenty-one in the world. I had never wanted to become a teenager, and now I had entered marriage without any preparation. My only sexual experience took place on stage and was pure fantasy. When Mr. B. had starred me in the role of the Swan Queen and created *The Seven Deadly Sins* for me, neither of us could have known that I would be married within three months and have to confront the real world, with Bert Stern as my tutor. In the weeks after I was married, I could barely dance because I was in such despair.

· · ·

On my first day back to work after the wedding, Mr. B. kept unguardedly casting his glance over me. I knew Mr. Balanchine's attitude toward marriages that were not his own. I presumed that someone in the company had told him about mine. As we began work at the barre, his eyes traveled over my body. This was a mystery and he was searching for clues. Perhaps he thought I was pregnant.

At the end of rehearsal, I walked up to him and said sadly, "Mr. B., I'm married now."

"Oh." He paused. "That's nice." He said this without emotion, and his voice trailed off a bit in a noncommittal tone.

I quickly assured him, "Don't worry, I'm not pregnant."

"That's good." He spoke in a middle-range register.

"I am a little out of shape, however. But we have a few weeks of rehearsal before the season starts."

Mr. B. shook his head once, up and down. He seemed to be saying, That's true but it's unimportant.

Typical of my relationship with Mr. B., what was left out of this conversation was the most interesting part. I did not say to Mr. B., "I've met a wonderful man, I'm married, I'm happy. I'd like to introduce you to my love. And please don't worry, I'm still here to dance for you."

He said nothing more, either, but continued to stare at me in puzzlement. He could sense my despondency. He didn't understand. Bert had come backstage once or twice, but there was no warning: suddenly I was married. My relationship with Balanchine had been based on its limitations. Now I had become removed from him in yet another way—marriage to Bert. Mr. B., the man who had re-created *The Seven Deadly Sins* on my psychic raw material, knew better than anyone that I was innocent. I read his true reaction, the one behind his calm voice. He was shocked.

CHAPTER NINE

It is memory that is the somnambulist.

—EUDORA WELTY,
THE OPTIMIST'S DAUGHTER

The Sniffen Court apartment I shared with Bert wasn't particularly light, but this was the one moment, in early afternoon, when the sun streamed in and added brilliancy to the green rug. I looked at it for a minute, then picked up the phone and dialed my sister's number. Bert and I had been married six weeks.

My mother answered, as I hoped she would, her voice young and expectant.

"Mom. Hi, it's me."

"Allegra, how are you?"

I hesitated and sat down on a patch of light. "My marriage isn't working out, and I know it never will."

"I see."

"Every day is like that party we had the day after we married when Bert was disgusted with me because my wardrobe disappointed him. He's not a kind person."

I could hear her thinking.

"I'm not going to change. Nor is he. I'll never be happy living with him."

"Shouldn't you give it more time?"

"No. We have nothing in common, and I'll fall apart. I can't dance when I'm this upset. I want to move back in with you and Wendy." I had been wrong when I thought I could keep my personal and professional lives separate. When I returned from Australia I had a success in *Swan Lake* followed by the triumph of *The Seven*

Deadly Sins, five months of rapid uphill events in my career. Immediately after my marriage to Bert, my dancing went into a downward slump.

Now I couldn't function well on any level. I had put ballet away for a while and done an accelerated course in human relations, but with all the important parts missing. There was no chance whatsoever for intimacy, warmth, or closeness in what I had just plunged into so quickly. I had tried to compress adolescence into a week. It had not worked out well.

"What made you decide so definitely?"

"Having dinner last night with two really ordinary but very decent people, Mother. Your first husband, Philip Leavitt, and his wife, Ruth." During the evening, having dinner alone with Wendy's father and his wife, I had felt a warmth and calm that was missing at Sniffen Court, and I decided to leave Bert immediately. My mother had left Philip and then married Harry, and for me to have dinner with Philip and then decide to leave Bert seemed symbolic.

Mother made a decision. "Hop into a taxi, Allegra, and come over. Can you?"

"Yes." I hung up the phone, threw on a jacket, put some money and my keys in a pocket, and went out. It was good to be alone, riding in a taxi and holding nothing in my hands. I knew I had turned a corner. The spring day held some beauty for me.

Wendy and Mother were both there. They had been roommates since I left six weeks before. We embraced as soon as I walked in.

Then Wendy started to speak while we were still standing. "Mother and I have been discussing your decision. Unfortunately, my plans are up in the air. If you move back, that might be just a temporary arrangement."

I looked around the apartment I had left six weeks before. Mother was in a housecoat. Something was cooking on the stove. I smelled dill and guessed it was a soup.

Mother added, "I'll help you find a place, something in a convenient location."

I slowly took off my jacket and hung it on a bentwood coat rack. This was a surprise. My plan had been to return to the family. "All right, then. I guess I'll have to live alone. Shouldn't we sit down?" The three of us moved to the dining room table and pulled out chairs. I was startled. I had lived with Wendy for two years rather successfully after I left UCLA and Utah. Now, at a difficult time, I was not going to be able to live with my family. I slumped into a chair and went on, "I realize that I have to find my own place. I understand more now than I did six weeks ago, so I'm a little more mature."

Wendy's voice was low, measured, and sympathetic. "I only wish you had lived with Bert before you got married."

There was a vase of anemones on the table. I placed them next to me and looked at the pure red one. "But Wendy, I felt I couldn't do that because of Christian Science. If the rules were true but not practical, I should have been told that years ago."

Wendy glanced down at her watch. I could see that she felt under pressure at this moment because of her job. As a TV soap opera actress on *As the World Turns,* she did from one to four live shows a week and had much to memorize.

I needed my family, but at this moment it wasn't possible. Trying to calm myself, I placed the back of my fingers on the glass vase holding the anemones and let the coolness seep into my skin. "I've made a big mistake, but now I have to undo it."

"I have to go to a rehearsal," Wendy said, rising and picking up a script from the table. "Allegra, today's *New York Times* is right over there." Wendy vaguely pointed to it. "You'll find something. I'm sorry this is such a bad time for you."

"Thanks, Wendy. What I really need to do is to get back to work as soon as possible."

I opened the newspaper to the unfurnished apartment ads. The School of American Ballet had moved to Eighty-second Street and Broadway, and when that happened, Mr. B. and many of the teachers had moved to the West Side to live near the school. But I couldn't think about the perfect place to live, just a place.

It was twilight at Sniffen Court on April 14, 1959. I had turned on all the lights. When Bert walked in, I snapped the radio off and waited until he hung up his coat. Then I got up and walked over to him.

"Bert, I need to talk to you."

"What is it?"

"Our life together is not working out at all. I saw a marriage counselor a few days ago, and I know definitely that I want to leave you." The counselor had asked me some questions and said, "I think you should leave."

"What are you talking about? We just got married."

I looked down as I tightly squeezed my left hand with my right, then released it.

"I knew this before I saw the counselor. He asked me some questions, and all my answers were completely negative. I have to do this. It will be better for both of us."

"Are you out of your mind?"

"No, I'm not, I've been in tears for six weeks. We fight about so many things every day. You would be happier with a different kind of a person."

"Don't tell me who I'd be happier with." Bert had moved to the kitchen. I followed him. He opened the refrigerator and grabbed a soda. I closed the icebox door.

"You thought I was that girl onstage that you saw in *Shinbone Alley*. I can play and dance that person, but I'm actually myself, and what is very important to me is to work and live without conflict. I can't stand the way we react to each other, but I am the one who is suffering more."

"Allegra, you just used this marriage to catch up on real life. You're a crazy fanatic Christian Scientist who wouldn't drink a drop of champagne at your own wedding. You refuse to grow up."

"I know we both have problems, but Bert, you're jaded. Ordinary life throws you into depression. You get gloomy with it. You need to alter life, dress it up, and costume it for a photo shoot. But it's hard to do that around the clock. There are tedious moments in a day. We have made a huge mistake."

"You can't do this." Bert put the unfinished Coke back in the refrigerator.

"I have to."

"I'm not going to give you anything."

"I don't want anything. I earn a salary, and I don't need your money."

"When do you plan to leave?" Bert left the kitchen, and I followed him into the bedroom.

"Tonight. I've taken an apartment and moved my little bed in." Mother and I had found a small apartment on East Fifty-fourth Street.

Bert lightly tapped his upper lip with two fingers. "Why not leave tomorrow morning?"

"All right." I said this quickly. I preferred to make a major move in daylight. And, in truth, it was difficult to contemplate the loneliness ahead. I wasn't leaving him for someone else. The minute I walked out Bert would have ten girls to call up, but I wouldn't even have my mother. My staying that night was prophetic. It symbolized the hesitation I would feel every time I left Bert.

The next morning I moved out and lived alone for eight months.

The day after leaving Bert, I took class again and caught sight of Mme. Doubrovska walking with her husband, Pierre Vladimirov, one block ahead of me on Broadway. I ran after them. Panting slightly, I said, "Felia, I've left my husband, and I'm going to get back in shape."

"Oh, darling, I hope you will be happier."

A day later, I spoke to Mr. B. "I've left my husband. It wasn't working out."

He was surprised, then concerned. He put his arm around my shoulder in a fatherly way. "It's all right. You'll be all right."

But I wasn't. I hadn't anticipated how lonely I would be. It was like joining the army. You don't know. You can only fail to imagine.

During this troubling period of living alone, my dancing was uneven. Physically, I couldn't sustain long periods of pure dancing. But if I took a break, I'd fall apart, then struggle to get back in shape. I also began to feel that my career had no importance in itself. For a while, I pondered if dance was only something to take up when all else had failed. Perhaps my deep love for ballet was something that had to be rooted out because it showed some sort of weakness. Yet there was an emptiness. When I wasn't dancing, I didn't know who I was. Dancing defined me.

So much was going on in my personal life that I may not even have noticed that Mr. B. was creating a landmark ballet. *Episodes,* with atonal music by Webern, had an opening section choreographed by Martha Graham and then a series of other pieces created by Mr. B. Martha Graham's segment was a dance drama about Mary, Queen of Scots, and Queen Elizabeth I in heavy costumes. Then Mr. B.'s dances continued in the stark leotard-and-tights look of *Agon.*

Before one rehearsal, Nicky Magallanes, Mr. B., and I watched Paul Taylor do his guest solo. It was wonderful. Mr. B. told me that one day he would like to do a pas de deux for Taylor and me, using our Silly Putty bones and our sinuous qualities to advantage.

When *Episodes* finally premiered, I was happy with my part and loved the way Melissa danced the Bach section. In the crowded City Center dressing room, Martha Graham found a tiny spot and wedged herself and her chair in between Melissa and me. We had never really met, and I was awed. Her makeup was very simple: a mauve smudge applied carelessly to each eyelid and just a touch of lipstick. With that face, it didn't really matter what she did. As an opening night present, she gave Melissa Hayden and me each a small Japanese carved figure.

One of the new dancers I admired most at the time, Violette Verdy, had another section of *Episodes*. She had joined the company as a principal just before Christmas of 1958. A one-woman theatrical event in the French manner, Violette brought a whole new continent into the company. Her stage makeup, with extended eye lines, bright red lipstick, and long black lashes, set off her beautiful cream-colored skin and transformed her into an exotic creature. With the addition of rhinestones, she glittered. She had long legs, strong insteps, and feminine shoulders. Violette was amazingly turned out, and Balanchine pointed her out as an example to follow. It was interesting to see how a dancer who didn't have everything—not over-the-rainbow extension or the height of the ideal Balanchine dancer—could really turn herself into something completely distinctive and original. Her musicality as well as her turnout went deep. She could extract the utmost charm and humor from a movement. Her radiant *Tchaikovsky Pas de deux* was thrilling. She had verve and sensibility, and her performances didn't seem to weigh heavily on her. She didn't arrive in the theater with mental handicaps that got in the way. She could always be counted on to deliver good performances and make the most of her abilities. Her endings were impeccable; just the way she would place her pointed foot on the final chord of sound made you want to cheer and laugh. Her simplest movement contained so much.

Our training had been totally different. She had started at the beginning and had absorbed it all. I had started in the middle, and some of my knowledge was makeshift, because those Russians in California hadn't spoken English. I came from the dithyrambic school of dance (Wild West division), while she came from Mme. Rousanne in Paris, Roland Petit's company, and American Ballet Theatre.

We shared one thing in common, however: stage mothers. One day Violette told me the origin of her stage smile. Her mother noticed that her gums showed when she smiled, so Violette always curled her lips under and smiled. Stage mothers do study their daughters' faces. Sometimes Violette's smile looked odd. I liked her natural smile, which was genuine, unstudied, and frequent.

I also liked the way Violette thought in startling metaphors, somewhat like Flaubert. Many years later in an interview, she said that Balanchine's ballets were like streets in Paris. I wondered if just a few of them resembled streets in Los Angeles: Melrose and Mariposa, Sunset and Fountain, or the La Brea tar pits on Wilshire Boulevard. I wished I could think in French as she did, but I spoke only English and, on special occasions, Arabesque.

She once gave me an unusual compliment. "Allegra, you are so long in the tibia."

"Is that so? Thank you! But Violette, what is the tibia?"

"The shinbone."

"Oh, great, I'm long in the shins. I'm going to tell this to some of my friends, particularly the ones who named their dachshunds after me."

"Oh, no, Allegra, not dachshunds!"

"Yes, and they thought I would be flattered."

These dogs were cute, but my knees weren't two inches above my ankles. My tummy didn't brush the sidewalk as I walked. My center of gravity was low, but not that low. I felt Violette had given me certification, like milk. Now it didn't matter about people's pets. Violette's ideas about proportions were important. It was good to know your assets.

When Violette joined the company, Jacques d'Amboise stopped talking to me for a while. I hadn't lived up to his expectations, and he thought she was wonderful. Jacques acted as if I had become invisible. This hurt. What had I done? But it wasn't permanent. A few years later he decided he didn't like Violette's dancing as much, but he once again liked mine, a complete about-face. From then on, however, there was a lot of caution in our friendship, on my side, at least.

Even with Violette's arrival, I was still the baby of the principals, the youngest. But new dancers, younger than I, from the school and from around the country were joining the corps. In the dark folds of the wings one day, I saw two serious, adorable Lilliputians doing a barre. Janet Reed was auditioning Suki Schorer from San Francisco. Suki had a beautiful technique. When she joined the company, I gave her a small gift as a welcome, some tiny thing. She told me it meant a lot to her because she had arrived from the outside. I knew what that felt like.

When Balanchine created the part in *Episodes* for me, this role was a continuation of his interest in the abstract use of the body and the man manipulating the woman. The pas de deux in my section of the ballet was a dance conversation. My partner makes his move. I react. He puts my foot a certain way and turns me, and that's where I must go. I respond by echoing his energy. At the end, with a last curl of my body, I move from upside down and become right side up, finding a sinuous solution. In the last segment, the four corps girls and myself join hands and never let go. I am like saltwater taffy being stretched to the left, to the right, lifted up high, and pushed down low. Nicky directed my movements from the center of his citadel of women. I was a dark pearl on a necklace, and the girls were my chain; they had to move with me. I loved the concept. The music was hyperactive, and so was I. Against the background of atonal music, a distance exists between the dancer and her emotions. Some reviewers thought I brought humanity to this stark pas de deux. Writing decades later, Anna Kisselgoff described my interpretation as "poignant." When I had heard that Mr. B. didn't like expressive dancers, I had rebelled and deliberately developed a distinctive style that incorporated an emotional subtext.

Offstage, my emotional life was stark. During this lonely time, I was unable to turn to my friends in the company, even Violette. Of all the contemporary primas in the New York City Ballet, Violette was the one I feel I could have gotten close to. I badly needed companionship, but I didn't have the confidence to initiate any meetings on my own. I withdrew and didn't realize I could turn to my old friends and develop new ones. I felt abandoned by my mother and sister, yet I neglected to look to the New York City Ballet, my other family.

Instead, I relied on dance itself. Any day that I took class and danced was a good day. When I woke up in the morning and I'd danced the night before, I felt clean in my muscles. There was a residue of feeling right. Some people complain that the morning after they eat a heavy meal, they feel like lead. The morning after I danced, I felt like quicksilver. Through the three ballet seasons that I lived alone after leaving Bert, dance was the only glint of light in my gray and lopsided life.

I had been living alone for eight months when my mother met Bert in the street, and he told her he wanted me back.

It was during the off-season, and I was restless. Mother was in the habit of overresponding to my every little up or down: Always something should be done quickly about a problem, as opposed to simply living or working through it. Mother had nothing to do but think about me, and now my mood touched her off. She was hatching another plan, deciding that my sexual future was in jeopardy unless I returned to Bert. He wanted me back, and this pleased her greatly.

That night Mother approached me with her ideas. "This might

destroy you sexually if you don't go back to him." When Mother said this, I did not ask her to explain this perplexing statement, nor did I explain that I didn't have a sexual problem. Mother liked him, and she didn't seem to focus on what my return to Bert would mean to me.

I repeated my reasons for leaving, reciting my minute-by-minute terrible unhappiness with him.

She seemed to listen, but then she said, "I still think you should go back."

I said again that I didn't feel I should, but she argued for it. It seemed that for every forward step I took, my mother campaigned for one step backward. When I had achieved early ballet success in "The Unanswered Question," she had insisted I have surgery on my face. Once I received solo parts, I should immediately depart for Utah. After my success in *Agon, Swan Lake,* and *The Seven Deadly Sins,* I should bow out and get married. Now that the marriage didn't work, I should go back to Bert and torture myself further.

Unfortunately, I listened to Mother with a critical ear on unimportant issues but followed her advice on important ones. She had created a myth about herself as someone with a unique vision of life. She did have depth and intellectual gifts, but she was treating my life as an abstract equation: if you marry, then you are grown up.

Bert sent me a flower book, and, even though the first six weeks with him had been terrible and I knew we weren't compatible, I decided to try it again. I went back to Sniffen Court with misgivings and a certain degree of hopelessness.

Why? Was it because I always listened to Mother? One of the myths of my life was that my mother had complete power over me. The reality is that many times I chose to follow my mother's advice, not my own instincts, and then blamed the results on her.

The truth was, I was lonely. I needed a friend, and my family was living without me. I wasn't ready to live alone. I had no social life. I wasn't meeting anyone in the netherworld of ballet. And I was shy. After a performance in New York City, I'd go home alone and eat— very often overeat—alone, then I'd play the same record over and over again, which was my style when depressed. I didn't ask any friends in the ballet if they were free or suggest that we go out.

From this point forward, I never really worked at dance again in the way I had done as a child, perhaps to keep things more equal between my mother and me. My pattern was now to advance and retreat, ad infinitum.

• • •

One day I was at my favorite spot at the barre, warming up for an Oboukhov class, when I turned around and saw Erik Bruhn at the top of the stairs. How I admired his dancing and his handsome Greek profile! I smiled hello and quickly turned away because I was shy and really didn't know what to do next. But Erik did. He came over to where I was standing, shook my hand, and told me he had just flown in from Denmark to join the company for the 1959 winter season. I was impressed to see him in class so soon after that ordeal and wondered how he'd hold up to the mad workout that was soon to begin. Mr. Oboukhov entered the room and Erik went up to him, introduced himself, and shook his hand. This is exactly what I didn't do with Stravinsky once when I'd had the opportunity. Erik had lovely manners. Class began, and, after we had completed a series of innumerable jetés done at the speed of sound, Erik gave me a look of pained disbelief. I flashed my eyeballs in sympathy. Mr. Oboukhov was hovering over Erik, really enjoying himself and the effect he had on the Danish dancer. Later, when Erik did some flawless turns in attitude, I gave him a look of disbelief in return.

Within a few months after I had returned to my marriage with Bert, I was paired with Erik in a ballet that Balanchine revived for me, the one I had fallen in love with as a child in California, *Night Shadow,* now entitled *La Sonnambula.* Erik was the poet, Jillana the courtesan, and I was to play the part of the sleepwalker. I had seen the ballet twice, once in Los Angeles, with Mme. Danilova, and once in Paris, with Marjorie Tallchief, Maria's younger sister (Nijinska had told them never to join the same company).

In the ballet, a poet attends a party and is captivated by a coquette, the mistress of the host. Suddenly everyone exits but the poet. When he is alone, a sleepwalker appears. She is the unexpected presence, a mysterious person who has a secret never explained. The sleepwalker's role was a continuation of Mr. B.'s woman-in-white theme, a figure who had appeared in a younger guise in "The Unanswered Question." In this ballet, I portray a woman not allowed to live a normal life, whose husband keeps her hidden. But on this special evening she does appear at his masquerade ball. In a surreal dreamscape the somnambulist enters and drifts across the stage with a lighted candle. My candle had a tiny, round, white lightbulb on the end. I asked a stagehand for a piece of thin orange gel and gave my flame a little peaked turban. I felt like a George de la Tour painting. The sleepwalker's fingertips see; her eyes do not. In a gliding walk on pointe, she is propelled forward. A silent alarm or air current could stop her at the very edge of the stage, but not a physical barrier. Abruptly she changes direction four times and then traverses the long diagonal of the stage with ever accelerating speed, running on pointe. She has supernatural powers and the brakes of a Rolls-Royce; uncannily, she can stop on a dime, particularly if the dime is Mr. B.'s. In some mysterious way she has escaped her imprisonment, but her route is dangerous. She floats urgently forward and backward. She pauses in front of the poet, yet she does not see him. Somehow, perhaps by echolocation, she knows he is there. She has found freedom in her dreams and, when the poet's presence is sensed, love. But her dream turns into a tragic nightmare when the host, in a jealous rage, kills the poet. In a most unusual ending, the poet's body is placed in the sleepwalker's arms, and she exits. When I first saw the ballet in 1948 and watched Danilova carry the male dancer offstage, the ending had left me stunned.

In this ballet there are no lifts for the poet, just one for the sleepwalker. The sleepwalker's carrying the poet, however, is stage magic. The choreography calls for the men to place the poet in my arms at the last moment before I back into the wings. It was really not difficult, because his whole weight was on my back and shoulders as he wrapped himself around me in a fireman's lift. This is a visual moment in ballet like a glance at the moon. It is something you want to recall, touch, and see again.

Mme. Danilova played a part in preparing to do this role. The sleepwalker's costume was important, and with two undulating movements of her hands Mme. Danilova had told me to be sure the costume had the right kind of sleeves. Her remark was fortunate because Karinska with the sky-blue hair had already produced what looked like a Bloomingdale's nightie with short puffy sleeves. However, I misinterpreted Danilova's hand gestures—she had meant tight sleeves with tassels. Re-creating Danilova's same ripply wave of the hand, I asked Karinska for wide flowing sleeves. This turned out to be a happy accident. At the next fitting the long sleeves, like butterfly wings, were in place.

To prepare me for his choreography, Mr. B. told me not to walk in time to the music, but I found that difficult. Endlessly, I practiced three or four different ways of walking. Melissa Hayden suggested that I move forward on slightly bent legs, and that was the secret to the fluent drift. There should be no sense of a brittle shifting of weight or bouncing, just a smooth flow of movement.

Because I knew I couldn't overwork my muscles, I planned how I was going to execute the dramatic level of the role. I practiced at home, alone with the music. The transitions were very fast. This wasn't a leisurely acting job where you had time to develop a response during dialogue. In this role I had to develop my next dramatic idea on the music exactly as the conductor was playing it that night. My interpretation had to read across to the audience. If a dancer feels dissatisfaction onstage, the audience senses that, and the performance is lost.

The woman who walks in her sleep has a deep disturbance in her life. She seems to be searching for something she has lost. At the end of their pas de deux, the poet kisses her. This is a Sleeping Beauty, Balanchine style. The kiss does not wake her; nevertheless, their love for each other is sealed. After the poet is murdered, she knows what has happened and mourns, but still she does not awake. In fact, nothing can awaken her.

This ballet of nighttime arrived in my life with uncanny timing. In some deep and obscure way, Mr. B. was again using the stuff of my life by re-creating for me this ballet from years before. Living with Bert again, I was falling into a deep depression, from which I despaired I might never wake. I knew I had stepped back into misery; my marriage would never be right. Yet it would take a decade for me to extract myself.

Night is the time when dreams take over and things you want to hold on to quickly slip away. Ballets are like dreams. In both we accept the phantasmagorical as reality. But the mere fact of a pointe shoe means reality is about to be transformed.

La Sonnambula finishes like a dream in a mist with a small light traveling upward to create the illusion that the sleepwalker is carrying the poet up a staircase. Even though there is death, the illusion of her carrying him upward suggests rising above mourning. Grief is somehow transcended through the beauty of the image.

In real life, I was a sleepwalker—dance my only light.

PART FIVE

1 9 6 0 — 1 9 6 4

Babies and Balletomanes

Allegra with Trista, Susannah, and Bret. Photo by Bert Stern. Inset: Bert Stern.

CHAPTER TEN

The truth is, I might as well have married some classical
dancer. A lesson at nine o'clock—that's sacred. That comes
before everything.

—COLETTE, THE LAST OF CHERI

I hurried to the barre in my favorite part of the room, along the east wall. Early in the class, I brought my foot out slowly from a fifth position to a tendu directly in front of me, emphasizing the conceptual presentation of my heel in a sinuous way. With this movement ending in a pointed foot, I created a triangle of heel, instep, and toe. Only my toe tip touched the floor; it became the apex. The geometry of dance was important. Once Mr. B. had said "make a rhombus" to four girls he was rearranging in that formation for *Scotch Symphony*. Everyone had perked up at the unusual word. What had interested me was his precision and exactness. Any old parallelogram would not do. He wanted an equilateral parallelogram. To me it became "the divine rhombus."

I glanced down in self-study at the round sphere in the center of my body, the part of me without corners, the stomach. When Bert and I had been back together about five months, I discovered I was pregnant. I had first noticed a physical change in myself at the beginning of the spring season in 1960; I had been restless, strangely exhausted, not functioning well. The season had begun without me except for an emergency when I stepped in and danced. I performed for a short while, dragging myself through the days. It was late May 1960. Then I saw a doctor.

The moment I learned I was pregnant, I bowed out of performing. My body was against it. I was not a superwoman like Melissa Hayden who could stuff herself into a costume and get on stage no matter what. Mr. B. had been very long-suffering about most of the events that happened to me in the past years, so this time I didn't call him up but told Betty Cage, the executive director of the company. She absorbed the news in her stoic manner and said she would tell Mr. B. for me. He did not believe ballet dancers should become pregnant. When Taglioni discovered she was pregnant, she said she had a knee problem and disappeared for the appropriate amount of time.

Even though I stopped performing, I still took classes. Mr. B. had just started to give very slow two-hour-long technical lessons, trying to fill in the gaps in technique that most of us had. The Bolshoi and the Kirov had visited New York City in 1959 and 1960, and I'm sure that it was seeing them that made Mr. B. want to raise our standards. The Russian companies had recovered from the war and were flourishing. Some of their dancers were magnificent; the leaps from halfway across the stage into waiting arms were breathtaking. I wished I had been trained like that. Until then, I had only seen films of Russian ballet and had loved Ulanova, Plisetskaya, and Chabukiani and their way of dancing.

Mr. B. wanted to bring us to world-class heights. We were one of the youngest major ballet companies around, not over one hundred years old but only twelve. The New York City Ballet was not even a teenager. Of course, we had something none of them had—Mr. Balanchine. And he had decided that the days of the ragged corps de ballet with their sketchy technical training were over.

The stylized finesse Mr. B. wanted us to have was perfect ballet technique plus his idea of what made a movement sublime. The haphazard was good for monster parts. What he wanted to see now was the perfect poem dancing in the center of the stage. These classes were grueling and in a slow tempo. He was set on bringing our standards up. This was something he had done before, individually with his wives; now he wished to do it with the entire troupe.

I looked down at my new central configuration and wondered if my pale green translucent nightgown, cut short for class, would hang gracefully over my growing girth. It would be some time before I was a poem on pointe again. It must be hard for a swan to fly just before she lays her eggs. Such intensive training couldn't have happened at a worse time for me. I needed to sit on the nest for a while. I was pregnant and also, it had been discovered, very anemic. Still, I came to class. These were the kinds of lessons I had needed at the age of fifteen. I appreciated the new precision Mr. B. wanted to teach us, although one day I almost fell asleep during a demiplié.

Iron pills helped me work my way back to classes each day, a psychological necessity with me. During these months of living with Bert again, when I could have fallen apart from depression, dance helped me maintain a precarious balance and, as always, gave me an intermission from my life.

Just before dinner Bert called and told me that a friend of his, whom I'll call Earl, was going to join us. It was a warm, leafy evening in June 1960. Bert had agreed to a move out of Sniffen Court to a very bright but terribly noisy apartment on East Sixty-fifth Street. With reckless hope, I had thought this sunlit apartment might help us, but deep within me I knew my marriage to Bert was just a temporary measure, even if I was pregnant.

Bert and Earl entered together after walking up the five flights, and we soon began dinner. Earl was the person who had once told Bert that I was involved with Mr. B.—he had evaluated a magazine article and jumped to that wrong conclusion. I shrugged. Earl must be between girlfriends, I thought. My sister had supplied some dates for him from her single actress friends, but Earl liked the women Bert discovered because they were spectacularly beautiful models.

"When are you due, Allegra?" Earl asked, sipping his wine.

"In December. I'm just at the beginning, but it's too hard for me to dance."

Earl directed his next thought to Bert. "I don't remember you ever talking about a baby, Bert." There was a hint of mischief in his voice.

Bert, feigning discomfort, cleared his throat twice and said, "It wasn't my idea, I assure you." Bert had caught Earl's drift and highlighted the word "my" in his delivery.

"I'm the person responsible for the baby," I interjected, rising and picking up a few plates.

As I moved around the table, Bert said, "You're right, Earl, I don't really want a baby. All those sleepless nights and baby-sitting."

"And changing diapers," Earl added joyously.

Bert glanced at me. "And look what it does to the body. Look what it's done to Allegra already." Bert pointed at me and laughed. "You can't dance and look that way."

Dancers and pregnant women have one thing in common: they constantly look at themselves. When she became pregnant, Isadora Duncan described her body as "marble that had been softened, broken, stretched, and deformed." But I loved being pregnant and had the irresistible urge to look at my new body all the time. Although I was not very far along in the pregnancy, I was already developing a mountain range with three peaks. Overeating to reduce nausea had quickly given me added weight. A part of me thought that didn't matter. Maybe my morning sickness would soon stop. Another part of me didn't like that sloppy, self-indulgent excuse.

"You know what?" I said, turning back to look at both of them. "I feel like the two of you are jeering at me. This conversation is making me feel very lonely."

"No, we aren't," said Bert with a small, self-satisfied smile on his face.

I went into the kitchen and placed the dishes in the sink. Nothing absolutely horrible had happened, but Bert's tone was upsetting with its needling edge. I didn't want to live with this all my life. I'd seen old couples who spoke to each other in mild, mutual hate—the battle of the sexes mixed with the battle of boredom. Tears crept into my eyes; anything could make me cry. It was all those baby-making hormones flooding my body. I had very little control of them. However, I could once again try to direct my life.

I walked into the living room and caught Bert's eye. "You don't care about me and my baby, and guess what—I'm leaving right now." Then I really started to cry. I rushed into the bedroom, picked up my keys and a sweater, and left the apartment.

The two men remained glued to their chairs. Bert made no move to follow me or calm me down. This hurt. Maybe I'd hoped that he would rush after me, throw his arms around me, call me "darling," and say, "I love you, and I want the baby." He didn't.

Downstairs, I proceeded to the corner and called my mother from a pay phone. "Mom, I just walked out on Bert. He was laughing at me. May I come over? I need a place to sleep."

"Yes, come over," Mother said with high-pitched intensity. She and Wendy were now living apart.

"Thanks, Mother. Bert and I see everything from very different standpoints. This will never work out. I don't want to torture myself any longer."

"We can talk when you get here." Mother's voice was supportive.

"I have nothing with me. I'm going to buy a toothbrush. See you in fifteen minutes or so."

It felt good to flee again. This was not the relationship I wanted for myself. However, it was definitely more complicated now. This time I was pregnant.

Within two days my sister called me. "If you are leaving Bert, you should get an abortion." The logic of what she said really made sense. But not to have a baby because of a second miscalculation in my attempt to escape from a doomed relationship was not what I wished to do. I felt I could have the baby, not go back to Bert, and still have my career and start life again on a fresh footing. My sister saw all the possible complications; I did not. The baby without Bert might mean a life very closely allied with my mother. But at the moment, I was only pregnant, and child care did not have to be dealt with yet. I told Wendy I was having the baby.

Bert was furious at me for disappearing so abruptly while he was having dinner with his friend. He suggested we go to the marriage counselor together, the same one I originally went to alone. I foolishly agreed. The counselor changed his view once he heard I was pregnant. He told me to go home and bake a pie for Bert.

But I didn't go back. Instead, I temporarily stayed with Mother and clung to my plan to have the baby alone. Certain things weren't necessary, like a good husband and father. They hadn't appeared to matter to my mother. Having children, particularly girls, for your old age was important. I didn't want to be like Mme. Doubrovska who had no family of her own creation. This was perhaps sooner than I had planned, but I was now choosing to do as my mother and father had done—recklessly throw my genes into the world's stockpile and have children.

With a lovely bouquet, Daddy met me at Union Station in downtown Los Angeles. Harry was dressed in a white shantung suit. He was very heavy—he must have been deeply discouraged and overeating. But he still was distinctively dressed, a personal emblem of some kind. Perhaps the white represented his medieval suit of honor. He showed me the apartment he had found for me in Hollywood near the ballet studios and then took off, forgetting to give me his telephone number. He had some property and a house in Fresno and was living there.

The sparsely furnished apartment he had found was perfect—small, clean, within walking distance of a food store, and only a short bus ride to ballet class. Also, there was a pool downstairs. I could float through my pregnancy.

When I had decided to leave Bert, I also decided to leave New York for a while. With only unemployment coming in and nothing from Bert, I would be in the city for the long, humid summer. I first tried to take a job in Mexico. A young choreographer at the school, Gloria Contreras, offered me a teaching stint in her hometown, even in my pregnant state. I accepted. But when I arrived at her home and started to work, I realized that my life had come to a standstill on top of a mountain in Mexico. I had made a mistake. I didn't know how uncomfortable I'd feel trapped as a houseguest in a foreign culture with an unfriendly altitude of five thousand feet. After one week it was time to say good-bye.

Back in New York City, I had again moved in with my mother and tried to arrive at a plan. Perhaps Los Angeles would be a better place to be pregnant and give birth. No one would be watching my body day by day and commenting on it. The company was going by train to Los Angeles in a month for their July Greek Theatre engagement. I could collect my unemployment out there and live modestly on that, away from the daily scrutiny I so disliked. When Betty Cage graciously said that the company would cover my train fare to L.A., I moved to California to have my baby.

Alone and pregnant, living near Hollywood Boulevard in a studio apartment, I cooked my fat-free, rather plain meals. In the morning, I'd swim and get ready for ballet class. At this time, I did not take classes with Carmelita but with a good-natured, very sweet Russian teacher called Michael Panaieff.

While I was in California, Bert became involved with the model Pamela Tiffin. I also became involved with someone—an artist, the son of a friend of my mother's.

When the friend first saw me, she stared at my loose overblouse. "How are you, Allegra?"

"Fine," I responded, knowing full well what she was thinking.

"Are you . . . ?" She wasn't being diplomatic, she was just surprised.

"Yes, I'm pregnant." I lay both hands on my stomach to define the shape the fabric had lightly veiled. "Five and a half months. And I've left my husband."

She looked up sharply from my middle to my face. "Is your mother with you?" She haphazardly touched one of her round Chinese earrings. Her mood had altered. She was thinking.

"No, I'm living alone out here. Ballet class is the big social event of the day." I smiled casually and kicked a leg up to the side.

"Oh, Allegra, where are you staying?" My mother's friend poorly concealed the fact that she was worried about me.

"I have a small apartment just up this street." I tilted my head in that direction. "With a pool."

"Do you have a car?"

"Don't be so concerned. No, I don't have a car, I use buses, and it's not so hard."

"Would you like to join us for dinner tonight? We live just up that hill." She pointed. "That way, northeast. Above Vine."

"I'd love to."

"Good." She smiled. "I'll send my husband or maybe my son. Did you ever meet my son?"

"I don't think so."

"I'll see if I can reach him. *His* wife left *him* a few years ago when she was pregnant."

And so I went to dinner and met the artist son, who was about my age. At dinner, he couldn't take his eyes off me. I symbolized something in his past that he missed. We became friends, and on our second date I slept with him because I was lonely.

The day after, I called Mother to tell her exactly what I'd done, as if to say, *Why were you making all that fuss, and don't worry about my becoming pregnant. I already am.*

I had found a male companion for my pregnancy, and I was less alone.

The dog raced ahead with great speed. It was near twilight on the beach. My brother, Gary, had brought me to Santa Monica to watch the sunset, and we were resting on a large towel I had spread on the sand. The dog, like me, loved being in the lead. He knew he was first and ran with exuberance. Occasionally, he looked back with a little smile for his human owner: *Oh, you slow creature.* I lay on the beach, pregnant in my eighth month, watching, wishing I were the dog.

I was no longer taking ballet classes, and I already missed them. My stomach was a large, round, hard dome like a planetarium, and I felt a little too big and ungainly. Vicariously I ran with the dog in his romp and stayed ahead with him in his pointed, cold-nosed power. His paws were half in and half out of the wet sand. One day I would feel as he did—when I danced again.

Then the sun sank lower, and there was a silver path in the sea, the column of light Turner loved to paint. I felt a little chilled and started to tremble.

Gary was concerned. "Do you want to go back now?"

"Yes, I think so. Thanks for taking me on this excursion. This time of day is beautiful."

I felt happy. I was rethinking all the aspects of my life in a Los Angeles tempo. I'd dance again, after my baby was born and cut loose for me to cradle and love. I thought of my artist friend. It would never work out in the long term. His life was in Los Angeles, and mine was absolutely tied to the New York City Ballet and Mr. Balanchine.

Jack London's description of lead dogs came to mind. They loved their position in the front rank—like prima ballerinas. Some dogs resembled Violette Verdy, so turned out; others were like Lupe Serrano, excelling at a double sky twist. But they all knew that the best way to get over a barbed-wire fence was to leap.

I woke up in a semiprivate room at UCLA Hospital. I had found a doctor who charged two hundred dollars to deliver my baby. Natural childbirth was cheap.

The doctor placed my newborn daughter on my stomach. Feeling the weight of the little raw creature upon me before she was cut free was a precious moment. This baby was happy to be born. Trista was named after Tristan of *Tristan and Isolde*. I liked the sound. I knew the meaning but assured myself that people also call their children Dolores and Salome. I did not know that the woman Bert had dated while I was in Australia was named Dorothy Tristan; I knew her only as Dorothy.

Only Mother was in attendance for my labor. As midwife, husband, and nurse all in one, no wonder she felt all our actions to be a partnership. But she had not attended any class or rehearsals for this particular performance. I had expected it to be easy. I had taken natural childbirth classes religiously and done the exercises perfectly. I thought it was going to be like knitting instructions: You followed the rules in the guide and the sweater came out as pictured.

I had truly believed there would be no pain. The doctor disappeared; he also seemed to believe my perfect training would carry me through. My horrible surprise was how wrenching giving birth was for me.

Although childbirth was disconcerting in its reality of bodily transformation accompanied with panic, I had not lost control for a second, and I had taken no drugs whatsoever. I was proud of myself and thrilled with my daughter. I felt like a giant sequoia tree with its seedling. And—this was important—I had chosen not to call Bert. I simply wondered how I'd function as a single parent.

I was still recoiling from the shock of what I felt was a torturous experience, when Bert walked into my room.

"How did you know?" I said, trying to cover myself up.

He told me that Wendy's new husband had called him. Bert looked at us, baby and me, and said, "You both look beaten up."

That was a deflating sentence. What I had been through was rightly called labor. I thought he might have been elated, and maybe he was, but he didn't express it. He didn't stay long, and just before leaving he told me he had a job in Los Angeles in about three weeks, so he'd be back to see us.

Meanwhile, Trista, my mother, and I settled in, and my daughter helped me grow up. More and more, I began to doubt Christian Science. Prayers hadn't helped me at all, nor did the childbirth books. There was pain. I felt it, as did others—denying its existence didn't diminish its reality. Christian Science no longer made any sense to me. And now I had a tiny baby completely dependent on me. Was I going to take responsibility for my daughter, or leave her well-being to pure prayers? I didn't want to make life-and-death decisions. I thought of Tanny. Trista and I were going to get our shots like everyone else. I left Christian Science almost overnight. This religion was not for my baby. She needed a practical mother.

A month after Trista's birth, the phone rang in my tiny Hollywood apartment.

"Hello," I said distractedly. I was in the middle of nursing my daughter. Awkwardly I released one hand.

"Hello, Allegra, this is Betty Cage. How are you?"

I was thrilled to hear her voice. "Betty," I almost shouted, "really good, and the baby is wonderful." As I spoke I was trying to reposition Trista and hold the telephone with my shoulder.

"I'm so happy for you, Allegra. Everyone sends their best." Betty said it kindly, but then her tone became businesslike. "Mr. B. wonders if you'd be ready to dance *Ivesiana* in two weeks. Have you started to practice yet?"

"Well, Betty, no I haven't. I feel like I have a hole in my stomach. It's as if my middle were ripped apart." My muscles were so strong that they had resisted the expansion. "It's been one month, and I was just thinking of going in to work out. This may take me longer than I thought."

"Okay, Allegra, I'll tell Mr. B. that you're going to start to practice. Call us when you're ready. We want you back." I could hear relief in her voice. She was thinking that maybe things aren't so bad. Allegra's alive and says she can dance.

"Thanks so much for calling, Betty." Balanchine was well known for saying that ballerinas should avoid three things—getting married, having children, and dancing "expressively"—and he was harsh in his enforcement of this code with everyone except me. I was guilty of all three, yet I was still in Mr. B.'s mind when he thought of casting, and that made me very happy.

The next day I was at Eugene Loring's Hollywood Dance Studio just half a block away. My muscles were nonexistent; they would have to be developed, coaxed, cajoled. Maybe I'd be ready for the spring season.

When Bert showed up again, my mood had changed, and so had his. He looked at his daughter and fell in love. Taking out his camera, he became a serious man, a handsome photographer with a great eye, and the father of our baby. This was the part of him I admired. I asked him to show me how to take a picture, and he did so.

I decided things might work out if Bert had therapy. I knew he wasn't eager to have me back, but because of Trista I decided to try. The idea of what therapy could do became a new hope, and as with my old feelings about Christian Science, I thought it could work miracles. I got a doctor's name, and Bert agreed to call him when he got back to New York. Maybe psychoanalysis could make incompatible people compatible.

Back in New York, Bert, Trista, and I, plus a maid, worked at living together on East Sixty-fifth Street, and Bert began seeing a therapist, whom I will call Sheldon Hertzberg. As I left Christian Science behind, I embraced a new religion, psychotherapy.

One evening in July 1961, outside the Metropolitan Opera House, I caught sight of Lincoln Kirstein. We both had been attending a performance of the Royal Ballet. When Lincoln saw me, he said, "Good news, Allegra, we are going to do *The Seven Deadly Sins* again next season."

I was back to dancing and fairly strong, but the surface of my body had changed.

"I can't do it." My voice began to rise, then sink. "I have stretch marks on my stomach." I hadn't seen anything like it on any other woman who had babies. I didn't see how I was going to do *Sins* again with its brief costumes.

Kirstein had rarely focused on me. He was very tall, and his eye level was above me. He would move toward exactly what he wanted—usually the current star principal dancers and Balanchine. Now Lincoln cast his eyes down to my middle region, trying to visualize what I meant. He looked horrified. "But, Allegra . . ."

"No, I can't do it. It's impossible. My stomach was ripped apart."

"This is terrible news, Allegra. I'll tell George." Lincoln's voice had drifted into a monotone.

I would love a second chance to respond to Lincoln, to go back in time and say yes. I could have consulted Karinska and had her invent a new costume and add a thin transparency to cover nakedness as needed. I had no understudy for this part. No one else had or would do this particular version. The company never got *The Seven Deadly Sins* on again. I remember thinking then, *Even though I can't dance this, my time in the company is now.* Still, I cautioned myself, there would be a time when I would no longer be in such a position.

I never dreamed of how depressed I'd feel when that time arrived and of the problems I would have in accepting that position—and eventually no position.

"I won't do it." Bert folded his arms resolutely. "I've never heard of anything so dumb."

His voice filtered over to me, then I blacked out. When I came to, I repeated my plea. "Bert, please make the call."

"I'm furious at you, Allegra. Why don't you use your head sometimes?"

"Bert," I said very softly, "I need your help. Please call the doctor for me." I tried getting up to call myself but felt weak again, so I waved my arms at him to signal the urgency and then fainted again. Coming to, I heard Bert say, "I don't like it when you wave your arms like that. You look crazy."

"Please don't be mad, Bert. I was trying to get your attention."

It was January 1962, and I had been bleeding for five hours from complications arising from having my wisdom teeth removed. By seven o'clock that night, the bleeding was worse and I started to faint repeatedly. When I begged Bert to call the doctor and carry me into bed, he hesitated. I was shocked. He actually couldn't see the urgent necessity for some action.

I had had all four teeth removed without thinking even once about Christian Science. Much to my surprise, it was Bert who had a problem with my impulsive action; he had his own ideas on how wisdom teeth should be removed. Deeply annoyed, he told me that four was not the wise way. He was like Mel Brooks's two thousand-year-old man stuck in his ways, who never ate fried food. Unreasonably furious, the day I had it done he could barely talk to me just because he personally had never heard of more than two being removed at any one session.

Now, one week later, the doctor's probing during a follow-up visit had caused my gums to bleed. The doctor had given me some gauze to bite on because he, too, thought the bleeding would soon stop, but during the barre in my ballet class, the bleeding had increased and interfered with my dancing. I was quickly running out of gauze. So I asked Mme. Doubrovska for permission to leave early and went home to assemble dinner and lie down.

Bert had walked in about two hours after I did and found me in the kitchen. "What's that in your mouth?" Bert had asked in a not-too-friendly tone, when he saw me looking like a chipmunk and hovering over the sink.

"It's gauze," I said, removing the wads and dumping them in the garbage. The salty taste in my mouth wasn't a good sign.

When Bert saw the blood, his face tightened. "It's those wisdom teeth, isn't it? That was stupid of you to have them all removed at once."

"Bert, I didn't have a problem last week when I did it. The problem started today." I held up a hand. "Don't look, I have to spit."

"That's not very romantic, Allegra."

"I'm sorry." I had glanced back at Bert after I ran some water to wash out the sink. I needed help, not romance. "Anyway, when the doctor checked my gums, I started to bleed slightly. The trouble is, it hasn't stopped."

I leaned my arms against the counter and stuffed two more wads in my mouth. Then, weakly, I walked over to the couch in the living room and slumped into a corner. Bert, following me, continued shaking his head, then sat at the opposite end of the couch and glared in my direction until I fainted.

Now I woke from another faint feeling helpless. The room had darkened. Only one light had been turned on. I made another attempt to get up but knew I was going to faint again. When I came to, I had a new message. "Please carry me into the bedroom. I can't get there on my own, and I'm frightened." I passed out again after I said this.

Finally, Bert picked me up and carried me into the bedroom. I lay still, and he quickly left the room. He came back with the report that my surgeon was unreachable for the weekend. He stayed in the doorway as he spoke, with his body silhouetted by the hall light.

This bad news was upsetting. I was still bleeding. "Bert, don't you have a personal friend who is a dentist?"

"Yes."

"Please try to reach him."

He hesitated. "All right."

I lay in bed until he finally reached his friend's answering service. Ages later, when the doctor finally called back, I was told to bite on a tea bag. The next morning my skin was white; I thought of Robin Hood and Lord Byron. A medical examination showed that I was extremely anemic.

In a depressed state, I built up my strength slowly, managing only a portion of a barre a day at home, as I took my iron tablets and B$_{12}$ shots. Even though Bert was in therapy, our life together was not better. I didn't have the energy to pack everything and move out, but I knew that one day I would.

Although Bert didn't know how to take care of me when I was sick, he did come up with an idea—a better apartment with a wrap-around terrace. The new place was very light with a southern exposure, and he was going to have a professional gardener plant a terrace for me. I was glad to move and try to leave past unpleasantries and disappointments behind. Although I thought I had dropped all of Christian Science, I hadn't. I still believed that a certain kind of pain was unreal, particularly the hopeless torment of an impossible situation. This made me reluctant to move out of old patterns, and it made me strange about money.

In Christian Science, "laying up treasures in matter" was an "error," according to Mary Baker Eddy. Christian Science did not foster my self-protective instincts. I didn't spend money, but I let others control it. Even though Bert's business was thriving, I started giving my paychecks to him. I had no idea how much money was coming in and going out, and I only suspected that nothing was being saved or put away. But this didn't seem reckless, because he was doing so well. I didn't put anything away for myself, as I had as a teenager, and Bert started to buy everything through the business.

He also, on the whole, began living two lives—his lavish studio style, with the best and most expensive dishes and furniture, and his home life, with broken-down furniture and second-best everything.

In the spring of 1962, Bert decided that he wanted to photograph Marilyn Monroe for *Vogue* and instructed his secretary to send her three dozen red roses in Los Angeles. Then *Vogue* stepped in and arranged the details for the sitting. When he told me about the roses, I complained that I had never received three dozen red roses from him. Mr. B. once sent Alexandra Danilova one hundred roses when she complained about not receiving opening-night flowers. But Bert was not Mr. B. He left for California without saying good-bye.

While Bert was in Los Angeles photographing Monroe, I went on an American summer tour with my mother and baby. Coming up in September was a long European tour with two months in Russia, something that would complicate my life even more. Should I do it or not? Trista was one and a half, and I was worried about leaving her for such a long time. We would miss each other terribly.

I enjoyed my baby with her adorable ways and her curly hair, so impossible to comb. One day while I tried untangling the knots, she squirmed and wouldn't sit still. In desperation I said, "Trista, face me." She looked at me in startled wonder while some realization dawned in her eyes. Then she slowly lifted her hand and put it gently on my face. I was overjoyed with the new creature's method of thought. Quickly I picked her up and whirled her around the room. Then we both settled down to see what the comb could do.

CHAPTER ELEVEN

Why am I going? I kept asking myself. What is awaiting me there? . . . loneliness, restaurant dinners, noise, the electric light, which makes my eyes ache. Where am I going, and what am I going for? What am I going for?

— ANTON CHEKHOV. "THE WIFE"

Before the curtain had risen on *Serenade* at the Bolshoi Theater in Moscow, two national anthems were played. In my long blue tulle-skirted costume, I warmed up to the "Star-Spangled Banner." Fast chaîné turns danced to "Oh, say, can you see" had helped me feel ready. *Serenade* was to Tchaikovsky's music and Mr. B.'s first creation in America. Now it was first on the program in Russia. My twirling warm-up helped me subdue terror, my personal version of stage fright.

It was the height of the Cold War—the fall of 1962—and the New York City Ballet was performing in Moscow, the first stop in Russia where we would spend two months. The tour also included Lenin grad, Kiev, Tbilisi, and Baku. Tbilisi, in Georgia, was Balanchine's hometown, and after a hiatus of almost forty years he was taking us to his country, a troupe of strolling players. We were still a young company—just sweet sixteen—and not an institution, a group of sixty-two dancers or so. Firebirds no longer dwelt in the forests of the U.S.S.R., but they could come to life on stage in a Balanchine creation. Nikita Khrushchev himself was sitting in a box out front. Opening night was the time for Communist party members to attend.

The audience's response to *Serenade* had been exquisite but not ecstatic. Now Arthur Mitchell and I were in the wings warming up and stretching before our second entrance in *Agon*. The first complex ensemble section had gone well, and the pas de deux was coming up. As the time grew closer, I said, "Arthur, I'm nervous. I'm dying inside."

"Just relax, Al-e-gara," Arthur said. "Remember Julius and

Darva." Arthur, sleek, elegant, and unruffled, always said this to me. It was a ritual, like Maria's crossing herself before going on. I will never forget Julius and Darva, even though I never knew who they were. I didn't investigate. Arthur couldn't have been more professional or serious, but a little playfulness helped to lighten the load of responsibility we both felt that night. Would we be good enough? Or were the doubts only in my head? Arthur and I were a contrast in temperaments. Handsome, dark-skinned Arthur was supremely confident with a positive outlook, while to me future events were definitely foreboding.

I was filling in for Diana Adams, who was nursing a bad foot. The pas de deux in *Agon* was created for two tall dancers. The colors of skin and leotard were contrasting in sharply bordered areas, and the choreography called for odd formations with large horizontal and vertical sweeps of movement. I felt I had given this role my personal stamp and elastic style. I was not as tall as Diana Adams, so I tried to extend my lines to the utmost and mesmerize the audience. It is good to be tall, but illusions of height can be created. I am lucky in my proportions. My neck is long, my wrists are thin, and my penchée— the six o'clock look of the legs—is perfect. Still, while Arthur was keying up, I was losing my spirit. Mentally, I was in the backseat of a car crossing America, but now the bears outside the windows were Russian. I lengthened my spine. It was time to move into the driver's seat.

"Allegra," Arthur's voice cut into my thoughts, "will you stop worrying? You're driving me crazy. You can't miss with this pas de deux."

"*Da, da,*" I responded in Russian.

In a bass-baritone voice, eyes twinkling, hands on his hips, he said, "Now, wait a minute, Al-e-gara. This is just a small town." I laughed. Opening night in Moscow, the heart of ballet country—a small town.

I gave myself a small, silent pep talk: *Allegra, get over your fear and dance. It's too late to worry about what you don't have. You don't need technique for this pas de deux. It's easy, it's great, Arthur's great, the choreography and music are sublime, and you have decades ahead to judge yourself. So just dance—not in the wings—but on stage. Just dance.*

Arthur counted two beats after Melissa's bow and only then indicated that we should go on; he wanted the stage bare for a brief interval of nothing. The discipline and formality of his approach were reassuring. I came back from my small trip in erratic fear and placed myself on an even keel. We walked out and posed in a waiting silence until

Robert Irving, our conductor, gave us the cue. Then I tore across the stage, spinning and lunging with Arthur right behind me on the first fiery downhill diagonal, lunging and twirling recklessly. Stravinsky and Balanchine were back in Russia.

The Russian audience went wild over *Agon,* particularly the pas de deux. There had been no clues that it would be so well received. It was a thrilling moment for me. When it became apparent that I was the Russians' favorite woman dancer, Mr. B. cast me in every performance but one.

Two days earlier, I had stood with the company in the doorway of the main rehearsal studio of the Bolshoi Theater, a room with brilliantly blue curtains. Our wardrobe people, stage managers, and crew were already at the theater, and the whole miracle of putting a visiting ballet company on stage was under way. As I looked around the enormous room with the raked floor, waiting for the Russians to finish their class, many emotions had run through me. Some of the greats of the Soviet ballet were at work inside the Bolshoi rehearsal hall, and the leisure moment gave me the opportunity to compare myself with them. Judged by technique alone, I was paltry in comparison. I had asked myself what I could possibly show these dancers that they couldn't do better.

When the Russians had finally finished, we entered and began our class and rehearsal. The room was a wonderful space to work in because the architect had not forgotten windows. The rehearsal studio also had exactly the same angle of rake as the stage, so we could get used to it. The body does this automatically, but it takes a few days. Choreographically, *Agon* and the rake were compatible.

As Mr. B. conducted the rehearsal, he had seemed neither anxious nor nervous. He showed a face the K.G.B. could never read. I'm not sure what he felt inside, but he wasn't going to show the Bolshoi dancers, who were now peeking in at us, his real feelings. He acted in his usual manner, quiet, thorough, and completely absorbed in the moment. His eyes took everything in. After all, he was the one who had to get us on.

I was surprised by the Russian audience's reaction to me. They had great dancers. I was raw, all emotion and desire. I had strange muscles that would die on me, and, to an extent, my style was an interpretation of ballet. There was a bit of Isadora and mountain goat in my dancing. I felt embarrassed about my lack of technique, and sometimes before going on stage, I had to say, "Forgive me, God, for what I'm about to do. I wish it was better." And then I'd do it.

Although I admired the great technicians of ballet, I knew, of course, that dancing isn't totally technique. When Mr. B. demonstrated, it was beautiful. He was so fascinating because dance was a revelation of his thoughts; you could read his mind by watching him move. Dancing is a quality of motion and an interpretation of rhythm. I've seen very good technicians who didn't interest me. They lacked spontaneity. They weren't even surprised that they could perform miraculous feats. Some excellent technicians were so used to being perfect that they didn't astonish themselves. They might astonish the audience, but it wasn't quite the presentation of the unknown. I longed to be a great pyrotechnician and have it all in my grasp.

I was thrilled that the Russians saw something in me, the girl who wasn't quite perfect technically. I was both surprised and honored to be their favorite.

Arthur Mitchell had the devotees right in the palm of his hand, and Edward Villella—who also was not a perfect technician—was the favorite male. Eddie won the Russians' hearts on his appearance the second night. Jumping powerfully high, Eddie gave them his all. He was young, handsome, and generous. Many important years had been missed in his teens while he was in the Merchant Marines, but his naked attack was appealing. He made the audience feel like teenagers. When he went up in a leap, they went with him. I watched him from the wings, waiting for his usual unusual happenings. The audience would not stop applauding after Eddie's high-flying solo in *Donizetti Variations*—his intense animal energy brought down the house. The Russians were going wild, and there was only one thing to do: repeat the variation, even though an encore was contrary to company policy. Eddie motioned to the conductor and shook his head in a gesture of *I guess we must*. It had been a thrilling dance the first time, and it was a thrilling dance the second time. The only dance encores I had ever seen were Eddie's, Maya Plisetskaya's, and those by a few Spanish flamenco dancers. In Moscow, all of us watching in the wings were caught up with the excitement. We were proud of Eddie; our boy was having a runaway success. Twenty years later, Eddie told me about Mr. B.'s instructions to him in Russia. "Stay upstage and always wear black"; in other words, be unobtrusive and inconspicuous. I never knew if this was Mr. B.'s joke with Eddie, or Eddie's joke with me. The Russian bureaucracy didn't want us to perform *Prodigal Son* because it was a Bible story, but Mr. B. forced them to accept it.

Diana Adams finally did one performance. I have no idea of what she went through to do it. She had traveled halfway around the world to dance and then realized she was in too much pain to do so. By the time we reached Vienna she understood that. But she was determined to appear once in Moscow and got herself up for it. Her performance was great. In my mind I can see her dancing, but the ballet remains nameless. When I see something like this I'm very much a part of the audience. I become a fan. In great excitement I went back and complimented her. She had created a singing line of movement inspired by, as she called him, "the Boss." Diana was uncomfortable with praise. When I danced, I always tried to touch something elusive or sublime, and sometimes it worked. When it worked for others, I was the first to tell them. I wanted her to accept my genuine enthusiasm. Giving a compliment shouldn't be such hard work.

Not all of our performances were at the Bolshoi. Two weeks later, in the dark folds of the wings of the enormous stage of the Palace of the Congresses, hidden from the audience, dressed in a wisp of white chiffon, I stood warming up and testing my shoes.

Tonight and for the rest of our stay in Moscow, we were right in the Kremlin itself, that gigantic ninety-acre triangle of government buildings, museums, churches, and embalmed bodies. Russian soldiers in long, full winter coats guarded the walls. The golden onion domes of St. Basil's Cathedral could be seen from the theater's canteen window; the Middle Ages were only a few yards away and could almost be touched. Perhaps the embryo within the gleaming gigantic onion might still be alive and sprout overnight.

The ballet had already started, and soon I would appear, the unexpected presence, the mysterious woman who has a secret never explained, the role Mr. B. had re-created for me, the sleepwalker of *La Sonnambula* who dances within her dream.

Before the rehearsal for that night's performance, I had studied the expanse of the stage in fear and horror. Why did everything in the Kremlin have to be scaled to giant proportions? A huge amount of space would have to be covered when I ran the long diagonal of my very first entrance—the sleepwalker's fifty-yard dash done on pointe. I prayed that the music wouldn't be too fast. All those tiny bourrées that propelled my character forward and in all directions were done on the tips of the toes, and many more were necessary on this huge stage. To enhance the perception of danger, Mr. B. wanted me to cover the distance and reach the very edge of the stage. He wanted the audience to feel I was going to fall off.

For that evening's performance, the shoes I had prepared earlier in the day were too hard and noisy, not supple enough. The sleepwalker is a creature related to the unearthly beings of the Romantic ballet. There is some unknown sorrow in her life that makes her crepuscular and sensitive. Any thuds from the shoes would completely destroy the illusion of ethereality, and they would jar and distract me as well as the audience. This was a pair of poorly made shoes that I must have rejected and tossed into the wrong pile.

I tried to soften them in the traditional ways. I whacked them against the floor, the table, and a metal post until my arm was exhausted. The time to go on was creeping up on me. I was desperate. The sleepwalker was not supposed to be a tap dancer. I wanted my first entrance to be like a floating feather, a filoplume that drifted soundlessly. I had watched others bob about, and it was wrong. A pompous ballet walk was out of place; the body should just progress eerily forward. Soon it was nearly time to go on, and my shoes still weren't right. Quickly I dipped my entire foot with the shoe on into the ever-ready pail of water that is always backstage, then dipped the other. The sensation of warmth and wetness felt good. This procedure didn't always work, though—sometimes the pointe shoe became too slippery or soft. But this evening in mid-October it did work. Readjusting a ribbon at the last minute, I straightened up and glided across the stage following the tiny light of my candle. I became at one with the part of me that could fall into the sleepwalker's shoes, the single-minded searcher who never gives up, who persists and dances. My world would be governed by music.

After the performance I removed my makeup, got into the bus with the others, and returned to the hotel. I had trusted the moment. The moment had touched me, and now I could rest briefly.

On October 20, 1962, when we had been in Russia less than two weeks, suddenly the Cuban missile crisis was upon us. The world looked as if it might blow up, but I couldn't miss a beat with my preparations for dancing or else I'd fall behind. No matter what happened, I had to keep sewing ribbons and elastics on my pointe shoes. Pat Wilde was out for a week, and that meant more ballets and extra rehearsals for me. I went through many, many shoes that I myself prepared. I was running my own sweatshop.

My muscles, mind, and shoes had to be ready because, despite the crisis, the audience didn't stay home; they kept cheering *Agon* and all of Balanchine's ballets.

• • •

When we were given our first precious twenty-four hours off in Moscow, Violette Verdy, Mimi Paul, and I ventured over to the Bolshoi school to watch class. There was an invitation on our rehearsal call-board, but very few N.Y.C. Ballet members wanted to go. The teacher, wearing a regular everyday dress, sprinkled the wooden floor with water shaken from a watering can. This was the way a slippery floor was tamed in the ancient regime. Immediately, we entered an era of the past. The little girls had large bows of filmy white tulle in their hair. These charming children, with their innocent hopes, were disciplined and serious about their work. No one spoke. These students knew how lucky they were. As ever in the ballet, the children were chosen by body and ability. Democracy prevailed in this area, as it did in the days of the czar. Sports and ballet, the great equalizers.

In the afternoon we were invited to go to the Kremlin museum, and now most of our company showed up. We saw crowns rimmed in sable with myriad glittering jewels set in gold. Someone remarked that all the jewels had been replaced with the jellied candies known as Jujubes. If they were, it didn't matter; I was lost in a meditation of the past. Some beautifully crafted tiny pieces of gold filigree were said to have been done before the magnifying glass was invented. Our guide explained that they were created with the use of the enlarging effect of water in a glass. Some days when I forget my glasses I read a menu through a glass of white wine. The lesson was learned in Moscow, 1962.

Other wonders were Catherine the Great's summer and winter coaches. If she wanted to travel between St. Petersburg and Moscow in the middle of a blizzard, nothing would stop her. The winter coach had sled runners and a stove. Catherine grew heavy as she aged, expanding from a tiny little thing into a huge creature. Her royal dresses showed the ballooning progression of her figure. For some brief moments I was happy thinking about the empresses, the Tatars, and the boyars of old Russia.

I also thought about what I had with me in my trunk, my own clothes. Mr. Balanchine had had strange fashion advice for us. In our meeting back at home to outline the tour, instead of telling his dancing girls to polish up their pliés, he told us to be glamorous at all times. No babushkas were to be worn ever, or pants, only nice sweaters, skirts, and dresses. The Russian grandmother look, above all else, was the one to avoid. As representatives of the free world, we had to look good onstage and off. Somewhere in my head, the place where re-bellious ideas were born, I remembered a photograph of Bardot wearing a gingham minibabushka with lots of eye makeup. The effect was quite fetching. I included a small red felt kerchief with my things and insisted on wearing it occasionally on the streets of Moscow. I found it hard to be glamorous on call. I had to stumble upon glamour in an encouraging atmosphere of experimentation.

I must have told Mother about Mr. B.'s glamorous-clothes speech. That was a huge mistake. She seemed to think that shopping for the right dress was of the utmost importance; taking class was the extraneous activity. Mother had a grandiose formal gown in mind. She visualized me making an arresting entrance at a ball in old Imperial Russia, like Natasha in *War and Peace*. I was just distracted enough to follow her lead on through stores, floor by floor, an exhausting and fruitless ordeal. Going through the furniture section of Lord & Taylor, Mother spied some rose-colored upholstery fabric in a thick luminous silk. She gave me instructions. Perhaps Karinska herself, the great Russian costumer, would design a gown. "After all, you are a favorite with her."

For some strange reason Karinska also fell into a reverie of the past. She, too, saw me making an entrance in old Russia and added a train to a very long dress. Now all I had to do was go for the fittings. Mme. Karinska's shop was on Thirty-eighth Street, not so far from the old Metropolitan Opera House but miles from the School of American Ballet. Would I ever get to class? I was in a panic. This was not the way to get ready to dance. All the time I was with my mother, I felt I should be practicing. Again, I wished Mother had a full-time job.

I was to carry Karinska's creation all through Russia but never to wear it; it stayed in my trunk the entire time. Mother had taken me on a wild swan chase. My destination was the U.S.S.R. in the 1960s, not Russia in the early 1800s.

Despite my excitement at being in Russia, I still felt a terrible conflict about being there. I had never been away from Trista for longer than two weeks, and, as much as I wanted to go, the thought of the trip threw me into turmoil. I also felt that if I didn't go, I might as well quit dancing forever. Why was I pursuing this difficult existential exercise if I said no to every engagement?

And Russia had special significance to me. How could it not? It was the place where the great ballerinas were born as well as most of my beloved teachers. In the century just past, fairy tales sprung to life onstage with music by Tchaikovsky. This was the huge reach of land that produced fanatics and geniuses who had rhythm and dancing in their blood and where most of the population were connoisseurs of ballet. During my troubled teens I had read Turgenev and Dostoyevsky for consolation. Of course I wanted to go—the land held a magic allure for me. Maria Tallchief had abruptly left our company two years earlier so that she could perform with American Ballet Theatre in this mecca of dance. This was a startling move; she couldn't resist the opportunity to appear with Erik Bruhn and show the Russians her technique. But as much as I had wanted to make this trip, there was my daughter.

Finally, I decided to skip the first weeks of the tour and join the company during the end of the European leg of the trip, a few weeks before Russia. Entrusting Trista to Bert, a nursemaid, and my mother, I took a taxi alone to the airport. But I wasn't really ready, and the conflict I felt over leaving my new baby stayed with me throughout the tour. Shouldn't I be home with her? Dancing, perhaps, was too selfish a thing to do. All of the Christian Science dogmas had not been extracted or expunged from my thinking; some residue remained. Even then, at twenty-five years of age, one part of me was deeply sure that I could have a good life if only I quit dancing. Sometimes in the unbearable grip of stage fright, I thought that ballet was ruining me. This was something my mother made me feel also. The exact opposite was actually true. Onstage I could throw myself into the business at hand and not think and ponder so much. Offstage I was always questioning.

When I arrived in my room the first night in Moscow, I felt as lonely as a traveling salesman. The space felt adequate, like a room in an old hotel in downtown Fresno, one of the lesser places my father might have visited when he was on the road with his dress line, Nardis of Dallas. The company had arrived together on Aeroflot, the no-frills Russian airline that feels like military transport. We were flying in the outside shell of an aircraft with no interior lining or decoration or pressure. We landed in Moscow on a cold, dark evening in early October. Once bureaucracy was satisfied, we were put on buses and taken to the Hotel Ukraine, a massive place of dehumanizing proportions, one entire city block built in huge cold stone. The elevator didn't stop on several floors because listening devices were located there. The guests came from all over Russia and looked grim.

I parked my suitcase in a corner and went down to the dining room. All our meals would be served here in a special area reserved for the ballet company alone. We had arrived in the land of group action. I would see my dancing friends day and night, eat with them, rehearse with them, be driven crazy by them, and perform with them. We were to arrive in Russia as an ensemble and leave the same way. Intourist would escort us almost everywhere and supply interpreters. I wondered what it would be like to work in a police state where citizens disappeared forever in the gulags. Maya Plisetskaya's romance with a British diplomat had been broken up by the government, and Rudolf Nureyev had defected a year earlier. He could not live and work in that system.

But here we were, and throughout our time in Russia I kept asking myself what I was doing there. Shouldn't I be home with my child?

The person I did not feel torn apart about leaving was Bert. Our marriage had not improved. As a photographer, Bert was very caught up in the world of beautiful women and models. He had another life. I had heard rumors that he was out at the Peppermint Lounge every night with a young woman, but at the same time he wrote that he missed me. Again, as long ago in Australia, I was confused, hurt, and powerless because of the distance.

Finally, I received a telephone call from Bert. I asked how Trista was and received a one-word answer, "Fine." The big news was that Bert was coming to visit me. He was feeling very depressed and wanted to see me. Why did he have to come halfway round the world to Russia when I didn't even want to see him? It was always this dichotomy, the confusion he felt over his relationship with me. With him it was a deeply ingrained attitude: the many lovers; the one wife.

His arrival didn't change my schedule. I was busy from morning till night, and in my free time I sewed ribbons on shoes. His arrival put even more strain on me, so I sent him out to sightsee and eat caviar with the injured dancers. Bert's presence was just another pressure. I was sure our marriage would not work out. I had left him twice already.

Standing in the wings of the Kremlin Theater waiting to go on in *Symphony in C,* I placed my hands on the waist of my tutu. The bodice of this costume was a radiant pure white silk satin. I was ever so briefly resting. The wardrobe mistress, Mme. Pourmel, came up to me and asked if I was comfortable. I did not detect any undercurrent in her voice and simply said yes.

"Well, get your hands off the costume." Madame's tone had changed, she was furious.

Tears started to form in my eyes, but I fought them back. I did not want to lose control and sob during my entrance. But I was exhausted and on edge. The men could touch the costumes offstage and on while partnering us. In fact, Jacques d'Amboise used to pick me up by the costume, dog-fashion, by the scruff of the waist. Once he lifted me so violently that the crotch ripped open. This happened just before a performance when my entrance was only moments away. The overture had begun, and quickly Mme. Pourmel—as always standing backstage with a threaded needle, scissors, and other emergency repair items—sewed up the crotch. Nothing else anchors the costume down. She hadn't been angry at Jacques. The men could touch the costumes because this was necessary.

But in the wings the tutus were under her jurisdiction. In Mme. Pourmel's mind, a costume was not an armchair or a couch on which to rest. It was a sacred object that enhanced theatrical magic. It did not matter to her that I was a principal dancer appearing nightly on a very grueling tour or that my hands were clean and my touch was light. She was working, too: packing, unpacking, washing, mending, adding on second sets of hooks and eyes—and counting. Balanchine was lucky to be able to call up Karinska and have his dancing girls clothed in the costumes of his dreams, but it was up to Mme. Pourmel to maintain their perfection, and she did. One or two costumes can't be lost or misplaced overnight. The organizational abilities of a wardrobe mistress are phenomenal; we traveled with fifty or more trunks of costumes. I could forgive her. At the end of the performance, Madame unhooked me, and my costume was hung upside down like a roosting bat on a high pole, as were all the others. She was worried about intense fabric fatigue but not mine.

I was pushing myself because so many of the women were unable to dance. When I had joined the company in Cologne, injuries were already taking a toll. Diana Adams and several other key people were out. The next day, still jet-lagged, I was taught the central role of *Concerto Barocco* and danced it. Within four days of intensive dancing I was exhausted and prayed for a masseur, but all the hotel could offer was a hot bath. In Frankfurt, our performances ended very late at night. My feet hadn't toughened up yet, and I finished with blistered toes. The next day I took class as usual, a dancer's daily ritual of exercise and discovery. What does this body feel like? What can this body do today?

By the time we arrived in Russia, a pattern was developing. Whenever someone was out, Mr. B. put me in. Whenever he had to substitute a different ballet, it was one that featured me. I felt I was carrying the company. After the first weeks in Moscow, I was sometimes too tired to sleep. In a photo of the company, my eyelids are drooping. When I saw it I wondered, *Who is that miserable looking creature slumped in a heap at the end of the row? Oh, it's me.* I recognized myself by the bathrobe.

Even though it was hard for me to rest or relax, I knew that if I somehow could get to the Bolshoi's masseur, Genya, my muscles could be coaxed back into elasticity. I discovered him while we were performing there. Genya gave very hard, deep massages, and they worked; he knew what he was doing. We should have had a physical therapist and a masseur with us on this trip, but unfortunately the days of sports medicine had not yet arrived. One day in Moscow, I pressed a tip into Genya's hand, wrapped up in an old sock. "Genya, *spasibo.*" A tip not disguised couldn't be accepted; it would be admitting that a Russian's salary was not sufficient. I wanted to show my appreciation and also to get my way in this small contest with Russian policy. Genya accepted the sock.

It was near midnight in Moscow. I was sitting in the backseat of a car going to an unknown destination. The vehicle moved quickly without many stops. There was very little traffic and not a lot of illumination from street lights. I was wedged like a piece of cheese in a sandwich between Jacques d'Amboise and Kolya, our pianist. In the front seat the driver and the interpreter were speaking in Russian.

With my stage makeup still on, I had jumped into the car as soon as I finished the last performance. I thought about the night before when Mr. B. had waved to me from the wings to attract my attention after a performance of *Agon.*

"Allegra, please come over here." He waited until I was an arm's length away. "That was a wonderful performance. Very good."

"Thank you. I'm glad you liked it. The Russians love Stravinsky."

"Allegra, I want you to stay warm. Where is your robe?"

Quickly I retrieved my wrap and returned to Mr. B.'s side. "It's right here," I said, putting it on.

"Allegra," he repeated my name. "I have to ask a very special favor." As Mr. B. spoke, his eyes roved, changing their focus several times. He almost seemed embarrassed, if that was possible. "Remember the special evening when the Russians performed for us?" The Russians gave us a joyous performance of ballet and music-hall comics. At the party given in our honor, I danced the twist, which one of Bert's secretaries had taught to me just before I left New York City. "We are supposed to reciprocate," Mr. B. said.

I raised my eyebrows into a question.

"There is a literary club here that is scheduled to meet late tomorrow night, and they want us to dance for them." Mr. B. paused. "I know how hard you are working, and I hate to ask, but it will be a special favor to me if you say yes." He gently shook his head. "You have the matinee and the evening tomorrow—four ballets altogether." His face had lost its nervous quality and was more tranquil after he had said what he wanted to say.

I smiled. "Oh, Mr. B. Of course. If you want me to do this, then I want to do it too." I had been dancing with him for ten years. To me he looked the same, with just a tiny bit less hair. He was now fifty-eight, a handsome man with beautiful bones. There was no doubt about it: Mr. B.'s love, approval, and even requests were a drug, a drug that imbued me with energy. He had chosen me.

There is also a certain gratification in attempting a marathon workload. (Oh, you think this heavy schedule will do me in? It won't.) I wanted to do this literary club performance for many reasons: for Mr. B., for the abstract audience and the real one out there that seemed to love me so much, and the other audience in my brain where I put the production onstage and also sat and watched and judged my own performance from the first row.

Mr. B. smiled back. "Good. That will be good." Then he said, "The stage is very small." Mr. B. held out his arms to encompass a wingspan. Mr. B. thought the *Midsummer Night's Dream* pas de deux, which could be danced on a postage stamp, would be perfect. "Jacques will do it with you, and we can rehearse between the matinee and the evening performance tomorrow. There is a free half hour at five-thirty. Mme. Pourmel has the costumes; she brought them along just in case." Mr. B.'s face had definitely lost its nervous edge.

I had begun to slip a few hairpins out of my French twist. It was time to let my hair down. Then I had another thought. "Oh, Mr. B. Will we be able to get dinner afterward? It will be so late when we finish."

"Oh, yes," Mr. B. said emphatically, turning his head slightly and looking at me in a devilish way from the corner of his eyes. "I will speak to the hotel and they will save some food for you, Jacques, and Kolya." Then he laughed under his breath.

I had thought, *He's laughing because he's the man who got* Agon *on stage in Russia. He can choreograph and deliver a ballet of great complexity behind the Iron Curtain. Surely he could figure out a way to get three dinners on the table slightly after hours.* I put my hands together and, in suppressed gaiety, whispered, "The body must be fed."

Now, here I was in the backseat of this moving car, underdressed with my pink dancing tights, the first of many layers, and a winter coat, the last, in a measure to retain the heat in my muscles after a twelve-hour workday. Mr. B. seemed excited to present us, but he wasn't joining us. He had convinced us to appear. That was enough.

On my lap was a giant puff of tulle and pale gray silk encased in a clear plastic cover. It sat upside down, the favored position for this kind of garment. Our costumes were like yoga instructors; they liked to rest in reversed posture. Not only were dancers subject to gravity, so were our costumes. Tartan and tulle easily became limp.

My mind drifted to the literary group. Were they good Party members or could they be a clandestine wing? The latter was impossible. Would they have an intellectual demeanor or a Tolstoy look?

The driver stopped the car. This was it. We followed our interpreter guide through a nondescript facade and into an elevator. After walking down a long hall, he pushed a door open, and there we were in the midst of a sea of men, all with accordions in their laps. There were hundreds of accordions, portable pianos that can go out to the field, bagpipes with keyboards.

They looked at us and smiled, all five hundred of them. Or were there a thousand and one? We smiled back. I had never seen so many accordions in one spot. This was the literary club. How books had become accordions, I didn't know. Perhaps the request had filtered up and down through fifteen functionaries and slowly pages were transformed into pleats and nouns became notes.

I wonder if this group is still holding its midnight meetings in Moscow with refreshments and visiting entertainers, or have they composed a concerto in many parts?

My alarm rang at seven, a low, reverberating tone, not too unpleasant but not a sound I wanted to hear. It was too soon to leave my bed and my nighttime thoughts. Outside it was dark and cold.

Leningrad was very far north. A muffled but continuous sound of traffic and motors accelerating and halting drifted in. Some of our matinees were at eleven in the morning. This early hour was not unusual for the Russians, but their ballerinas did not appear eight times a week as I was doing. When I danced the last ballet at night and the first one in the morning, supper and breakfast seemed to converge.

I dragged myself out of bed and at the same time carefully tested my muscles. My calves, hamstrings, and shoulders were tight. My body felt stiff and unworkable. The blood wasn't going anywhere, and my muscles didn't want to elongate. I walked cautiously into the bathroom, not jarring my exhausted body, and turned on the hot water, then added a little cold. While the tub was filling, I packed some essentials for my day—tights, two extra sweaters, and clean leotards. I had danced *Apollo* and *La Sonnambula* the night before.

By Leningrad the strain was getting to us all. I began acting in a maniacal fashion, calling Lincoln Kirstein "uncle" and joking and horsing around in crazy ways. It was the pressure and also the pull. Bert had traveled with us to Leningrad, but I rarely saw him. Shouldn't I be at home with my baby? It also looked as if Mr. B. was having some sort of breakdown. He hadn't really wanted to go to Russia, and his personal success and the company's was definitely a surprise, but that didn't make it any easier. He began to look gaunt and haggard.

When the bath filled, I climbed in—all of me, one little girl with four hundred muscle groups and ten thousand overworked tendons. The immediate warmth was a consolation. My spine lengthened somewhat, and my hamstrings gave up some of their tightness. The ballet juice in my blood started to stir and move. It whispered, "Wake up, Allegra. It's almost time to go to work." There was a moment to stretch and elongate in my watery retreat, the miracle of ordinary hot water in a tub. I thought of the day ahead of me in a state just beneath terror. I was already judging how I'd do in a performance that was four hours away. Something was wrong with my psyche.

After soaking and putting on a conventional wool sweater and skirt—what I'd worn the day before—I packed up my necessities for the day and went downstairs for breakfast. Our group was nearly assembled. The company comedians, especially Billy Weslow, were already holding court. Our entertainers had absorbed new material overnight and had their preview audience engaged. It was too early for me to laugh, so I walked over to a table where Mimi Paul sat alone, sewing ribbons on her pointe shoes.

"Hi, Mimi. Dare I ask how you're feeling today?"

Mimi looked up and said in a moderately cheerful voice, "Oh, not too bad, I suppose. And you?"

"About the same," I said, sitting down and surveying the rolls. "Those look good."

"They are." Mimi guided the needle and thread into a knot and cut off the excess. She was preparing her shoes for the matinee. "I'm not in love with these breakfast performances, but I guess they're nice for the schoolchildren." The matinees were attended almost exclusively by young students.

I broke open a roll and put some jam on the plate. "The audience is such a surprise. Some fan in Moscow gave me a beautiful lacquered box, and now she is here in Leningrad. I'm sure she works very hard to get by, and this woman is probably traveling illegally without permission." The wonder was the Russians' response; they were enthralled with Mr. B.'s ballets.

Mimi poured some deep amber tea and asked, "Are you taking John Taras's class at nine-thirty or working alone?" She tilted her head from side to side, stretching and cracking her long neck.

I watched in fascination, then responded. "I need the group's collective energy today. I don't have any of my own. Even though it's early, I must take it. I'm that tired." John Taras knew how hard this tour was, and he gave us the steps we needed to wake up and warm up.

Walking upstairs to the studio for class, dressed in many layers of wool plus a robe, I met young Russian girls in practice clothes, as always with the big white bows in their hair and their dreamy, unspoiled faces. They looked deeply happy. There was something wonderful in their idealistic expressions. I guessed that they were eleven, the magical age. We were performing in the old Maryinsky Theatre where so many of the greats first danced, and these beguiling creatures, these young swans, were a continuation of that tradition. The theater's curtain was threadbare, but that didn't matter; the air was thick with the atmosphere and aura of the past. This was the very stage where Pavlova, Nijinsky, Spessivtseva, Doubrovska, and Balanchine first danced.

Today was going to be one of those apparel marathons when I'd change from street clothes to practice clothes to costumes, going back and forth between real life and theatrical outfits thirteen times or more. It was too boring to count after thirteen. This was why I felt my gray woolen garb of the day was unimportant. I wouldn't spend much time in it, and maybe by supper Billy Weslow, our comic genius, would have a few new jokes and ballerina imitations worked up for his devotees. His wicked mastery of an imperious Russian *assoluta* from the Bronx was unequaled, and after the day's work I could appreciate him. Sometimes his Balanchine and Danilova imitations were touched with the cackles of a barnyard but still sublime.

On my one free morning I rushed over to the Hermitage, but it was closed. I was in shock. It was the anniversary of the October Revolution, a holy day to the Russians. I had missed my only chance to look at works I had longed to see.

One night after Bert left Leningrad, I relaxed alone in my room. The long day was over. I had danced, eaten, bathed, and scraped off the makeup. The work had gone well. Just a few hours earlier, my partner and I danced feeling very attuned to each other. We had painted a picture with a filigree of steps to beautiful music. I felt we had gone a little beyond our best performance. I was lying in bed in my pajamas feeling clean and fresh from my immersion in the delicious warmth of a bath. I had decided not to do my stretches tonight. I would take a rest from dedication.

There was a knock at my door. It was one of the male dancers. I invited him in. We both felt exhilarated with each other, our work, and the deeply perceptive Russian audience. He sat next to me on top of the sheets and we spoke, then started to kiss. Our kisses had no past; they were without recriminations and were for this moment alone. I craved some intimate warmth from this man, and perhaps this was the moment for it. I knew that my marriage would never work out and would never be what I wished it to be, so I had a ready excuse for unfaithfulness. There was nothing so very wrong in what might happen. Dancers casually sleep with each other. Sometimes it appeared as if no one ever stayed alone at the New York City Ballet Company for very long. If a couple broke up in the morning, they had connected with new partners by the evening.

But my mind slowly changed. This easy solution to loneliness on tour wasn't for me. I had decided never to become involved with someone in the company—it would be too difficult to function afterward if it didn't work out. And what would performing with this man be like in the future after such an affair was over? Perhaps near impossible. I also didn't want to be on his considerable list of conquests. My nature was too vulnerable for this kind of entanglement. Also, the person next to me was married. That made him off-limits, and what he could offer was also limited. He was not abandoning his marriage. He displayed unusual warmth and grace this evening, and, even though part of me wanted to, I told him I could not sleep with a married man. He very graciously accepted what I said and left my room. I was a little sad to see him go, but if I were going to take a lover I wanted someone who could be my very own.

Besides, my pattern of stretching every night meant that dancing took all my time.

Sitting in our new dressing room a few evenings later as we prepared to dance, Violette and I realized we were tired before the performance had even begun. It was mid-November, our sixth week in Russia, and we were in Kiev. The city felt dark; none of the lights seemed to be fully on. The day before, Violette and I had left the hotel bundled up warmly and trudged through cold, crisp air over to the theater to see if the stage held any surprises for us. It did. The rake was even more extreme than the Bolshoi's; it looked like a slide. I was scheduled to dance *Symphony in C* the next night and saw that the middle adagio section would be a problem, particularly the part where I simultaneously changed directions, whipped the leg, let go of my partner, and found my balance. My arabesques would have to be acute, as well as my en avant. Obtuseness had no place on this stage. With one obtuse arabesque, I might easily end up perched on someone's lap in the first row.

Violette looked at me through the jungle of her freshly applied long eyelashes and gave a little consoling high-pitched lapdog bark. I responded with an adolescent coyote howl. Violette answered back hyena, and we were off in an under-and-over dog conversation. Soon a whole team of Alaskan huskies was calling in the wilds of our dressing room. We had hit on yelp therapy, decades ahead of the primal scream school. I don't know what the Russians backstage thought of the howling ballerinas; perhaps they imagined it was a ritual we always performed before pliés. Luckily, Mr. B. didn't hear us bark. He had returned to New York City for a desperately needed week's rest. I knew he wanted decorum, not deviltry. He didn't want us to wear babushkas, let alone dog collars.

Violette and I stirred up some animal energy from somewhere, and we both danced well that evening. We exchanged knowing glances at the final bow: one more day was over and we were a tiny bit closer to our return. The next day in John's class, I noticed that my jump had returned. I hadn't had it since before Trista's birth. At least the long stretch of performing consistently had been good for my dancing.

By the time we opened in Tbilisi, we knew the pattern to expect in our Russian audiences. The first-nighters were all good Party members, and our reception was cool. On the second night the real devotees were able to get tickets, and their appreciation was deeply gratifying. A party was thrown for us, and the Georgians danced and drank like wild men. A toast was directed toward me. While never interrupting his stare, a young man lifted his wineglass higher than his lips and suggestively kissed the bulb of the glass where it connected to the stem. It felt as if he had touched me in an intimate way. With involuntary swiftness, I modestly crossed my arms over my chest. If I had been Gypsy Rose Lee, I would have jumped on the table, given the orchestra its cue, and gone right into my act, finishing in a perfect fifth on the tips of my black Georgian boots with a few wineglasses in strategic locations. I have never seen a toast like this anywhere else.

The eight performance-packed weeks were over, and at last we were flying home. I thought about an important conversation I had had with Mr. B., one that I had pushed aside, not thinking about it until now. It took place at the Kremlin Theater, as I was on my way from a rehearsal to the canteen.

I had noticed that Mr. B. was striding purposefully down a long hall toward me. His eyes were thoughtful and narrowed. I gave him a quizzical smile. What more could he possibly ask me to dance? The first two weeks in Moscow had become a whirlwind of work and preparations for me personally. Mr. B. took my hand.

"How are you, Allegra?"

His voice had reflected genuine concern and I was touched. He ceased to be someone who just had to get the performance on that night. I smiled in appreciation. "Good, I'm holding up."

"Not too tired?"

"No." I was, but I didn't want to say so, because Mr. B.'s look had changed to wistful. The Kremlin Theater was inhuman, vast, dark, and cold. Maybe I could cheer him up with a smile and lighthearted conversation. "Guess what? I've discovered a masseur at the Bolshoi, and I stretch in a split before going to sleep at night!"

I had never told Mr. B. about the split before. It was a secret. My muscles did not recuperate quickly, and by this trip in 1962, I had to stretch extensively at night if I had a typical dancer's workday, which might include a class, many hours of rehearsal, and then another warm-up for a performance of one or two ballets, or nearly twice that amount if there were both a matinee and evening show. I understood my physical limitations, but Balanchine didn't totally understand them. He thought I was a natural dancer. Lying in the split was my passive way of coaxing the knots out of calves and hamstrings. But I did not want to admit what I had to do to dance. It was almost embarrassing.

"You do that every night?" There was surprise in Balanchine's voice. Even though he knew I had a fanatical side, the split must have appeared excessive. Had I said too much?

To be safe, I backed down slightly. "Almost every night, then I don't feel so stiff in the morning. My muscles require a lot of stretching. I just lie in a split and read." One day I had exercised with Violette and the next day felt crippled. She had been trained from a tiny child and gone through the syllabus in the accepted manner, in the French style. She was exquisitely versed in the alphabet of ballet, but I couldn't do the extensive preparations she did.

"You know, Allegra, when we return to America, I want you to work and work at ballet and at technique. Work like this." Mr. B. made his hands into blinders, such as a horse wears to obliterate distractions. "Forget your husband, forget your baby, only work, work at your turnout and on your feet. It's not too late. How old are you now? Twenty-five?"

"Yes."

I watched as he turned his palms to indicate a spectacular turnout. Then he presented his hands as feet, beautifully pointed. "You must *work*."

Since my marriage to Bert and the birth of Trista, something in me had begun to change. Mixed with my ambition was a core of deep discouragement and hopelessness. I could no longer devote my entire life to ballet. When I had returned to dancing after Trista's birth, Mr. B. had asked me to learn a part in *Liebeslieder*, and I refused; it seemed like too much work. He saw the conflict in my face. "Not now, Allegra, but when we return." He may also have detected a manic tinge in my voice and was trying to calm me. There was something pulling me apart, and he could see it. I was here, but shouldn't I be there, at home with my baby? Could ambition still be false as I had once been told by my mother and my Christian Science practitioner?

However, I saw there was a time reprieve. Mr. B. did not wish to add to the pressure of this tour.

"You know," he added, "Spessivtseva was a wonderful dancer. She was like a beautiful diamond, cool, distant, and perfect."

We both seemed briefly to enter the realm of the imagination where the perfection of the past could be held, captured, and seen. Mr. B. took me with him on this nostalgic trip to the time of his youth in Russia.

I nodded in agreement, a tiny bow. I wanted this too, but I wanted it through magic, not hard work. The routine he pictured was unrelenting and grim. "I wish I had seen Spessivtseva dance. I know how much you admired her. Didn't she go mad? Like Nijinsky?" To try to approach perfection was frightening. I responded in a trance of interest and fear.

"Not exactly. When she was older, she did have a problem, but it wasn't with her dancing." Mr. B. wanted to minimize that particular observation. "Allegra, it's not too late for you to work at technique, but first we must get through this tour." He ran his hand across his throat as if the Russians were killing him. "It's *awful* here, not civilized." He understood the undercurrents of this country.

I tried to steer our talk to less important observations. "This tour is hard, so I've brought a trunkful of fruit juices, chocolates, and a bottle of blackberry brandy."

This statement startled Mr. B., the great wine connoisseur. "You like blackberry brandy?" He made a horrible face as if he might have to drink that peculiar beverage. "Be careful. Chocolates are fattening."

I felt a little bit like Buttercup in *H.M.S. Pinafore* describing her wares ("I've treacle and toffee, I've tea and I've coffee"). "The brandy is for cramps, and the chocolates are to give away as presents. They're my toys. It's cold and scary here."

Mr. B. put his hands on my shoulders and looked into my eyes as if he were trying to hypnotize me. He did not want me to forget his message. "Remember, when we go home, *work*."

"I'll remember."

Mr. B. had delivered his message and his face reflected hope, hope that I would resume the unrelenting work habits of my teens. He pushed any women with whom he was deeply involved to perfect her style. He did it with Maria. He had helped her remake her technique. He was just starting to do the same thing with Tanny when she became ill.

It hadn't always been technique that interested Mr. B. It was something else that fired his creativity, and he was very attuned to this special something in its earliest forms. He could see it in a mere child. Years earlier, he had said to me, "Don't listen to anyone!" He liked the primitive, untutored forces within me. He may as well have said,

"I don't want you to be perfect." He had a devil's advocate in him. But now he no longer wanted my off-course development to go its own way. Balanchine was pleased with the Russian reaction and my dancing there, but at that point he decided that the weak portions of my style had to be strengthened.

Now he wanted my something else coupled with technique.

During that conversation, I sincerely believed I would work very hard when I returned to America, but at that moment home felt very far away, and reality did not have to be faced. We could both believe in his fantasy of unrelenting work, so easy to talk about but so hard to do. Now, with our return, the reprieve was over.

I had probably used up well over one hundred pairs of shoes on the trip. I had danced nearly every performance in Russia—about sixty-four—and I was deliriously happy to be home. Trista, Bert, and my mother were at the airport. My baby was exactly two, and she was talking.

As I held Trista in my arms, I knew I couldn't live only to dance as I had done in Russia. I couldn't take Mr. B.'s entreaty to work on my technique seriously.

CHAPTER TWELVE

The street is lined with cars. There's not a breath of fresh air in the neighborhood. The grass won't grow anymore. You can't raise a carrot in the backyard.

—ARTHUR MILLER,
DEATH OF A SALESMAN

Oⁿe bright sunny day in December after my return from Russia, Bert asked me to make breakfast in bed for him, and I said, "Sure thing." I decided to become a short-order cook. "What would you like?"

"Bacon, two sunny-side-up eggs, orange juice, a toasted muffin, coffee, butter, and jam."

"Got it!"

Bert, Trista, and I were still living on East Fifty-sixth Street in the apartment with a wraparound terrace. The bedroom was cheerful and opened into the terrace with a tub containing a little weeping beech tree. I rushed to the kitchen. Should I use one frying pan or two? Maybe one, I'll start with the bacon. Put the muffins in the toaster, boil the water, find the tray, put on utensils, remember not to burn the bacon, and then degrease it carefully.

Finally, I walked into the bedroom with a proud, beaming smile, proceeded over to the bed, and placed the tray on Bert's lap.

He stared at it and then said in a disgruntled voice, "Where's the orange juice?"

I looked at the tray. There wasn't any orange juice, but there was everything else. Bert hadn't even said thank you.

He looked at me. "I want orange juice."

I walked back into the kitchen and squeezed a glass of orange juice. The fun had definitely gone out of the morning. With the juice in hand, I walked back into the bedroom. Bert smiled as he saw me. I walked over to the bed and, with a quick movement, threw it into his face. Bert was very surprised. I was a little shocked with myself, but the action felt good. Until I saw orange juice all over the sheets.

The best place to go then was ballet class.

After we had progressed toward New Year's Eve of 1962 without an invitation to celebrate, Bert decided to give a little informal party based on the four pounds of the very best caviar I had brought back from Baku at the amazing price of fifty-four dollars. He invited his old friends Nancy and Arnold Perl as the only guests. I could have invited some of my friends from the ballet, but this thought never dawned on me. We returned from Russia to work on the winter season *Nutcracker*, and I had had no chance to catch my breath. Now I wanted to forget ballet for a night.

In the youngest hours of 1963, Bert and I went to bed. I felt that he wanted to turn toward me more wholeheartedly but that something was holding him back. Lying in bed next to him and thinking about what made him tick, I decided on a little story. "Bert, something happened in Russia that I didn't tell you about. One of the male dancers asked me to sleep with him."

"You're kidding! What happened? Did you do it? I'm so jealous. What city were you in?"

"Leningrad, just after you left. I felt that our marriage wasn't going to last, so it didn't matter what I did. Anyway, I'm not going to tell you what happened."

"Allegra, I can't stand this! How could you do this to me? I traveled halfway around the world to be with you in Russia, and the day after I leave you're playing around! I made the trip because I was cracking up without you. I brought you chocolates and even visited your grandmother's brother. You were too tired to visit your *own* relatives."

"I couldn't move that day. I was sick with exhaustion."

"I want to know what happened. Did you sleep with that creep or not?"

"Yes, I did." I lied, to see what effect it would have on Bert. The game was on. Bert was deeply upset with my made-up story of infidelity, and we stayed up all night talking. He seemed to enjoy the torment and strived to use his jealousy to transform himself into something he wasn't—devoted. I had used the lie as a tool to make things better between us for the moment, but I knew it couldn't solve our long-term problems. And not all the problems between us were Bert's. In those days I was a very narrow creature who was far more likely to say no to a vacation or a party with my husband than yes.

By morning I told him the truth, that nothing had happened, but our relationship was better for the next three months. But I didn't want the glue of our marriage to be meanness and lies. Something else would have to hold us together. I had been hoping that it would be love. At the moment, however, that something else was the excitement of jealousy.

Mr. B. asked that I développé very high to the front while holding my foot in both hands. His next instruction was a small rotation and there we were, face-to-face, body to body, Eddie Villella and I, with my legs perpendicular in a front split. Next Mr. B. instructed Eddie to press me very close. Oh, this was a sexy pas de deux. Eddie and I were both a little shocked when Mr. B. asked us to do movements that seemed to consummate a sexual encounter. When Balanchine asked me to spread my legs to the audience, I gave him the shocked look of a Salvation Army major—which he disregarded—so I did what he requested. The physical contact and intent in this ballet were so revolutionary that during the first rehearsals, as Mr. B. showed Eddie what to do or gave instructions, the understudies stood around with their mouths hanging open.

It was late January 1963, and Balanchine was creating a new ballet for Eddie and me—*Bugaku*—with a duet that was the most sexually overt of its time. The choreography reflected Mr. B.'s love of surprises. His genius could present a look at sexuality that was more titillating than a merely X-rated work, and Mr. B. was having a good time creating it. In other, more abstract ballets, the body is used merely as a supple substance. What does it matter if a crotch becomes an apex of a triangle if the dance is abstract? But in this dance, if it looked sensual, it *was* sensual. Our bodies were used as bodies. This duet represented an off-branch, a white rose growing on a pink bush, a mutation, in Balanchine's evolutionary themes. This was a more explicit variation on the stark, modern pas de deux that first surfaced in *Apollo* and continued in dances like *Agon* and *Episodes*.

After seeing the ballet, Arlene Croce said, "Balanchine seems to have derived his inspiration for the pas de deux from Japanese pornographic prints," and Allen Hughes, the *New York Times* dance critic, was shocked, but Mr. B. didn't care.

One of Balanchine's inspirations for *Bugaku* was the gagaku, a group of male Japanese dancers and musicians who performed ancient dances on a raised platform. Lincoln Kirstein had invited them over to open every program in the 1959 season. The mesmeric movements and sound of the gagaku took one back to feudal times in Japan, and Mr. B. cast Eddie as a samurai warrior for his new work. As I watched Eddie dance this role, I thought he resembled Toshiro Mifune in action. Had Mr. B. seen *Rashomon*? In a role even more erotic than my part in *The Seven Deadly Sins,* I was cast as a Japanese creature having an arranged first-time sexual experience, a ceremonial coupling. Was I a wife, a concubine, or something else? It didn't seem to matter. The ritual was the important thing. The ballet opens in a formal setting and proceeds toward a ceremony that sanctions the physical. After the couple's physical consummation in the sensual pas de deux, our translucent trains return in the arms of our attendants, and we go back to courtly manners, back to formality. The ballet presents the two sides of courtship—the mannered and the sexual, the classic and romantic.

I had understood immediately how I was going to study for the role. I wanted to portray something of the look, beauty, and mystery of Japanese women, particularly as I remembered them from two Kurasawa films, *Throne of Blood,* a version of *Macbeth,* which I had seen in Japan, and *Rashomon,* the movie that had startled the entire film industry. My objective was not Lady Macbeth Japanese-style, only some intangible quality that would evoke the haunting aura of this ancient culture. For refreshment I invited Mimi Paul, my understudy, to come to the movies with me so we could slip into a different world and century with the huge images of make-believe. The Japanese words were sounds and tones I didn't understand, so they became extra music. I decided that more should happen in the eyes and body and less on the face, that a perfectly simple ritualistic movement could be rich with currents under the surface, as the famous No puppets illustrated. Liquid movements were a favorite with me because of my love for the water, so I tried to contrast the fluid with the sudden, and the straightforward with the sidewinding. The music for *Bugaku* sounded like movie music, so I decided to accent a dramatic sound with a dramatic move, as Hollywood would do. It was the time to be obvious.

After the first rehearsals, Mr. B. handed the ballet over to Eddie and me, and from then on we usually rehearsed alone. This was the first time we had been teamed together in a new work, and I was very excited about it. As usual, our first clue had been a call sheet on the bulletin board. It was odd: Balanchine had an Italian boy from Queens and a Polish girl from California who had both made a success in Russia, and he now starred them together in a Japanese ballet.

I had known Eddie only briefly at the School of American Ballet, and when I had joined the corps de ballet, he was in the Merchant Marine Academy and got his degree there. Like many American dance careers, his had proceeded in a not entirely straightforward manner. Then one day he had come backstage to meet Jacques d'Amboise after a performance of *Shinbone Alley*, and I was struck more than ever by his good looks. He was studying ballet once again, and soon he was in the company. Around 1958 we had danced *Afternoon of a Faun* together. One of the lifts hadn't gone well, and I was upset. By that time I was used to Jacques, who no matter what happened could always reach out and save me. After that I wasn't eager to dance with Eddie, even though I admired his dancing tremendously.

But now working with Eddie was refreshing. He didn't coach me to the fingertips or do cruel parodies of my mannerisms in the name of being "helpful," as Jacques did sometimes. Eddie had the intelligence and the foresight to allow for creative development in his partner. It was exciting for us to see how what we did together grew and evolved.

I couldn't truly become creative about this ballet until it was complete, however. I had to see what it was in its entirety, and *Bugaku* turned out to be easier to perform than rehearse. In rehearsals, Mr. B. always wanted more space covered, with the legs higher, and when he wanted something to happen, he always said "Bang" with eye-opening immediacy. But with this ballet, Mr. B. entrusted the final product to the heat of performance. What developed in *Bugaku* was not only a result of what Mr. B. gave us but also what happened between Eddie and me. The stage lights added a hothouse warmth. Tanny called me a "rubber orchid" in this role.

Bugaku is a ballet that can go wrong very easily. If it goes astray, it is with the woman's interpretation. Arlene Croce said that my performance "brought out the acid below the surface," that I achieved "complicity carried to the point of mockery—so the piece becomes nearly a feminist statement," and that I made "the movements look insinuating and delicious at the same time." I found her comment about my interpretation uncannily perceptive. She could have been describing the way I was conducting my life.

Mr. B.'s choreography also called for a certain level of self-consciousness on the part of the woman. This is a controlled situation.

There are people who take the capes off us and leave and come back and put them on. Everyone is involved in the ritual coupling. Even though the court leaves the stage for the consummation of the pas de deux, the entire court knows what we are doing. The ballet reflects the duality—the two sides of a relationship, the public and the private. Even though the whole audience is looking, it is the people in the court who create the sense of invasion for the female. It is the sense of the court knowing what has been prescribed that creates the self-consciousness for the female dancer. Although I was dressed in tights, a bikini, and a bra, I never felt more exposed on stage than at that moment. Offstage, before entering, I used to say to the girls, "Tell me quietly if everything is all right." Of course, they weren't about to say in the middle of a performance, "Your stretch bra is off the mark, honey." But I always asked them to tell me anyway. What is exposed is not the woman's body but her intentions. There is privacy but no secrecy. It was a duplication of my real life. I projected what I was experiencing offstage—a sense of self-consciousness at others' intrusions into my sexual life. It was me and my mother, my not liking her intrusions into my bed. When my attendants removed my train in preparation for the conjugal pas de deux, I always felt naked, even though I was lightly covered in a costume.

When I arrived at Karinska's for the first fitting, Mr. B. was there, taking delight in the breathtakingly beautiful costumes. Eddie's outfit was also elegant, a short kimono with golden lamé inserts, like fans, and a long transparent train. My headdress of black lamé was light, with two little nests of Japanese sparkling decorations and toys. I had a fuchsia chrysanthemum-petaled tutu with rhinestones, a white flowered bikini top and bottom, and a gossamer kimono with my own long train of white transparency edged in translucent tubing. I recommended a stretch bra, a concept that had just arrived. Mr. B. was having a good time.

As had the other ballets Mr. B. did for me, this ballet symbolized the evolving vision he had of me and of our particular relationship. During the rehearsals, I was very aware that he enjoyed partnering me in the sensual pas de deux of *Bugaku* with its very close body contact. As I understood it, my earlier fanatical religious beliefs and marriage as well as Mr. B.'s marriage had long ago solidified the limitations we had put on our relationship. When he pulled my body to him in a vertical split during rehearsals, it was the director and dancer at work. Unacknowledged sexual tension was, as always, a source of creativity for both of us, and partnering was within the bounds.

In early May 1963, Bert and I went to a party at Luchow's, and I danced with a newspaper columnist who asked me, "Do you remember your childhood friend from the company, Janie Mason?"

"How could I forget her?"

"She's adopted nine Aztec babies."

"Good heavens!"

I thought about Janie, one of my first real friends in the company. I remembered her black sheath and hat with the veil on Hollywood Boulevard. We weren't alike at all, but now we were both mothers. I had one child, and she had nine. I had been thinking of another baby. I was remembering how important my brother, Gary, had been to me when I was a child. With open eyes, we two small botanists trod the empty lots making discoveries. Everything was new to us. I wanted to give Trista a playmate.

This was five months after Balanchine's little talk with me in Russia. "Forget your husband. Forget your baby. Work, work, work." I decided I was going to do just as I pleased.

Mr. B.'s was not the only permission I didn't seek. By summer, it seemed that Bert once again had another woman in his life. There were certain unmistakable signs. His hours at work increased, and he wasn't always where he said he would be. He was sloppy. I knew I didn't have a marriage; I had a household unit, minus a husband. What was missing was more important than I understood it to be, but I didn't know that. I had grown up without a father. By the fall of 1963, I decided I wanted a baby no matter what was going on with my marriage.

I became pregnant Halloween night without consulting Bert. What he felt was immaterial.

I also quit dancing immediately. I wanted to rest. The company's performing base in New York City was going to move out of City Center and into the State Theater in the Lincoln Center complex. I knew that if I became pregnant, I'd miss dancing at the Lincoln Center opening. Something within me decided on the child and not the opening. I had invested a lot in my dancing, but like my mother I adored babies. They were surprise packages.

Besides, this career of mine was too hard, and I was ready for some time off. During this pregnancy, I did not take ballet classes at all. I felt too much pressure on my legs because I carried this baby in a different way. The company would still be there. I could get back in shape—I'd done it once before. I didn't want to think about my career for a while. I was twenty-five and had been a professional for ten years. The New York City Ballet had been my nursery through graduate school. At this moment, I needed a rest.

I have no memory of telling Mr. B. about this second pregnancy or my darling baby-to-be. But I do remember thinking he might not have cared as much now. He had a strong lineup of distinctive ballerinas.

I attended the opening of the ballet at Lincoln Center pregnant in a borrowed long red velvet dress.

After I became pregnant, Bert decided we should buy a brownstone. His business was doing very well, and he was in the mood for expansion. Also, something about the death of John F. Kennedy had triggered this impulse. Somehow, Bert thought of himself as cementing the strength of the family through property.

I agreed to his plan. I thought it would be wonderful to live in a house. Long ago, on Sunday drives in California, my father and I had traveled the avenues looking at houses with their gardens and trees. If only I could possess all that dirt and all those flowers! When I was six, we had lived in a house with a rose garden, but it wasn't ours. As a child and an adult, I had lived only in rented places. Always temporary. Owning a home sounded like a childhood dream realized. There was a big missing piece in this dream, of course. Bert was asserting the importance of his growing family through an exterior gesture, but he had no impulse to give any more of himself. But I ignored that. There would be a garden to plant, and I needed a larger nest with the new baby coming.

We found a light, bright brownstone at 243 East Sixty-first Street, a pretty block that appealed to us, and I gave Bert eleven thousand dollars toward the down payment of twenty thousand. He took my money but did not put the house in my name or even in both our names. He bought it through the business. I didn't question him. My interpretation of my former religion and my mother's tossing off the stuff of daily use as we moved from coast to coast made me very impractical in life, almost a masochist. I didn't try to hold on to things that were needed. I didn't take care of myself, and I didn't lay up a store to protect myself or my children financially, never dreaming that everything would one day disappear.

We wouldn't move in until the house was remodeled, but I ordered rosebushes with wonderful names and sterling attributes and, in the spring, put them in the garden of our new house. It was hard work. My stomach was huge and so was the shovel.

When Bert arrived home from work one evening late in June, I was sitting in bed trying to stay calm. He had tickets to the Norman Norell fashion show for that night, a presentation of sumptuous garments he had loved the year before.

"Bert?" My voice was low and serious. "My labor has started. I'm going to have to go to the hospital in a few hours."

"But you can't. I want to see Norell's show tonight. You told me this morning that the doctor said you weren't ready." Bert looked at me as if I were a traitor.

"Well," I answered impassively, "that was true this morning. But it isn't true now. My contractions have started, really started. There is no way I can go to that show." I looked down at my huge, round stomach. "Nothing can stop this baby. It's time for it to come out."

Bert inhaled and walked over to me. "You are doing this on purpose, Allegra, just because you don't want to go." Bert pursed his lips. "I'm going to call the doctor and see what he says."

"Bert, I'm the one having the baby." A strong contraction started as my body followed its own timetable and its own rhythm. I started to do the correct kind of breathing, even though I had already discussed with my doctor how I was going to have this baby. I wanted medical help this time—not a lot, but a little. I could not go through natural childbirth twice.

Bert stood watching my contraction in silence, then walked out. I felt a restless anxiety. This time the father of my baby was present, but he was acting strangely. It was not better than my first labor in Los Angeles.

Finally, I convinced everyone—Bert and the doctor—that I must go to the hospital. If I didn't know my body, who did?

Not so very much later, lovely round-eyed Susannah Amanda was born at seven pounds, thirteen ounces, the same birth weight as Trista. This was my child. The numbers were right. Her round eyes were intensely blue. Later there would be just a touch of gray iris in them, the flower and the perfume. My new baby was a tender, sweet creature, a primitive bundle.

Two weeks later, in mid-July, we moved to a rented house on Fire Island for the summer, where my sister also had a rental. Between us, my sister and I now had four babies. My mother galloped back and forth between our two households, arranging rendezvous with Trista, three and a half, and her cousin, Jennifer, three, who were very close. Once, before a party, the caviar diminished rapidly. Trista and Jennifer, who loved it, made trips to the refrigerator at odd hours, when no one was watching, scooped out teaspoonfuls, then ran into the bathroom where they ate it and laughed.

Bert, the perfectionist with a great eye for detail, supervised the construction work on the brownstone while we were away and came out for weekends when he could. Although he loved the way the brownstone was turning out, during this period there was a sharp downswing in our relationship. I realized that owning a home wasn't going to change anything, but Susannah and Trista made me euphoric. Ballet and babies were my life now.

A month after Susannah's birth, I began to practice in the kitchen, holding on to a counter for my daily barre. The serious task of remaking my body—regaining what I had lost—would take time.

When we moved into the top two floors of the four-story brownstone, it was with very few odds and ends. Bert had had most of the furniture at our apartment built in, so we couldn't move it. It remained where it lodged. In our new home, we had beds and tiny bureaus in each bedroom and a redwood picnic table and some porch furniture on the top floor. The children and I were camping out, with the two lower floors empty.

The better furniture was in Bert's studio. He had furnished his workplace with antiques and fine paintings. A Cy Twombly and an Allan Jones hung in the office, with an antique Spanish sideboard, an antique desk, leather couches, and wrought-iron baker's racks. Bert had bought entire collections of leather-bound vintage books, all of Dickens, and classics that he'd never read. The furniture and the books stayed at the studio. Bert could not share them with his family.

I did not question Bert about the money, but I thought he must be saving for the future. How could he not? As a star photographer, Bert was raking money in, and he became grandiose in his ideas and expenditures. One day, he told Trista that we would all live in a castle and she would be like a fairy-tale princess.

I asked Bert not to talk to her that way. But I did not ask him to spend more time at home. On evenings when I felt lonely, I'd invite one of my girlfriends over. We'd eat dinner and play with the children. Trista was extraordinary at improvising. She listened, heard the music, and danced in a unique way for a four-year-old. Muriel Stuart confirmed my observation when she visited one afternoon.

I was dividing myself into pieces—the dance part, the mother, and the salvager. I was still hoping somehow to rescue my marriage, and I had begun seeing Bert's therapist, Sheldon Hertzberg. I didn't like Hertzberg, but I thought that might be part of what the process was about. He told me he thought that Bert and I would become compatible and that some transformation would occur. His basic answer to my problems with Bert was, "He loves you."

In the meantime, Bert hired a landscaper to "do" the garden without consulting me, and the man ripped out the rosebushes I had worked so hard to put in and replaced them with very expensive varieties of trees. More money for him, no roses for me. Eventually the house would reflect nothing about me—not its ownership, its garden, or its future.

"How are you, Allegra? You look stunning. When will you be ready to dance?"

It was the fall after Susannah's birth, and Mr. B. had come from the wings when I had appeared backstage during an intermission to say hello to friends. After a hug and a kiss, Mr. B. stepped back to look me over, carefully searching for the damages of childbirth. There were none. My hair was caught up in two bunches, one over each shoulder. The style was a bit juvenile, but Mr. B. liked it. He put one palm under each ponytail. For the moment he had me gently in hand. I was in his grasp. I felt like a Georgian princess. His eyes and upper lip expressed expectancy. What he said was wonderful. He wanted me onstage and dancing because he loved my dancing.

I smiled. "My wrists are always thin, like the rest of me, but I'm not strong yet. I'll be ready for *Nutcracker.*"

"That's good news."

The warmth of his welcome thrilled me. My presence in the company was still important to Mr. B. But then a change on his face foretold an important message; I had received others from him before.

He was thinking of its presentation. In a tone of a legato seriousness, Mr. B. said, "Now, Allegra, no more babies. Enough is enough. Babies are for Puerto Ricans."

I smiled and thought, *And for little Polish girls, too. No man can tell me what to do when it comes to babies.* I had not even consulted Bert about having a second child. This was my realm.

"Promise me!" As he spoke he pointed his finger upward in the direction where all important messages originate.

I delivered a soft-spoken and playful "All right," but thought, *I must have one more baby on this little speech alone. You may direct the New York City Ballet, but I direct my own life.*

When Mr. B. put my name on the board for the the new production of *Nutcracker* opening night of the winter season, December 1964, I wished I could give him a guarantee of how I'd dance during a performance, like an electric mixer or some kitchen appliance. But it went well. Mr. B.'s only correction was that he thought I wore my crown too far back, but that was just the way I dealt with royalty. I was happy. I had come back from a second pregnancy.

I didn't realize that I would never be really back, not in the same way. I hadn't known it at the time, but *Bugaku* was the second to last ballet part Mr. B. was to make for me. During the time I bowed out of performing to have my second baby, Mr. Balanchine had turned his energy away from his fantasy relationship with me to a flesh-and-blood possibility—Suzanne Farrell.

PART SIX

1965 – 1970

Family and Friends

Photos by Bert Stern.

CHAPTER THIRTEEN

Am I to live forever in a barricade of perennial innocence like chickens in a cage?

—WILLIAM FAULKNER, THE WILD PALMS

It was a boiling-hot late afternoon at Kennedy Airport, not a day to travel. I found a phone booth, walked in, and threw some coins in the slot. "Hi, Mom. I just checked my suitcase and I have lots of time. There was no traffic." I'd taken a break during a European tour to visit my children on Fire Island for two weeks, and I was leaving to rejoin the company in London. My voice resembled a descending scale. I didn't like traveling to Europe alone. "How are the kids?"

"Allegra, the children are fine. But there is something in the *Post* I think you should know about." The breathless pattern in my mother's voice depressed me.

"What is it?" I could almost guess.

She hesitated. "Bert's name has been linked with a model. He's seeing her every night. It's horrible." Mother's unchecked vehemence was growing rapidly. "Buy the paper and you'll see what I'm talking about. It's an insult to you and the children."

"All right, Mother." I closed my eyes. I felt exhausted, completely defeated. "I'll buy it."

Awkwardly, I pushed open the door of my phone booth and walked over to the newsstand. The bad news was mid-column. Bert's name was linked with his favorite model of the moment. Only four weeks earlier he and I had been in Paris together. He had wanted to be with me and flew over to France while I was performing with the company at the glorious Paris Opera House. Now, as I prepared to rejoin the tour after my intermission, this was my send-off. I knew about Bert and other women; I'd always known. But this was different. Now Bert was announcing his personal infidelity to the world. I felt sick. It was still a long time until my flight took off.

Impulsively, I walked over to an airline employee behind the desk. My body felt limp. In a dry voice, I said, "I've decided against this trip. May I please have my suitcase back. I'm really sorry to bother you, but I'm staying put. I can't travel at this time."

"Are you afraid to fly, miss?"

"No! It's a personal matter that must be taken care of. I just received some news." Embarrassed, I set the wheels of retrieval into operation. The spirit of travel and dancing had gone out of me. Crushed, I would just go back to Fire Island and figure out my next move. But first I'd hug and kiss my little girls.

A month later in front of the State Theater, Maria Tallchief stepped out of the taxi I thought I had hailed. She wanted to talk to me, so I motioned for the driver to move on. We were on the corner of Sixty-second Street and Columbus, near the stage entrance.

"Allegra, why didn't you return and dance in London?" Maria looked directly in my eyes. She had very much wanted me to dance *Bugaku* in England. She expected an explanation. This woman could have been a marine drill sergeant. She was furious at me.

"Bert put something awful in the newspapers that upset me very much. I can't dance when I'm unhappy and there's chaos in my life." I felt like sinking into myself. Maria's presence in person was as commanding as it was onstage.

"Oh, Allegra," Maria said impatiently, "husbands come and husbands go, but your dancing is the thing that's important."

What Maria suggested was a very sound course of action. She had had three husbands and maintained her career, but her advice made me feel weak and miserable. I started to sob and jumped into a taxi to escape. Maria never took me quite as seriously after that.

Maria was right. I should have gone to London. After I had retrieved my luggage and returned to Fire Island, no one had seemed that happy to see me. What was I doing there? I was supposed to be at work. Mother had taken over my position at home, and my returning did not resolve the situation with Bert.

But my unease had been justified. For the first time, Bert felt divided about his next action. He thought maybe he would leave me for the model. But I didn't know how to fight. Instead of confronting him, I became fearful. I hadn't developed another plan. I had no sense of independence, and I despaired that I couldn't juggle a career and children while searching for a new man. I felt more secure staying in the marriage, as horrible as it was. Bert was actually living two lives, and I chose to accept that.

Bert's new TV-commercial business was on the runway, had accelerated, and was starting to fly. He was inventive, and he was hot. The major agencies eagerly employed his company. He bought a schoolhouse, a huge building at Sixty-second Street and First Avenue, which became his new office and business. He also had a condominium at the San Tropez on Sixty-fourth Street, and he went on lavishly furnishing his spacious four-story office and studio and now his nearby condo with deluxe objects, fragile hand-painted Limoges and costly antiques.

In contrast, the children and I were still camping out on the top two floors of the brownstone. Wherever I lived, I brought my childhood sense of poverty to the place. The two lower floors remained unfurnished. Bert did not make funds available. I worked—took care of the children with the help of a housekeeper, danced at night, and rehearsed by day. I could have bought some furniture, but that wasn't my way of doing things. A part of me still felt impoverished. And I was. I was giving my checks to Bert, and nothing was in my name. Mr. B. said I didn't need a raise because I had a rich husband.

I was still clinging to the hope that psychiatry would make us compatible. When I complained of Bert's infidelities, Dr. Hertzberg advised me to stay in the marriage. He told me, "No matter what happens, that doesn't change Bert's love for you," and he implied that eventually Bert would improve.

This was the era of the open marriage—and the double standard. That was clear in what I would allow myself. Even in Russia, knowing that I didn't have a marriage, I still wouldn't sleep with a married man, not even for fun. There wasn't anything Bert wouldn't allow himself. And I was not the kind of wife who was jealous of someone's work. I believed a person should have other passions—such as work, friends, family, or botany. I did not, however, believe the other passions should include women in bed with you.

And Bert always gave me a glimmer of hope, even when he was at his most unfaithful. He thought he could have everything he wanted, and that included his family. He seemed to enjoy the prestigious implication of a marriage to a ballerina, while resisting the drudgery of having a wife.

My ideas of how to live life hadn't worked out. Bert was an

unlikely candidate for a husband or father; this play had the wrong male lead. I was not a genius casting director.

Slowly, I began to overeat. By refusing to board the plane, I had accomplished nothing. I had lost some credibility with the company, and I had placed myself in limbo.

One evening in 1965, while I was making up for *A Midsummer Night's Dream,* Mr. B. and a young man knocked on the door of the dressing room I shared with Suzanne Farrell and came in. From the conversation I learned that Mr. B. thought Suzanne should have a special coiffure for that evening's performance.

This came as no surprise. Mr. B. had always had an interest in hair. Just as higher extensions and greater finesse in technique led to the evolving look of ballet, so did the appearance of our hair. The classical Victorian helmet that I had struggled with at fifteen was for the most part passé. Mr. B. wanted a modern look, with the ears exposed and the strands swept into a French twist or a neat sculptured shape. Diana Adams was one of the first to wear the neoclassical look, in *Symphony in C.* Soon everyone had adopted it for *Apollo, Agon, Concerto Barocco,* and *Stars and Stripes.*

Balanchine also understood hair tossing and often used loosened locks for dramatic emphasis. Originally there were no hair changes in *Serenade,* but later he requested that just before the waltz girl falls to the floor, her hair should tumble free. Then the ballet proceeded toward the "Elegy" section with a more emotional context. This followed a tradition: when Giselle, one of the most famous heroines of the Romantic ballet, went mad, she lost her mind and her hairpins simultaneously.

Once while performing in *The Cage,* Jerome Robbins's deadly insect dance, I did not fasten my sleek black beetlelike wig securely, and by mid-dance it was hanging near my ear. I ripped it off in disgust, full of self-hate, feeling very sloppy and unprofessional. My own hair fell wildly about my head. But Mr. B. came backstage beaming. He thought I should lose the wig in every performance to show more clearly the lethal development of Jerry's mate-consuming mantis. The hair reflected her ominous maturity. Mr. B. knew how upset I was with the performance, and it was generous of him to de-emphasize the mishap. He had looked at *The Cage* with a fresh eye and did not find it at all disturbing that I was having a bad-hair day.

However, on this night in the dressing room it was not my hair that concerned Mr. B. The young man with him was a professional hairdresser, there to arrange Suzanne's coiffure. This put me in a competitive mood. Suzanne was getting special attention, but no one cared how I looked. Mr. B. didn't even glance my way.

As new muse and love object since 1963, Suzanne was now given first choice of roles and performances, and Mr. B. created most of his new works for her. They seemed to need only each other, and the rest of the company be damned.

Balanchine's interest in Suzanne had come as a surprise to me. While we were dancing in Ravinia near Chicago, just before the European-Russian tour, there had been an emergency. One principal woman was out in *Serenade* and a young new member was put in: Suzanne. This was my first awareness of her in the company. She had been just sixteen. The Ford Foundation grant allowed Balanchine's talent scouts—in this case, Diana Adams—to tour the country, find talent, give young dancers scholarships, and bring them to New York to study. Suzanne was one of those, and within a year she was to become Mr. B.'s obsession.

The opening of *Don Quixote* upset me particularly. Suzanne was in the starring role, and it was clearly a statement of Mr. B.'s love for her. But Tanaquil, his wife, was in the audience. How could Tanny bear this? I never was able to look at the ballet again; all I could see in it was gloom and disloyalty.

I looked sideways and saw that Suzanne's hairdo was growing by leaps and bounds; bigger and bigger fake strands were attached and teased, spray was added, and a giant bouffant was built. Mr. B. was nervously buzzing around Suzanne's beehive. This infuriated me. Perhaps a little austerity with my hair and some good dancing would be the very thing for tonight. I got out my metaphysical fencing foils and sharpened the blades. Determination to dance well and romantically in the gorgeous pas de deux fired me up. Jacques was the ideal partner for this particular piece. The dance was about love, off-balance swoons, and floating lifts, so I could do without the hairdresser.

After the performance Mr. B. came backstage and spoke to Suzanne. Her hairdo had been a bust; it was too big and ungainly. Then he came over to me and gave me a most genuinely felt compliment. I knew I had really danced well, and his guard was down.

I gloated for a second or two, then in a furious voice I snapped, "That's the first thing you've said to me in six months."

Mr. B. froze on the spot. The temperature, including the windchill factor, might as well have been ten degrees below zero. Balanchine blanched as he stood in the uptown side of dressing room A, my toehold in the State Theater. I couldn't let him enjoy that moment and refused his favorable words and his right to deliver them. Another one of those confounded compliments. Mr. B. should have known better.

Mr. B. shut his mouth and didn't speak to me for the next year. After that, our exchanges were confined to "Oh, hello, Allegra," as if he were addressing a stranger back from the Yukon. He developed a special tone for me; it divulged nothing, protected everything, and was merely polite. And, in our dressing room at the State Theater, Suzanne was always very silent as she prepared. There was none of the easy flowing talk there had been with Violette.

I must say in all honesty that when I had first noticed Suzanne, I wasn't struck with any particular attribute of hers. This was in contrast to my first view of Gelsey Kirkland. I was in the practice room of the old American School on Eighty-third and Broadway when a youngster entered and started to practice with total seriousness and dedication. I had been immediately taken with Gelsey, a little bullet, a pint-size perfectionist with the fabled grasshopper muscles. Eventually, I could see that my style of dancing was a strong influence on Suzanne. But some of my ideas came from Carmelita. It was interesting for me to trace the lineage. *What a strange influence to come out in Suzanne's dancing*, I thought.

In the early 1960s, just before Suzanne joined the company, Balanchine had taken the names of the dancers out of the newspaper—it was just the New York City Ballet. Maria Tallchief's name had been first when I joined the company 1953. Then Mr. B. abolished the word "ballerina," and we became principals listed alphabetically in the program. He was the first to do that, then many other companies followed.

Did he do this to make the company more democratic or to make himself the only star? The answer depends on who responds to the question, but I think he did it to shift the focus of the audience away from a particular dancer to the program. So casting became a secret to most people except reviewers and insiders. It was almost always posted as last-minute information, even for the actual cast. This confirmed Mr. Balanchine as the center of the company, and he really saw the dancers as extensions of himself. Nor was he democratic in his treatment of his ballerinas. Now he was in love with Suzanne. His talent needed fresh raw material for inspiration, and she embodied that.

Many of the ballerinas were demoralized by Mr. B.'s obsession with Suzanne. Some were enraged. Pat Wilde and Mimi Paul left in despair in the 1960s. Maria came back for her final round of dancing at the time when Suzanne was very important to Mr. B., and she found this insufferable. In pain from bursitis, she soon quit, but her afterthoughts about Suzanne's talent were extremely—and appropriately—generous. As always, I followed Maria's example.

Early in 1966, John Taras, one of the company's ballet masters, took Melissa Hayden and me to lunch at the Schrafft's near the School of American Ballet and told us he was very interested in our well-being and in the company as a whole. He was "on call" for help. Very soon afterward, he started to work on *Jeux* for Melissa, Edward Villella, and me. At the same time, Mr. B. started to work on a ballet called *Brahms-Schoenberg Quartet* with various principal men and women heading each of the four sections. Mr. B. placed me with Eddie, but I felt disappointed with our movement. It was more for the ensemble than for us, although Eddie had a spectacular variation. The piece did not give me the chance to do what I was best at—unusual movement with a subtext or dramatic understory. John's *Jeux* did. I asked John if I could wear bell-bottom trousers. The story is a three-way love affair, two women and a man. He let me have them, and Karinska made two versions, both beautiful and all in white.

During the same rehearsal period I asked Mr. B. if I could understudy Patty in *Harlequinade* and Melissa in *Pas de Deux et Divertissement*, but his response was evasive. I felt it was a roundabout no. So I did not attend rehearsals or learn the parts. Even though *Jeux,* to Debussy's music, was very satisfying to perform, as a whole, I was discontented with my life at the ballet.

I had been the baby in the family, the youngest child. The focus had been on me. Now there was a new baby, Suzanne, and I was a middle child of the ballet.

Late in 1965 a friend and employee of Bert's told him about an amazing doctor who mixed special vitamins and other substances together and injected them directly into the patient's vein. The miracle serums gave energy, endurance, and a buoyant outlook. Bert expressed interest, and his secretary took him over to Dr. Robert Freyman's office in the East Seventies for a demonstration. Bert tried a sample shot and became a devotee of Dr. Freyman's art. Reality receded, and a new repainted one in beautiful colors came forward.

Bert was enchanted with the wonderful way he felt. Medicine had advanced.

There was one disadvantage. When the shot wore off—and it might be as late as two or three A.M.—Bert felt peculiar, uneasy, and deeply anxious. This was distinctly unpleasant for him. The very next morning, exhausted, he could hardly get up. However, for Bert the good was so good that it outweighed the disturbing aftereffects. What Dr. Freyman, or Dr. Feelgood-C, was actually giving Bert were intravenous amphetamine shots.

To unfaithfulness, Bert was now adding drug addiction. As more work arrived, Bert had more demands on his time and creativity. The number of injections he took per week began to increase. He found it exhilarating to move at the speed of sound. He would leave the brownstone at seven in the morning, arrive home by midnight, and then stay up for at least two more hours. During the day, after a shot, his judgment seemed fine. He was energetic and his concentration was focused. But at night sleep and rest were elusive, and euphoric fantasies replaced logic. He wanted desperately to sleep, but as the shots wore off he couldn't.

During this period, he became my tormentor. The drugs began to change Bert's personality, and our family life, always precarious, started to suffer even more. He was often away on jobs—sometimes he'd tell me one place but he'd be elsewhere. As Bert accelerated his dual life, I became a recluse within the marriage. The only thing in my life I could count on was dance. When I went onstage, I could close the door on my personal life. And I needed to.

I had been given the conditions for my life by my mother—Christian Science and psychiatry. But it was my own fears that bid me stay with Bert. I had to keep trying to make an impossible situation just a little less impossible. There was some happiness in my life when I went to do my pliés or when the children were original and spontaneous and we had fun together. But it was also sad. Bert as I wished him to be wasn't there.

One time during the season Bert came home at the uncharacteristically late hour of three in the morning. He usually came in around midnight and told me he had been working on a job—he couldn't get the ad cut correctly—or he had clients to entertain. There was always some excuse for why he left before the children awoke and was never home until long after they were asleep.

This time, however, he had stayed out until the middle of the night—with a woman, I was certain, probably in his condominium. Even though I knew it happened all the time, a mix of idealism and naïveté had marked my refusal to confront the truth about Bert and other women. Now he was forcing me to. I had a temper tantrum. My methods weren't entirely rational, but then neither was my life.

Exhausted and betrayed, I took a hammer and smashed his Tom Wesselmann watercolor, both the glass and the painting beneath. It pictured a naked woman whose breasts looked as though they'd been molded in plastic. In black magic marker, I wrote "You are a destroyer" on it and left it at the foot of the stairs for him to discover. I had very little sleep that night and had two ballets scheduled for the matinee. Bert, of course, was furious with me for destroying his property; his conduct was not important.

I woke to a call from Una Kai, the ballet mistress. Could I do Melissa Hayden's role in the *Pas de Deux et Divertissement* in addition to my other roles? This was one of the parts I had asked Mr. B. to understudy but received no encouragement. Now I was already doing too much. I had the weekend ahead of me, eight ballets. It was a torment to be called in and to know that I could have prepared the steps at leisure if Balanchine had encouraged me. In despair and fury over Bert's conduct and exhausted from no sleep, I was asked to perform a dance that I didn't know but could have easily understudied. Despondently I said yes. Weary and disgruntled, I went to the theater early, but no one seemed to know the steps. I went onstage and let out a tremendous scream of frustration. Why weren't things at the theater cared for in a better way? Somehow Una, Conrad Ludlow (my partner), and I pieced together the missing steps, and Mme. Pourmel took in a costume for me, the costume no one liked.

I went on. It was a performance of the moment. I danced each step with a certain tension but also calm. It was slightly above me technically, but I did know the music. I decided to take possession of my entire body. I told my fingertips, my toes, and every part of my body, *We are going to dance this piece together, you and I. I don't quite know the dance, but we are going into the ballroom together, we will be elegant and gorgeous, a partner will choose us, and we will dance. It will be nearly right. Or maybe it will be entirely right.* Circumstances were merely a detail. My body and I loved to dance.

I gave a terrific performance and then did my other parts with a sense of relief and power. Some people think that great performances can't come out of such a situation, that great dance can occur only with exhaustive preparation. I've been criticized by some reviewers who thought that I didn't rehearse enough, but it's one of those gambles. This time, however, I had been forced to gamble.

Only the night before, I had been in deep despair. But I had left my personal life on the East Side, transcended my frustration at Mr. B., and gone on the stage to dance. As always, ballet made me forget that I had lived my life incorrectly. I said a prayer: "Thank you, inventors of dance, creators of this precious beautiful thing, an antidote to real life."

But I was preparing to give up dance for a while after that season. It was time for an intermission.

That summer, in bed, just barely awake at my rented house on Fire Island, I pressed my fingertips into my stomach just above my pubic bone. Underneath the strong fibers of the surface, I traced a small avocado shape. I was pregnant again. I knew every inch and sinew of my body so well that I could detect any subtle change. It was June 1966, and in a few weeks a doctor could confirm my findings with a test, but it was unnecessary. I already knew, because this was a deliberately planned pregnancy.

I had always wanted three children. Even though I no longer had any illusions about my marriage or about Bert as a father, somehow I was capable of knowing this brutal truth and being idealistic at the same time. And on one level Bert did want us; he behaved as if we had a marriage and family. Within the limits of what I had to work with, I thought I could create something that would pass.

What made me happy were my children. And I wanted one more. I wanted to create my own allies and friends and to relive my childhood. Having a father present was not essential—I'd grown up knowing that. Even if Bert wasn't there, I hoped that the children would know that he loved them the way I had always known my absent father loved my brother and me.

And if I wanted another child, Bert would have to be the father. I didn't have an alternative, and I wasn't looking for one. Finding a new father for my family would require a lot of energy and many auditions or dates. I was a mother and a ballerina, and I had a difficult body to care for and maintain.

Rebelling against Balanchine's "Sermon on the Mount" was also a factor in my decision to have another child. His never-to-be-forgotten backstage speech about the precise number of children I could have had ruffled my feathers. I had known then that I was going to have another baby. My personal life was mine alone to direct. Why didn't Mr. B. say to me, "Allegra, we'll give you a cash bonus of ten thousand dollars not to have any more babies"? That's what they do in China.

Why wasn't I pursuing my career more avidly? In another month I would be twenty-nine. Ballerinas didn't have three children in their twenties. These were precious years. The moment for great achievements could easily be missed. The body is twenty only once. However, many of my dancing teachers expressed regrets because they had put off having a child until it was too late. For various reasons, many ballerinas in the thirty-five and upward age group found it hard to conceive.

I had many loves in my life, and I wanted them all. I had created a pattern that seemed to work well for me, alternating two or three years of intensive work with a rest and a pregnancy. And I needed the rest. My muscles had been giving me trouble; they cramped easily. Much of my day was taken up with making certain they would not fail me during a performance. Part of my routine was a daily massage, and, after a working night, one hour of stretching, in a split, to counteract the physical stress of ballet and dancing on pointe. It was time for this round-the-clock dedication to stop. In a profession famous for injuries, I suffered very few in my career. I often thought that this pattern of long breaks combined with daily massages was responsible. Now it was time for me to enter the other part of the cycle. I wanted more time to play with my children, read books, and stop living a lopsided life.

However, at the very moment I was planning to step more deeply into family life, Bert was again preparing to bow out. I had made a terrible miscalculation.

Days after I had stopped using birth control, as I embarked on my plan to conceive a third child, Bert rang me up from out of town to say he loved me and that it was raining.

I said, "Oh, that's funny. It's raining here also," and then we talked on for a bit.

Five minutes later my mother called. "Allegra." There was great tension in her voice. "I just saw Bert on Second Avenue walking hand in hand with a blond woman."

"But, Mom, that's impossible. He's out of town." The pain of betrayal caught in my throat, leaving me barely able to speak. I was humiliated and could not go on denying what was happening. My mother was a witness. I thought of the news item a year earlier. A public affair meant that Bert was thinking of leaving me again.

I resumed using a contraceptive on the slim chance that my plan had failed, and I confronted Bert.

Caught in a lie, he furiously defended himself. Bert always expected me to take him back and accept him as he was. Then he would become enraged with me. He accused me of not being a wife, of never doing anything with him, of never going on trips with him, and of spending all my time dancing. But he did not ask for a divorce.

I, however, began thinking seriously about one. And for the very first time, my mother wavered. After she had witnessed Bert and the blonde, she was as uncertain as I was. My life was beginning to resemble hers: she, too, had had three children without a reliable husband. Although she agreed that I should leave Bert, she worried that I hadn't put enough money away. There was no new partner lined up for me out there, and I didn't have the assets to do it alone. In the end, she counseled me to stay.

Ultimately, Bert didn't want me to leave him, and I bowed to the advice of my psychiatrist and my mother. Although Bert was unfaithful and loved his models and the power he had over them with his camera, I had a strange secondary role in his life, and he never really tried to make a real break from me. And I was guilty of a passivity that resembled my mother's. Only in dance did I assert myself and assume my real nature, just as I had as a child.

Now, as I lay alone very still in my bed touching my stomach, feeling the tiny shape that would be my third child, the stupidity of my timing overwhelmed me. What a fool I had been, but it was too late. I was building a family, but it had no foundation. I had stayed with Bert, refusing to admit to myself that he and I were living separate lives. We were married but not a couple.

That night Bert arrived in Fire Island for his obligatory overnight visit. The girls and I walked over to Seaview to meet the pontooned seaplane that landed in the protected waters of the bay. The cockpit door opened, and Bert hopped out holding a small briefcase. I would have to tell him my news. As with my last pregnancy, I had not discussed this with him. He had no idea that I hadn't protected myself for that brief period.

That evening, after our two little girls were asleep, while Bert was sitting at the dining room table constructing a ship model, I sat down at a right angle to him. He was gluing two tiny sticks of balsa wood together. For a moment, I watched him at work. "Bert, I'm pregnant."

Bert raised his head with a quick turn to look at me. "Are you sure? Have you had a test?" He put the delicate pieces of wood back in the box, pushed it away from him, then resumed staring at me.

"I don't need to. I'm sure."

"Did you plan this?"

"Yes."

Bert pinched his lips together and let out a low whistle. "Thanks a lot for not consulting me."

"Are you happy about it?"

"Are you out of your mind? Don't you want to be a ballerina?"

"I thought I'd try for a boy."

"Oh, God."

"Bert, our marriage is coming apart, and it's your fault."

"No, it's yours. You're not interested in me, in what I've done and achieved."

"Well, I'm pregnant now. I'll have lots of time to be very interested. I won't be dancing for a while."

Bert wasn't enthusiastic, and, after he left, I felt depressed. There must be some action I could take to help my family.

By Friday I had an idea. Perhaps I could knock the other woman in question out of the picture. But who was she? How could I find out? It was easy. I called Bert's secretary and casually asked her the name of the blonde who was helping Bert decorate his apartment. She was a junior Ford model.

The next call was to Eileen Ford at her modeling agency. At first she seemed taken aback, but then she readily gave me the number of "Bert's other wife," as the model was referred to in the studio. I was in the middle of making an apple pie when I decided to act. I washed my hands, and, still standing up, not even dragging over a chair, I proceeded to dial.

"Hello." The voice had a pleasant timbre, rather sweet, not very aggressive. That was good.

"Hello. This is Allegra, Bert's wife."

I heard her take in a breath. She was shocked.

"Do you love Bert?"

"Yes, I do."

"Do you know that I'm pregnant?"

"No, I didn't know that."

"I have to tell you that Bert, at this time, is going ahead with his marriage. He knows about the baby and is happy. I'm sorry. As you must know, this will be my third child with Bert. This situation with you can't go on. And it's hopeless. You'll never get him."

Bert's other wife very softly began to cry.

I had thought I was the underdog, but now I felt sorry for this young woman or for any woman involved with a man who was merely a playboy. "I'm sorry. The children need their father." I could tell she was not a fighter.

Within an hour Bert called. I was afraid of his reaction, but he was thrilled with the drama and the scenes. He loved being topic number one. His girlfriend had called him, but so had other people. The Ford agency was buzzing. Rumors were flying. Bert was the center of a scandal. Women were fighting over him, and he loved it.

To Bert, a winner was very appealing, and I had delivered the knockout punch. He began to extend his weekend visits, sometimes by a few hours and sometimes by a day. However, he showed no more interest in the children than before and spent the time he was with us sleeping until he could return to the city and his shots.

I had temporarily knocked Bert's "other wife" out of the picture, but Dr. Freyman was still deeply etched in it.

And there were two important people who still did not know that I was pregnant again: my mother and Mr. B.

As she had done during other summers, Mother lived on Fire Island with Wendy and her children, running between her household and mine, being *prima* child-care *persona assoluta* and a grandmother. The woman had energy. She was caught up in the lives of her girls and our little ones. When she took Trista to nursery school she'd announce, "This is Allegra Kent's daughter."

Late one morning, Mother found me lying in bed in my dark green velvet bathing suit. I felt queasy. "Mother, I may be pregnant."

"Oh, no, Allegra, how could you at this time?" The blood rushed to her face. She was deeply alarmed.

I immediately said, "Maybe I'm not."

But she could read me. She was tuned in to my body. She closely inspected my physical posture and shape on the bed, and she knew, too.

I let her think it was an accident and hoped she believed me. It was best. I didn't want her rancor at the moment; it wouldn't help.

I never told Mr. B. directly about the baby. That July, a summer dance project was a film of *A Midsummer Night's Dream* that was designed to make Suzanne a star. I was asked to do the pas de deux, which was something I did well, although it hadn't been choreographed for me. I was one month pregnant in the film and hadn't prepared as much as I should have. Already I was directing my energies away from my career and focusing back on my personal life. After the filming, I went to Fire Island with my girls. Eventually, I told my dance friends about the pregnancy and knew it would filter back to Mr. B. It was common knowledge that my marriage was a disaster, so I surmised that Mr. B., too, would think this pregnancy was an accident.

At this time I had been seeing my therapist for four years. All I had known was that he was a genuine, certified psychiatrist who had had the training, but his advice was starting to bore me. It was always the same. One day I got up and left his office mid-session and never returned. I was going to have my third baby and solve the problem of my marriage to Bert by myself.

"Hi, Bert. I've just bought a mimosa tree in full bloom, and it's given me an idea." I spoke to him from a phone booth on the street. "I'd like to throw a birthday party for you in the house." His birthday was a week away, on October third.

"Allegra, there's no furniture in the house." It was the fall of 1966, and I was four months pregnant. I had given up on psychiatry, but— again trying to convince myself that my marriage was redeemable— I embarked on a plan to bring more warmth to the family. I would give us a more comfortable home. "But there could be furniture, if you send some over from the studio—some couches, lamps, tables, chairs, and paintings. We can invite your friends from the art world and have a great party. How about Richard Feigan, Babs Simpson, and O. K. Harris? Give me a list."

"Can we have orange mousse for dessert?"

"Yes, and a cake with candles."

"I'll put Evelyn on this right away." Bert was actually showing some enthusiasm.

"Good. This will be fun."

In my heart, I knew there was an element of calculation in what I was doing, but it was working. With one phone call, I would have the house in livable shape and furnished.

The party was a success, and the house seemed less empty and hollow. It would be a nice place to bring up my new baby.

Unfortunately, at this time Bert's daily shots from Dr. Freyman were inspiring him to even more grandiose plans. During one of his sleepless nights, Bert told me about an idea for a store of objects and clothes created by artists. I voiced a conservative and negative point of view. Lately, some of Bert's commercials had lost money. Now he wanted to engage in the wholesale-retail garment business, and he knew nothing about it. But his solution was to be lavish. Bert believed in Hollywood extravaganzas with Klieg lights and stars. Red roses should number in the hundreds, particularly if they were for Marilyn Monroe. Allegra received a dozen. To Bert, the budget was merely an invisible boundary. When I raised my objections, he claimed that I was "not audacious," and he went ahead with the store, named On First. He put two hundred and fifty thousand dollars into it and took on a business partner who lent him capital for the venture. At the same time, Bert told me that his shots were a "real bargain," only twenty dollars a vial.

My son, Bret, arrived on March 6, 1967. I had a new child, an unknown creature, a little person who would inspire high hopes and would be greeted warmly by his parents.

Just nine days after Bret's birth, on the Ides of March, the store was born. Bert opened On First with a gala party—a dinner at Maxwell's Plum and a huge guest list. I attended the party briefly and then went home to breast-feed my baby. Again, Bert arrived home at three in the morning.

The life of the store was short. The objects were too quirky, expensive, and impractical. I took a look inside after the store had been operating for one month. The walls and floor were densely covered in rugs. It was heavy and oppressive. The salesgirl and myself were the only people there. How lonely for her. There was no action in this mausoleum. The name of the store was taken from the famous baseball skit of Abbott and Costello, but Bert hadn't made it to first base with this venture; he had struck out. He had made a huge mistake and had jeopardized his family's well-being.

Two weeks later, while I was nursing Bret, Bert told me he wanted me out of the brownstone. He said it would be easier for me to be in an apartment all on one level, but in reality he had found a way to leave his family and separate from us physically as well as emotionally. He took an enormous ten-room apartment around the corner for us. I consented to this plan. So I was moving again. Bret was four months old. I was exhausted.

I packed only clothes. The furniture was staying—Bert liked the house furnished. Now that it had chairs and paintings in it, he had rediscovered the charm of the brownstone and he wanted it empty for parties—or, as I surmised, rendezvous. I didn't know whom he was seeing now, and I didn't consciously try to find out, although when I looked at his ads in magazines, I assumed that the models photographed in particularly sexy poses were probably his girlfriends.

We moved without Bert, but then he began to show up at the apartment every night. He was not a strong presence in our new group portrait, but he couldn't let go of us either. Our life continued its confusing pattern of Bert's withdrawals and returns. Like the prisoner who has to shift his energies to the limited things possible for him to do, I focused on my children and turned back to dance.

For my sanity—but also from love—I would transport my body back to class and train it again to dance. I would come back from a third pregnancy. I was still young and I could do it. This was my pattern. I had had the rest and the pregnancy, and now I would return to my career. Rebuilding my body after giving birth was slow and hard for me, but I had managed it before. Dancing, the surprise discovery of my childhood, could take a backseat at times, but now it was time to resume my career—slowly, step-by-step, to reawaken the muscles, the sense of coordination, the small spring upward, then the bounding leap.

One lonely weekend, when I missed everyone so much, I decided to surprise the children and visit them on Fire Island. It was the summer of 1968. I was dancing again and had decided for the first time to spend July with the company in Saratoga, leaving the children with Mother on Fire Island. Dancing was all that I had. I did not have a marriage and I did not have assets. And I had not figured out my next move. By spring 1968, a year after Bret's birth, Mr. B. had given up all speeches about numbers of offspring and welcomed me back into the company. There was greatness here as well as generosity. He had let me break his rules again.

I took an airplane, then a seaplane, and, for the final leg of the trip, walked to the house in Fire Island. With wild joy, I rang the bell. My mother opened the door and stared at me in shock. Then, angrily, she said, "Why are you here? I told you not to visit us. It's too hard on the children. You shouldn't have come."

I was astonished. I had given my mother a role as my stand-in, and she was guarding it tooth and nail. She wanted no interference from me. With her, my babies had an excellent caretaker, and I was superfluous. She couldn't imagine that my children would enjoy seeing me, even briefly, the equivalent of a visiting day at camp. She totally ruined the happiness I felt at that moment, but then my little ones gathered around me, and we kissed and played. They loved the surprise.

I was visiting my mother and children in the new house Bert had bought for us. Unfortunately, my mother had already made it unlivable. In a frenzy of decorative inspiration, she had thrown out or given away all the furniture she didn't like—which was nearly everything—and pulled up the rug. The furniture dated back to the 1930s and was in the shipboard art-deco style, but that was not my mother's style, and it had to go. The ground floor of the house had remnants of rug where the carpet nails held it in place, and there was no furniture, so in this place too we camped out on the top floor. The only souvenir from this house that I have to this day is a gray granny-square afghan.

While my mother was busy throwing out furniture in his Fire Island home, Bert had been busy buying more and more objects for the brownstone. That was the drug at work. It made him possession-crazy. He bought more books, including an edition of the Encyclopaedia Britannica, glass bells, rooms of antique furniture from dealers and friends, and many more paintings. But nothing from Joseph Cornell; two sandboxes had arrived from Joseph on speculation, but Bert did not buy them. Because of my friendship, Bert had hoped those collages and boxes would be gifts.

His bizarre behavior began to escalate. On one working trip, Bert saw a blue car, and the purity of the blue startled him. The color gleamed like ground lapis lazuli, the ultramarine of medieval paintings. The magical blue covered the surface of a Corvette Stingray, but Bert was in Los Angeles and so was the car. There was a euphoric tidal wave flowing in Bert's veins; it made him want to sweep up that car—absolutely no other would do—and transport it home, three thousand miles away. This was not a car created on an assembly line; this was a vehicle with mystical properties. Bert had the car flown home. When I heard the story, I visualized the Corvette's nose covered in hundreds of canceled airmail stamps. The postage was two thousand dollars.

One of Bert's secretaries told me about this escapade. She could barely believe it herself. The car could have been bought at any location in America.

Reality and the family were slipping away. The car had only two seats; there was no place for the children in it. Obviously, it was bought for another woman—not me—to sit in.

CHAPTER FOURTEEN

*There is health in these concoctions and they are safe. No
need to worry.*

—DR. ROBERT FREYMAN,
AKA DR. FEELGOOD-C

I was shocked to see Bert roll up his sleeve and expose multiple
bruises on his arm. Dr. Freyman prepared Bert's mixture and then
turned his square face to me. In a flirtatious manner he said, "You
have beautiful veins. They are so prominent. Would you like a shot?"
His words made me cringe. The man had secretly been inspecting me
and my anatomy.

It was spring 1969, and I was still rejecting divorce as an option to
solve the breakdown in my marriage. This was yet another of my
attempts to bring Bert back in the family: I went with him to Dr.
Freyman's office. Freyman had told Bert he wanted to meet me, but
I had my own agenda. I wanted to talk to him about what was going
on with Bert.

We arrived at around seven in the morning, and the waiting room
was already packed. However, Bert and I were ushered in ahead of
the others. The doctor had a pecking order and selected patients according to his favorites.

Robert Freyman spoke with a German accent and had white hair.
He smiled graciously and shook my hand. Next he told me that he
was an expert on hepatitis and gave me some mimeographed papers
to read.

I asked, "Are these shots necessary for Bert?"

Freyman, inspecting me closely, responded, "They are like another
cup of coffee."

This didn't make sense. All the people in the waiting room were
drinking coffee and anxiously waiting for their visit.

Then once again he glanced at my veins and asked if I'd like a shot. "No, thanks. What's in them?"

"B₁₂, B complex, and other vitamins. Are you anemic? This would help you enormously." Dr. Freyman took my skinny wrist, turned it over, and looked at the inside of my arm with fetishistic delight. "Let me give you one."

I wanted to reject his advance on my arm but thought maybe I should know exactly what was happening to Bert and experience it. Reluctantly I agreed.

"Sit down and take off your shoes while I get your medication ready."

First, Dr. Feelgood-C gave Bert his shot. Some happy change registered on Bert's face—a look of satisfaction and assent. He had climbed a mountain and was on its peak.

I watched as Freyman filled a syringe for me with bright-colored liquids from various vials. Maybe this wasn't such a good idea after all. But before I could say anything, Dr. Freyman turned my left palm upward and tied a rubber tourniquet on my upper arm. Just after unsheathing the needle, Freyman positioned my feet on his crotch. I wanted to squirm free but was afraid of getting hurt. The doctor hovered briefly over my arm to find his entry position, then quickly he inserted the needle and looked at me for a reaction as he slowly emptied the contents of the syringe into my vein.

The vitamin mixture gave my blood a warm rush, almost orgasmic. I had just received a drug. My body felt ready to dance a full-length ballet or two. Then the soles of my feet felt some activity in Freyman's crotch area. The doctor smiled. He was thoroughly enjoying this salacious delivery of medicine. I had to believe that the good doctor acted out this little ritual with every female patient.

Bert, usually a very jealous man, had not uttered a word about Freyman's behavior and his symbolic sexual assault. Bert was clearly in his thrall, too desperately needy of the sick concoctions. His judgment was altered.

As we left the office, Freyman said, "Now remember. If any of your ballet friends have hepatitis, send them over immediately. I can cure them."

The man was not a humanitarian. He wanted more patients, and if they had the beautiful bodies of dancers, so much the better. I was skeptical, but I should have been horrified. It was not widely known then exactly what was in his mixtures.

I never went back, and I told Bert it was time to stop this madness.

rt Stern

La Sonnambula

with Erik Bruhn

Martha Swope © Time Inc

top, *Symphony in C* with Nolan T'Sani;
bottom left, *Diamonds* with Peter Martins;
bottom right, *Brahms-Schoenberg Quartet* with Conrad Ludlow

Swan Lake
with Nicholas Magallanes

top, *Jeux*

with Edward Villella;
bottom, *The Concert*

Martha Swope © Time

Dumbarton Oaks

A part of him knew it must end, so he went on abstaining during weekends, spending his time sleeping and eating. His appetite returned when he was abstaining, but when he wasn't sleeping and eating, he was peevish, snappy, irritable, and exhausted. He had moderate temper tantrums over very simple things, or sat in a stupor, smiling. He went through withdrawal during his time reserved for the children.

I knew the marriage was over as far as intimacy, warmth, or caring were concerned, but rather than confront the reality, I turned my energies to dance.

The heated pool was surrounded by giant delphiniums in sky colors, feathery astilbe, and beguiling begonias. I was sitting on a step at the shallow end when Mr. B. described his idea for a new ballet with music by Gershwin, in which I was to have the starring role. The step I was sitting on was indeed a "Stairway to Paradise." My heart did a loop the loop and so did my leg, with an over-the-rainbow extension to the sky. Mr. B. laughed. We were at the home of Mrs. Odgen Phipps, who had thrown a party for the entire company the final night of the summer 1969 Saratoga season.

I was jubilant. Things were changing. The spring 1969 season had been exciting but with one major disappointment. The strength and elasticity I had lost during my third pregnancy had returned, and I had danced in Jerry Robbins's new masterpiece, *Dances at a Gathering.* Robbins had returned to the company after an absence of ten years on Broadway. Originally, *Dances* was to be a pas de deux with Patty McBride and Eddie Villella, but when Mr. B. saw a rehearsal, he recommended that Jerry expand it. The choreography was exquisite, but the main female part seemed to be Patty's, and I was discontented with my sections. I was not alone. Jerry wanted all of the principal dancers present at rehearsal in case he had an idea. In the final version, Violette, for example, was there to perform only a short dance of about three minutes. The principals all preferred Mr. B.'s style of working. There was very little sitting around with Mr. B. He called whom he needed and worked with them during an allotted time. Jerry wanted everyone present in case he decided to do a dance for ten or six or five. He was used to working on musicals and also with his experimental group.

I was no longer a teenager. I had three children, and my time was valuable to me. And I had another, more alluring possibility. Mr. B.

had announced plans to bring *The Seven Deadly Sins* back into repertory for the spring season, and I was to do my original role as Anna II. I had not been forgotten. This unique piece of dance-acting and contorted movement would be mine again. This time I felt we could modify the costume to hide my stretch marks. My alter ego and vocal half was again to be Lotte Lenya. When I heard this, I jumped for joy and sang some of the lines from the opening section and then added some stray stanzas from Lust, Gluttony, and Sloth.

I had decided I had enough work with the regular repertory and my starring role in *The Seven Deadly Sins,* so I bowed out of *Dances with Robbins.* I quit by telegram. I envisioned someone in a Philip Morris costume with shiny buttons and a pillbox hat delivering the telegram to Jerry in the main rehearsal hall. It said, "I love what you're doing, but I think I'd rather sit in the audience than appear in your work as a secondary player. Much love as always."

However, Lotte Lenya was unable to take the singing role in *The Seven Deadly Sins,* and other performers, such as Barbra Streisand, whom Mr. B. wanted were not available to take the part. Thus I was disappointed to find myself suddenly with only the regular repertory, except for a fun little piece by John Clifford, *Prelude, Fugue, and Riffs,* until Jerry convinced me to rejoin the cast of *Dances at a Gathering.* I had met him in the hall. Staring into my eyes, he had said, "I know you're disappointed about *The Seven Deadly Sins.* But I want you back in *Dances.* Let's work together again." He was honest, and I felt he had reassessed me as a dancer. I said yes and was very happy about returning.

Despite Mr. B.'s plans to revive *The Seven Deadly Sins* for me, Suzanne had still been the center of his universe—offstage as well as on—in the spring of 1969. Once the season was underway, he had been formulating plans for his future. He was taking Suzanne out to dinner almost every night, and then he flew to Mexico for a divorce. Even though it was possible that Mr. B. and Tanaquil would have split up if she hadn't gotten polio, as a result of Tanny's illness his life had not continued in the same pattern of his wives breaking with him after seven years. It was unthinkable to me that he would ever leave her. Now, when he actually did divorce, I still thought it was unthinkable.

Rumors flew: Suzanne and Mr. B. were going to marry. As I had observed as a teenager, he married his dancing girls when they were between the ages of fifteen and twenty-three. In 1969, Suzanne was twenty-three and Mr. B was sixty-five. It was time.

But the unexpected happened. Mr. B. had included a third person in his dinners with Suzanne, Paul Mejia, whose dancing and choreographic abilities interested him. Balanchine had obtained a divorce, but Suzanne married Paul. This happened in the middle of the spring season, just before a gala. Mr. B. took away Paul's roles on the evening of the gala, and Suzanne issued an ultimatum: if Paul wasn't given his roles back, she would leave. It didn't work, so Paul and Suzanne left the New York City Ballet that night.

Mr. B. always said that his wives left him, which is true. I think that happened when their focus shifted and they wanted a different kind of married life and perhaps children. Tanaquil was a professional at fifteen who married Mr. B. at twenty-three. I often wondered if she had ever dated and how she felt about Mr. B.'s abandoning her. But Mr. B. was abandoned also. He was divorced, but Suzanne was unavailable.

The company had a brief summer tour scheduled in Monte Carlo, and without Suzanne many of us quickly had to assume her parts. Mr. B. began to notice his other dancers once again.

During a late-evening supper party at the palace that Princess Grace held for the company's principals after one evening's outdoor performance, I saw Mr. Balanchine walking toward me. I thought he was going to say something about the performance. As the evening's sea fog had rolled in, I had taken a tumble on the wet, slippery outdoor stage. I had stayed near the back where it was drier and therefore safer, but the choreography bid me to come forward. My fall was perfect for a Chaplinesque comedy, but out of place for the darkly romantic sustained adagio section of *Symphony in C*. I often enjoy being a clown, but not in *Symphony in C*.

I waited.

However, what Mr. B. said was, "Allegra, please be dignified tonight."

I looked down, wondering if Mr. B. had noticed that my dress was a nightgown: as usual, I had had trouble finding a nice little schmatta. In its favor, it had a beautiful impressionistic mix of pale colors and subtle tones. The other principals assembled at the Hôtel de Paris and looked handsome, Patty McBride outstandingly beautiful in a white creation.

"Okay, Mr. B. Don't worry." He knew that sometimes I had irresistible urges that might be out of place in a palace.

At dinner the food suddenly appeared in front of us held by servants with gray gloves. However, Princess Grace, who wore a long patchwork quilt skirt and a blouse, had not overdressed for this occasion. When I went to the bathroom, a guard accompanied me almost all the way in. I guess they were afraid of souvenir hunters. My daddy would have carried something off, preferably some sheets and pillow-cases for a little nine-year-old to take to boarding school, but I be-haved myself and returned with the company to complete the summer season with this Saratoga run.

At the pool on that final night I was wearing a leotard that may have been slightly transparent when wet, and I often wonder if I wasn't trying to remind Mr. B.—in the abstract—about my body, the raw material of many of his successful creations. Perhaps I was trying to remind him that it was my dancing and what I could do with my body—not my behavior in a palace—that he should care about.

Now, surrounded by the fragrant flowers of a garden at night, I learned that my old position with Mr. B. was within reach. The Gershwin ballet was mine, and I had just learned from one of his assistants that *The Seven Deadly Sins* was scheduled again. I would have two starring roles in the new season.

I was about to be sent back up into ballerina space.

One by one, I counted the stitches: one hundred and two. This kind of operation was not yet sophisticated. For the second time, cosmetic surgery would have a negative effect on my dance career.

While the company was laid off for August, I had decided that it would be the perfect time to make a little improvement on my stomach. Then I would be physically free to appear in the scanty panties of Pride and the padded bust of Lust and be avaricious without shame in *The Seven Deadly Sins*. I went to the hospital before my birthday and came out with a fourteen-inch curved scar. I lost a lot of weight and had an inkling that the sewing job might mean a long recupera-tion, because I was a slow healer. Furthermore, the doctor had cut a little too deeply on my right side, and the top of that thigh muscle was numb and tingling. My stomach was improved if not perfect, but I was not ready for class at the end of two weeks.

Meanwhile, things had not improved at home, where I had left my mother in charge. I had been away most of the summer, and when I arrived back in Fire Island for August it was obvious that Bert's drug use was escalating. He brought a masseur to our house on Fire Island weekends, saying that the massage eased him out of the shots. But Bert was introduced to more "doctors" and a "dentist" who sent over syringes of amphetamines, and Bert began to increase his usage. He'd start the day at Dr. Freyman's and then supplement that with drugs delivered to his office and self-administered. I knew Bert was heading toward a point of no return, and I was helpless to prevent it.

One incident soon after my surgery was particularly disturbing. We were on the beach at Fire Island, and the two younger children were with us playing in the sand. Bert began giving me instructions about how to stay warm in a rough, icy sea. "Walk into the water with your palms up. The rays of the sun will enter your body through your hands, and you won't be cold."

I sat back down on a towel. "Bert, I've changed my mind about swimming. It's only been nine days since the operation. I'm not up to a dip in the ocean yet." I had just returned from the water's edge after testing it with my toes and announced that the water was too cold and the waves too large.

"Allegra." Bert's voice displayed irritation. "You have to do it. I'll show you how." His eyes blazed like a fanatic's, and he jumped up. "The sun's heat goes directly into your palms." He assumed the described position. "If you don't go in the water, I'm leaving the beach and the island immediately." Bert looked to Bret and Susannah and then to me.

Susannah cried out, "Oh, Daddy, you just got here."

"Don't go," said Bret, getting up and taking his father's hand. "Stay here."

"Bert, don't go. The water is cold and rough." I looked down at my ninety-eight-pound body in a black bathing suit. I hadn't been this thin in a long time. "What if a wave knocks me down?"

Bert started to shout, "You must do what I tell you to do." When Bert unhinged Bret's hand from his, Bret started to cry.

"Bert, calm down. You're upsetting the children." I stood up, speaking softly. I didn't want a scene on the beach. Where had Bert's anger come from? It had flared up so quickly.

"Like this, Allegra." Again Bert turned his palms up as if he were carrying a platter. "Go in the water or I'm leaving," he screamed at me.

Susannah and Bret were both crying now.

"Bert, I'll do it tomorrow." I tentatively touched his upper arm in a conciliatory promise.

But he jerked his arm away from me and picked up his towel. "I'm leaving."

I tried to calm the little ones down. "Your daddy is very upset today. He's going back to the house to shower and then he'll feel better. Shall we take a little walk? Let's build a sand castle."

"No, I don't want to." Susannah looked at me with her round, wet, blue eyes.

"I want my daddy." Bret started to wipe his tears.

"Don't rub your eyes, sweetheart, you'll get sand in them. I have a Kleenex." I reached in my beach bag.

Bert was deranged by the shots and absorbed in cultish fads. This was a new problem. To argue with him would not help: his point of view had nothing to do with reason. I felt powerless and wanted to cry myself, but instead I tried to distract Bret, two, and Susannah, five.

When Bret was about seventeen months old, he had watched us stringing beads. It was the 1960s. He began pointing to the needle and beads—he wanted to do it too. I remembered my dreams of imaginary needles entering my body. Reluctantly I gave him the needle. Even though he was a baby, he had the skill to do it. He was dexterous. While other babies were trying to put huge round blocks in square holes, he could put a needle through the tiny hole in a bead. But he couldn't reach his father. No one could.

Depressed, recovering from surgery, unable to dance, and watching Bert disintegrate, I called up my old friend Joseph Cornell, and we had a long telephone conversation. Even though we'd been corresponding for many years, for the first time I was struck by some of the sad aspects of his unconventional life: his aloneness, his life with his mother and brother before they died, and some of his beliefs based on Christian Science that I felt kept him outside of usual human relationships as they had me.

I decided to visit him. He requested a book on erotic art, so I went into a bookstore and said, "A book on erotic art, please, any one will do." I also brought along a mocha cake.

That afternoon we sat in his garden while he ate most of the cake. He later sent me a spoon, a plate, and a napkin. There was always this kind of exchange of gesture between us, rather like a Japanese tea ceremony or, in this case, a cake ceremony. I also gave him Joseph Conrad's short story "The Secret Sharer." I once sent him the *Life* book on birds because I felt he would like to read about these creatures built for "the world of air" with their delicate bones and scientific design. I still have a little book, *Secrets of Flowers,* that he gave me as a remembrance of this visit. It's a book on Victorian meanings of flowers. Underlined with tiny red dots in the book are "iris—message," "rose—grace," "cactus—endurance," "zinnia—thoughts of absent friends," "orchid—beauty, magnificence, love, refinement." He stapled my name between "violet—faithfulness" and "woodbine—fraternal love." There was also a piece of torn white paper on a page with forget-me-nots.

I wish there was a rose named after Joseph. It would be fragile in appearance but exquisite and deceptively strong—very resistant to the elements, very fragrant, almost always in bloom, and of an indescribable color somewhere between coral and tawny. Perhaps it would be a descendant of Spring Morning and Peace or Garden Party as the father and Souvenir de Malmaison as the mother. It would be a chance seedling from a great French hybridizer. I read rose catalogs and constructed dream gardens. In this imaginary landscape there would also be an iris named Allegra.

In his real backyard that day, I remember making and wearing a tent-shaped newspaper hat because the sun was so bright. We lost ourselves talking about music, nature, and shells. I have a passion for shells; they possess the dynamic spiral, and I collected them with my brother Gary.

Another thing Joseph and I did that day was look at his boxes on a tour of the house. It was a complete vacation from reality, and I felt I was in a timeless trance. Joseph adored the Romantic ballerinas, and the funny thing was that I didn't dance their parts. I could dance ethereally, but I always had more than a hint of the true world in my dancing. Even though he loved the ballet, it had become impossible for him to walk into the State Theater. He had become too claustrophobic.

I returned from the visit happy. I had experienced what usually transpires between human beings—communication and rapport, something I had never had with Bert. The connection I felt with Joseph was spiritual, an empathy. For some reason, he was very apart, and I believe all he wanted from me was just what we had that day: communion with another person. That afternoon, he told me he wanted to be my double. And I wanted to be anyone but myself.

In September, I received a startling invitation from Bert. He was going to St. Tropez to shoot a Coca-Cola commercial and wanted me to come. A maiden carrying a Coke and singing "Those Were the Days, My Friend" would be in the foreground, and the Mediterranean would be in the background. This surprised me because I'd seen a photograph of Bert with his girlfriend at Colombe d'Or, a famous restaurant in Provence. He took his girlfriends, not me, to Europe. When I had confronted him about the photo, I commented on the beauty of the terrace gardens there. Was this invitation perhaps a peace offering? Was Bert finally trying to go off the shots and hoping I could save him? The clients were going with him on this shoot, and perhaps he wanted a certain look of respectability. His motives were unclear. Maybe he was just in between girlfriends.

I thought a bit before deciding. I had no illusions that the trip was going to save a hopeless marriage, but I was despondent because of my slow recovery from the surgery and was not yet able to take class. Furthermore, I had loved Monte Carlo. The sea there beckoned to me. In fact, en route to the airport to leave with the company, realizing that we had an extra fifteen minutes and that the water was sparkling with reflective highlights, I had decided on one last dip. I had the taxi pull over to the side of the road, took off my shoes and hat, and jumped in with my dress on. Later, I climbed on the plane salty. Now I hoped that a return to this beautiful part of the world might revive me.

I decided not to worry about Bert's motives. His feelings about me were as mysterious to him as they were to me. His withdrawals from me and the family were always followed by a return.

In Europe, Bert was gone most of the time. I thought his work on the commercial was going well, and I wondered how he was managing without his shots. But on the second day while rummaging in the little fridge in our room, I saw many filled syringes hidden behind a fruit platter. Bert said they were there just in case, but their number decreased.

I focused exclusively on my physical recovery, and at the pool in our hotel I made a wonderful discovery. The previous June, one of my friends in the company had bought newly styled water wings, circles of air enclosed in plastic. These bracelets of buoyancy were for children to wear before they learned to swim. Trista at eight and Susannah at five already knew how to swim, but the water wings intrigued me. I was attracted to them at the time but didn't buy them. With my return to the Côte d'Azur, I bought four pairs. Back at the hotel, I blew them all up, strung them on my bathrobe belt, and went to the pool for a dip. After a few laps, I thought, *These wings are for the arms so I'll put them on my ankles.* Standing in the water with two bracelets on each ankle, four in all, my legs went up in a split. Luckily I was holding on to the pool rim.

The concept flashed into my head: I had created an antigravitational condition. Upward movement was easy, but down was difficult, the exact opposite of land exercise. The water, which was elastic, enabled me to move through it or stay on the surface. I could also use wings on one leg at a time and do most of the steps in a ballet barre or be off balance if I chose. I could stretch and strengthen my body. If I put them on arms and legs, I could do an upside-down split and keep moving my legs until I did the equivalent of a water walkover. There were so many possibilities that I was exhilarated. The water had become my choreographer. The hotel guests were laughing at me, but I knew I had found a way to get back in shape. The next day, I went back to the store and bought more wings. "I have a dozen children," I explained to the storekeeper, "*beaucoup de bébés.*" Eight years later, in 1976, St. Martin's Press would publish my *Water Beauty Book* detailing these exercises.

When we returned to New York, I called Dr. Freyman and told him, "Bert is addicted. He gets his first shot from you but then has other doctors send filled syringes over. Even the dentist is sending them."

Freyman said, "Oh, that crazy guy," but offered no solution.

Dr. Freyman's sham respectability disgusted me. At this point, I called the doctor's wife at home—we had met once—and asked her if she knew what was going on. I also told her a rumor I'd heard about her husband and a female patient. She reported this to her husband immediately, and Dr. Freyman called and threatened me with violence to my body, the only thing I had.

Two years later, Freyman would find a way to discourage Bert from ever coming back to him. He gave him a bad shot. He stabbed him repeatedly near the vein with the needle but always missed.

In any case, my phone calls to "Feelgood" were immaterial. Bert had other sources. Massages were very important to Bert as an antidote to the speed. On his next trip to Europe, Bert took the masseur—not me.

Even though my water-wing exercises did help me tremendously, by the middle of September I was still not ready to take class, let alone rehearse. My recovery always was slow. I was reticent about telling anyone that the operation had been a tummy tuck. Since the shape of the scar was like a half-moon, I decided to say that I had fallen on an anchor and had to be airlifted from the Fire Island bay in a helicopter. When Mr. B. was ready to create the new Gershwin ballet, ultimately to be called *Who Cares?*, I was able to put him off for a while, but then, exasperated with me, he called Patty McBride in for the leading role opposite Jacques d'Amboise.

As a result of the first operation, I had lost my face and never really wanted to show it again. As a seventeen-year-old, I had withdrawn at the very moment my career was beginning to flower, with a damaged soul. Now, because I had temporarily lost the use of my body—again because of cosmetic surgery—I sacrificed an important moment in my mature career. What I did not yet know was that my inability to dance at that time would cause me to lose my unique position in the company forever. Trying to fix my body, I had lost it and had taken an irreparable backward step.

Ironically, I was soon to learn that the surgery was not my only physical problem. In early 1970, I was still struggling with my body. My muscles weren't responding to exercise. I was doing enough work, so it was obviously a medical problem. I needed to see a doctor. My metabolism had probably changed in my late teens, but I had never investigated a medical solution because of my Christian Science training. I had been brainwashed. Although I immediately consulted doctors for my children over the years, the basic message—don't turn to doctors—had stayed with me.

A friend sent me to her physician who prescribed medication for an underactive thyroid. Almost immediately, the medication released my muscles. Within a month, I suddenly had a great arabesque, one I did not have during the entire period of the 1960s. It went up a foot and a half. For ten years, my body had been against me, because I had needed thyroid supplements. When I saw photographs of myself from the past with bunchy thigh muscles that I now no longer had, I realized I'd been at a disadvantage throughout much of my young career.

With my new muscles, I was about to embark on what many reviewers described as my best decade of dancing. But my physical renaissance came too late. Even as I was about to reach my apex as a dancer, I lost the intuitive gifts of my choreographer.

I would dance in the general repertory for another thirteen years, but Mr. B. would never again—as he had for a decade and a half—design an entire ballet for my special abilities, a ballet uniquely created for the peculiarities of my body and psyche, one that used my psychological raw material. For fifteen years my personal emblems had been woven into dances created just for me.

I had lost the Atlantic Ocean.

From Center Stage to Scarsdale

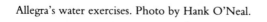

Allegra's water exercises. Photo by Hank O'Neal.

CHAPTER FIFTEEN

The princesses had made them drink something of a philtre, which froze the heart and left nothing but the love of dancing.

—*"The Twelve Dancing Princesses,"*

The Red Fairy Book

One night in early 1971, Bert left Trista, who was then ten, alone at an evening's performance of *Follies*. I thought he was taking her out to dinner, but he called from the lobby during intermission to say he had to leave, because the musical's poster had caught his attention and disturbed him. It contained a woman's face with a deep crack, a sculptured, broken face reminiscent of an ancient ruin, and it had frightened him. Bert saw a portent of danger for himself in the image and also in the spelling of the word *Follies*. The double *l* was "ominous," and he was compelled to leave the theater. Had he never noticed my name had a double *l* in it too? He said he would give his ticket stub to an usher, and I was to hop into a cab immediately and join my child.

Luckily I was home in the apartment with Susannah, Bret, and a housekeeper, so I was free to go. I rushed over to the theater where I found Trista sitting in her seat looking very brave. I kissed her, and she took my hand, smiled, and pressed it. The second act had started, so we did not speak. I would not let this happen again. I had to be ready to take my children away from Bert. It was time for me to learn to drive.

I called a driving school and began lessons the next week. Thirty-three and one-third years old was not too late. Was I not Harry Cohen's daughter?

Over the next two months, Bert's behavior took on a new cast. He was becoming irrational. One afternoon he walked into the apartment looking deeply upset and pointed to a newspaper headline.

There was some development in South America, which meant that I couldn't dance that evening. Bert had come to believe that he had psychic powers and could foretell the future by interpreting messages. He told me that if I danced, "there would be terrible repercussions for the whole family." One manifestation of his growing paranoia had been his habit of bullfighting with shadows. Like a toreador, he'd edge away from them and let them slip past him. But now he was seeing dangerous penumbras, shadows from the future—from another hemisphere—that threatened his family, not just him.

I listened calmly to what he said, wondering how I should handle this. I promised nothing and controlled my anger. He couldn't read me, but he was suspicious, so he stayed, watching me closely. After an hour, I hoped I could quietly leave, but he was guarding the entrance. I needed to get to the theater and prepare for the performance. I strolled in the direction of the door and then started to run. This is what Bert was waiting for. "I like to play football, too, Allegra." He tackled me and pinned me to the floor.

The children were crying, and the housekeeper was incredulous. She kept saying, "Mr. Stern? Don't do this!" I didn't want this scene to take place in front of the children, but Bert was out of control. In the moments when he relinquished his grip, I tried to escape, but he was too strong. After ten minutes of wrestling on the floor—one moment up, one moment down—Bert changed his hold, and I was able to stand up and squirm toward the exit. Then Bert leaped forward and caught my wrists in a bruising clench. I started to cry.

When I gave up, Bert sat down and watched my tears flow. At this point I probably could have made my escape, but I was too upset. What if Bert came to the theater and created an incident galloping around backstage, disrupting the crew and other dancers, or popping up in the orchestra pit, knocking over the sheet music and adding an extra drumbeat to the "Wedding March" that would be played that night during *A Midsummer Night's Dream*?

I gave up dancing that evening. I called the theater and spoke to the first person available, describing exactly what had happened. The company manager understood my peculiar situation and said, "Allegra, I'll explain it all to Mr. B. and tell him it was not your fault."

Now that Bert was so volatile, I knew I could no longer protect my children or myself. Since we had to get away from him, I started a secret account. Nothing had been in my name, and, because of the shots, Bert had now lost his business, the schoolhouse, the home on Fire Island, the condominium, and his credibility. No one would hire him. I would be head of the household, sole supporter of three children, active ballerina, and single parent.

It was late June 1971, near Susannah's birthday, when I greeted my father at the airport. At my request, Harry had come across the country to help me drive the children to Saratoga Springs for the summer. Taking the children with me was a natural opportunity for our separation from Bert.

I didn't say anything to Bert, but when he saw me packing, he was suspicious. I packed only clothes, but his animal instincts were on the alert, and he became overly interested in exactly what was leaving the apartment. He seemed to understand that our leaving might be a final break.

When I finally walked in with my father, the original and the copy were face-to-face. Bert became more wary. He wondered why my father was in New York City. To avoid an incident, I left one day earlier than expected, and we moved into a Holiday Inn—the three children, Daddy, and me all in one room. At first, the children were charmed with Harry's Buffalo Bill impersonation, his fringe of beard and absence of mustache, the look of a folk hero from the West arriving to rescue the kiddies. One of Daddy's favorite songs was "McKinley Calls for Volunteers." But in bed that night, none of us could sleep. Was a chain saw gang cutting down a forest at the Holiday Inn? Or was it merely my daddy's ten-decibel snoring? The next day, weary, we headed out of the city in a rented car.

I had obtained my first driver's license just a month before. Although I did not become a stunt driver like my father, I often drove through empty expanses with my left leg extended straight up and out the driver's window or with one foot on the ceiling. However, I struggled with my inexperience in highway driving when we encountered a monumental rainstorm. I drove a little farther, but finally Daddy took the wheel, and once it was in his hands he wouldn't relinquish it again. A Texas fanatic had taken over. Hunched forward, eyes alert, here was the stunt driver from my youth. We were still the fastest car on the road, but visibility did not exist. Nervously I requested that we pull over and wait for a lull in the storm.

Daddy glanced at the side of the road and saw a symbol. "What are those C-shapes?"

"Daddy, those are emergency telephones."

"Let's keep going."

I closed my eyes and hoped his vision and reflexes were all right.

Four hours later we arrived in Saratoga and settled into a rented house over the July Fourth weekend. Harry returned to Los Angeles a few days later. As usual, he was restless and eager to move on, and we were now safe. As far as I knew, Bert did not know our whereabouts.

One night I woke up suddenly. Someone was in my room. If the children awakened and wanted me, they usually called out. A large dark shape was moving across the room from shadow to shadow. I screamed. It was Bert.

As he dashed over and grabbed my wrists, Hilda, the housekeeper, and the children rushed into the room. Everyone was wide awake.

I sat up, pulling against his grip. "How did you get up here?" I knew he'd lost the blue Stingray and his driver's license. The car had been repossessed.

"A friend lent me a car."

"Bert, you're hurting me. Let go." I calmed myself and tried to deflate the situation by distracting him. "Are you hungry?" I could see that he hadn't shaved or eaten in a while. He was very thin.

"Yes." He let go of my wrists.

"Hilda and I will make you some food. Let's go down to the kitchen."

Somehow I lured him downstairs, fed him, and got him out of the house. I'm not sure what he did for the rest of the night. I couldn't sleep, so I moved into the children's room. Bert's entrance was a mystery. The house had been locked tightly. For a decade after that I didn't want anyone, even the children, walking in my room without announcing themselves.

Back in New York, Mother and I were in the kitchen of the East Side apartment packing up dishes when Bert walked in. I was attempting to move the most important functional furniture and belongings to my new secret residence without running into him.

With one look, he knew what the cartons meant. "Where are the children?"

"They're with friends, and they're fine." I moved to the entrance of the kitchen.

Bert looked at the packing boxes and glasses on the kitchen counter and, with a furious sweep of his arms, knocked everything off. There was a huge clatter of smashed crockery and broken glass.

Toward the end of our Saratoga stay, I had come to the city on a free day and located a new place for the children and me to live that fall—a residency hotel called the Bancroft on West Seventy-second Street. The little place was much smaller than the top floors of the brownstone the children and I had occupied for years. In our new home, I would sleep in the living room, Trista and Susannah in one bedroom, and Bret and the housekeeper in the other.

During the month of August, before we moved in, I had arranged for the girls to attend camp, but when I had tried to drive them there, I got lost, and we ended up at a bowling alley. So the children and I had been camping out in various friends' apartments in the city until now, when the Bancroft apartment was ready. We had been able to avoid Bert until today.

I screamed, "Stop it! The children have to eat on these dishes." I had tried to think of something logical and simple that might snap him out of his madness.

Bert continued to kick and shove at the crates and stacks of dishes. Then he formulated a new plan. With a quick burst of energy, he ran out the front door to the elevator, to confront the moving men, I supposed. I had hired some friends of friends and unemployed actors, because they were cheap.

My mother had stood transfixed throughout Bert's tantrum. When he was gone, she surveyed the depressing destruction of our efforts.

"Mom, I want to finish soon and leave quickly. Don't bother to clean up."

Mother put down the shards of a plate she had picked up and said apologetically, "I guess I never realized what you were going through with the man all these years." She shook her head. "Allegra, I hope you can salvage the rest of your life."

The remark stabbed me like a knife. I expected to live a long time. She was telling me that it was almost inevitable that, from this moment forward, my life would slowly disintegrate. I was thirty-four years old.

I never forgot my mother's words. She seemed to have made her own decision about my life: she hoped it could be saved, but she doubted it. I rejected her statement but also took it in, and a part of me gave up for a long time to come. After leaving Bert, I never tried to save money and buy the children and myself a house.

The movers told me that Bert had argued with them about their right to move his furniture and then had walked away. I hoped it was the last we'd see of him. Everyone on my team had instructions not to tell Bert our destination, and they left early before he could return. Then I sent my mother to pick up Bret and Susannah, and I went for Trista.

But Bert had gotten to her school first. He was walking down the street holding her hand. As I approached, he said, "Don't take my child away from me," then added, addressing Trista, "Don't you want to stay with me?"

Trista started to cry.

"Look what you've done to your daughter," I told him. I took Trista's other hand and knelt on the sidewalk. "Don't cry, darling. You can see your daddy when he's better and off the drugs." I looked him steadily in the eyes. "Bert, stop confusing her and let go of her hand. She's not choosing sides. She'll see you when you're well."

I feared a tug-of-war might ensue and tried to switch from emotion to logic in my appeal to him. Trista was standing between us in a sidewalk scene that was attracting attention. From crying, Trista started to sob, and somehow that reached Bert. Or maybe he had glimpsed what was involved in keeping a child. Children require care. When he finally gave up her hand, I hailed a taxi before he could have second thoughts, and we left.

By that evening, we had the apartment at the Bancroft assembled. There were beds and sheets but no chests of drawers for anyone. With a few calls, I located a cast-off bureau and we all crashed into sleep.

In the morning, as I emerged from confusing dreams, I knew I was sick. It was mononucleosis. I wouldn't be able to return to work until I was better. I'd put away nothing, and Bert had lost everything. My salary was five hundred dollars a week when working, one-half that for rehearsals and nothing for the layoffs, about nineteen thousand dollars a year. This was not enough for the children's schools, the housekeeper, rent, and expenses.

A friend sent over Natalia Makarova to buy some of my old furniture, but she didn't want any of it. She had recently defected, and was almost my age, but her career was about to ascend while I had only "salvage work" ahead. I couldn't forget my mother's words when I saw myself surrounded by flotsam and jetsam. And the great Russian ballerina didn't want any of my jetsam.

As I spent two months recovering from mononucleosis, depression took over. It was the hopelessness, the feeling of waking up and realizing I had lost everything, of knowing that I hadn't demanded that Bert put something away for the children. What he'd gone through was so much.

Then a golden arrow came through the window. Jerry Robbins

located me at the Bancroft. His voice was sincere and caring. "How are you feeling, Allegra?"

"Better. I'm over the mono. But I'm so depressed, and I haven't danced in two months." As the purposelessness of my life had overwhelmed me, I started overeating. I hadn't yet learned how to manage my depression and my body's reactions to it. The movement of class, performing, and swimming—my daily routine of action—had been the key to fighting off depression. I had become very, very thin from the mono, but, as I began to recover, I started systematically building my weight up again. Eating replaced thinking. Sweets were an effective medicine for forgetting and deflecting reality. I ate raspberries, whipped cream, ice cream, and as Lotte Lenya once sang to me, those tiny biscuits filled with honey. Exercise never started. I was embarrassed about my weight, so I didn't go to class. I needed to pick up the pieces of my life and my dance technique, but I had become immobilized.

Jerry's voice was kind. "I'm sorry. Come back and let's work." He had moved past any problems of previous years and talked of what was important to both of us—work.

I promised to start the next morning. Eddie Villella also called and invited me to do a concert with him.

I hadn't been forgotten.

Bert hadn't forgotten me either. Although he hadn't found us yet at our new apartment, he did find me. Early one morning after the children left for school, I headed for the State Theater only to find Bert pursuing me on a bicycle. I was able to flag a taxi, outdistance him, jump out at Sixty-second and Columbus, and run down the stairs. The sacred, familiar stage door was right there. As always, one guard and one telephone operator were behind the barrier. Because a full class might be too taxing and I didn't want to show anyone how out of shape I was, I had decided to practice by myself for a few days. It was early, and I would be alone in the building. I explained to the guard and switchboard operator that I was being followed by my ex-husband. They said I was not to worry; they were at their posts.

I was in the fifth-floor bathroom, stripped bare, rummaging in my practice bag for a leotard when the bathroom door swung wide open and the uniformed guard stepped in. "Have you seen your husband? He broke in and is running around backstage." He paused to look at me. "Oh, excuse me for barging in."

I had placed the leotard in front of me, but the bathroom mirrors were right behind me. At this moment, however, modesty was a secondary consideration. "Thanks for telling me. I'm not staying here."

How did Bert get past the guard? Trembling, I quickly dressed and cautiously retraced my steps to the stage door and fled home. I had to return to work, but I didn't come to the theater early again.

At first there was no response when I asked who was there, only more insistent knocking.

"Who is it?" I asked again.

Silence, and then finally a voice said, "It's Bert."

My heart sank. I had known he would appear one day, but I had hoped it was far off. Our reprieve was over.

In March of 1972, Bert had been hospitalized by his brother for a drug cure but escaped from Gracie Hospital with Dr. Freyman's help and moved into the only piece of property left, the brownstone. He had no jobs and was still taking daily amphetamine shots, not vitamins. Bert was now schizophrenic, but he was coherent enough to keep searching for us. The search was what kept him alive.

He had finally realized he could follow Trista's school bus on his bicycle. From this vantage point and perch, he could watch as each child left the bus, and that led him to the Bancroft.

"I'm hungry, Allegra, and I want to see the children."

I opened the door as much as the chain allowed. Bert was thin, unshaven, and had round, dark bags under his eyes—the amphetamine look. "Bert, please don't upset the children. If you want food, I know a place that will feed you and take care of you."

"I don't like hospitals."

I made him less than half a peanut-butter-and-jelly sandwich and passed it under the chain. I wanted Bert to stay hungry. Food was the lure I hoped would get him into treatment.

After a week of this, I convinced him to go to Metropolitan Hospital with me, where he was locked up on the thirteenth floor. I was able to talk him into this by promising to visit him and bring him presents.

On the first visiting day, at Bert's request, I brought him pineapple-pecan ice cream. I found him in a wheelchair drugged on Thorazine. In Gracie Hospital, Bert had had a private room, so he was upset with the dormitory arrangement in the locked ward here. I, too, was horrified. The look of this place was frightening. He was also unhappy with the drugs they were giving him.

At this point I went to the brownstone, wondering if there was anything left that I could sell. I also wanted to see how Bert had been living. It was the home of an out-of-control drug addict. Bert had painted the rooms black or red and put white crosses on many doors. His natural imagination made him a genius at being mad; drugs and creativity blended in a destructive force. There was evidence of small fires started and extinguished and candles put in holders at dangerous angles in front of broken mirrors. I felt deeply uneasy.

I was scheduled to leave the children with Hilda and tour with the company for two weeks in Munich. I finally decided I could safely leave with Bert in a locked ward in the hospital. I needed to fulfill my dance contract, now that I was in charge of supporting my family. Trista was twelve, Susannah, nine, and Bret, five.

I stood on the sidewalk in front of our brownstone waiting for the police. I was expecting either a squad car or men in blue. The dispatcher had told me to wait in front of the house. With key in hand standing near the front door, I placed myself in a blind spot so that I could not be seen by anyone looking out of the window.

A car pulled up and two men in casual dress got out. They looked at me and I looked at them. They were not in uniform. Tilting my head slightly to the side, I pointed at them and then at myself, silently asking, "Are you looking for me?" They acknowledged me with an almost imperceptible shift in their posture and walked over.

"Are you the policemen?"

"Yes."

"But you're not in uniform."

"No. It's better this way."

"I'm the one who called."

When I had arrived in Germany and called home, all was well. When I called the second time, Hilda told me Bert had escaped from the hospital and was standing outside the door begging for food again. The children didn't want to leave the apartment.

I had been stunned to hear Bert was on the loose, that even a locked ward couldn't contain him. But I was powerless to do anything until I returned. Upon my arrival home, I called Metropolitan Hospital and asked what had happened to Bert Stern. I was told he fled to freedom while being sent down to the dentist. "Do you want him back in the hospital?"

"Absolutely."

I turned, opened the front door, and led the policemen into the entrance hall, which now was covered with erratic streaks of black paint. I made a sharp right turn, and the three of us walked into the kitchen. It was empty. I went to the refrigerator, opened the door, and raised the cover of the butter compartment. The gun was gone.

I hadn't told anyone it was there. When I had been at the brownstone three weeks earlier, I had checked in the refrigerator for old food that should be thrown out. When I had lifted the little flap and opened the butter dish, I had found the pistol. My blood had raced. What if the children had found the gun and thought it was a toy? I had picked it up carefully and examined it. It looked dangerously real, but the nozzle seemed to be blocked. I didn't want to carry it around. Since Bert was in the hospital, I had put it back in the butter dish and thrown out the garbage, trembling the whole time.

Now I tried to calm myself by breathing as I had during natural childbirth, and I shut the refrigerator. I said nothing to the policemen about the missing gun. I felt that they were poised waiting for my directions. A sharp, acrid smell was in the air. Surveying the room I saw that a dance photo of myself in *Bugaku* had been damaged. Jagged burnt edges bordered my bending silhouette. A lighted candle, placed next to it, was stuck at a precarious angle in a bowl of sugar. It could easily topple. I blew it out.

My attention shifted. The man I had married twelve years earlier stepped into the room. He was smiling but staying very close to the door. When his focus changed to the two men, I spoke his name. He turned and ran. We could hear his feet running up the stairs. I wondered why the officers didn't give chase.

They seemed hesitant. Hadn't they been told what they might have to deal with? They inspected the other rooms on the ground floor and spoke quietly to each other. Then one of them said to me, "He's gone. When you find him, call us, and we'll come back."

"Please, you can't leave. He may still be in the house or on the roof." I decided to take charge. "One of you go to the roof and the other stay with me. If we all go up and he's hiding on another floor, he might slip down past us."

The officers agreed to help me. I was amazed. These trained policemen were following my lead. It wasn't a perfectly designed strategy, but it was something.

On the second floor the miniature dragnet split up. I went toward the front. In the library a mirror with a roughly painted yellow cross had been smashed to pieces. Another dance photograph, a group portrait including Balanchine, had also been scorched. There was no sign of Bert. On the third floor there was another symbolic sign of destruction: a silk scarf of mine had been ripped and cast on a pile of clothes dragged from open drawers.

As we reached the top floor we heard shouting and then a gunshot. I felt paralyzed with fear. Was Bert dead or had he shot the policeman? I looked at the other officer's face. It was frozen. His partner was on the roof with a crazy man. I should have told them about the gun. I was overwhelmed with guilt and remorse.

Both of us stared transfixed at the metal ladder leading up to the roof. Slowly the square roof hatch opened and Bert struggled down, his hands handcuffed in front of him. As the policeman climbed down after him, I understood how lucky we had been. Thank God no one had died.

Bert, however, didn't look particularly upset. He loved dangerous experiences—he saw them as exciting entertainment. At this very minute, he was starring in his own B movie as actor, stunt man, and scenic designer.

I broke the silence. "Can we take him back to the hospital?"

"Not now. This guy had a starter pistol that could have been converted into a real gun. He's under arrest."

It was not over. They told me I would have to come to the local precinct, the 19th, so that Bert could be booked.

I looked at the two men. They were so decent. "Thank you for not killing him."

Walking the six blocks to the precinct house, I wondered if I would ever be free of this disastrous marriage. When I had had Bert committed to the hospital, I had remembered again what my mother had said: "I hope you can salvage the rest of your life." Perhaps I couldn't. But I vowed never to help Bert again. It was too dangerous. It could involve innocent strangers, and the outcome was too unpredictable.

Bert was taken to the Tombs and eventually bailed out by a friend. Back at the Metropolitan Hospital, the new admitting psychiatrist gave him a test and found no reason to hospitalize him again. He said that Bert didn't need to be admitted. All charges were dropped. My interference had not done one bit of good. I went to the Bancroft, and Bert went back to the brownstone. Did I want to overeat after this? Yes.

With Bert loose, I decided that I could not make a return trip with the company to Russia, the land of my earlier triumph.

Bert was finally getting what he'd always wanted: he was keeping me from dancing. He had tried to make me choose him over ballet the first week we were married. Now at last he was succeeding.

Although Bert was now free, the brownstone would not be his home indefinitely. Within a month of this episode, Bert was going to lose his right to stay there. This was the last of the properties to go. I had heard stories of Bert's former employees carrying off valuable loot when the business collapsed. Disheartened, I called Joseph Cornell to tell him about the foreclosure, just to talk and pour out the news.

"Allegra, that's terrible." His voice reflected dismay. "I'd like to give you twenty thousand dollars or twice that amount to save the brownstone."

His generosity startled me. I hadn't called for financial help, just to talk. I thought for a moment. My mother had told me to try to salvage the rest of my life. Anything connected to me might be a hopeless endeavor; my future and the years ahead were going to spiral downward. And so I felt compelled to say no to him. I refused the money. There was no reason to fight. I'd just watch the inevitable losses in a passive stance.

Cornell had spent the second half of that summer with his sister on Long Island. He had been hospitalized in June and was recuperating. His letters from his sister's home described nature and music. A butterfly ballet arrived folded in an envelope, and he wrote of the blue color called cerulean. In another, he said, "Everybody is making money but Tchaikovsky." Near Christmas, I sent him a book on dolls. He was one of my first fans, and I treasured his friendship.

Early in the New Year I was shocked to receive a message that Joseph had died of a heart attack. In quiet sadness, I took out a note he had once sent to me and read it again:

> *Who shall inquire of the Season*
> *Or question the wind where it blows*
>
> *We blossom and ask no reason*
> *The Lord of the Garden knows.*

My gift to him came back unopened. A chapter had come to an end.

• • •

After one cramped year in the Hotel Bancroft, I found a spacious three-bedroom apartment in the Lincoln Towers complex just a few blocks from the State Theater.

On day of the move, I had many rehearsals and a performance. I drew a diagram of my new living room to show the placement of the furniture and gave the map to Hilda, my elderly housekeeper. She pointed to Bret. "Give it to him." Bret was five and not in school that day because he had a cold. He looked at my map and understood it immediately. Before I could tell him, he told me where everything went—couches, lamps, pictures, and chairs. It was out of my hands, and I went to work.

When I came home that night, everything was in place, a small miracle. It was like Hollywood—a painless transformation. The next morning, the children and I looked at the Hudson River from our balcony on the twenty-second floor. The light and view gave us all an expansive feeling. All the bedrooms had windows on the terrace facing south. This was a good move and one I engineered entirely alone, except for the help of a five-year-old.

I loved my new apartment and envisioned a forest primeval on the terrace. One of my first purchases was twenty huge pots and a half ton of dirt. Next, I ordered the roses, which would arrive by mail in late March. Deciding what to order had been difficult. I read about the parents of the Peace rose and the fragrance of Varigata di Bologna and Reine des Violettes. Each fragrance was rated and described. Some varieties had fruity scents, others spicy, some had an intense perfume and others a light one. The Sea Foam and the little Fairy rose had none at all but were easy to grow. The moss rose had a thorny look and the cabbage rose had hundreds of petals. I thought about the history and ancient age of this branch of flora. Billions of years ago a plant said to itself, "Today I will become a red rose." Yes, I loved my apartment.

But the rent was higher and the move was expensive; I was desperately trying to stay afloat financially. Extra money came in doing concerts with Eddie Villella, and a friend who knew how eager I was to obtain my own bookings brought Henley Haslam backstage one evening after a performance to help me. Henley had successfully run a huge dance school of five hundred pupils in Birmingham and could take rehearsal, be a wardrobe mistress, or do anything necessary to help run a small touring ballet company. We shared many views about what makes a great dance and dancer, and I loved to attend performances with her. We became friends, and she generously offered to help me with her expertise and connections. Together, we prepared a brochure with photos and sent out seventy or so folders. But very few concerts came in through them, so I was glad to receive more work from Eddie and a job offer from Jacques d'Amboise.

On a bitter cold day in the third week of March, as I was to leave town to do a concert in Santa Barbara with Jacques, the bare roots of my roses arrived. They had to be soaked in water for twenty-four hours, so I threw them into the bathtubs. My house-keeper flatly refused to do the planting for me, so Henley dug the holes, mounded the cones, spread the roots, covered them with more dirt, stomped on the soil to push out the air bubbles, and then carried buckets and buckets of water out to drench the roots. She spread a little mulch to keep the naked stems warm and then de-frosted her hands for two hours.

Meanwhile, in California for the concert with Jacques, I stayed with a college provost and his wife. They admired my dancing and gra-ciously opened their home to me. However, as a houseguest I was difficult. I was going through a sleepless stage and would wander around at night, eating, reading, and trekking through their home. One evening, in the middle of the night, I opened their fridge.

The apple pie looked good. I thought it might be interesting to combine it with lemon ice cream. *I wonder if they want this salmon for their dinner. Well, too late now.* In a jet-lagged, neurotic state I consumed most of my hosts' dinner for the next night. Then I started wandering in the garden looking at their camellias.

My friends liked my dancing but not my eating patterns.

I decided to move in with friends of friends who also lived in the area. They had a heated pool covered with tiny black tiles, and I hoped a dip at night would put me to sleep.

My original hosts looked relieved. If I left they would know what their food supply was at any given moment. Just before packing, I questioned them about three unusual trees I had seen in their garden. The fruit or nut on them was very hard and a lot were on the ground. It was something I had never seen before.

"Those are macadamia nut trees."

"How do you open them?"

"There's a special machine for it."

"Could you use a hammer?"

"I guess so."

"Would you mind if I took a few with me? My children have

never seen macadamias dressed up in their shells. Only naked and in a jar."

My hosts knew I was leaving that day. In relief, the wife said, "Okay, take some. When is your ride?"

"In half an hour. And thanks for the nuts and for letting me stay here."

Eagerly I ran out to the garden and the trees. There was a thick layer of nuts on the ground. I considered the situation. If I had these trees, I'd scoop up all these beautiful little spheres and bring them in. Maybe these miracles of nature meant nothing to my hosts. As I started to harvest the rich crop, the farmer in me felt inspired by such beautiful abundance, and I kept slowly increasing the amount I had planned to take. These poor little nuts were neglected; I'd take them to the ball like Cinderella. By the time I'd finished gathering, I had half a suitcase full of them. I had taken the entire harvest of the three trees, an expensive crop, maybe worth a thousand dollars.

Back in New York City, my children found them as fascinating as I did. But their advance publicity was accurate: they were hard to open. When I approached one with a hammer and missed, it fell off the counter and started to roll toward the living room. I gave chase, and tried again. I thought of myself in Vienna when I lost my chocolate confections called Mozart Balls and had to go after them as they waltzed away, pursuing them to the tempo of the "Blue Danube."

Bret came home from school and joined me in the search for all the escaped nuts that were rolling around on the floor. The living room was a giant slot machine. We had hit the jackpot.

We did this every day until the supply gave out. I would have liked to have had a tree like that, but on a floral map we were two zones too cold. This was the climate for roses.

Henley's efforts had stunning results. The blooms were resplendent in the summer, and I had a rose garden in the sky.

But roses, stolen nuts, my dance salary, and the concerts were not enough to support my family, so one day I was excited to get a call. "Allegra, you've got the part." But it was not a dance role.

While I was still with Bert, I had done a commercial for Noxzema, and during the early 1970s I'd been trying out for television commercials as one way to supplement my single-parent income. A former employee of Bert's was making a commercial for M&M's, and all present at my audition agreed that I should get the part.

On the simple set, merely a table covered in black against a dark background, I was the goddess Shiva who possessed eight arms. The TV commercial company rented a golden pagodalike costume for me and played music from *The King and I* to create a Southeast Asian mood. I sat on the table in a lotus position, and three girls in black sleeveless leotards sat behind me. Their arms and mine fed the one hungry little mouth. As each hand arrived with its M&M offering, my eyes looked delighted and a little surprised; my chin moved from side to side like a lawn swing, always level and always sinuous. After downing a dozen M&M's for one take, I requested a spittoon.

At the end of that shoot, after chewing up but not eating almost seven thousand M&M's for seven hours, I was supposed to dance my acrobatic part in *Goldberg Variations*. I'd been sitting for too long in a lotus position; my body felt like a cast-iron pan gone to rust. I groaned at the thought of the preparations, the warm-up, and the shoes to break in. But a surprise gift from heaven arrived with a phone call. A few key people were out and *Goldberg* was replaced with two other ballets, two that I wasn't in. I had a chocolate-free evening to recuperate.

Another commercial I did was for Mitchum's deodorant. Peter Martins and I did an on pointe pas de deux while a voice-over spoke about how dry and scintillatingly sexy I was under my arms.

For years I continued to receive residuals from these two commercials. The one for M&M's won an award.

However, I didn't get all the parts I hoped for. After one audition, the casting director called me on the phone with the reason. In his words, I was "not nubile enough. Could I recommend some *jeune fille* of the ballet, aged eighteen to twenty?" His voice dripped with honeyed sadism.

"Oh, gee, I just can't think of anyone that young, and you happen to be a tactless numbskull."

I began to think I'd taken a vow of poverty. Mr. B. had once said to the company, "We're like butterflies and birds." We don't need material things was the implication. Everyone else understood what he meant, but they didn't start to live it. I did. When I was so depressed I could barely carry on, I didn't try to hold on to things. One major symbol of my failure to hang on to things was losing the brownstone.

I was living on the edge. After one of my performances, Edward

Gorey sent me a note saying that my dancing was the cat's pajamas. I sent back a message: "It's no wonder. I've been wearing the cat's pajamas for a month."

Despite my financial difficulties, dancing during the spring season of 1973 was going well for me. I would wake early, before my children, and briefly study the outside world. It felt expansive. Then, lickety-split, I would pad to the kitchen for coffee. When the children awoke, I made them toast. Then I made two lunches and put them in brown paper bags. By this time, Hilda was up and had taken over. Next, I took a hot bath before going to the theater. If John Taras was teaching, class would be fun. Next there might be two hours of rehearsals for a ballet in progress or for one in the program. After that, I'd wander over to the health club for a swim and maybe a massage. I had placed a masseur I knew and liked in this health club. All this closeness was very convenient. When I needed a late afternoon rest, my apartment was right there. If any of the children were around, I visited with them. Then back to the theater to put on makeup, do the hair, and warm up the body again. Perhaps an actual rehearsal and then the onstage dancing. The discoveries of the day were realized at night during a performance. This was where real life was lived. Afterward, home—and more food—and a hope that everyone was asleep and well. My home life was fairly stable, and my rosebushes were in good shape. The children seemed all right and were in their individual routines of school and friends.

I had been in the New York City Ballet Company for twenty years and felt that my dancing still had a special quality to it. Of course, in a certain way, I was an old-timer. Makarova remade her technique here in America—as Arlene Croce said, "She modernized it." But I was just hanging on to mine, although I started to gain momentum as we progressed through this particular season. Even though the company had been operating for decades, a mid-season crisis was still the usual event, no matter how many understudies were called in. As I was getting stronger and stronger, company injuries started to mount up. The number twenty comes to mind, inclusive of corps and principals. Everyone was counting. Nevertheless, I was fine. The season felt a bit like Russia when I had so much to dance and could do it.

One afternoon as I was leaving a rehearsal, the door to the small studio opened, and Mr. B. stepped out. He was looking for me.

"Oh, Allegra, could you come in here and show Linda how you do this lift in *Episodes*?" Because I had been removed from this ballet to dance in two others, my part in *Episodes* was being taught to Linda Yourth.

Mr. B. looked pleased that he had caught me before I escaped into the outside world. The small windowless studio blazed with fluorescent tubes. Everything showed up in this workroom of harsh white light. Mr. B.'s presence offered the necessary warmth. His familiar work clothes, a plaid shirt and blue jeans, added a touch of humanity to the enclosed space.

As he opened the door wider, I could hear the atonal Webern music of my section on the piano. Each new sound was followed by a measured pause like a reflection, like new ideas presented in a conversation.

"I'm not in practice clothes. Should I change?" I was in bell-bottom trousers with ruffles.

Mr. B. shook his head. "No, just this one lift. Linda needs help." Mr. B. took my hand and brought me into the center of the room. The music stopped. "It's in the first section, where you hold onto your leg in à la seconde." I took this position. Mr. B. knelt down and grasped my supporting leg in both his hands. He was in a mood of participation and wanted to do the lift himself. He clearly wanted to dance with me. I was worried. Mr. B. was very strong, but he did have a bad back.

"Are you sure you want to do this lift?" I asked. Luckily, Nicky Magallanes stepped forward promptly.

"Mr. B., let me do it." Mr. B. let go of me and allowed himself to be replaced.

Nicky buttressed his shoulder against my leg, held it firmly, and lifted me straight up.

My gingham ruffles were in the air. From on high I explained to Linda, "If your leg is close to your head, your weight is all in one place, and it's easy for Nicky. You can't be like the Leaning Tower of Pisa and fall away from him."

Mr. B. was smiling at his creation. This step was a snap for me and Nicky because of my limberness.

"Allegra, show Linda how you get into the arabesque."

Mr. B. walked over and held my left leg with Nicky. He liked to have the raw material of choreography in his grasp.

I continued my explanation. "Keep your leg as high as you can and keep your weight over Nicky when you change from à la seconde to penchée arabesque."

I did this maneuver and then Nicky put me down.

"Linda, you try it now." Mr. B. gestured to her with his hand. I moved next to him so we could confer if necessary. Linda was still having trouble; she wasn't as flexible as I was. Mr. B. offered help but not criticism. "Lean to your left. It will work out."

He clapped his hands. They would start from the beginning again.

Mr. B. thanked me at the end of this *Episodes* rehearsal. Despite my latest problems, he still wanted my help. He still admired my dancing. Even though he had injunctions against ballerinas allowing their personal lives to intrude on dancing, he had invited me into the room to dance with him. Was he letting me know that I was still the exception to his rules? He used to describe me that way in interviews.

I also wonder if, at this time, Mr. B. was beginning to sense my impending withdrawal from the very thing I loved—ballet. Mr. B. was loyal, taking an opportunity to remind me that I still had my ballet family. About this time, he asked me to learn the *Tchaikovsky Pas de deux*. He still believed I could do something challenging, and he had placed me in the special category of expert on the leotard ballet *Episodes*.

I was happy. "Well, good-bye, Mr. B.," I said. "How do you like *Episodes* in ruffles?"

One morning, mid-season, Susannah came running into my bedroom. "Look at my face," she said in distress. One side had grown large and swollen. It baffled me for two seconds, and then I understood. It was the mumps. In a reasonable length of time, Bret came down with them, too. I couldn't remember if I had had them or not. My wondering stopped one morning soon after. My face was lopsided and huge on one side. To be out with the mumps seemed absurd—overwork or injuries were more acceptable reasons. The gods, the Greek ones who floated around in the sky in various attitudes—particularly Mercury and Athena—must be laughing. With a preamble of apologies, I called in sick.

Any change in my daily routine was precarious. My best chance was not to ponder but just to keep moving. Dance every day, water the bushes, and pray that the little insidious white flies didn't find my terrace and start to multiply. Just as I was gaining strength, I lost my forward motion again because of the mumps. Perhaps my mother had been right. The road for me was downhill now.

And ballet, the thing that had been my refuge and escape, now had become a necessity. I had to dance. As I became more and more financially unsettled and grew more and more depressed, dancing—what had been the glitter and fairy dust in my life—was becoming more and more difficult. Had work become work?

The questions I was asking myself about my ballet career, however, were minimal compared to the confusion I was experiencing in my personal life. In my early thirties, after my separation from Bert, I began to do what I should have done as a teenager: date. Unfortunately, I didn't have the equipment to enter the scene with any level of sophistication. My only dates had been with Bert. This had not prepared me for the rest of the world, and I had some unrealistic goals. I was looking for a rescuer.

A man I had started to see just after my split from Bert had helped me move into the Bancroft. It was nice to have a male friend, someone I could talk to during that difficult separation. However, when I told my friend about my plans to move from the Bancroft to the new apartment with the terrace, he had looked a little stunned and then instantly replied that he was going on vacation. I thought, *So, he chooses to be out to lunch, lounging in a lower latitude, temporarily adrift.* Out loud I said, "How can you *go* on vacation? You're unemployed. In my book you're *on* vacation." This friendship would soon end.

I had thought dating was going to be as easy as joining the ballet company. That had happened with no effort on my part. However, this scene was much more difficult to conquer. Many of my friends seemed to have met their husbands in college, and I had negated male dancers as an option. I was not in the right world in some sense, and, in the world I lived in, no one astonishing turned up.

I also kept rushing the stages and hoping that after one date I would have found a life partner. All that learning about someone took time, but as with my mother, the less I knew, the more I could imagine. Anyone who seemed on the surface just all right or showed an interest I saw as the rescuer. Other men I dismissed quickly by fastening on some quirky detail. I rejected one man because he had a yellow velvet couch (his decorator probably chose it, anyway) and another because he wore too much Cartier jewelry. I rebuffed a third candidate because he voted for Nixon. Then I'd call friends up indiscriminately and ask them if they knew anyone.

"Well, yes, I do, a professor," said one girlfriend. "Unfortunately, he was very unfaithful—with his students, in fact with everyone. Then his wife left him for a younger man and he was amazed."

"Really, do you think I should bother at all? Your character review scares me."

"Well, he's intellectual."

"I see, the pain is intellectual."

One friend arranged a date for me with a younger man, but he was just a pretty face.

For a while I dated a minor dance critic. When I saw that our coupling had no future, I became despondent. Then one man I had liked abruptly stopped calling, and I was devastated. Single life was difficult, and I had a lot to learn.

As always, married men didn't interest me, but those were the men who called. When one phoned me, I actually arranged a meeting, knowing I wasn't going to keep it. As the hours crept up, I decided to send a telegram. "Off on a month's vacation starting today in another hemisphere which will have a different season. You see I do want to stay in touch."

After I finished the telegram, the telegraph taker said, "Have a great time."

I even took a job that I hoped would lead to a romance. Walking by the New School, I noticed that the institute was soon to have its first cultural cruise. Some of the caryatids of culture were Viveca Lindfors, Dore Ashton, and David Schoenburg, plus liberal Democratic candidates, poets, politicians, and the press. Maybe this would be a good place to meet a man. I went to the New School office and offered my services—a lecture-demonstration on ballet. They liked the idea and I was granted a free trip on *The Adventurer* in return for giving two lectures. My friend Henley decided to come with me and help with the recorded sound.

The entire group flew to Puerto Rico and there boarded our Cunard ship. But my suitcase never arrived. In a small carry-on bag I had pj's, a few leotards, my swim wings, and, luckily, the small cassette of dance music. An intensive search did not help. The suitcase had gone astray, so the New School management agreed to just one lecture. Many elegantly dressed women on board generously offered to lend me clothes, but I decided it was easier just to wear my pj's daily. After all, they were bought in a very fine thrift shop, and they were hand-sewn, pure silk, and burgundy with tiny white dots, made by "Olga." If I looked the same every day, all conversations on style would be kept to a minimum and everyone would understand that my suitcase was vacationing elsewhere.

The lecture went very well, but no one knew what it was about, nor did I. A description might have read, "Tonight's stand-up co-median will wear pajamas and bend over backward." It was a hit. After that performance I met an expert on Caribbean politics—a champagne Socialist and courageous currency changer who fearlessly walked around Geneva with a suitcase full of money. The political observer wanted me to store twenty cases of Mt. Gay rum and his camel-hair coat in my apartment, and so our shipboard romance was on. For him infatuation was fun and practical; he found lodging for his bottles. I was learning that my suitors didn't want to rescue me, they wanted storage space.

The political expert, however, was good-looking, with a home in Cork and an engaging charm. He also had a boxer's nose that looked as if it had received a few direct hits. I called him the flower of an hour, after the quickly fading hibiscus of the islands; he, however, corrected me, saying flower of *the* hour. I had it right.

One week after the cruise, on New Year's Eve, my suitcase was delivered to my apartment in New York City, with all my possessions intact. Two hundred moonstones on a string came back to me, but I didn't have a date. After two years, I had not found someone new. I thought I would have met a great man by this time and be married and secure. I thought life was like graduating high school—I'd done my time, now things should be in place. I was ready for the next stage, but it wasn't there. And I might not have even recognized it if it arrived. I was still struggling. As terrible as my marriage had been, there was a certain stability. Now I was searching, and it was exhaust-ing. I had not yet learned that I had to rescue myself.

Meanwhile, Bert, broke and homeless, left to stay with a friend in Spain, taking with him fifty cartons of newspapers and some negatives he had salvaged from the brownstone. One single ring in the middle of the night meant Bert was thinking of us, but he sent us nothing.

"But, Your Honor, she was unfaithful to me." Bert smiled at the judge, my lawyer, and me. He was unspeakably happy to have the scene set, lit, and ready for his appearance. Bert had cast himself in two roles for this particular drama. He was playing his own lawyer and himself. And he had arrived late. Coming from some girlfriend's apartment, Bert had walked eighty blocks in his bare feet to the courthouse and arrived only ten minutes late for our divorce hearing. He hadn't had the money for a subway token. Now he stood before the judge, in jeans, with his feet bare. Often Bert's nature was unreliable, but if he wanted to be somewhere, he'd get there.

I stared at him. Acting as his own attorney, he was questioning me on the stand. He continued: "She ruined my life. She didn't care about me, only her career. And now I have no money." Years later, Bert said he defended himself because "I had a fool for a client," but on that day, he was smirking with happiness. Some actors will do anything for a part, even if it's offstage. He was taking the proceedings seriously, but he wanted some comedy. He looked around again, judging the judge and those present, delivering his punch lines, and waiting for their reception.

Flabbergasted, I put my hands on my hips. "Now, wait a minute. There is a little inaccuracy here." I was about to explain that we had been separated when I started to date, but I didn't continue. Nor did I bring up his long list of models. I just wanted to get rid of him. Bert had nothing to give me or the children. Our future had not been secured or considered. My lawyer, Robert Groban, had refused a fee; occasional ballet tickets were his only request. I wore an old rag of a dress to court which my mother had bought for me in a thrift shop. Now most of my clothes would come from that source.

After the question of child support was referred to family court— a process that would take a year—the judge granted the divorce, and I gave Bert a subway token and a little mad money. I wanted and received my old name back, dropping the Stern forever, as my mother had once done with Cohen. Bert congratulated me on the divorce and went to Spain. He eventually got off all drugs and successfully resumed his photography career.

He had hardly given me anything for the children since our separation in 1971, and now, in the spring of 1975, my situation as a single parent was very precarious. Expenses were climbing. I had to find a solution.

CHAPTER SIXTEEN

Never were so many beautiful princesses seen together at one time. . . . They danced on till the shoes of the princesses were worn into holes.

— "THE TWELVE DANCING PRINCESSES,"

THE RED FAIRY BOOK

I arrived for my first class early, dressed in leotard, tights, and a short dance skirt, and swept the floor in our minuscule studio. I was ready, or hoped I was. The first class of twelve young girls ranging in age from eleven to fourteen were eager to begin their pliés. I smiled at them and began to demonstrate how we would start. The pliés, the equivalent of saying grace before a meal, are traditionally the first steps of a class. The space could barely hold the twelve at barre. The room was claustrophobically small, and when everyone came into the center, it was even worse. There was no room to move, no path for a series of big jumps. With two runs and one leap the students were across the floor from corner to corner.

From the first day I felt imprisoned in this room. I had wanted my students to love and enjoy their classes. Some might have been interested professionally, but I hoped the others would enjoy their lesson as they would a tennis game—as an end in itself or something complete in itself, like dinner, an exercise with wonderful music where you could zip up your lips and just use your thoughts, muscles, and imagination. The room was impossible, however. No one's imagination could enlarge it.

This was my most desperate plan yet to augment my income. When I saw a newspaper article about a business called "Love Letters Anonymous: $50 per letter," I wondered if I could write letters for others, too. It was somewhat of a tradition in my family. My shingle could read, LESSER LOVE LETTERS ANONYMOUS, for lesser loves. They wouldn't be as grammatically correct, and the spelling would be impressionistic, but they'd be cheaper. I also thought about being a governess, like Claire Claremont, or a sea captain. Anything would have been more realistic. The Allegra Kent School of Ballet was a terrible solution.

Free public schools and a life plan designed by my new psychiatrist convinced me to endanger my already tenuous position at the New York City Ballet by moving from the city to Scarsdale and opening my own dance studio.

I had been seeing a new therapist since 1971, when I had replaced Hertzberg with a female. I still believed in the psychiatric profession. I wished to investigate my life, and I wanted someone on my side. By the time I divorced Bert, I was financially teetering, I was having some sort of breakdown, and it had become increasingly difficult to dance. My new doctor, whom I will call Geri, had the answer. Unfortunately, this therapist loved opera and hated ballet. She supported my decision when I withdrew from the thing I loved—performing—and opened a ballet school, even though I was not in love with teaching. Furthermore, her solution included my moving to Scarsdale. She was going to help me increase my income and improve my social life.

During a session with me in early 1975, in a fit of creativity, we agreed on an elaborate strategy for my redemption:

1. Leave the city.
2. Move to Scarsdale.
3. Open a ballet school there.
4. Enlist my friend Henley Haslam to be my partner in the venture.
5. Convince Mr. B. that I was too old to dance but not too old to receive a paycheck.
6. Enter the Scarsdale matron's lifestyle by running around shopping centers with Geri.

Most important in her mind was that this plan would rescue me from my loathsome profession, la danse, le ballet. She even found me a studio. Again, there was nothing affordable in the right location. At last she found the fourteen-by-eight upstairs space where my first twelve students were trying to coexist. When I had expressed shock at the dimensions, Geri said, "Pack 'em in." Next she put up posters everywhere.

I stopped taking dance classes and began to take solace in food. Her plan made me out of shape.

Next I had to schedule a meeting with Mr. B. He laughed when I said I was too old to dance at thirty-seven. Melissa Hayden retired when she was near fifty. Alicia Alonso would never stop dancing, and Margot Fonteyn, near sixty, had not given up either. Mr. B. laughed, but he allowed me to have my way.

On the morning of the move, I had nearly had a nervous breakdown. The children and I had accumulated many things, and Scarsdale was forty-five minutes from Broadway. I left most of my rosebushes, because the terrace of our new apartment was tiny. I was leaving the home I loved and my personal Hanging Garden of Babylon. In addition, the dance school was an unknown. The parting was not easy for me or the children.

Geri's advice to bow out of ballet when I was thirty-seven was as wrong as my mother's to leave performing when I was seventeen. It was the worst thing I could have done. But I allowed myself to follow this well-meaning woman's plans for me.

Geri had been in the new studio the day before it opened, filling out forms and registering pupils, but registration had been going on for weeks. She loved to be a part of the operation, placing students and talking to the mothers. We had two hundred seventy students enrolled, even though the room was way too small for more than seven at a time. I was amazed. My name plus the convenient location of the school and Geri's relentless efforts at spreading brochures, photos, and information had brought them in.

Now we were officially open, and though we had many students, we could put only a small number of them in any one class. This meant classes had to be scheduled back to back from three-thirty to seven-thirty, the precious after-school hours. Then at seven-thirty Henley offered an adult ballet class. Henley and I decided to have a pianist for every class, using records for emergencies only, but the piano took up room. More space taken. Why had we abandoned our common sense when Geri showed us the space? There was no room for dancing; it might have passed for a singing lesson.

And the size of the studio was not the only problem. I would be in Scarsdale almost every evening teaching in a community of mostly married couples. If I had a date with anyone, it would probably be in the city. I was in the wrong place for a single woman. Also, where would I take a class for myself? How should I arrange my life in this suburb? Daily, Carmelita Maracci practiced alone. It is only rarely done—the work needs the combined effort of a group. My head was full of all these thoughts while I tried to look thrilled my first day teaching at the Allegra Kent School of Ballet. But immediately after that class I recognized the truth: I had imprisoned myself in a suburb and in a dancing school.

As I left the school that day, I fell into a deep depression. I was still young. It was too early for me to start teaching; I needed to dance and perform. But I had just told Mr. B. the exact opposite. I had isolated myself from the things I loved and was overwhelmed by the stupidity of my situation. I stopped sleeping, and my weight began fluctuating. I wasn't as thin as I needed to be. At one point, I had the children chain up the icebox. The chain had links the size of golf balls, and only the children had the combination. One morning, I wanted coffee with milk. It was too early to run out to a coffee shop, and there was milk in the chained refrigerator. With Bret's metal saw, I sawed open the chain. It took half an hour. By the time I got in, I was ready for a Canadian breakfast—after all that exertion, I felt like a lumberjack. Someone else gave me an alarm for the icebox, but that didn't work either.

I started reading biographies during the middle of the night. At the train station in Scarsdale, I had met Nesie Breines, a reading fanatic who recognized me as a dancer and perhaps as myself, and we started to converse. She did recordings for the blind and made them in a few languages, including Yiddish. I became interested in what she was reading, and it was easy to follow her lead. One of her favorite books was a biography of Shelley by Richard Holmes, which I read and liked so much that I branched out to Byron; Shelley's wife, Mary; her half sister, Claire Claremont, and her illegitimate daughter, Allegra; Mary's mother, Mary Wollstonecraft; and Blake. I hoped to find an answer in the lives of other people. I read about Trollope's mother, the *Indomitable Mrs. Trollope;* Madame de Staël, who was *Mistress to an Age;* and the great female orators of the last century like Anna E. Dickinson, who gave campaign speeches for Ulysses S. Grant. Olive Schreiner found that plants never were argumentative. Gordon Craig's mother (Ellen Terry) spoiled him, and Louisa May Alcott's father didn't favor her. I learned that massage had helped Edith Wharton when she had her nervous breakdown (I had started massages at twenty-one and knew it was indispensable to my mind and muscles). I tried to find insights in the lives of Fanny Kemble, Mrs. Patrick Campbell, the Von Riffenhoff sisters, Diana Cooper, Vera Brittain, and Rebecca West. I read about mothers of famous authors who favored another child in the family and fathers who hated their daughters with dark competition or taught their sons Latin at eighteen months of age. I read about a man who could only marry a woman called Harriet, who also had a mother called Harriet. I read the biographies of George Eliot, Charlotte Brontë, and Isadora Duncan. I always read the acknowledgments, and almost every contemporary biography I read included a thank-you to Lincoln Kirstein, the brilliant authority on dance who had founded the New York City Ballet with Balanchine. His name appeared at the beginning of a book on T. E. Lawrence and also in one on Eugene O'Neill. At two A.M., when *Lives of the Saints* failed to hold my attention, I tried lives of the criminals. Dillinger was eccentric and liked to jump over the bank counter; this made him dangerous. He probably should have danced. I ate and read in the middle of each night, but I never found the answers to my life.

During that dreadful first year in Scarsdale, Mr. B. agreed for a while to let me have my salary with limited performances. However, in 1976 Mr. B. told me I had to dance more. I was delighted and hired substitutes to teach for me. But I was still almost an hour from Broadway and without a car.

During the commute, I wrote letters:

Dear C,

At this moment, I'm stuck on the train; all signals are out of whack. The wait thus far has only been half an hour but the future looks uncertain. I'd like to jump out the window or go to the nonexistent bar car. "I'll have a drink of nonexistent champagne, please." I did well in class today. Oh, dear, I'm so confused, lots of people are walking.

With love, Allegra

Dear H,

There is no power; my train has lost its energy source. We are somewhere on the tracks. I'm reading, napping, also stretching and chatting with other mystified passengers. We are picking up stray conductors and proceeding at a snail's pace. We are wailing our wailing device for extra caution even though we are crawling along at a ludicrous mile per hour. The still point was at Crestwood, the stop just before Scarsdale. I might be home for dinner. We are passing many inactive trains. You will read about this tomorrow; it will make page 30 in the New York Times, *tessellated.*

Lots of love, from Allegra

One day on the commuter train I had a realization: I was not only stalled most of the time, I was always going in the wrong direction.

Occasionally help arrived from unexpected quarters. About this time, Edward Preble, my tenth-grade science teacher, arrived with a solution to my transportation problems. He must have been following my career, and he wrote me a note at the State Theater. He was working out of a storefront in Harlem buying life stories from people who walked in the door. He had won a bet and asked me if I wanted to go to Puerto Rico with him. I hadn't seen him in twenty-five years. I said no to Puerto Rico but yes to *Nicholas Nickleby* with Trista.

That night I told Mr. Preble how upset I was with my secondhand car. Geri had switched gears, and now I had to have a car. I had called the vehicle the "Dawn Treader" after the C. S. Lewis book; its muffler was hanging out and it had other problems. I didn't have the money to repair it. Edward told me to give him the key; one of his lieutenants would drive it to Harlem and fix it. It was a present. I gave him the key, and the car disappeared early one morning and returned a week later in perfect running order for a lemon.

Mr. Preble had descended from sea captains. I had found the name Edward Preble while I was reading a book about great sea battles and started to scream when I saw it. "Could it be? Could it be?" Edward Preble, like Decatur, was one of the heroes of Tripoli, but no street in the South was named Preble, because he fell into disgrace. I asked Edward about this, and he was indeed a descendant. The eldest son of all Preble offspring was always named Edward. My tenth-grade teacher was the tenth Edward Preble.

I asked him, "How come you were such a great science teacher?"

"My field was English, but I took the only job available. I stayed one step ahead of my students, so all the material was fresh and interesting to me."

I sighed. I was falling a step behind in all aspects of my life, not just dance.

When my father was in his middle seventies, he also found himself many steps behind. He was in a penniless state. He had made great deals and had possessed extraordinary properties, but somehow he had always sold out at the wrong time. At this point, even a few hundred dollars would help. "Something has *got* to happen," he told me.

Something did. He got the idea of appearing on *The Gong Show*.

I settled down to watch the program with Geri, who was still playing a role in my daily life.

Soon Harry appeared on the screen. He was dressed as an egg—all in white except for a little triangle of a yellow T-shirt that showed at his neck. His hair and beard were nearly pure white. When young, he was handsome, in his fifties he looked like Jerry Robbins, but now he looked like a cross between Mark Twain and Doc Holiday, two of his heroes. Over the years he had been writing little stories and poems for children. One was about his regret at having killed wildlife when he was a youth. He started to recite his poetry eloquently. Whenever there was a rifle shot in the poem, he would grab an egg and crack it over his head. Soon egg yolks were dripping all over him. Watching him, I didn't know whether to laugh or cry. Finally, he was gonged.

When stagehands came to drag him offstage, he said, "But you can't do this to me. I'm Allegra Kent's father." Someone on the panel said, "Who is Allegra Kent?" Someone else said, "The ballerina."

"That's her father?" The voice sounded surprised.

It was over. Before I could open my mouth, Geri remarked, "That was absolutely pitiful."

What could I say? I was proud of him. It was an offbeat idea. He had no regular talent, but he still had developed an act. Later, he told me the show was replayed and he received a residual. He wasn't afraid to appear in an undignified way. He was never mean-spirited.

After that, I had no further contact with Geri. I sold my "dance academy" and returned to classes at the Ballet Theatre School. From *The Gong Show,* Daddy went on to *The Dating Game* and was a great success. Of course, he was chosen to go on the date. I was still waiting for the right man to choose me, but I had begun the salvaging process. I was dancing again.

Much later I would have an allegorical dream in which my life was an ostrich egg that I didn't know how to cook—should it be boiled or coddled? It was already scrambled. The people of my life reappeared, but there were no hors d'oeuvres for dinner.

Even though I was dancing again, my position with the company didn't feel completely secure. In the fall of 1977, I was still living in Scarsdale and collecting a full salary for increasingly limited performances. Although I had ups and downs with Mr. Balanchine, he felt a loyalty to the past. I thought this wasn't an entirely unfair agreement because in the past, when I had danced almost every performance, my pay was very low.

However, Lincoln Kirstein was apparently furious about this arrangement. He had liked me at one time and this feeling was mutual. I liked him. When he brought Balanchine to America it changed all our lives. But now I was no longer a valuable company member. One day, on the street, he suddenly yelled at me, "Not one fucking penny more!" He was talking about my salary.

I was surprised, for just moments before he had greeted me with warmth and interest. "Oh, Allegra, how are you?" We were standing in front of the Red Flame coffee shop, my destination. Kirstein had reached out to embrace me, and in that movement suddenly his face distorted, and, caught in a charge of emotion, he hurled that phrase at me.

Sono Osato, a dancer who was standing there with us, heard Lincoln's words and was more shocked than I was. I blanched, but she turned green. This was unexpected. Did George Balanchine feel the same way? At that very moment, for all I knew, Mr. Balanchine might have been at the Russian Tea Room having borscht, blini, caviar, and sour cream in some combination, knowing nothing about it.

Lincoln had been on the verge of being hospitalized for a mental problem, but I didn't realize that and took his words literally. After an hour or two, I called the ballet office to ask in a trembling voice if I had been fired. The reply was no. I took it to mean not yet.

PART EIGHT
1978 — 1983

From a Change to a Chance

Allegra's dressing room. Photo by Hank O'Neal.

CHAPTER SEVENTEEN

After class one day at the Ballet Theatre School with Pat Wilde, I took off my practice clothes, dressed, and walked over to the elevator, a bit sweaty but exhilarated. My body worked, and dancing was fun.

Twyla Tharp and Mikhail Baryshnikov, in conversation, came over and stood close by me. They were waiting also. I wanted to say hello to him. I thought of him as a golden plover, one of the world's great flyers. This particular bird can travel more than two thousand miles without a rest or weight loss. I pondered whether to be my reserved, shy self or break my pattern.

By this time the elevator arrived and we all went inside.

"Hi. I'd like to introduce myself. I'm Allegra Kent, and I adore your dancing."

"You're Allegra Kent?"

"Yes."

Misha took my hand and shook it. He looked genuinely pleased. "This is Twyla Tharp." He gestured politely to Twyla.

"So nice to meet you," I said, shaking her hand. Then, looking at Baryshnikov, I said, "One of your friends I met in Oklahoma told me you are very eager to dance Balanchine's *Apollo*. If you ever do, I'd love to be your Terpsichore."

Misha's eyes assessed my height in comparison to his. It would work; our sizes were compatible. He was thinking about *Apollo,* leader of the Muses. "My teachers in Russia saw you dance in 1962. They told me about you."

I went to my rehearsal at the theater happy. What a talent! And for once I hadn't been shy.

About two weeks later, Barbara Horgan called me. "Misha wants to dance *Apollo* with you at a dance festival in Chicago. Mr. Balanchine has agreed to a shorter version, with the birth scene cut. Pat Neary will stage it and the two other Muses will come from American Ballet Theatre."

I was thrilled. A lot of negotiations had already transpired. It was going to happen, and Mr. B.'s office would negotiate my fee.

My conversation with Baryshnikov and my engagement to dance *Apollo* with him all happened because of the writer Paul Scott.

Early in 1977, I had read a book review of Scott's *Raj Quartet* and decided to buy it. When I got the book home, it weighed in at three pounds, about one thousand pages. This might very well be a fight. Who would break down first, it or me? For a commuter carrying practice clothes, pointe shoes, wallet, snacks, and other necessary *objets de la danse,* a three-pound book would be a terrible burden. I pondered the matter and was slightly horrified with my solution. I understood that the only way to read it was by cutting it into eight-ounce portions. After reading it in sections, I could unite the pages with a blue ribbon and pass them on to my friend Henley.

This is how I started to divide and conquer certain books. I steadied myself as I ripped off the hard cover and put a razor to the spine of the binding. It felt wrong, destructive, and strange; a book becomes an object of sacrifice. I tried be very neat with this first paper surgery.

But cutting up was in my genes. My mother told me that as a child she had loved to cut, and she applied her scissors to clothes, mainly destroying them in the process. As an adult, she loved to re-create, reconstruct, and refashion clothes and jewelry. During my sleepless nights, I often cut up my clothes and made new things out of them. Always something else. I would turn a dress into an apron, or a skirt into a hat. One time when Trista returned from a trip and asked me where a certain dress was, I had to tell her reluctantly, "It's now a belt."

Soon after reading Scott's book, I had almost said no to a *Nutcracker* engagement in Tulsa, Oklahoma, until I read that Scott was teaching a creative writing class there. In Tulsa, I had lunch with the author of the *Raj Quartet,* who was very ill at the time but thrilled that a ballet (which he pronounced "belly" with his English accent) dancer had searched him out in the oil fields. It was in Tulsa that I met Baryshnikov's dancing friend who told me about Misha's interest in *Apollo*, a meeting that led to my bold offer in the elevator.

Just before going to Chicago to dance *Apollo* with Misha, I called my father.

"How are you, Daddy?"

"Not so good." There was despair in his voice.

My father never admitted this kind of information. He put on a performance with everything he did, adding color to his voice and to his clothes, and large curvy arabesques to his handwriting. Now, for the first time ever, he admitted to not feeling well. I called my brother. It was true. Harry was not doing well at all. He had cancer. Until this moment, no one had let me know how seriously ill my father was.

"Gary, I'm going to Chicago for a week to dance with Baryshnikov. Should I come to Los Angeles first?"

"No, go to Chicago and dance."

Gary understood how hard it had been for me to get ready to dance. Released at last from the school and Geri, the previous season I'd danced every dance in my repertory. During this period I had got down to my ideal weight, one hundred pounds, and was a real member of the company again. I was doing some of my best dancing, and my confidence had returned. This time I was really ready; my strength and weight were right.

After speaking to Gary, I wondered why for years I had been so dismissive in my conversations with my father. I was still living out some of my mother's instructions. Gary and Wendy thought more for themselves than I ever did. I left for Chicago, leaving my hotel phone number with the housekeeper.

My body was ready, but I also had to defeat my psychological demons to go onstage in Chicago with Misha. Wandering through the city after rehearsals and before each performance, I prepared myself to perform by conducting an internal dialogue with my Dostoyevskian devils. I told myself I was not a funambulist on a rope between the World Trade Center towers; I was merely a dancing girl. Although in ten years I would put this debilitating panic in its place, in Chicago I had to work hard every day to defeat it before each performance.

The occasion for my dancing *Apollo* with Baryshnikov was an international dance festival sponsored by a very wealthy Chicago woman. European dancing stars had been flown in for this event.

Misha had three different partners, one of whom was Natalia Makarova, who was dancing Jerome Robbins's *Afternoon of a Faun* with him. I was curious to see her in it because it was not in her style. She also had just cut her hair very, very short, and long hair was part of the choreography—Jerry had written a little hair-tossing into the dance. But gestures involving long hair don't make sense if the principal girl doesn't have it. Makarova's *Faun* didn't work. It's a choreographed piece that must look spontaneous—made up on the spot. A movement takes place, a dance response is given. The reviews weren't good, and Makarova decided to leave after the matinee—with her costume. *Faun* was scheduled for that evening, but Natasha and costume had taken a walk.

When Misha asked me to replace her, I cut up some white practice clothes and dyed them blue. Misha thought it went really well. Peter Martins had made the trip to Chicago with Heather Watts, and he told me I outdid myself in both *Apollo* and *Faun*.

I did some of the best dancing of my ballet career in Chicago, and I had not called California once.

In a surprise move, Misha changed his dancing arena after Chicago and joined the New York City Ballet. But just at the moment that the great Misha—the golden plover, my new partner—was joining the company, I was about to fall into a deep sadness and begin withdrawing from dance.

When I returned to New York City, I learned that Harry had died. No one had called me; no one had told me. I have always assumed that my mother and brother made a decision for me: they knew I wouldn't be able to dance. But I've never asked.

I had lost another ocean.

I vowed to be as good to people important to me as I could be while they were still alive. Tears of regret and remorse were impossible. People should receive their bouquets when they're alive. Chances must not be lost.

Harry had done the best he could. In a letter of 1946 he wrote to my mother, "You R the loveliest one in the world and I love U." Attached was an informal will in his beautiful handwriting. He had felt guilty about all my mother had suffered, and one day he bought a replacement diamond ring for her—very small, just a long rectangle, not even graceful, but a genuine diamond nevertheless. It was a gesture carried out with spontaneity in remembrance of the past. The small bar of diamond would relay a message. He didn't know how to be a good father and husband, but he would do his best. He had tried.

In the fall of 1978 a suitcase full of letters arrived from California. They were my own. Daddy had saved every letter I wrote to him or Mother, the ones from boarding school from 1946 and even a cat collage from Miami Beach I had made at five. I picked up one written on thin paper:

Dearest One,

Your bouquet of flowers was sent to me via Barbara [Horgan] as it turned out for a rather special occasion, my first Swan Lake. I did it pretty much the way I wanted to after 3 rehearsals.

Love, Allegra

I went into a nameless mourning. I went to Denmark in August 1978 with the company but did very little dancing. On our last night, it was requested that all the dancers come back onstage in costume for the final bow. I had been out in Tivoli Gardens but I returned to the theater and put on my mustard-colored costume from *Dances at a Gathering.* I held Misha's hand. Suddenly it was raining flowers for the final bow. The Danes were throwing roses on stage. I felt a little something was missing. Flowers had become good-bye and thank-you notes. The flowers brought out the old Iris in me. I disentangled my hand and grabbed some roses to toss back. I tossed them from a pitcher's stance. Mr. B. and Jerry were onstage close by. They both gave me a surprised and disapproving look. Decorum, decorum. Had I made a deep mistake and done something undignified? I thought so from their faces. Misha acted indulgent. Later that evening someone jokingly called me "the florist."

I wanted to punish myself. Almost immediately after Denmark, I fell into a deep depression and decided to seek help from a new psychiatrist. That would be another search. Meanwhile, I began to perform sporadically. I became less and less reliable.

But one exciting dance invitation came my way, arriving by post. Edward Gorey had written a libretto for a ballet and was also designing the costumes. In his letter, he said he couldn't think of anyone he'd rather ask to perform in his work than me. Peter Anastos was to choreograph it, and it would be performed with the Eglevsky Ballet. When the time came for my costume to be finished, Gorey's special instructions were to place at random over the entire costume two thousand and one safety pins as a badge of my improvisational style. Offstage, I often wore parallel rows of them instead of buttons. When safety pins came into their own as a fashion trend, I had to abandon them.

The ballet was a delicious romp, and I met Peter Anastos, a wonderful friend. While talking to Gorey, I discovered that what I felt was one of my worst performances—my first "Choleric," which I did at seventeen—was a stage moment that Gorey loved. There is no accounting for taste and favorite dancers.

Despite this high point, I began a period of balletic decline, and I haphazardly read the letters Daddy had saved, the ones written when I was really dancing. If you can't dance, you can read about it.

One day in 1979, I stumbled and fell on the asphalt street in front of my apartment house in Scarsdale. A man came running out of the nearby drugstore—I thought to assist me, to pick me up.

"Why are you loitering near my car?"

I started to laugh. "I just fell down. Where's your gallantry?"

"Oh, sorry." The man rushed back into the drugstore.

It was the weekend before one of my rare appearances. I had an *Agon* rehearsal the next day, and I hadn't been in the State Theater in four months.

I knew the only reason I was still in the company was because of Mr. Balanchine's loyalty to the past. I hadn't been much of a presence in the New York City Ballet for the last seven years or so, but we had an unwritten agreement: he asked that I dance once a season, an even more blatant arrangement than the one that had upset Lincoln Kirstein. This situation was unreal and impractical. My wholehearted effort now went into abstract practice. The daily classes and swims continued, but not the performances. I was pursuing a full-time noncareer. Mr. B. left my name on the dressing-room door, a tiny windowless New York City apartment that I still shared with Suzanne Farrell. I dreamed of having a clothesline in New York City for my laundry. After class in the city, I stuffed my tights and leotards into my dance bag and carried my sweat back to Scarsdale with me. Even though I had to commute with my laundry, there was a place for me backstage. What did these rare appearances mean to me? Way too much. All my stage fright for a whole year would be concentrated into one day. It was insufferable. Now one of my rare appearances was two days away.

I put weight on my foot. It was not really bad, just a nuisance, a huge nuisance that would give me nightmares. I was feeling fairly prepared to perform again, and this had to happen. An injury was threatening my fragile arrangement with Mr. B.

I sat on my favorite part of my old sofa, the part that was three inches lower than the rest, and placed my legs on the coffee table and wrapped a plastic bag full of crushed ice on my foot. This was the place I sat when I was depressed, the place where I read biography after biography searching for something in other people's lives that would help me with my own. There was no denying it: that part of the couch was sinking lower and lower. There is weight to words that are read. It was something like St. Peter's toe in the Vatican. In that case, kisses had worn the marble down. In my case, pure biography had compressed the cushions into a single layer of foam. An older date had once visited me and he couldn't pull himself up from such a low position. I had laughed, invisibly, at his weak knees.

But at the moment I wasn't really worried about what an interior decorator would say about my couch. I was worried about what Mr. B. would say when I "marked" a rehearsal—attended but didn't fully participate. Someone does this who is overworked, injured, or, sometimes, lazy.

The next morning I tested my foot, and it was not good. I also understood from the type of pain that it was not serious, but this still was bad for me. The rehearsal was Friday, the performance Sunday. I thought deeply about this situation, and I decided I would be all right by Sunday.

The following day I went to the State Theater and changed into practice clothes. In my youth I wore colors, but lately I had been wearing only black. I had read a book on Edith Piaf and decided it was easiest always to dress in a monotone. This simplified life—if it were possible to simplify my life. So maybe I couldn't pay the bills, but I had one area of my life under control and pared down to one leotard, one pair of tights, and one practice skirt—all in black.

Balanchine was near the piano, so I made a sharp right and walked over to him. "Mr. B., I fell last night on my foot, but it's not serious. However, I must mark today's rehearsal and I'm really sorry about it. I know you haven't seen me dance in a long while, but I can do this performance, just not a full rehearsal today."

Mr. B., eyes alert, paid careful attention to exactly what I said. I felt lucky that this man was a listener. He was a great musician as well as choreographer who really heard all sounds, including conversations.

"It's all right, Allegra. Don't worry. Do what you can today."

This was part of Mr. B.'s uncanny insight into a human soul—and a sentence. He read me right. He understood my regret that I could not do the rehearsal full-out but that the performance was not imperiled. He had not seen me dance in six months, but he heard in my voice that I could do it and do it well.

Mr. B. was one in a million. Any insecure choreographer would have said, "*Auf wiedersehen, danke schön,* good-bye, thank you." But not Mr. B. He knew that what I said was true, and he was not worried.

Emotion welled up within me. I'd encountered greatness, true gallantry. All I could say was, "Thank you."

When it was time the next year to reappear for my obligatory performance, I felt emotion running through me like a tidal wave as I entered the State Theater. This time I was not ready. I had kicked a lead pipe out of the way of traffic on Madison Avenue, forgetting that I was wearing sandals, and my big toe was bruised. Dancing at this time was a mistake. And there was too much to organize. I was just not in shape. As I entered the main hall, I felt fear, happiness, despair, regret, and the knowledge that I wasn't up to a performance this time. People were nice, but this did not calm me. I was dying inside with tension. Would she dance again? Yes or no? The dance rumors had been spreading. I was adding to them.

Twenty-five years after my plastic surgery, I still felt embarrassed about showing my face in the theater. I later learned that I could be helped by an antidepressant, but they weren't quite in style yet. Besides, my mother thought of them as tranquilizers and was horrified at the mere mention of them. So, for now, whenever I entered the stage door after an absence, I relived the torture of those moments when I walked back into the School of American Ballet after my face had changed.

One day while I was in the pool doing my daily laps at the Parc Health Club, one of Bert's girlfriends showed up in street clothes at the shallow end. As my hand touched the rim, she started screaming at me. Even with earplugs and a bathing cap I understood the gist of her message. It was about the trials of dating Bert and his problems as a human being. I peered at her through my foggy swim mask. She looked crazed. I interrupted my swim just long enough to shrug my shoulders in a helpless gesture, then dipped back in and swam to the deep end. She ran at a fast clip around the pool and was waiting to receive me with continuation of her tirade on Bert. She was like a dog chasing a ball. Allegra, the ball, decided to get out of the pool and shower alone with the curtains drawn and lose the barking dog as quickly as possible. But she seemed to know where I was taking class and showed up there, mid-barre.

"I'm not Bert's mother, only someone who was once married to him," I told her.

She'd come to the wrong person. I'd never been able to solve the problem of Bert. At the time, I was dating a second-night theater critic, and I was learning what it was like to have insurmountable problems with men who weren't Bert. My current date was often unreachable. He told me, "I've gone out with hundreds of women, you know, because of the surplus. My friends advised me to play the field because it's so lush." I was troubled by his calculating description of the man-to-woman ratio. What a mean, unthinking thing to say.

I replied, "I don't consider myself surplus," and thought, *Why am I seeing him at all? Is there any warmth in an ice cube?*

I continued to meet many men who forgot me or were forgettable. During one of these years, I saw and slept with five men for exactly forty days each, and each one of them abruptly and cruelly said good-bye. I was living my life backward, trying to do in my forties what I hadn't done as a teenager—relate to men. I often used images to describe men I'd known. One I tagged as the iguana. My friends with pet iguanas objected.

I went out on hundreds of blind dates. I even crossed the Atlantic for one, an Englishman who had named his horse after me. I lost touch with the Englishman but continued to follow the career of Allegra, the horse who was at least one thousand pounds heavier than I am, who possessed a harder head, a softer muzzle, and who ran on her toes. I was a little upset years later when this man sold Allegra.

A friend telephoned from Los Angeles. "Allegra, a friend of mine is going to call you. He's rich; if you marry him, I want ten percent."

"It's a deal," I said, wondering, ten percent of *what?*

I dated a British identical twin who was brought up by a nanny and could fall in love only with American women. His grandmother lived across the street from me. A movie mogul I dated diverted a company jet to fly me to a gala Joseph Cornell retrospective at the Smithsonian in Washington. The only thing I remember about the mogul was that he complained bitterly when the chauffeur drove the limo to the wrong side of the airplane. Another man, whom I met through a dating service and whom I liked, never called after our first date. We had been having a good time until I asked him if he knew the name that Stephen Crane's wife gave to her brothel. He paused for a moment and then said, "I don't like gossip."

This time in my life resembled my mother's when she was in Florida dating the officers. No doubt my children felt I was neglecting
them in my search for a new companion, but I was compelled to find
someone.

In Scarsdale—living on a salary I received even though I almost
never performed—I also went on struggling to augment my income
as a single parent. For a while I had one iron in the fire. A man I was
dating introduced me to a professional writer who wanted to help me
write my life's story, and we started to meet once a week to tape our
conversations. Soon, however, I began to doubt the outcome. I felt
she was trying to use my life to prove her entirely negative point of
view about men. Still, when she wanted to meet Bert, I introduced
them, and she walked right up to him, skipped all preliminaries, and
said, "What is the state of your prick?" Bert looked stunned.

When he left, she told me she wanted sexual details about him.
Then she asked, "By the way, have you slept with anyone famous?"

"I don't think so." I loved disappointing her, but that was the end
of my life story.

By late 1980, I was afraid to be seen on the fourth floor of the State
Theater near the ballet office. Was I in or out of the company? One
source of my anxiety was a new souvenir book. It was in the process
of being assembled, and the principal dancers as well as everyone else
had been assigned various times to have their portraits taken by a
famous fashion photographer. My name was not on the list, and that
meant I would not be in the book. This upset me. Was this a delicate
detachment? I tried to determine if I had been deliberately left out.
Mr. Balanchine had just had an eye operation and was recuperating
and unable to oversee the early stages of the book himself. There was
no denying it; I was not a key player. I took class daily and barely
maintained my body. Unlike the U.S. Coast Guard, I did not live by
the motto *semper paratus*, always ready. As a matter of fact, I was always
"not quite ready to dance." After doing enough of class to get the
endorphins into my bloodstream, I'd quit. I took just enough exercises
to alleviate pain and mental anxiety. And that's what I did this day.
Then I boarded a train home to the suburbs. I could not plan my
future. I didn't have one.

At home I found a message on the kitchen counter: Barbara Horgan
had called and wanted me to call her back. Hoping it would not be
bad news, I dialed her number.

"Allegra, Mr. B. wants your picture in the souvenir program. You have just been put on the schedule for tomorrow. Do you know where to go?"

"Yes, it's on the bulletin board."

"Good, pick up your *La Sonnambula* costume and be ready for the photo at two-thirty."

"Oh, thank you, Barbara. I was wondering if I was going to be in the book."

"Mr. B. definitely wants you in it." When Mr. B. realized that I hadn't been asked to be in the souvenir program, he had insisted. This was a way of showing the Board that I was still in the company. I was still included, even though I was dancing only once a year. My career resembled the blossoming cycle of a tulip.

"How is Mr. B. feeling?"

"The surgery on his eye was successful."

"That's such good news!"

"It's the best. Now, don't forget, two-thirty tomorrow."

"I won't." Miraculously, I was still in Balanchine's thoughts even with all he had to do, even with his eye surgery. He had not forgotten me.

My photograph was taken in the long white chiffon sleepwalker's costume, first some head shots and then additional shots with Bart Cook as the poet, the man I enchant in the ballet.

One week later, while walking toward the stage door, I encountered Mr. B. "How are you feeling, Mr. B.?"

"Good, and I can see again. I saw the photos of you, and they're beautiful. How is everything?"

"Fine." I still had some time left at the New York City Ballet. But I had put myself in the position of being grateful for every extension, not a very good place to be.

I also appeared in another publication during that year. When I made a mistake while listing ballets I had performed for *Who's Who*, they reprinted the error. According to the 1980-81 edition, among the ballets in my repertoire was *Afternoon of a Swan*.

One day in January 1981, Mr. B. found me in the hall on the fourth floor. I didn't often hang around this area, but he was on the lookout for me. It was time to fulfill my unwritten agreement with him again. "Allegra, I have been looking for something for you to dance this season, and I'd like you to learn the young girl in *Bourgeois Gentilhomme*. It's a good costume for you; you won't have to worry about weight."

"I'd love to do it, Mr. B. When does it go?" I stared into his face with gratitude.

"The last one goes on Valentine's Day. That will give you a full month to get ready."

"Should I study the videotape?"

"No, Suzy Hendl can teach it to you. I want her to learn the whole ballet, so she can rehearse it."

I was delighted but also frightened. How would I get in shape? Because I was embarrassed about my weight, I hadn't been going to class. I looked worse, and that made me feel awful, so I ate a little bit more for consolation.

After a few days of practice, my calf was also in knots, so, soon after my conference with Mr. B., I slunk around a few corners, walking quickly past the office, and arrived at the therapy room where I quickly ducked in the door, avoiding conversations and chance meetings. I had not felt comfortable backstage for some time. As I furtively sped into the room, the physical therapist looked at me in wonder. What was this dancer doing?

"Marika, I think I need some ultrasound on my calf. That miraculous machine that helps my knotted muscles so much."

This was a new development at the State Theater. We had a physical therapist and a therapy room. The company doctor had thought it an absolute necessity for the dancers. The person selected for this position was Marika Molnar, a genius at healing, with a love for dance and a special ESP when it came to a dancer's body.

"Let me look at it. What's your name? Are you in this company?"

"I guess so. My name is Allegra."

"You're famous! Why are you creeping around backstage like a mouse?"

"I'm out of shape and self-conscious."

Marika looked at the total me.

"I have to dance in one month, and I'm terrified."

"You're a little overweight, but I could help you get into shape. Take class every day and then come over here. I'll invent exercises for you."

"How fantastic!"

"You'll have to work like a dog. I have no mercy."

I found that out very soon. She was a human machine, inventive and indefatigable. At the end of three days, Marika told me to start wearing pointe shoes around my apartment at night. I had to get my toes toughened up and desensitized again. In three days I also started to work with Suzy Hendl, an exquisite dancer who was now a ballet mistress. This was going to be fun; the ballet was humorous.

However, to work again reminded me of all the times I couldn't work. So there was a sadness in starting again. But I couldn't allow myself to think that way. I needed this income—my children's well-being was at stake. Sometime during this period, I started to write rehearsal requests on dry ginkgo leaves for luck. These flaky messages could easily crumble and disappear. I was gambling with my practice sessions.

But another kind of session had become steady. I had finally found an exceptional therapist and was on the antidepressant Norpramin. I took less than the therapeutic dosage, and it helped me keep things even. This was the medication I had needed for years. This was no time to wallow in what could have been if I had been able to be consistent; I just had to do this performance and do it well. Marika and Suzy were doing their utmost, and I had to do the same. It was almost Valentine's Day, and I felt fairly ready.

Suzy asked Mr. B. to our next stage rehearsal, and there he was, standing in his favorite position near the wings on my right as I faced the audience. After rehearsal he came up and gave me a kiss. "That was very good, and your arabesque has improved so much."

I was very happy.

The performance went well. Because it was Valentine's Day, Godiva chocolates were given to everyone. I put on stage makeup for the first time in a long while, and the face looking back at me, my own, looked good. Peter Martins, my partner, said I looked great, and the review from Clive Barnes was spectacular.

I brought the chocolates home to Scarsdale. Bret, who was fourteen, was still awake and wanted to know what was in each of the bonbons.

"I don't know," I said, handing him the gold box.

"I'll find out."

Bret dashed into the kitchen and came back with a corkscrew. He put the bottom of the chocolate on the tip of the spiral, pushed down the wings and started to turn the handle as if he was opening a corked bottle. I laughed. I liked his "turn of the screw" approach to chocolates.

"The performance went well," I told him jubilantly.

"Good, Mom. I want to see you dance next time, and I want a very good seat."

"You've got it."

• • •

Meanwhile, Bert's luck had also turned around. His book about pills—a lay version of *The Physicians' Desk Reference* with color photographs—was doing well, and a book of his photos of Marilyn Monroe had just been published in Germany. It was a big deal, or more accurately, there was a large advance. The future looked better. Bert had dedicated the German edition to me—"f ür Allegra"—and offered me a trip to Paris. I learned about the dedication on page six of the *Post* when one of my ballet teachers pointed it out to me.

So, in the spring of 1981, I found myself in Paris with Bert, his William Morris agent, and the agent's girlfriend seated at La Tour d'Argent, a four-star restaurant, a lovely place located on the top of a small building.

"Allegra, how about this one? It costs a hundred dollars a bottle." Bert pointed to a selection on the elegant wine list.

I looked. The price was in francs, so it looked exorbitant. "Whatever," I said in a resigned tone. "You have your own style when it comes to spending. Don't forget to save some of this money for Susannah and Bret; they want to go to college."

I couldn't believe I was with Bert, but when he invited me I had been assured that there were no strings attached. I had the good grace to wear the same old dress I had worn for my divorce. However, the barefoot contessa I was not. I accepted the trip on the understanding that our romance was over and I had my own hotel room.

Bert said he understood, but he didn't. Whatever had existed for all those decades of our marriage still existed in his mind. Over the years, we had always been in contact over children and money, our two favorite topics. The first inkling, however, that Bert was out to win me back was Bret's announcement, "Dad's buying you a car." Feeling guilty about the past, Bert indeed gave me a new car. The Dawn Treader could tread no more, and Bert had replaced it with a Toyota straight from the dealer. He had even driven it to Scarsdale for me.

Bert had accepted my request for a separate room but could not comprehend it once we were in Paris. There had been a misunderstanding the first night over the sleeping arrangements. "Allegra," Bert had asked me with annoyance in his voice, "why do you think I invited you here?"

"Bert, I said I'd go along for the ride and only the ride, or I wouldn't go." I did admire the fact that he never seemed to give up, but this was not a reciprocal-trade agreement. As clearly as I thought I had stated my position, it was murky in Bert's mind.

I may as well enjoy this meal, I thought, looking at the Tour d'Argent menu, because afterward there will be more confusion. There was. The trip was a minor hell for me, and after Paris Bert went on pursuing me, but with not quite the same ardor.

Meanwhile, I went on meeting warped and wayward men. I dated two fetishists, one of whom collected alimony from his ex-wife and saw himself as a saint. The other one pulled out large binoculars and looked up the tutu of the prima ballerina from our front-row seats at the ballet. The binoculars were huge and the eyepieces had compasses in them. He could measure everything under the tutu precisely, which classified him as a leotard chaser.

I was not quite ready to trust a man again. Many of my dates who were more promising than the fetishists were not interested in a woman with three children.

Trista was now a grown-up working as a dancer in Mexico. After her first year of college, there was no money for her to continue. John Avildsen had an interest in making Bert's story into a movie, and Bert thought Trista could play me. He suggested she take some ballet classes. I thought it was possible, even though she didn't want to pursue ballet. All three of my children were athletic, but I didn't encourage them to dance. I certainly could have. Maybe I was wrong, but ballet is such a hard career—a lot of it is luck and timing. And so many things are involved that one can't control, such as having the right body type. I couldn't seem to live my life and also be a dancer, and I think I didn't want my children to have that struggle. Some people could mix it better than I, and some had bodies that didn't require as much attention as mine. However, Trista had choreographic and dancing ability, and she used it. When the movie didn't materialize, she switched to jazz and began a professional career in Mexico, Japan, and Italy.

Susannah was the wild dancer in the family. She was like an untrained Russian as she executed wild flying leaps down Fifth Avenue. She was exuberant and spontaneous. Once, as we entered a movie theater together, she ripped our tickets in two. One of the two ticket takers had called out, "Both sides," and my daughter responded quickly, ripping the tickets apart and, with two halves in her right hand and the other halves in her left, simultaneously handed the ripped halves to both ticket takers. They were startled and laughed. Years later, when I visited her in Pittsburgh on the opening of a show of her paintings, a friend complimented her. She was pleased, but the moment was also unbearable. She was so excited that she threw up her arms in delight and accidentally emptied her can of beer in her friend's face. We don't take compliments lightly in my family.

Susannah also was psychologically astute, the philosopher of the family. Often she'd make an observation in one sentence that clarified everything. When I was upset one day because I hadn't heard back from a man who had abruptly stopped calling me, Susannah said, "If he doesn't like you, then you don't like him." Her words were an immediate consolation. From a young age she had an insightful side. At ten, she wrote a note and placed it next to a dead moth on my dresser just before I left to do a concert with Eddie Villella in Kalamazoo. It read, "This is a secret performance written in secret thoughts." Susannah understood my feelings and read the subtext of a suitcase packed with pointe shoes.

Bret was the entrepreneur. When he was twelve, he made the most money in his class in a mock stock-market experiment. They all bought stock, there was a crash, and Bret ended up with the biggest gains. He also liked to blow things up. One time, as a special effect for an animated film, he created a conflagration in the dining room. He placed three pans of alcohol with connecting wicks on a tabletop. We hoped the fire would spread from pan to pan. There were also flares and fake blood. I stood by with a bucket of water. No wonder our landlord hated us. However, the fire was magnificent, with flames of a surreal blue.

"Bret, you must admit I'm a good sport: not many mothers would allow you to do this."

Bret tossed a charming smile my way.

The closest Bret came to ballet occurred the time I asked him if he wanted me to break in his sneakers for him. In one of the great parent-child dance teams, Toumanova's mother used to break in her shoes for her. My offspring Bret just laughed and looked horrified.

My children were the one constant in my lopsided and unsettled life. I loved the way their minds worked.

The phone rang early in the day during the fall of 1981. It was John Taras. "Allegra, I'm afraid I have some bad news to tell you."

My voice became very small. "Have I been fired?"

"No, it's about Mme. Doubrovska. She died yesterday. But I want you to know she was very happy just before it happened."

"Oh, my God. What was it?"

"It was a heart attack, and it was sudden. She was shopping, selecting a new dress. She was hunting for something beautiful."

"Oh, John, I've always felt that I was her child of the ballet. She was so elegant and gave such gorgeous classes. She was so generous to me."

"She was one of the greats."

"I still have her card from a bouquet of flowers she sent to me when I was fifteen."

Tears began to flow. I thought of our first meeting when she was fifty-five and I was fourteen and I took my first class with her. In her seventies, she was alone. Vladimirov had died. She took a trip to Europe with her little dog, and during the movie the people in the airplane cabin complained about someone snoring. Everyone was saying, "Be quiet, be quiet, who's doing that?" Mme. Doubrovska lifted her pooch, "He is." She held her creature up for all to see, a sleeping, snoring little ball of fluff. She told me this story in a tone of radiant purity that I found touching, as if all the passengers were searching for the Holy Grail—a little grail that barked—and she was the person who found it.

Once, when she was in the hospital, I brought her a length of lace and a seashell. She thanked me, saying, "When I go to sleep, I can put on the lace and listen to the ocean." This woman could create an atmosphere anywhere.

Her funeral service was three hours long. Everyone stood for the entire time. Danilova was in tears. Although they were like sisters, Doubrovska had been competitive with Danilova and could become very involved with those feelings, even when she was eighty years old. They both had danced in Balanchine's *Apollo* in 1928; their history and connections went back a long way. I thought of Field Marshal Montgomery with a photo of Rommel in his tent, or Strindberg with a photo of Ibsen over his writing table. These men never gave up competing, nor did Doubrovska and Danilova. Luckily, I received only positive help from Madame. I was her ballet child, not her rival.

Candles burned and ate up the oxygen. Everyone's grief consumed the oxygen as well, and a few people fainted. It was the Russian Orthodox way of saying good-bye, of saying how much you were loved. This woman had danced and had created magic. Maybe she had once wanted a child of her own, but she had never had one. Perhaps I was her spiritual child. I saw so much in what she did. I had heard that the younger dancers at the school mocked her and said she was vain. But I knew otherwise.

Some of my past was slipping away. I wanted to hold on to it. I was certain Mr. B. felt devastated. He adored her so much, and they conferred on so many things. The world of ballet was beginning to change.

CHAPTER EIGHTEEN

Dancing should be like lace.

—FEDERICO FELLINI

In June 1982, Edward Villella asked me to do a benefit with him at the Metropolitan Opera House. There was to be an international array of dancers participating—American, Russian, Danish, English, German, South American—and Margot Fonteyn would be the on-stage hostess. I was thrilled to be asked, because I wanted to pull myself together again. When Marika didn't have time to be a human machine for me, I scheduled a week of Pilates exercises, seven in all, plus my regular class and rehearsals with Eddie. I could feel myself getting stronger day by day. I wanted to look trim, or I'd feel embarrassed appearing with such a gallery of greats.

Two days before this glittering event, Susannah graduated from the Scarsdale Alternative High School. The ceremony took place outdoors on a weedy hillside. Only eight students were graduating, but nine teachers were scheduled for "short" talks. If only it could have been like *The Gong Show*, but it wasn't. The teachers were wordy. Finally, out of sheer boredom, Bret climbed a tree and disappeared. Walking home was better than these speeches.

The graduation took three hours. While sitting, my calves and neck sent me messages of despair, and when I finally arrived at my apartment I called Eddie to tell him rehearsing was impossible. The ceremony had taken a huge chunk of the day. So instead of rehearsing, I read about Sir Ethelred, the secret agent. He reminded me of the famous eleventh-century Anglo-Saxon king, Ethelred the Unready. I had great sympathy for Ethelred the Unready.

On the day before the performance, I woke up at six and muted some pink tights with a tinge of taupe, sewed some ribbon on my pointe shoes, and weighed in at 107. I had toned down my tights in an attempt to deaccentuate my legs, and I liked the result. I considered wearing a string of bright red radishes to the diamond party after the gala as a necklace. De Beers had underwritten this event; maybe radishes could be my rocks.

When I eventually called Eddie to set up a rehearsal, I told him Ethelred would be a little more ready. The next day I was greatly relieved when our practice session went well.

On the night of the performance, I was placed in a dressing room with Doreen Wells, a former principal dancer with the Royal Ballet and now a marchioness. Eddie and I were placed second from last in the program, so I went out to the wings to watch and warm up. Baryshnikov was watching the performance, and that made me nervous. I said to him, "Please don't watch me, I'm not up to this. Go in the green room and smoke a cigarette." (This was the first time I ever encouraged someone to smoke.) Did he symbolize Everyman or the most ruthless eyes?

"Oh, don't worry so much, Allegra." He stayed in place.

Eddie and I were dancing his *Shenandoah,* a ballet I had done before, but this time I had trouble with the concept. I was supposed to be a figment of his imagination. I could dance as my own figment, but this evening not as his—it made me feel too wispy and intangible. I couldn't decide how I should dance as a vapor. By the end of the piece, I felt depressed. The dance had not gone where I wanted it to go. I had not imbued the steps with a special flavor of abandonment; I had only done a good job.

A bouquet appeared from somewhere as we took our bow, and I decided to do my special floral interpretation. I picked out one flower and began to offer it to Eddie, but then with a rapid change of heart put the one flower behind my back and gave the rest of the bouquet to Eddie, saving the one bloom for myself. It was a bow I occasionally did in remembrance of the greatest traveling salesman of them all. Gelsey and Violette sometimes borrowed it from me. You can't copyright a bow. I was jubilant when this particular audience howled, loving the switch. Sometimes it's better to have only one of something. Well, at least I'd given the audience a tiny piece of pure theater.

Back in the dressing room, Doreen Wells was changing for the party afterward. During the evening she had performed a tap dance, but now she had a long dress of forest green, in pure silk taffeta with a tight bodice. Assuming the role of Marchioness of Londonderry, she asked her personal dresser to put her shoes on for her. I was only Allegra Kent the Unready, so I put on my own shoes.

A week after the gala with Eddie, I was in the backstage area of the State Theater when I ran into Mr. Balanchine. I was just going in to pick up my unearned paycheck, a guilty mission I had to work myself up to perform. As I entered the long yellow hall that would take me to the office, there was Mr. B. at the other end, walking slowly, leaning one shoulder against the wall for stability. He had ear trouble, which was affecting his balance. I had never seen him look quite so vulnerable. He saw me, smiled, and continued to slowly progress. I walked over to him and we spoke. I asked him how he was, and he minimized his physical problems. I would have to ask someone else to find out how Mr. B. really was.

I knew I had to make an appearance at Saratoga. I had not danced well with Eddie and had not been onstage for a while before that. This worried me. While poring over the summer programs, I saw that *Apollo* was scheduled. *Apollo* was not that hard technically, but the costume, a white leotard and a short dance skirt, revealed the body, its beauty or its problems. I plunged into the conversation. "Mr. B., do you think I could dance *Apollo* this summer in Saratoga?"

Mr. B. looked thoughtfully at me. "I don't see why not."

"Oh, thank you. Can I help you get to the elevator?"

"No, I'm fine, dear. I just have a little ear problem. I don't need help."

"I'll start to prepare for this right away."

I walked toward the office but turned around to watch Mr. B. as he progressed down the hall. Mr. B. was frail. He must have hated this condition. Just a little while back, he could show choreography with his body—demonstrate precisely, express everything. Yet, in spite of all his problems, he understood that I had to make an appearance to justify my position. I would not forget to take class and I would try to diet. He seemed to be behind me in that conversation.

In early July, I received a call from the ballet mistress. "Mr. B. told me you want to do *Apollo*. Well, if you do, you have to come up here and show yourself and take company class. It's a leotard ballet. We have to see how you look in a leotard."

Her tone was unfriendly. Maybe I had asked too much? The company did not know the state of my physical body. But the way the ballet mistress put it made me feel as if my sinews and naked body would be on the auction block and the buyers were hostile. The atmosphere would be impossible. My psychological makeup at that moment was too fragile, and so I didn't show up.

The endings of careers sometimes come as a surprise. The body is not entirely predictable. Toward the end of her career, Melissa Hayden could barely function in the classroom, but she could function beautifully onstage. Sometimes if she had an injury she'd completely wrap up both legs in Ace bandages, like a mummy. Then she'd cover them with pink tights, add pointe shoes, and be ready when the curtain went up. She'd warm up in the wings with weights on her shoulders and have her oxygen tank and her tea with honey ready. She was near fifty when she quit. Her muscles were naturally strong and didn't lose strength quickly. When you are older you have to work harder to stay in the same place; the law of diminishing returns sets in. Melissa planned the way her career would end: with a gala performance and a work done especially for her by Mr. B. At the moment, it was very uncertain when I would appear again.

Although I didn't know it at the time, the night I danced at the Metropolitan Opera House benefit with Eddie had been a farewell performance. There would never be a gala for me, no symbolic gold watch. And my last appearance wasn't a success. I had fallen to the occasion.

In early 1983, the pattern in my life was about to reverse. The decline of my dance career was accompanied by something good in my personal life. On a blind date arranged by friends, I met the filmmaker and innovative editor Aram Avakian.

Actually, I had met him once twenty-four years earlier. Bert had brought him backstage during *The Seven Deadly Sins*. After the usual greetings, Aram had said conversationally, "I saw Nora Kaye in *The Cage* in London," and Allegra, the mongoose, had said sharply, "Name-dropper!" At that point, any man would have had to bend over backward to gain my trust. Tarzan's chimpanzee had better manners than I did; the chimp knew how to shake hands politely and give a friendly monkey smile to a newly met fragile human.

While dressing for my first date with Aram, I decided on a black skirt and blouse from the thrift shop. It didn't amount to much, so I added a few clothespins as a border. In an old photo, Buster Keaton dressed up his outfit by using a clothespin as a tie tack, a humble, inventive way of upgrading rags. Maybe clothespins were romantic too? The minute I met Aram, I could tell that he liked me, and so could everyone else, because he was so attentive. My clothing style didn't put him off; in fact, he seemed to like the comedians of the past.

It was during our drive home in heavy, dense rain that I introduced Aram to my former self. "Aram, my real name is Iris Cohen and my daddy was called Harry Cohen."

"Really? How wonderful. You have the nature of a wildflower. If you had used your real name, you would have had a greater success."

"Some day I want to plant a field of irises bordered by pointed conifers. In the spring, my old name will bloom in resplendent colors."

"I could be your gardener and mulch. By the way, does Bret tell his father about your dates?"

"I think so. Why?"

"When I call, I shouldn't use my name. Bert would go crazy if he knew I was seeing you."

Aram was right. Their history went way back to when they worked together on *Jazz on a Summer's Day,* the movie that Bert made in the summer of 1958 while I was writing him unanswered letters from Australia. These two men were very competitive, and one of Bert's girlfriends had become Aram's first wife. I did not want Bert to know about Aram's entrance into my life. Bert still wanted to remarry me. I remembered his attitude when Clay Felker married Pamela Tiffin. To Bert it was inconsequential that he'd been married to me when he was involved with one of these women; his jealousy crossed borders.

When we arrived at my Scarsdale apartment, Aram looked around. I had styled the entire living room after a Joseph Cornell collage, and near the glass door many succulent plants from California were grouped.

I told him, "These plants solved their survival problems by becoming succulents. Their leaves are fat and juicy in case of drought. But when I did the same thing, Balanchine complained I was overweight, and it imperiled my survival as a dancer."

"I like you the way you are."

Aram and I sat on my broken-down couch. I apologized for it. "All my money goes into expenses. Susannah calls this object part couch and part barbecue pit. It's on the verge of disintegration."

When we exchanged histories, I told Aram that I'd like to write a book on four hundred men, all called Harry Cohen, and tell their life stories. I wasn't the only one with a Harry Cohen in her past.

When he asked if I was still dancing, I told him about my fears that my dancing life had no real form to it and that I was neither in nor out of a career. I told him about my poor performance with Villella and my worry that I would be fired. I couldn't seem to take class, and, worse, I couldn't move in a new direction toward a new goal. Mr. B. was ill. It was uncertain if I would ever put on my pink tights again. I was terrified of the future. I told him about trying to send Misha to the green room the last time I had performed.

"Why don't you remember the best time instead of the last time?" he asked me.

I liked Aram. When he kissed me good night, I said, "Your skin is so silky. Does everyone go crazy over it?"

"Every time I cross the street."

I called Aram five days later, and we got together. He, too, seemed to be in a terrible depression. There were certain similarities in our pasts. Our careers had taken odd and discouraging turns, and for long stretches we both were responsible for the total support of our children.

We walked by the river and watched the winter sun, a red ball of fire, descend on the New Jersey horizon.

I told Aram, "I've just gone out with two men in a row who were fetishists. Doesn't that beat the law of averages?" I described my sad dating history. "I met so many cruel, selfish, mean-spirited cranks. I needed a ton of love, and they couldn't give me an ounce."

"So. They've all been lightweights?"

"The newspapers say ideal weight is a slippery concept."

"Oh, Allegra, why didn't you call me up years ago?"

"I wish I had."

"Give me a kiss."

I did.

"Thank you."

Aram thanked me for every sign of affection and every touch.

The night we made love, I put on a red nightgown with giant pink flowers. We had a sweet time.

In the morning, I asked, "Do you need coffee?"

"No, you woke me up, Allegra. Allegra, Allegra, Allegra, you're beautiful and you flipped me with your big toe."

"It's leverage. Aram, you are adorable."

"Yes, I know. It's also because I adore you. I'm in love with your body."

"I'm happy. Aram, you're my first man. It took me forty-five years to find you."

Aram repeated my name hundreds of times.

"When did you first feel something for me?"

"Instantly."

"Oh, Aram, I like the way you make love to me. It's true love."

Later that morning, when I called Aram, he asked, "Are you still crazy about me?"

"Yes, I'm as crazy about you as ever. Did you start to worry?"

"No."

"That's good. I've been living by my wits all these years and I have fewer of them than most."

"I think you have more. You know what I like about dancing? The big leaps."

"Me too."

"I like it when a man and a woman dance together, then they go off and return separately; then they come back and dance together."

"That's a pas de deux," I told him.

"Barbara, is it *over* ?" I sounded alarmed and wished I didn't.

"I'm afraid so." Barbara Horgan's voice came over the phone in a very clear connection.

Cold lead collected in my throat with a welling up of sorrow. It had really happened. I'd been fired after thirty years with the New York City Ballet—and by my friend. "I don't know what to say." I looked outside my window; it was a new season, spring. I'd never dance with the company again. There would be no more seasons for me there. Maybe I'd never dance anywhere again.

Barbara continued, "I'm sorry, Allegra. The Board asked me to do this. Please know it's not Jerry or Peter, and it's not what Mr. B. wants either. The Board has just taken directive control of the company. Unfortunately, Mr. B. is no longer able to do so."

This was true. A few hours earlier I had read about it in *The New York Times*. Mr. B. had been in Roosevelt Hospital for the past eight months, and Peter Martins and Jerome Robbins had just been named balletmasters-in-chief. But I had not understood what it would mean to me personally. Now I wondered what I was going to do. I lived on the exact edge of my salary. I owned nothing and had nothing saved, and I'd been unable to develop an idea for my future.

"Don't think that the Board hasn't expressed concern. They want to know if Bert will help you."

I managed to say no. Bert had been out of my life for more than ten years. I didn't receive alimony, and my child support was now seventy dollars a week. Although Bert's interest had rekindled a few years earlier when he gave me the car and took me to Paris, he was not about to take care of me.

"Come in and see me. We'll talk."

It was over, but as a formality I had to drop in for a meeting. As I passed various people in the hall on my way to the office, I wondered if they knew. Did I detect pity in the receptionist's hello? Unlike Melissa's career, mine was not finalized by a triumphal gala, just an ignominious phone call. I had not held on tightly to what I had but had let it slip out of my grasp.

In Lincoln Kirstein's windowless room, Barbara told me, "I'm sorry, Allegra. The company will give you a salary for a short while— maybe we can even stretch it—and then you can collect unemployment insurance."

My emotions churned. Secretly I wished I'd worked for the post office; at least I'd have had a pension. Tears were forming, and I tried very hard to suppress them. Somewhere along the line I had lost or given away everything that was important to keep. Why couldn't I hang on to things?

At the same time, I had made the mistake of staying too long in the company. As I left the office, Barbara looked at my bag.

"You need a new purse."

I had just slipcovered it, and I guess it looked shabby. What I needed was a new profession, not a new purse. I didn't get either. Since that day, I have yet to purchase a pocketbook. I make mine from old tights and cut-up dresses. The legs of tights tied together and hung over the shoulder work well. The natural closings get opened. The crotch is opened, and the waist is closed. I didn't envision needing tights for anything else.

This blow was not unexpected. Oftentimes during the previous two years I had anticipated a similar message. I had danced and danced well for many of those years since the split with Bert, but not consistently. A review of the late 1970s read, "It has been a good season, generally, for the company. Even the elusive Allegra Kent showed up for at least one performance."

Although I had appeared once a season in 1981, after that I danced only once a year, making me the highest-paid performer per performance within the company. Mr. B. would carefully think of something uniquely suited to my ability, a role that was not psychologically frightening. Then he gave me a month to pull myself together for one performance. Probably if he had said to me, "You've got to dance," it would have been the best thing. But he wasn't that interested in me anymore. By 1983, it had been seventeen years since he'd created a ballet for me.

I felt deeply humiliated. I was the very first piece of deadwood for the new management to weed out. There must have been a lot of resentment about my peculiar position.

When he was well and running the company, Mr. B. had seen a wild humor in my rare appearances, and so did I. He assigned a dressing room to me every season so that I had a place. But at the time I was fired, I hadn't actually danced in a long while, over a year. That season I had hoped to see *Bourgeois Gentilhomme* on the program, a ballet I felt I could gracefully and humorously bow out on; instead there was *Episodes*. I felt less limber in 1983 than when I last performed it in 1980, and rather than do it less well I chose not to do it at all, or anything else. I had reached an impasse in my life and could not make a move in or out of the company. My position had no dignity, and it was impossible for me to formulate future plans. Mr. Balanchine would pass me in the hall and smile in surprise as if to say, *Delighted to see you, but are you still here?*

My father, when he was alive, had suggested collecting garbage, another job that had what mine did not have, a pension. This seemed unappealing after the heady perfume of ballet. It was one of my father's more curious ideas.

I wandered into a ballet class and began to cry during a port de bras to the back. Melissa Hayden noticed this and told me she understood. Her words were comforting. I didn't feel so alone in my back bend of despair, an echo from *The Seven Deadly Sins,* but I saw that dance doors were closing, not opening, for me.

As I left the State Theater, the future filled me with terror. I was still recoiling psychologically from Bert's huge financial loss twelve years earlier when I felt as if my life had been smashed. Supporting myself, the housekeeper, and the children took everything I had. When I called my mother with the news about the end of my career, she told me, "No matter how badly off Wendy is, you're worse." She exploded with laughter at her reading, and so did I. Wendy's husband had left her, and she was struggling as a single mother of five children. Mother had impeccable comic irony.

For a week after I was let go I called my ballet friends and left a message on their tape: "Orchids in their configurations conform to internal rules." I thought that irises must conform also, but their rules are different from orchids'.

A few days later, I spied Joanna, a new friend of mine who worked in the New York City Ballet's press office.

"Hi, Joanna. How are you?"

"I'm fine, Allegra. The publicity department is emptying out your file, giving your photos away to anyone in the office who wants them and throwing out the rest. I tried to get most of them because you should have your photos."

"Oh, yes, thank you. I would have thought they'd call me on that."

"I know." Joanna made a face. "While I was out at lunch, the office received a memo to discontinue your file. When I returned, they had already given a lot of your photos away."

"Why are they acting this way? Am I paranoid? Somehow I think they're trying to pretend that I was never there. I feel like a nonperson." I put two fingers on the edge of my cheekbone and touched my face. I wanted to feel its stability. I didn't want to disappear so easily. "This is a little thing, but it hurts a lot."

"I'm sorry, Allegra. They didn't handle this very well. I left the photos I saved with the guard at the stage door with your name on them. There is one of you and Eddie in *Scotch Symphony* and even one when you were Miss Maple Syrup of 1958."

My full-time noncareer had not provoked only resentment. Annihilation was more accurate. It was as if ten dark birds flew over my head, the creatures that close off the past.

One week after I was fired, Mr. Balanchine died. Barbara called early on the morning of April 30 with the terrible news. "He's not with us anymore."

I went to Balanchine's funeral with Suzy Pilarre, Renée Éstópinal, and Debbie Flomine, my friends from the ballet. A great era was over; a genius of dance had died. Again, the Russian Orthodox service lasted for three hours. All the mourners stood for the entire time in a numbing sorrow. Two thousand candles blazed, and again a few women passed out, but Mme. Danilova stood the whole time in proud respect, defying her age. The great man was gone.

My detachment from the company had been impossible until Balanchine's death. I was there only as long as Mr. B. was there. It had been an informal gift. The tie was finally severed, but I couldn't do it myself. I had to be fired, and he couldn't live forever.

Aram was away in California during this devastating week. We were unable to connect by phone. When he returned, I told him my news and broke out into uncontrollable tears. He hugged me tightly while repeating "It's all right" many, many times. He said he would take care of me forever and gave me what I desperately needed—time to figure out my next step.

For me, ballet—the continuation of my childhood dreams and the way I chose to rebel against my mother, visually but soundlessly— was over.

I had a dream about performing a ritual to prolong Mme. Doubrovska's life. It occurred to me it was not Madame under the blanket but Mr. B. It was the end of so much. I was so deeply upset that I didn't clean my refrigerator for the next two years.

From my dressing room in the New York State Theater, I moved to the lockers. Eventually, I decided to move out of the locker room, but this took years. A part of me still thought I was on the verge of another comeback. My pink tights looked as if they would soon be moving again.

Although my stay at the New York City Ballet was over and there would be no ceremonial jewelry and no gold watch, a stunning piece of glitter did arrive. Freddie Grzyb of the opera wardrobe called. He had a *Swan Lake* pin to give me, a diamond swan swimming in an amethyst lake, a picture pin with a fairy-tale story. An allegorical gift from a friend, an exquisite consolation prize.

Five months after Mr. B. died, I pursued a job with the show *On Your Toes*. Thirty years earlier, during my first European tour, Mr. B. had received a telegram asking him to revive this Broadway musical. The day he received the offer, he came into class beaming and asking Maria Tallchief which one of the boys he should take with him as a comedian. He tap-danced around the room and sat at the piano and played "Slaughter on Tenth Avenue" and a boogie-woogie. After a few moments, it was over, and he resumed his familiar no-nonsense attitude. He said, "Let's be conscientious," and we began pliés.

The star of the current production, Natalia Makarova, didn't want to do matinees, and the producers seemed interested in me. I auditioned, and my friend Suzy Pilarre coached me in acting, but very soon afterward I understood that they wanted a Russian to do the part, and many were available. "That's show biz," I told Aram. I wrote the following letter:

September 13, 1983
Dear American Guild of Musical Artists:
   I'd like to withdraw from the union as honorably as possible.

                                                   Allegra Kent

The next day I went to the Scarsdale YWCA, famous for its dance courses, and spoke to the director. She wanted me to teach a series of classes and suggested starting with one a week. She would give me forty dollars per class. Well, it was a start. The first class would be the next Tuesday at eleven. The night before my middle-aged return to teaching, I found myself in a panic, going over and over the format and the steps. I wasn't this nervous for the *On Your Toes* audition. Would I have to wow the students with amazing combinations?

The next morning I prolonged my self-torment. I called Henley for advice. Her recommendation was, "Keep it simple." My panic, out of proportion to the actual event, was not easy to subdue. Counting to eight four times seemed beyond me. When the appointed time edged up on me, I drove over to the Y, changed clothes, and walked into the studio, just after the preceding class had finished.

About three minutes later, one person walked in; that was it. There is group energy in a class of students, but now I would have to generate all the enthusiasm. I told the pupil we would wait five minutes for possible stragglers. I started to stretch with a hopeful eye on the entrance, but no one else arrived. So I gave a private lesson but did all the steps together with my devotee of the dance so she wouldn't feel lonely, thinking that my overblown fear should be saved for journeys to the moon. Teaching wasn't so terrible or dangerous.

The dance director reconsidered the time slot and moved me to three afternoons a week. That hour was better for aspiring young dancers. I didn't make much money, but it was something, and it was honest work.

I went on taking a discreet number of ballet classes in case a job appeared. Given our family's style of message collecting, I may have missed some offers. One evening I asked Bret, "Were there any phone calls today for me?"

"Yes, but I forget her name—it has five letters in it and two vowels." Bret had style but was too impressionistic to be a secretary.

"Thanks a lot."

Aram asked, "Do you know who that is?"

"No."

Finally, I told Bert that he had to help me until I got on my feet. I was down to the last of my money.

I was desperately afraid of sinking so low economically that I'd never be able to get out of it. A New York City subway mouse lives and dies underground on the tracks between trains and incomprehensible announcements. It is trapped for life. I didn't want that to happen to me.

Aram sent me a big check to bounce over to the bank and bounce out my minus. He didn't want me to pay him back; he wanted me to buy a new couch and a new bed. The old couch was twenty years old, eroded by reading.

"You're so generous. I'm so down right now that the children can locate me when they hear a moan."

I was still reading biographies—*Memoirs of an Anarchist* and a book about W. H. Hudson, the author of *Green Mansions*. Also a book about Elsie de Wolfe, mistress of the externals. She had azure hair on the Côte d'Azur and advocated white flowers only for gardens and bouquets.

Aram told me he wanted to read what I was reading, and he surprised me one day by saying, "You're an intellectual."

I really laughed at that. "I don't want to think. I don't even want to think about clothes. I don't want to be compelled to look or dress a certain way."

He told me, "I like you the way you are."

I realized Aram would be loyal. For once, I'd be the only date palm in the entire Sahara. For the first time in my life, I was in love.

One of the fetishists called and I told him, "Give my worst to your mother."

In December of 1983 Peter Martins announced his plan to retire as a dancer so that he could devote all his energy to running the company and choreographing. His last appearance would be *The Nutcracker,* in which he'd be partnering Suzanne Farrell with Jerry Robbins as Drosselmayer.

I took my things to Henley's apartment in the city and invented an outfit for the performance. A dress that had disintegrated was now an apron, which I put over my black slip and thereby avoided having to iron anything. Then I colored my hair and checked Henley's mail for bills because she was out of town. I still had about one and a half hours. I was nervous, almost as if I were giving a performance. I looked at one of Henley's ballet books, waiting for Aram to arrive and take me to the theater. Aram loved my outfit.

Before the performance, I learned there was to be a party afterward. I wasn't invited; I wasn't a part of this group anymore. My personal regrets overpowered me, and I watched the dancing with difficulty. A performance and a party seemed to be the way to finish a career, but I was no longer in the company. My name had disappeared.

The next Saturday night, my friend Judith Yeargin called.

"Allegra, have you read the Sunday *Times*?"

To my surprise, an article by Anna Kisselgoff about Peter's retirement was also about me. Kisselgoff had not forgotten that I had once danced with the New York City Ballet, although the company never acknowledged my disappearance.

That Christmas, I went to the bank and discovered a three-hundred-dollar miscalculation; I had no more money. I bought a Christmas tree for the children, a cheap one with very few branches. The tree looked so pitiful that the only thing to do was buy two more trees, which I did the next day, and place them on each side to add fullness. So I had three trees and no presents, and I was penniless before Christmas. I found some ties for Aram, in the thrift shop—total cost $1.50—but my children didn't want clothes. This would be my first Christmas without a salary. Bret told me he was going out to play poker and he'd bring something back. He sounded remarkably like his grandfather, Harry Cohen. Bret returned with sixty-five dollars in quarters, nickels, and dimes.

"Bret, will this ruin someone's Christmas?"

"No, Mom, these kids are rich."

"Well, then, let's buy a bottle of champagne."

"I'm going to put a down payment on an iguana."

I told the children they would get rain checks for Christmas, but they were busy trying to keep the iguana warm and happy. Bret had bought it for Susannah with his poker money. He paid with quarters. Then he put a down payment on another iguana.

Aram arrived with money and his mother's antimacassar. I wore it as a scarf to the Christmas party at my sister's house, which was gloriously festive, and I finally introduced Aram to my mother.

"I just met this man in the Village. His name is Aram."

"Hello." Mother smiled with interest as she scrutinized his jacket and face.

"Hello." Aram extended his hand.

"What do you think his profession is?" I asked with a touch of mischief.

Mother guessed, "He's a writer."

"Let's ask. By the way, Aram, what is your profession?"

"Hardware."

For Christmas, Aram bought me a new bed.

"Thank you, darling, we will celebrate its birthday in a year with champagne and a pillow fight." I thought, *Could anyone care more about me than Aram?*

I began to worry that Aram would stop loving me and maybe start acting like a madman. I'd never encountered someone whose love was constant. Certainly not Bert. And with Joseph Cornell and Balanchine it was the next woman who provided inspiration. Their love hadn't been reliable either.

But Aram's was. I had watched Aram give serious attention and devotion to a degraded, exhausted, and broken-down geranium plant found in the garbage. He encouraged it and mulched it and even gave it showers. Occasionally, he crumbled a leaf to smell its pungent perfume. He was fiercely joyous when the plant formed tiny buds in the summer. It would bloom; his faithfulness had been rewarded.

In the year after I was fired from the company, I was like that geranium plant, and Aram gave me care and empathy. Even two years after Mr. B.'s death, I was still crying. I continued my dance career at night while sleeping. I dreamed that there was a revival of *Ivesiana*. The rehearsal went well, but during the performance, the male dancers hindered my progress. They had to pass and hold on to me simultaneously. Afterward, I got ready for the next ballet. I seemed to be dancing really well. I gave the boys constructive criticism the way a ballet mistress would do. It was an all-Balanchine program, and he was still alive.

I had many dance dreams in this period, and during them I always did exquisite star turns. In this realm it was easy to do many, many beautiful pirouettes in a high proud passé, the position that creates a beautiful triangle of leg, thigh, and tibia. I also cried in my dreams.

When I needed comfort, Aram would hold me and say repeatedly, "It's all right, it's all right." Some things have to be said at least five times.

From Allegra to Iris

Allegra and students. Photo by Gayle Corkery.

CHAPTER NINETEEN

Life is all memory except for passing moments.
— TENNESSEE WILLIAMS, THE MILK
TRAIN DOESN'T STOP HERE ANYMORE

When I'd been out of the New York City Ballet for a year, Peter Martins decided to revive *Bugaku* for Heather Watts. I felt terrible. They wouldn't do it while I was still there. Then Heather called. "Allegra, I have two job ideas for you. I know a woman who wants private ballet lessons, and I'd like you to help me with *Bugaku*. Are you interested?"

"Absolutely, I'd love to help you with *Bugaku*, and I can teach ballet. Who is the woman?"

"She's the wife of one of the richest men in the world. Her name is Lamia, Mrs. Adnan Khashoggi. She's adorable, charming, and interested in exercising with a ballerina. You could also bring your water wings, because she has a pool on one of her floors."

"Are you kidding—a pool *in* the apartment?"

"Honest. She has three floors in Olympic Towers. Now, Allegra, don't start worrying about it. If anything, you are overqualified for this job. A portable barre is going to be delivered today."

When I showed up at rehearsal to help Heather with *Bugaku*, I pointed out as many things as I could in an hour. At the end of our time together, a ballet mistress walked in. When she saw me, her face froze; she seemed to feel insulted. Once in an interview, John Taras had remarked, "So often in Balanchine's ballets, I find that the dancer the work was made on is what the ballet is about. When the cast changes, the work survives, but it's not the same; it becomes diluted." But the ballet mistress was upset. Even though the part was created for me, she felt that my presence was unnecessary. Heather sensed this and never asked me to help her again. Not only was I no longer a member of the company, I didn't even feel welcome in certain areas backstage.

However, the wife of one of the richest men in the world still wanted my help. I proceeded toward the Olympic Towers with my string of water wings, some practice clothes, and a bathing cap.

When security cleared me, I went up to the thirty-third floor and arrived at the kitchen door. Two men, who were, I presumed, body-guards, were watching a closed-circuit TV set. They put me in a room to wait. Heather had told me this might happen and suggested reading material. A book, however, was already part of my standard equipment for the train. At this very moment *Lord Melville* by David Cecil was tucked into my bag. Before plunging into the nineteenth century and learning more about Queen Victoria's adviser, I looked about at my twentieth-century surroundings. Giant elephant tusks framed the doorway, and there were so many bouquets of long-stem roses, they were almost boring in their repetition. The area was conference space; upholstered pieces in brown and beige implied "office." The waiting made me nervous. Soon I would have to act like an expert and some-one at ease in this lavish atmosphere. I must not appear too needy; that had no dignity.

After about a half hour, Mrs. Khashoggi's secretary came for me, and we made our way up to the less formal quarters. Lamia, Italian by birth, was tall and had long black hair and a huge diamond ring. She greeted me warmly, and we changed in her boudoir where the floor was natural canvas inlaid with blue stripes. The bathroom blazed with solid-gold fixtures. However, it did not contain her lapis lazuli tub, which was near a window overlooking the city. We were high up. The top of the AT&T Building was a few yards beneath us. During the barre work I felt like an exercising eagle hovering over a vista of skyscrapers.

After the ballet part of our workout was over, we changed into bathing suits. Lamia gave me a giant-size terry-cloth bathrobe from a closet that contained fifty or more, all in white and all from Yves St. Laurent. We were on our way to the water.

The pool was surrounded by plants, marbleized mirrors, and an-other magnificent view. Once in the warm water, Lamia put the Schwimmflugels on her ankles and let her leg drift up to the side. "This is genius," she told me. She understood the principle of it right away. Up was easy, down was hard. She was genuinely mad about the exercises. When she told me that she used to be an expert diver,

I gave her a dive mask to try an upside-down split. "As a matter of fact," I told her, "you can have it. This one doesn't quite fit me, and I use it only to cut onions." Lamia laughed.

While she was in this topsy-turvy position, her husband walked in. She was upside down in the water with her legs spread apart, orange air wings on her ankles.

"Hello, darling," she said to him after she surfaced. "I want you to watch this." She went upside-down again.

Mr. Khashoggi was of medium height with a rounded build. He wore a regular suit, but in some of her bedroom photos he had on an Arab headdress. Later, when I asked some friends if Khashoggi was in oil, I was shocked to learn he was an arms dealer with thirty-six domiciles, a yacht named after his only daughter, Nabila, and a jet or two.

Lamia was going to pay me two hundred dollars an hour, including waiting time, and I felt like an expert. We made a date for the next day's ballet class. Lamia was very happy with the workout; chaîné turns were her favorite.

The classes came to an end when Lamia left town. She paid me, and I went to Grand Central Terminal and counted the money in the pay toilet. As I left the station, I saw a bag woman who had a little poodle dressed in a basketball shirt asleep on the floor on the lower level. What a contrast.

It was Palm Sunday, and my palms felt greased.

Unwelcome at the New York City Ballet and having lost the tuition of my one pupil, I was now desperate for income and something to give my days purpose and shape.

One thing that made me feel creative during this empty period was a late-night session with some scissors. One afternoon while going to see the physical therapist in the theater, I detoured to visit with Freddie Grzyb of the opera wardrobe. After our hellos and greetings, some iridescent glints from his garbage pail caught my attention, and I walked over to inspect. Freddie noticed me hovering over the basket and said, "You can take that if you want. They're scraps from the *Kismet* costumes."

"Oh, thank you. I love the variegated look."

While rummaging, I thought of myself as fate's mouse receiving an invitation to forage for destiny's fabric in the opera's recycling heap.

"These will go somewhere, Fred. On a letter, or a package, or on me. Their destination is not yet known."

That evening at midnight I pretended I was Mme. Karinska creating some concoction of velvet and collected snippets, sculpting satin with scissors and crocheting green chains as Madame used to do. I felt that Karinska's memory must have dated as far back as her grandmother's tales, which might put us in the year 1830. Maybe her grandmother was born when Pushkin was still alive. Her memories of the old regime had their reverberations in the tulle, peau de soie, and ancient laces of her work. Many of her costumes had an understory as well as an underskirt. This gauzy fabric fueled my personal stockpile; Freddie's garbage pail had become one of my vacant lots.

At this time, Arthur Mitchell and the Dance Theatre of Harlem seemed like a possible direction, and I called his school looking for work. I was told he was out of town and left my number. Within minutes, Arthur called and said, "You've got the job."

"What will I be doing?"

"I don't know. We'll figure something out. What job did you apply for?"

"One in the abstract."

"You've got it." Arthur laughed.

"Where are you, Arthur?"

"On tour. I just got the message that you called, and I think you have a lot to offer. Call the office and make an appointment."

I did, but then I canceled it at the last minute. At the time, I was too insecure and wasn't taking ballet class. When I was back in shape, I called again, but my timing was off. Arthur couldn't understand such massive insecurity because he didn't have it. He had the qualities in his dancing of spontaneous joy and deep security. Was he lucky!

I liked Kurt Vonnegut's short story "Harrison Bergeson." It's set in the year 2081 and, to make everyone equal, the special and gifted are given handicaps. There are some ballerinas on TV, and they are masked and burdened with sash-weight bags of bird shit. The viewer in the story is thinking that perhaps ballerinas shouldn't be so handicapped. Harrison's son appears at the station and liberates a ballerina. They jump up together and kiss the ceiling. In Russia, Arthur had done his best to liberate me. But now my nerves had taken over, taken flight, and handicapped me.

Even though I had missed that opportunity, I decided not to review myself or focus on lost chances. It would make me too pessimistic about my future.

However, one year after being fired I was still in a financial crisis. Betty Cage had once said I could borrow money if I ever needed to, but she had left the company in late 1984. That option was gone. I hadn't foreseen that I'd be this long without money. A friend got a good job in ballet working in Fort Worth, Texas. I wished something would fall into my lap, but I didn't want to be under- or over-privileged.

Someone once said, you always have to have a second idea, and I was still looking for a new profession. Many of my dance friends, such as Robert Blankshine, were also finding themselves in this position. Bobby was an extraordinary dance talent but difficult to place. When he stopped performing, he started to teach classes. I used to do his combinations with an unusual emphasis to surprise him and make him laugh. His life, like mine, had come to a cul-de-sac. He had extensions, line, and a finesse that many ballerinas envied. When he came to New York, Joffrey had told him to select a male dancer to emulate. He chose me. Now we were both offstage, and his wonderful classes cheered me up.

Another thing that meant a lot to me at this time was a comment Jerry Robbins made about me in one of the many news interviews appearing about the New York City Ballet without Mr. B. In one long article, Jerry said, "I miss Allegra. With all my vast admiration for our ballerinas, no one brought such complexity to her roles. Even her walk was complicated." I deeply appreciated his remarks at a time when I felt so forgotten, so useless, and so humiliated about how my career had ended.

Meanwhile, a second idea refused to fly into my butterfly net, so I started a book. Instead of dancing on a stage, dancing in my dreams, or teaching, I would try to write about dance. When Jacqueline Onassis told my friend Judith Yeargin that she was very interested in a possible autobiography, I began hoping that this was a way to bring a little something in.

In 1985, after Bret graduated from high school and left for college, I moved from Scarsdale back to the city into Aram's apartment on the Upper West Side to continue my tussle with the text. My three children were now out of the nest, living in Rome, Pittsburgh, and Bridgeport. When I moved in with Aram, he gave me some clothespins and a washer/dryer. I could now do my laundry at the drop of a leotard and devote the rest of my time to my book. My fairy godfather, lover, and friend had given me a secret grant.

• • •

The morning of January 17, 1987, I found Aram asleep on the couch with his glasses on. That was not usual. I went into the kitchen and made some coffee. When I came back to the living room, Aram had not moved. I studied him. He looked too still. His eyes were closed. *Oh, God, let this not be what it appears to be.*

Aram had not been feeling well during the second year we lived together in the city. I worried about him but didn't want to become a nag. However, I had forced him to have a checkup. He would not allow me to go with him to the doctor's office, nor would he show me the results of his tests. His report was, "Everything is perfect." I thought the doctor a nitwit but was powerless to do anything.

All month Aram had been dragging himself through the day. The symptoms were deep depression, total exhaustion, and shortness of breath. He could barely get out the door. By mid-month, I knew we had to visit the doctor together, no matter how he resisted.

Now he was lying still on the couch. The previous day, he had seemed to have the flu. When I had asked if I could get or do anything for him, he asked me not to hover. I had felt a little like an over-enthusiastic dog panting at its master's feet, with Aram saying, "Quiet down, girl."

That previous night had been bad. He told me he felt awful, then said, "I'm at the end of being myself. I can't put two and two together anymore." Aram had never spoken quite like this before.

A wave of terror flooded over me. "I think we should do something. May I call a doctor? Please."

"No, Allegra. I don't want a doctor." From his tone, I understood that what he said was exactly what he meant.

Many nights I used to get up with Aram to see how I could be of help, but the night before when he got up he strongly requested that I stay in bed. He had closed the bedroom door behind him, and I had heard him moving toward the kitchen.

Now he was motionless on the couch.

I said his name a few times and then began to scream it. I put my head to his warm chest but could hear nothing. "Oh, Aram, this might be the very worst thing that could possibly happen."

Maybe he was not dead, maybe it was something else. I called Aram's brother. "I can't wake Aram up."

I ran into the bedroom and threw on some clothes. Aram's brother and sister-in-law arrived. Very soon I knew it was the very worst. Aram had died, and I had not said good-bye.

This was the first time I was so close to death. Aram's father had died at ninety-three, so he had felt that he would, too. He was a very great love of my life, and he told me I was his. I'd known him for less than four years; we hadn't married, but we had planned to when he felt better. Tears and sadness overwhelmed me, but one thing helped: I knew I had made him very happy. At this time, his family said it, too.

And Aram had made me happy. He had helped me master my problems: my weight was perfect, and I was rid of debilitating stage fright. Some of the things Aram told me made this possible. He said I should be proud of everything I ate, and that statement transformed my eating patterns. With him I also learned to erase shame and guilt over my past. Somehow, I had been able to become a teenager again and could go back and really enjoy my life.

Aram may have known he was very ill, but he did not want to take steps to save his life. He was afraid of lingering on for years as an invalid.

He was only sixty years old. I thought of a line in a letter that Ibsen wrote to Rose Fitinghoff: "Parties are often like life; people do not meet until they have to say good-bye."

Aram had been dead only one week when the reality of my position became apparent. I found myself again with nothing, not even my youth. I didn't have a book contract, or a job, or a source of income, and I had nothing saved. I was a single woman near fifty without assets, health insurance, or any credit cards. My sole possessions were a library card and a driver's license. The landlord said I had no right to live in Aram's apartment because my name was not on the lease, and he was going to evict me. Aram's family wanted me out of the apartment, too. It was merely a rental, but it was stabilized and spacious. I decided not to give the family any room in my brain.

Only one of Aram's friends would ever talk to me again. There were very few phone calls. However, I was very touched when Bert rang up with a sincere, consoling message. He was very sorry to hear the terrible news.

Eventually, I began to receive small coaching and teaching jobs. The first was with Arthur Mitchell's Dance Theatre of Harlem, where I helped polish a production of *Bugaku*. Then John Taras got me two teaching jobs, one at the School of the Arts in North Carolina for two weeks and a second with Maria Tallchief's dance school in Chicago, and there was a wonderful letter from Maria waiting for me in her office before my first class. Another friend, Kathy Brynner, secured a week of teaching for me in Bermuda. I also taught three weeks at Harvard, a week in Texas, and one week at Miami's New World High School. When I found a palmetto bug in my room, I considered asking the hotel for police protection. This insect may have reminded me of some of my early phobias. I taught at the Kansas City Ballet School, and I sent out hundreds of letters offering myself as a teacher to universities, schools, and dance camps. Wherever John Taras went, he never forgot to speak about me and request work.

I also called Carmelita, who immediately had an idea for me. The University of California at Long Beach was in the process of searching for a new professor of dance. I decided to try out for the job. Three letters of recommendation were needed, which Peter Martins, Jerome Robbins, and Arthur Mitchell readily agreed to provide. The generosity of their letters made me cry. I needed some money to stay afloat while I was in search of regular and freelance teaching, and I received help from Jerry Robbins and Herbert Ross through the Doubrovska trust at the School of American Ballet.

I set up an audition date and flew to California one afternoon in April. My classes went well, but I wasn't what Long Beach envisioned. I decided to stay a week and proceeded to a local class. Ballet was helping me with my grief.

Before Aram's death I had been taking classes haphazardly. However, almost immediately after he died I began going every day, just to survive mentally. This was not so much for my body. I went to classes just so that I wouldn't fall into such despair that I couldn't climb out again. At this point, it never occurred to me that I might dance again. Or perform.

There was a low but constant hum in the semi-airless room, very much like the assertive whirring motor of a helicopter. The space was formerly a bowling alley. There were no windows in this huge cube with the pumped-in oxygen, but it contained the necessities for dance—barres, mirrors, and fluorescent lights. I tried not to focus on these drawbacks. Stanley Holden's studio in Los Angeles was a place to stay more or less in shape and say hello to dance friends.

Arriving late and rushing over to obtain my favorite spot at the barre in the brief interval between classes, I didn't look around until I staked out my claim with personal possessions. Then, while swooping into an extravagant stretch, I saw John Clifford across the room, smiling madly.

John Clifford joined the New York City Ballet in 1966. He had creative choreographic ability and created *Fantasies* in 1969, which I admired tremendously. Another ability was his quickness in learning choreography. Almost with one look, he had it memorized. John and I had been great pals at a time when Balanchine was barely speaking to me. Clifford would come bounding backstage with corrections or admiration for the good sections. It's not easy to dance in a vacuum, and he filled that for me. John's generous nature always surprised me; he was genuinely happy when others had good luck in their work. This was unusual in show business.

"Allegra, my love, what are you doing out here?"

"I just auditioned at Long Beach for a job, professor of dance. I won't get it; my class was too interesting." We kissed and hugged. "John, stand next to me so we can talk. How are you?"

"Really good, and I've got lots of ideas at various stages of realization." During the 1970s, with Balanchine's blessing, he had formed the Los Angeles Ballet Company. It was quite successful for a while, but then it fell apart because of problems with the board of directors and funding. Now John was setting Mr. B.'s ballets for various dance companies around the world and also creating his own dances and teaching.

While John spoke, I took my left foot in my right hand and extended it over my head with a flexed foot finial. "Where are you living?"

John rolled his eyes upward, toward my foot, and laughed. "On Primrose. How's your penchée arabesque?"

"It was perfect yesterday." Changing feet and hands, I did the stretch to the other side. "I'm limber because I've already gone swimming this morning." During class I told John about Aram and my great need for an income. Midway through the lesson, after we had left the barre and done a few combinations in the center, John said, "Allegra, you can still dance, I mean really dance."

"Do you think so?"

John gave me the once-over. "I just saw what you can do. It's all there, and your weight is perfect."

"Yes, now that I'm out of the field I've mastered that problem. I've been taking lots of classes."

I, too, thought I could dance again, but I needed confirmation. I believed that if I had a fresh chance to go on stage and dance, I could defeat the sheer fear that had possessed me for so many years. My grief would somehow protect me from stage fright. Although my fear still existed under the surface of my tendus and développés, I felt I could move through it and past it with motion.

"John, thank you for saying I can still dance, that means so much to me. I've had a strange career."

John and I went on talking in the intervals between combinations. Finally, he paused and rested an elbow on the barre. "Allegra, seriously, I've got an agent and we have a tour planned for early 1988. Do you want to do *Apollo*?"

The pianist was playing a waltz from *Der Rosenkavalier*, and I thought of my past. "You tell me. Can I do it?"

"Yes."

"John, a bus tour is too exhausting. How about one performance in a locale close to New York City? I do only one entrechat-six per month now."

"Well, save it for January."

"Please don't tell anyone."

I was thrilled. After a six-year hiatus from performing, and only intermittent maintenance, my body had not betrayed me.

The day was cold, bleak, and overcast. Driving out with John's agent to join the other members of Clifford's touring group at Red Bank, New Jersey, to dance *Apollo,* I thought about Aram. He used to watch me dance around the apartment and say, "You should still be dancing." I was following his advice, but I wasn't so sure. Someone in heaven or hell was laughing or crying right now. By eleven o'clock that night, I'd know which.

I looked out at the rain. All those years I thought I would never dance again, and now, at fifty, I was performing. I always wanted to ask Alicia Alonso, "Who is your gynecologist?" When the hormones of an actress diminish with menopause, she can still be an actress. Not so the dancer. But Alonso danced impressively at sixty and beyond—a phenomenon among phenomena. I had done a walk-on with Clifford at an AIDS benefit in California, which had served as an icebreaker. After a hiatus of six years, I had been on pointe and on stage again, even if it was only for ninety seconds. As we headed for Red Bank, I still had the fears, but I had been able to quell them, fold them up, and put them in a drawer.

Usually I called my dance friends for advice, but this time I told no one I was dancing. This was to be "a secret performance written in secret thoughts." A fortnight earlier I had had some sort of peculiar stomach virus that put me in bed for a week, leaving me only seven precious days to prepare. In addition to class, I did one-on-one Pilates sessions with Renée Estópinal every day for a week.

Now the moment was here. Because my vision had changed, applying the makeup was difficult, even with a magnifying mirror. I felt as inexperienced with makeup as I had at my first performance at fifteen. Now I understood why Martha Graham had fingered in two purple smudges. I inadvertently followed her lead, only using grayish umber. My biggest worry was the hair, but one of the girls in the group was an expert in the coiling of a French twist, and she did it for me.

Now I had to dance. The review of my dancing at the benefit said that I had "a strange attribute" in my bones that gave my dancing "a sort of lunatic quality." *Apollo,* however, required genuine dancing. I had not been on stage in a serious work since 1982. Six years. Was I mad? Maybe not. I could do now what I couldn't earlier—get ready to dance and get to the weight I wanted. All because of Aram.

The performance went well, and I felt wonderful. One person from the New York City Ballet showed up, Damian Woetzel, now one of the company's stars. I trusted his judgment and eye, and he loved the way I did *Apollo,* especially my entrechat-six, the step that Tolstoy describes in *War and Peace* as "jumping high and striking one foot rapidly against the other." I received five bouquets, and my living room became a garden in the middle of winter. Just after my father died ten years earlier, I had been overwhelmed with sadness, a feeling that I'd always be alone. A hopeless depression made me bow out of dance and life in general. Once at a store buying Susannah and Bret clothes for camp, I became too panicked to execute this simple task; I had to sit in a chair while Trista did this for me. My inability to function, even on the most mundane level, hadn't helped my buried grief, it only intensified it. During my middle thirties until the day I was fired, performing had been something I feared. Stage fright wore the costumes with me, an exhausting other presence that I couldn't outdistance.

Aram had somehow brought me past that phase, and, after his death, I had moved in the opposite direction and welcomed a chance to perform again. Because of him, I was less afraid of being myself.

There was also a practical factor in my return to dance. I had no injury that impinged on my range of motion. All the stretching and massage had protected me. I was under no delusion about my age, however. I was not an aspiring adolescent, and ballet had no room for the equivalent of a Grandma Moses. I could probably dance for four or five years more in the right parts.

Early that following Monday morning, Henley called me to ask, "Allegra, did you just dance in New Jersey this past weekend?"

"Well," I took in a huge breath, "yes, I did. How do you know?"

"There is a review in *The New York Times*."

"I didn't think it would be reviewed. I needed the money, so I just didn't make a big fuss about it."

"Well, the review is great."

I was changing. I wanted to perform, but I didn't want or care about comments and points of view, particularly if they were negative. Aram's memory had traveled with me to New Jersey, and now I knew I could function on stage again.

The fact that I had the chance to dance once more gave wings to my life.

In late 1987, Barbara Horgan called me up about a job. It wasn't a job as much as it was a bluebird flying by my window. The Royal Ballet of London wanted two Balanchine ballets for a mixed program, and *Bugaku* was to be one of them. Barbara, head of the Balanchine Trust, told their artistic director that she'd like John Clifford to set the choreography and me to coach the ballerinas of the first, second, and third casts. She requested and received a large fee for me, plus living expenses and transportation.

After the *Apollo* performance in Red Bank, I took twenty-four hours to recuperate and take ballet class at Steps—one of New York City's largest dance schools—packed, and hopped into an airplane with a volume of Gorky's autobiography. I was off for my job coaching *Bugaku* with the Royal Ballet. Following Erik Bruhn's lead, I headed straight to work after dumping my suitcase in a claustrophobically small hotel room. The bed would be for later.

Working with the Royal dancers was a wonderful experience. The lovely ballerina selected was Bryony Brind, and Wayne Eagling was her Japanese warrior. Everything was magical except the hotel, but, with Bryony's help, I located a homey bed-and-breakfast on

Maiden Lane where the bathtub alone was worth the weekly rate.

I took class with various teachers at the Royal in the theater and also in their school in an interpretive, delighted fashion. A born-again Iris had made an unexpected revisitation to dance. The English dancers looked at my movements and laughed—they found something joyously eccentric in my style. Class was still my kindergarten. I lived in the Covent Garden area near a health club called the Sanctuary. In contrast to my frugal life in New York, here there was momentarily a little luxury. Naked women swam in an idyllic pool with swings, and a huge area was crisscrossed with streams containing large goldfish and turbaned women. It had a decadent feel, even at eight in the morning. The price of the dip was also decidedly decadent. I had found a place for myself and my water wings, my bracelets of buoyancy.

Trista, who was in Italy at the time, joined me for the final weekend in February, inclusive of the 29th. This was the occasion when girls get to propose to boys; however, I had no one to proposition. Trista and I were each other's dates for the theater, the museums, the pool, and the watering holes.

I hoped this would be the first of many jobs like this one—it gave me a very happy time and money in my pocket—but it was the last. Very soon afterward, the bottom went out of the ballet market. There was a great economic shift, and these lavish ballet productions would be scarce.

In June of 1988, I owed the landlord about twenty thousand dollars in back rent. He had not accepted my checks while he was trying to evict me. A complicated lawsuit ensued, and I had to hire an expensive lawyer. Somehow, many friends, including the New York City Ballet and my brother, Gary, stepped forward with cash—a small miracle.

Along with this new security in my living space came another gift, but this too evolved from a tragedy. It wasn't just Aram who had disappeared from my life. There was another loss in 1987, that terrible year. Robert Blankshine, who had told me that I would always be a guest in his class at Steps, died very suddenly. However, after Bobby's death the owner of Steps, Carol Paumgarten, came forward with a fantastic gift: she granted me a scholarship. I was both deeply grateful and honored that at forty-nine I became their oldest aspiring dancer. Through her generosity, I felt as if Bobby were still there to help me. Now both my apartment and a place at the barre were not in peril.

The scholarship gave me a chance to maintain my technique, but I still needed to earn a living. I was picking up occasional teaching jobs, including many weeks at Harvard, but teaching was not the perfect career for me. I had found myself saying to the students, "Please notice what part of your body is on the floor. It should be your feet. If it isn't, stand up immediately."

I hadn't found a new profession yet.

In the fall of 1988, for the first time since Aram's death, I started to consider looking for a new companion as well as a new profession. I was surprised to receive a remarkably perceptive letter from the father of Bert's agent. I called him.

"Hi, Jesse, this is Allegra. How are you?"

"Fine. I haven't heard from you in a long time. How nice of you to call."

"Well, actually, Jesse, you sent me a letter."

"I did?"

"Yes, you answered my *New York* magazine ad." My latest "boy wanted" bio had been deliberately unusual:

Pseudologia Phantasmagoria?—No, only the truth. Are you a lover of ballet? Then, perhaps, you have seen me in Moscow, Sydney, or on West 62nd St. (Lincoln Center). I have been described as elegant, supple, antic, spellbinding, and beautiful. My interests are reading, inventing, collages, oceans, lakes, and lianas. (I consider myself a non-married widow). Hope to meet a man who can distill thoughts and experience, who sees a little and then knows a lot, who is passionate and fun, perhaps is 45–60 or so, and happy in work (relatively). A letter please. Photo/phone.

"That was yours?" Jesse was surprised. "I thought the woman was a bit overboard about ballet."

"You were right."

Jesse and I had dinner, although neither one of us wanted to date the other. It was just an odd coincidence.

My ad did net more interesting results, however. A man wrote me who knew Jacques d'Amboise. I found that a relief. Trusting a voice over the phone was something I would not do quickly, and revealing an address to a stranger was frightening and could be dangerous.

My second blind-date-through-an-ad and I hit it off. One morning, I was almost out his door when he said, "Allegra, look under your pillow."

I registered a baffled look. "Did I lose an earring?" I felt my earlobes and glanced at my wrist. My jewelry was in place. My smile had a questioning curve.

"Go take a look," said this new male in my life. It was easy to see that some plan was afoot.

I walked back to the bedroom and lifted the pillow. There was a hundred-dollar bill. "Oh, thank you so much. The tooth fairy lives on the West Side!" I embraced my friend and gave him a kiss. He knew that I was struggling financially, and his gesture was very nice. However, it was curious that he chose to help me out in a bedroom setting. The curtain had gone up on a new kind of mating dance.

About a month before Christmas I started to see my new date almost every other night when I was in town. Otherwise, I was on the road as an itinerant ballet teacher or performer. We were thinking of putting our lives together. Two days before I was to leave again, my friend and I had returned to his apartment from dinner and a movie. I was in bed, but when I looked at him I could see he wasn't ready to join me, not at all ready. "Why are you cleaning your apartment now?" I asked.

Not waiting for an answer and feeling more than a little annoyed, I threw *Pride and Prejudice,* the book I was reading, at him. Of course I hit my mark, squarely. Luckily it was a paperback.

He was taken aback, but he also hastened to finish his cleaning. I thought my bad behavior would end our budding relationship, but it didn't. When he finished cleaning, suddenly he was asking me, "Allegra, what do you rely on for cash flow?"

"Cash flow?"

"Income."

"Just my teaching. But it's not good right now. This time of year the dance schools I worked for have all plunged into *Nutcracker* productions. I have no work teaching or performing until January. That's why I had time to make those Christmas decorations I brought you." I had made them from clothespins.

"They are beautiful and original."

"Thanks. The idea was born in depression and poverty, the look of Paris blended with the clothespins of Buster Keaton."

My friend picked up my hand. "In some ways you are the sweetest person in the world. I'm going to do something to help your cash flow until January. Where is your money belt?"

"In the living room, on the coffee table." I put three fingers lightly on my upper lip. Was a miracle taking place?

My friend jumped up. "Don't look until tomorrow when you get home." He threw a devilish glance my way.

I almost started to cry. I was so grateful, but I hated to feel that needy.

The next day when I followed my friend's instruction, there was a check for three thousand dollars in the zippered pouch. Again, this man's generosity flabbergasted me.

But after a while our relationship did not work out.

"Who writes your scripts for you? Do you know what? I hate them," my male friend said to me one night while we were sitting in a restaurant.

"I don't have scripts written for me. I talk like everyone else, with spontaneous answers or messages or observations. I put my own sentences together and always have!"

"Sometimes you have the worst behavior I've ever seen, and you almost never wear a dress."

"Well, that's true. But you're just angry at me. It dates back to the evening when I threw *Pride and Prejudice* at you. I wanted to sleep, and you were cleaning your apartment with a Q-tip. Anyway, I guess it's time to say good-bye."

I thought of my daughter Susannah's statement, "If he doesn't like you, you don't like him."

I assumed that our relationship was over, but it wasn't. When I left to go on a new tour put together by Clifford, the man-who-answered-my-ad took a list of my locations, with dates, and asked me to call him while I was on the road. When I did so from San Francisco, he started to question me about my dresses again. My attention was not on clothes but on survival and dancing.

Waiting in an airport, I later started a letter to my almost ex-boyfriend:

Dear_____,

Don't give up with all women just because of me. Ninety-eight percent of those you will meet will behave better, have nicer clothes, be more at ease with their doormen, have thicker hair, do a better split, and be less defensive.

Suddenly we were boarding and the letter never got sent. I found it six years later. In the end, we dated for five months, including a coda.

The final curtain occurred while we were eating out. I sneezed and my glasses splashed into my soup. He thought that I had done this on purpose, that it was another example of my "worst behavior." But the glasses were just loose.

I made up another ad:

Lyrically Limber Lollapalooza—with toehold and magical career in ballet, has been described as elegant, spellbinding, spontaneous, and fun—with a love for flora, fauna, forests, oceans, theater, and travel (has been to Botany Bay, Baku, and Boulder Dam), hopes to meet a man, 46–60 or so, who likes the unusual, hears grace notes, has an antic eye, is creative, passionate, and secure, has exquisite sensibilities and perhaps a sense of the absurd.

I used a lot of alliteration but had no luck.

I missed Aram when the air was fresh. He was a redwood. In the dating game, I often felt as if I were in a forest of bonsai trees.

Although my personal life was not very successful, my dance life was blooming. In 1989, I toured again with the smallest ballet company in the world. John Clifford had put another group together, but this time travel was by air, lots of air. Sometimes we had three connections to make in one day to get from one engagement to another. I called it the B tour—Beaumont, Boise, and barres (or bars).

John's exuberant voice and proposal had crossed the country and greeted me in my own living room through the receiver. "Come to California. I've got a piece in mind set to Schubert's *Notturno,* and it's gorgeous music. If we have time while touring, I'll put together a Mahler ballet also." He explained that some Russian dancers, who had been stranded in the States when their tour fell through, would be joining us.

"Yes, I'm interested. I now work for my landlord. Send the ticket. I'll be right there."

"And I have a wonderful partner for you—Mark Lopez, who used to dance with the San Francisco Ballet."

Now we were thirty thousand feet up on our second jet ride of the day, with just one more air trip to go. Our destination was Boise, Idaho. Over the loudspeaker a voice said, "If you look out the windows on your left, you will see the Great Salt Lake."

Oh my, I thought. *That's where I didn't go to school for four years.*

Going to the University of Utah, I had followed my mother's directive, but it took me only four days to know it wasn't the place for me. I had searched for solace in music and wrote Mother fourteen letters wondering how I could solve the problem of making both of us happy. The only thing to do then was leave. I remembered feeling gloriously free on the flight back to New York City. Now, as I looked down at the lake, I felt tired but elated once again. Those ninety-six hours in Utah had taken place thirty-three years earlier. I thought about that as I picked up my pen. My present style was to write in a notebook and, after a week, place the pages in a sealed envelope. My diary looked like hundreds of unsent letters to myself.

I listened to the hum of the engines and thought about tonight's performance in Idaho. I was dancing more on this tour than I had in the final years of my career. I thought Aram must be laughing, because I was. Much of the travel seemed like a surreal exercise in planes, air terminals, and packing luggage, with three air flights every other day.

At the moment, there was a restless energy in our little group. No one had exercised yet. We had awakened way too early, before sunrise, to make our connections.

I heard a *thwack*. I looked around and saw that Alla, our Bolshoi ballerina star, had just hit her husband, Vitali, over the head with a pillow and then ducked behind his seat. Mark, my partner, tossed Vitali a puffy square for a reciprocal thump. I put my book back in my bag and tossed my pillow to Alla.

I could get involved with these antics for about three minutes. I was on tour to work and prove that I could still dance. I felt closest to George Vargas, a dancer in the group who was also an extraordinary painter. He inspired me to pull out my notebook and start drawing.

After Boise and San Francisco, we traveled south by bus. One of our stops would be Fresno, the heart of Armenian country in America, where my father lived for many years. Aram had once told me that when an Armenian son left home, he was given a horse, a tent, and a rug. Aram had given me the rug he received as a young man from his father, along with the metaphysical strength never to give up. I loved William Saroyan's book *My Name Is Aram* and used to present it at parties to clarify the name of my date. It was not Ouram, Avram, or Arum. Many people were confused, but not if I held up the book.

Now, looking out the bus window at a landscape that had caught my imagination at eleven, I was mesmerized. Our chartered vehicle traveled through exquisite countryside into Santa Clara. Then everything changed, and we entered a live-oak, hilly landscape of sunlight and shadows. We had arrived in Cupertino.

While on the bus, I read about Natalia Makarova. She was appearing in Leningrad while I was touring small towns. We had had very different careers as well as different mothers and muscles. I could wear only my own shoes and work with my own body. Although I admired Makarova and other dancers my age and younger—such as Patty McBride, Gelsey Kirkland, Lis Jeppersen, and Alla Sizova— neither she nor they were a force in shaping me. My contemporaries were not the icons of my youth. The dancers I studied, the ones who gave me ideas in my formative years—particularly, Maria and Tanny—were all older than I. They were from farther back in time, but their vivid stamp lived in my memory. The critics and public wrote and thought about the more current group, but I didn't. I dwelled in the dance past.

That night I had a pointe shoe problem. I was using what remained from six years ago, and there were not many pairs left. Their days were numbered. One dancer suggested that I put Krazy Glue in the tip to help squeeze a few extra performances out of a pair, but, in testing, they didn't soften up with alcohol. I sounded like an elephant tap dancing, and this would ruin my performance. A pointe shoe needs to offer support but also be broken in to make it soundless. I had been trying to get the sound out of my shoes ever since I submerged my foot in a bucket of water in Russia. These shoes were old, and a panic started to grow within me. I had to take myself firmly in hand: *Don't be so negative; it will work out. Persist. Quiet down. Don't give up easily.* I went on giving the shoes an alcohol dose every ten minutes for an hour to cool my heels, or in this case, my toes. At the last minute the shoes gave in, so I decided to give a special performance. In a solemn oath I swore off Krazy Glue forever. Two days later, I received a very good review in the *Los Angeles Times.* The trees of my childhood had inspired me, old trees that took a long time to grow. John called my performance "transcendental."

I was deeply happy on this tour. John had developed two vehicles just for me, and I detected in him the same quiet confidence, admiration, and encouragement that I had felt from Mr. B. when I was twenty-one. I had been given a second chance at my youth. A second chance to dance.

At the airport the next morning our flight was delayed because of freezing sleet, snow, and wind. When a three-hour delay was announced, George Vargas and I drew pictures of our company companions and read newspapers. It's hard to use airport waiting time wisely.

Our group finally arrived at Galveston at five o'clock. We had a quick bite, got to the theater, and threw ourselves into the dance. Later that night we placed ourselves on a bus and were off to Dallas, or as one of the Russians said, "the American Siberia."

The next morning there was a freak blizzard and our matinee audience didn't exist. The Texans didn't know how to drive in a slippery snow, but Natalie Krassovska, a resplendent star of the old Ballet Russe de Monte-Carlo, traveled by Jeep, hair and makeup flawlessly in place. She arrived early with a group of young male devotees—her students, no doubt—and came backstage to say hello.

As two o'clock edged nearer, our Russian prima ballerina from the Bolshoi, Alla, didn't want to dance because there were so few in the audience. John implored earnestly, "It doesn't matter how many are out front, Alla." I said, "We dance for abstract reasons and for abstract benefits." But her henpecked husband said, "Shut up and dance." She listened to him.

I thanked John for giving me a little adventure, even if it turned out to be negative. It was still an adventure.

John was undaunted. "How about coming to Russia in October?" he said to me the next day in the parking lot beside our bus. The chef in the kitchen was improvising.

"I'm game if you can arrange it, John. After this tour is over, let's give out Mother Teresa awards. I want to win one." I had acquired a roommate because my rent was so high. My new roommate's rent check had bounced in New York, so I was happy to think about more work in another country. I settled down next to John and listened to a fresh set of stories. John had one about Alicia Alonso sprinkling rose petals on the corps de ballet after *Swan Lake,* and one about Gelsey Kirkland's partner taking a walk before a performance. A pas de deux became a solo. Midway through the dance, Gelsey waltzed over to the pianist on stage and whispered frantically, "Faster, faster."

Finally we arrived at the Sarasota airport, where George did a tropical *Dying Swan* for us. It was a natural reaction for dancers on tour to try to give an entertaining cast to some of the frustrations of travel. I had seen variations on it since I was sixteen. Vida Brown once conducted a rehearsal of *Western Symphony* in the Manila airport. She had the time and they had the space. She had needed to position a substitute for opening night in Sydney.

In our run-down motel that night, I continued my hobby and prepared a new ad. I was still hoping for other possibilities for myself in the companionship department. My limberness ad hadn't netted anyone I would have gone out with more than once—no starfish—so I decided on a spunkier style:

Have Moxie, Imagination—An eye for the magical; wish I had echolocation. Nevertheless, hope to meet a man, 48–60, with warmth, passion, and depth of perception, who is fun, secure in work. My fascinations are with reading, rhythm, theater, the great cities, and oceans. I have been called lithe, loving, a good friend, beautiful, exuberant, and sometimes a hellhound. My work has been described as an exquisite, existential exercise, which means I'm a Danzatrice. Letters/phone/photo.

I had no luck with this ad, either. These ads were getting costly with little return.

Our last appearance on the tour was the Purchase campus of the State University of New York, near White Plains—the place where Aram had taught film. I had two pieces to dance on the program, and it was St. Patrick's Day, March 17. I told my friends in New York about it this time in case they wanted to attend. I thought that the critics might appear, and that made me a little nervous, but then I decided to free myself up. I remembered Arthur Mitchell's remark in Moscow: "It's just a small town." But this time it was. I had just performed with John's Ballet Company of Los Angeles in Dallas, Naples, Sarasota, Oklahoma City, Stillwater, Fresno, Cuppertino, Oakland, Miami Beach, a place somewhere in Virginia, Elmira, Beaumont, and Boise. I wasn't going to be stricken with fear; that was mastered. I was just going to dance for a few people in heaven or hell and whoever was in the audience.

Two reviews, received a week apart, were gratifying:

THE WASHINGTON POST:
The ever remarkable American ballerina Allegra Kent broke her retirement from dancing (she's 50) to perform in Clifford's *Notturno*. . . . Kent has left a trail of golden memories from her career

at NYCB—she was always a dancer of extraordinary personal cha-
risma. The wonder is she's lost none of it with time. Artistically,
the high point of Friday's program was her typically vivid, musically
acute and expressively poignant dancing in *Notturno*. . . . Kent's
very special quality, still very much intact, was always an emotional
abandon mysteriously and implausibly registered within a classical
line of breathtaking perfection—Gelsey Kirkland was the only
other dancer I've ever seen who could work this particular magic.

THE NEW YORK TIMES:
This visit included Allegra Kent, a former ballerina of the City
Ballet, who seldom performs these days, but whose magic is leg-
endary. Miss Kent, who is 50 years old, is still a ravishingly lovely
performer, with all the delicacy, radiance, and buried hint of daf-
finess that made her so beloved at City Ballet. . . . It is Miss Kent's
lyrical arms that stand out in *Notturno*. Here, it is her carriage and
head and neck so delicately yet intensely expressive of the subtlest
degrees of emotion.

All those years I thought I would never dance again, and now, in my
fifties, I was back in ballerina space, back as the wild Iris, not Allegra.
I thought of the dog I had watched running on the beach when I was
in California, pregnant with Trista. Suddenly I was no longer the
woman sitting on a towel on the beach trapped by the conditions of
my life. For the first time I was the dog running free on the sand.

CHAPTER TWENTY

But the truth is, brother, I am a—I am a kind of weed,
and it is too late to plant me in a regular garden.

— CHARLES DICKENS, BLEAK HOUSE

After the performance at Purchase, John Clifford had only one more dance date scheduled for the group. I could not safety-pin my hopes on a vague offer. That would not pay the rent. I needed another idea.

Suzy Pilarre came up with an inspiration. A ballet school in Stamford, Connecticut, needed a new director. It was an academy that Carole Sumner had started and that produced the Balanchine *Nutcracker* at Christmastime, importing principal dancers from the New York City Ballet for the starring roles. The Board of Directors expressed enthusiasm and interest in me, and an audition was scheduled that consisted of teaching two classes. I got the job. It was thrilling to have regular work, even if the pay was modest, but they allowed me to take outside work to augment my income if I replaced myself with a substitute.

It was fifteen years since I had taught in my own school, and I noticed that there was a difference in the students' responses to difficult combinations. Many of my new scholars wanted to discuss the steps with each other instead of placing the challenge on their own muscles. Dance became verbal. Orthodontics and jewelry were also examined. I needed to be a strict disciplinarian, and that was not part of my nature. I also taught mostly with records, a deadly, scratchy affair. The sixteen little girls in my preballet were adorable, but this level was not ideal for me, and I soon trained someone for that position.

I also learned when not to show up at all. On Halloween night, I suspected that trick or treat would take precedence over tendus and turns, but, when questioned, the children had said unanimously, "I'll be there." I arrived and there was only one child present. She looked upset, and the heat had been turned off. I decided that a never-stop moving barre with a run around the room during the small intervals between combinations would keep us warm. We did a follow-the-leader class during which I called out what we would do seconds before we did it. Luckily, my one pupil was a rapid study. One hour of this aerobic rompery was enough. My total traveling time was four hours. Henceforth, I decided to cancel class on special holidays.

My daily schedule in my new job was an exercise marathon with a backward commute starting in early afternoon. Before leaving the city, Allegra cast as the fanatic would swim and then take a ballet class. The day finished at nine in the evening, when the work-weary creature started to cook dinner. New York City was the wrong location for a Connecticut job, but I never planned to dwell in the suburbs again. Looking back, I considered the time in Scarsdale as my personal Babylonian captivity.

The second careers of many dancers don't always slip gracefully into place. I had taken this job because I had to. But whatever happened, my own class and swim were incorporated into my routine, because my future might still include performing. Ethelred the Unready was part of my past. I was now ready, willing, and able to dance—I needed only to be called. My new motto was sometimes on my answering machine: "If you are calling to give me a job, I accept it."

In the spring of 1990, I had the chance to dance again. I took a two-month leave of absence to appear with Gary Chryst in some concerts. Again it was time to polish the pas de chat, make them go higher, and desensitize my toes. Renée Éstópinal was not teaching Pilates at that moment and suggested I call her friend Patrick Strong. The version of Pilates I did at twenty-one was excellent but made me muscle-bound. Patrick's method of Pilates was perfect for my body. He'd stretch me out like a rubber band and literally hold and sit on me during an extreme stretch. I wish I had worked with him for decades, but at least I had sessions with him now. It's easy to cultivate "if only" in the blue garden of regrets. My daddy had done it with real estate.

After the tour I went back to my job at the Stamford City Ballet School and back to Grand Central Station. Finishing work late and waiting for the train to take me home at night was a sad moment in the day's routine. My biggest wish was to develop another life for myself—but what and how? One night I had a dream of taking a trolley across America. The trolley looked like a Metro North train with the power antennas reaching up for electricity. My commuting years and childhood had merged into my own streetcar named desire. Something Mme. Danilova said to me helped: "You can get used to anything." This was a simple but profound statement. You can even get used to good things and not appreciate them. One meal, one cloud, and one tree. But this was not the job for me, primarily because of the commute and my wish to dance. I had not yet bowed out of the field.

In the fall of 1990, Peter Anastos called with great news. He was creating the dances for the movie musical *The Addams Family* and wanted me for Cousin Ophelia. Glory hallelujah! The money was good. Perhaps this was a new career avenue opening up, lined with dawn redwoods; the trees would cast the fragrance of a forest over my future. The rent could be met easily. Two lines of dialogue in the film made me an actor, not a dancer, and the difference was a first-class ticket to Los Angeles.

On the set in full Ophelia makeup, wearing a muted sea green costume and a diaphanous headpiece, I made my film debut in front of a gathering of eccentrics. Accentuating my last spoken line with a piqué into arabesque, my black candle became punctuation when I pushed it forward like an exclamation point. But the director had a different idea of how he wanted the little scene enacted. "It should be like Vivien Leigh playing Blanche Dubois. Can you do a Southern accent?"

"I'm not sure," I said, wishing I had been told that earlier. But Anjelica Huston swiftly walked over to me, smiling. "It's easy," she said with reassuring command. "You get very sweet." An aura of honeysuckle seemed to float around her. Then she spoke my lines and sat into her hips. The final words were, "Where am I?"

With wide eyes, I gave an echo-perfect reflection of her reading and swung my hips, catching a "that's it" from the director. I had been delighted to meet Anjelica Huston, who told me that her mother had once danced for Balanchine and that her sister's name was Allegra. No wonder I had always admired her acting so much. Great actresses have a touch of the ballerina in them, sometimes in their genes. I loved her coaching style. By the second take, we had it. Raul Julia said, "Very good." I was certified.

I fell into a routine during my two weeks on the set. Before sunrise, at around six, I went swimming, as I did every workday, to be ready for makeup around eight. Then I whipped off a barre while hanging on to a piece of the set, an architectural wonder of bentwood railings, wrought-iron trim, and cobwebs. Miracles can happen in the twinkling of an eye in Washington and Hollywood. Decades earlier, Violette Verdy told me that while she was making movies in the 1950s she did her ballet barre five times a day to stay in shape. That was impressive, but after one swim and one barre I usually put on my sun hat over my Ophelia headgear and read. *Bleak House* was the book of that moment.

Although on Valentine's Day many of us in the cast exchanged cards that had a gothic tinge, this job would not be a social stepping stone. One night when I had been invited to a Hollywood movie star's party, shooting ran deep into midnight overtime, and I finished the long day by crashing into sleep and letting my subconscious write its nighttime story. No nightmares that evening, and no socializing.

This work held a special happiness for me. It was retrace and re-place. I had said no to Joseph Cornell's film proposal thirty-five years earlier and purposely thwarted my other chances at film over the years. Now I could accept and fulfill an assignment in a professional manner without feeling ashamed of my face or my body. Unfortunately, most of the dancing and my two lines were cut. Nevertheless, the work gave me a respite from Metro North and, to my delight, continuing health insurance. This made me think that Peter Anastos should be president: he did what many politicians could only promise. Maybe we need a choreographer in the White House.

Soon afterward, a mysterious filmmaker from Flint, Michigan, named Wendell B. Harris Jr. became a regular caller, and his plans gave me hope for another six months. He had won the top prize at Sundance and while there had seen a documentary film I was in called *Dancing for Mr. B.* by Anne Belle. Wendell wanted me for his next movie. We had long conversations, and he told me, "You can call me anytime, anytime, anytime."

I once called him at a hotel in Los Angeles, asking to speak to Wendell B. Harris Jr. "Look, lady, we don't have any juniors here, or even any seniors. You don't know what kind of place this is—it's a fleabag motel." The man was incensed that I gave a complete name with initials and paternity and that I acted as if I were calling the Ritz. I was distressed but glad my friend was not there. I could call him anytime, anytime, anytime, but not anywhere, anywhere, anywhere. I always liked people who spoke in triplicate. However, I never met him. He remained a voice over the phone that gave me hope, a very important mental state. Like my mother, I couldn't live without it.

Yearly the Stamford school produced the Balanchine *Nutcracker* but nothing else. It was time for a June extravaganza. The children lost interest in ballet by April. Attendance decreased. Two Italian movies gave me story ideas—Fellini's *And the Ship Sails On* and Rossellini's *Miracle in Milan*. For the music, I selected seventeen Verdi choruses from eight or so different operas. Another inspiration was the Dover fairy books with their various colored covers. A friend had given me my first one, in lavender, in 1985. I loved the tales and adored the illustrations. These make-believe people wore beautiful clothes, allegorically fey costumes, and they never gave up. With and without magic, they accomplished superhuman feats out of sheer determination, valor, and luck.

My production, in which I also appeared, was called *La Donna Pipistrella,* who was, as I announced, the Italian cousin of the Fledermaus. During the performance, the students' fathers were overwhelmed with gratitude—the running length was only fifty minutes. I had never forgotten the day when a father described a four-hour ordeal. I was pleased that my invention met with success. Everyone, but especially the children, loved the music from *Nabucco, La Traviata, Aïda, Rigoletto,* and *Il Trovatore.* I choreographed seventy-five percent of the dances, wrote the script, and slipcovered La Donna's kite in black lamé because she flew only after twilight. The hardest part was slipcovering the kite.

The following year I did a continuing story of the Bat Lady woven in with the real tale of the Twelve Dancing Princesses. My version, set in the Roaring Twenties, had music and lyrics by the Gershwins. When everyone in the original story came to America, there were changes. The Tap Dancing Queen renounced royalty, went to work, and became a boarding school headmistress, where ballet and botany were emphasized. In this position, she renamed all her pupils from the Burpee seed catalog. So there was Hyacynthia, Ginger, Iris, Larkspur, Tulip, Tansy, Evodia, Little Wild Rose, and onward through the student body. Every night the girls went out to dance at the Clematis Club and wore their shoes to pieces doing the Charleston and the Castle Walk. The bat, which I played, became a vegetarian and switched from insects to the fruit of the giant saguaro cactus. Additional characters were a six-foot-tall freelance fairy and Agnes de Mille bouquets. The headmistress watered her cactus only when it rained in Arizona. (She must have learned that from my brother, Gary.) Balanchine often recycled some of his best ideas, so I called this recital "The Lyrically Limber Lollapaloozas" after my personal ad. We had rhythm—some of it obscure, but most of it fascinating. The exquisite title pages for both programs were drawn by Mary Ellen Moylan, a very great ballerina and a wonderful artist. I have noticed that many dancers were painters. They had the eye, but so did cavemen.

A month before the second annual school performance, I sandwiched two jobs around it. The first was dancing in an opera titled *Welfare* produced by Fred Wiseman based on his documentary film; the second was an on-pointe version of Myra Kinch's *Giselle's Revenge* at Jacob's Pillow. Although I was receiving some good offers, I didn't have the constant flood of them I needed to meet expenses.

This was my situation in June of 1992, when Trista came to America as she did every year for her annual visit. She had been working in Rome since 1985 as a featured dancer on Italian television. This trip home was different. Her Italian boyfriend and she were considering marriage, but she was uncertain. She arrived on a one-way ticket. One morning two weeks after her arrival, Trista and I sat on the couch reading the newspapers. Our furious work schedules had come to a halt. Inertia and depression had set in for both of us. I looked around the living room, feeling sapped of energy and confused. "I guess I'm not that interested in the apartment. I haven't bought a coffee table yet."

Trista and I had our feet on an improvised arrangement of upside-down drawers taken from a discarded chest, something that would never be pictured in *Architectural Digest*. Sensing how down I was, Trista brightened and said, "Well, you bought the rubber ants!" She was trying to cheer me up by reminding me of some small action I had carried through. I had purchased the latex insects to decorate a package in a natural-history style by creating a sort of elephant walk executed by ants.

In a low tone, I said, "I guess I'm better at packages than living rooms. No one has ever accused me of being an interior decorator." We looked at the room again and laughed. It didn't fall into any known category. "Mom," Trista said, taking charge and folding the newspapers, "go take class. I'll swim, and then we can take in a movie or go to the museum. Remember that great Italian futurist show we stumbled across at the Met?"

"Okay. Let's take a few hours' vacation from real life."

Daily Trista thought about her future. Should she return to Italy or stay in the United States? The scale tipped back and forth. I offered no advice whatsoever. I could not settle my own life.

The Stamford school closed for vacation in June. Not only did I have no extra employment that summer, I was also losing heart because there was a lull in my dating life. The people I met on the job were children. I was in the wrong world. Because the gentleman callers were few, I tried to fool myself about one man who appeared. However, I had merely fallen into my old pattern and wanted to think I could be rescued from loneliness. My dreams were tormented. He was not it.

Then things changed for both of us.

On the last day in July, Trista decided to return to Italy and bought her ticket. However, on August 3 she met a handsome New Yorker and canceled her flight. In September she received a proposal and was planning a wedding in December.

In October, my life changed too. Judith Yeargin called; she had a date for me. And so a bass-baritone voice over the wire brought a new man into my life.

"Hello. Is this Allegra?"

"Speaking."

"I'm Bob Gurney, Judith Yeargin's friend."

"Oh, yes. I heard that you might call."

"Is Allegra Kent your real name?"

"Well, no. It's Iris Cohen."

"I thought no one could have that name from birth."

"But someone does. The genuine Allegra Kent. My ambition is to meet her. She lives in London."

"I like your voice. You're not a New Yorker."

"I was born in L.A., but I've lived here for forty years."

"What are you doing right now?"

"Making a shoulder bag from a Russian scarf."

"I'd love to meet you. Can I come by? I'm leaving town tomorrow."

"Give me a half hour."

In a short space of time, I opened the door to a new era. Bob Gurney had kind eyes that had recently suffered. His wife had died earlier that year. He wanted to rebuild his life. I understood; I had been rebuilding mine. It was not easy to do. He was at an age when he couldn't spend years in mourning. He was charming, and after we went out for a drink he bought me some braided border for my sewing project.

For some unknown reason my professional résumé had been changed and I had been described to Bob as a "retired ballroom dancing teacher." Politely, my new date requested information. "Tell me about yourself. Did you work for Arthur Murray?"

"Well, no," I said, feeling surprised. "That wasn't what I did. I'm one of those classical dancers. That thing called ballet, which was and shall be my everlasting pursuit. I may never perform again, but I will never retire."

Bob had never seen me dance. The athletic side of life did not interest him. However, when I asked in mild curiosity, "Have you ever heard of Balanchine?" he said yes. That was promising.

The next day, he called again, delayed his flight, and asked me to lunch. With gallantry and grace, Bob offered a European trip to me as a gift. We would leave on Buster Keaton's birthday. I accepted. He sent the matchmaker a bouquet—which somehow arrived in my apartment—and covered the cost of hiring a substitute at the ballet school.

After a splendid sojourn in Italy and Spain, Bob encouraged me to take a leave of absence from the Stamford school: he liked to eat dinner earlier than nine o'clock. I thought that was a wonderful idea and agreed with a curtsy and a kiss.

With this wonderful gift of a furlough, I could catch up with some of the neglected areas of my life. I thought of resuming work on some of my old projects. Work on the book had ceased five years earlier. And there was something else I would have time to do. Trista wanted some input on a special day she was planning, the event that Elena Kunikova, one of my Russian ballet teachers, called "the divine hassle."

Outside, Sixty-ninth Street was dark and icy, but inside a special ceremony brought us together in a wintry spirit of warmth. With their arms linked, Bert led Trista forward as she looked at him with love. My daughter looked gorgeous while exchanging vows with Eric Wright. Her idea of a simple column of fluid white silk velvet was perfect for a winter wedding. This was an emotional moment of great hope. All of my children were joyously there, and my sister, Wendy, and some of her children were present. Although Gary and his family could not attend, they sent their love three thousand miles to Trista, and Mother—with a burst of determination—had crossed the country, flying in from California for the celebration.

During the dancing, a chair was carried forward, and all at once Trista, the beautiful bride, became a circus girl held on high. Our spirits and gaze rose with her. Our feelings were drawn skyward. The wedding showed me again that you must not give up too easily, because the unexpected can happen. Trista's eyes were opened when

"Love Walked In." This Gershwin song became my daughter's theme. A tiny bit of luck, a chance meeting, and two rivers alter their course.

Just three months earlier, it looked as if our branch of the family was struggling for all it wasn't worth. Although the near and far past could not be altered, at this moment there was no reason to focus on the past. Through the generosity of many cousins, friends, and even Bert, we had proved that luck could change and the feelings between two people could swirl and sweep into the "Wedding March." This was the night to acknowledge it.

For many years I held a deep bitterness toward Bert, but not this day. He had made this celebration possible, and we were polite. However, I did not introduce him to my new date. I had invited Bob with caution and asked that he keep a low profile because I didn't wish to upset Bert. Although Bert and I spoke only every other month or so about the children, and he had brought someone to the wedding, he still felt possessive about me. Bob sat at my table, but his presence there was unexplained. Quite a few of my single girlfriends were sitting near me, and he could have been with any one of them.

Mother met my first serious suitor in a long while with a casual hello. The bitter cold of a New York winter plus the long flight deflected some of her natural radar toward any change in my life. She did not know that this was the man who had taken me to Europe. I was deliberately discreet.

While Bert made the wedding celebration possible, I was able to contribute the flowers for the ceremony— all white for Trista's table, blue irises for mine, and, for each of the other tables, one color from every corner of the botanical paint box. Trista's bouquet of white lilies and freesia had some tiny pinecones scattered throughout in honor of Mr. Harry Cohen, the conifer with a cowboy hat.

Everyone danced at this gathering. Age, ability, and affluence were mere details. Different families specialize in different interests. Some prefer verbs and adverbs above all else. Mine loved the parts of speech but also treasured silence and motion. Watching them in action on the dance floor illustrated that anew to me. My mother, the woman who wanted to go dancing every night in Dallas with my father, received an invitation from Bert to come out and do a turn on the boards. Her face reflected her deep happiness.

Susannah, in blue velvet, danced in free-form style with a young man she had been seeing for quite a few years, and Bret brought Barbara, the woman with whom he lived and was going to marry.

And now Trista was in love with Eric and he with her. My children were capable of relationships. I was grateful. Like my own mother, I hoped I hadn't failed my offspring. Whatever my mistakes as a parent had been, my children seemed all right. I studied their faces. They looked happy. Susannah, once an editor, now had a job inventing clues to boggle the minds of crossword puzzle addicts. However, her greatest interests were painting and philosophy. Bret had become a cameraman for commercials and film and sometimes took directing assignments. My children had not been done in by having me as a mother. They seemed glad to have been born.

This was a wonderful day.

Four months later, in the spring of 1993, I visited California with Bob, and our first stop, direct from L.A. International, was my mother's apartment. She looked young and beautiful. We had not seen her since her trip east for Trista's wedding. She was thrilled to talk to Bob again. He delighted her because he had brought me to California.

"Bob, you look good," my mother said, exuding ebullience.

Bob took my mother's hand. "Allegra has become my personal trainer. I'm in much better shape than when you last saw me." Then, with a triumphant smile, he added, "And it wasn't that hard, except for constant hunger."

"Bob's eating tempo was too fast." I demonstrated rapid forkfuls of food entering the mouth. "So I slowed it down with a conductor's wave." My hands indicated a languid rhythm. "I became a Toscanini of the tiramisù, the tarragon, and the thyme. Bob is amazing. He didn't find that intrusive or insufferable."

Mother looked closely at Bob. She was weighing his soul. She really observed people, how they held their teacups—if their pinkies went up straight or curved like a comma. Mannerisms never escaped her scrutiny. The supersleuth was as sharp as ever. Bob passed her test.

I looked at my mother with pride. She was then eighty-seven and had very few possessions, but what she had, she kept in meticulous order. If she acquired too many dresses she immediately gave some away. She could move easily at the drop of a hat (preferably Harry's). She did not want to be burdened. Her eye for clothes and color was still excellent, and she loved to buy me whole wardrobes from the thrift shop in Santa Monica, where she now lived. She could still make something very enticing.

That day I needed to sew up a hole in my sweater, but she would not give me the needle; she wanted to do it. I had to beg and fight for the needle and thread. I saw afresh that she could imbue a small, regular task with theatrical suspense. She made me feel lucky when I finally got the needle from her.

The small scene reminded me of my mother's passion for change. She loved to vary a dress or piece of jewelry. The object might be almost right but need just a touch of alteration; if she did the work herself the results could be disastrous. She told me that as a child she had an obsession with cutting fabric. I tried it myself, particularly during sleepless nights, and found it exhilarating. Recreation or total destruction—the outcome was not always known. Like a gambler you could watch and hope.

Mother wondered if I was still taking ballet classes.

"Of course." I added, with a crisp intonation, "Do you remember what you once said to me?"

"Yes, I remember. It's not the classes that you take that make you a ballerina, but the ones you don't miss." Mother quoted her exact words with satisfaction and smiled.

I smiled back and told her, "Darling, you ruined me. Here I am at fifty-six still living by your motto and feeling terrible if I don't follow it."

"Allegra, you can forget that now. Travel, do what you like." She gave Bob a sly look while she said this.

When I gained her eye again, I said, "I can't. It's a compulsion. If I do skip a class, I feel I'm in the wrong place. It's the thing you felt when you took to the road and moved us across the country."

In a visit two years later I saw that one of my mother's prize possessions was her view of the ocean. She had moved to a better apartment within the complex. After setting her sights on this particular spot, she had been unrelenting in her efforts with the landlord. The reward was a small apartment with a huge vision of the sea, sky, and sunsets. Now, at eighty-nine, my mother was a kind of Jewish monk with a taste for exercise and reading. She had just hurt her back doing a yoga shoulder stand. It did not dawn on her that perhaps it was not wise to attempt such a thing at her age. She did not wish to accept limits.

As I think of my mother now, there are so many things about her to admire. I remember her love and appreciation of babies. Even when she just said hello to a tiny new person, she was extravagantly enthusiastic. It was as if she was saying, Who are you? Who will you be tomorrow? As a child, I had watched her plunge recklessly into the swim of cross-country currents as the star of her own travelogue. During the war years she was a determined heroine without a cash cushion to help erase mistakes. Yet lack of money never stopped her. As a single mother she constantly sought what was best for her children and herself.

Mother tried to save me from what she saw as dangers, and some of her fears weren't so far-fetched. I read in a newspaper of a teenage dancer who had a romance with an artistic director. The relationship placed enormous responsibility on her. In the young woman's desire for perfection, her body cracked, and she did not dance for two years. But just as a director's love could be a liability, so could a parent's. My mother may not have envisioned this particular aspect—love as a danger and a trap. Her main fear was an unseemly age discrepancy in the director-dancer relationship.

My desire to dance had been a serious decision. In Ojai, depressed and lonely, I had an insight into my own possibilities. And my message to Mother met with luck. Remembering her own childhood love of dance, she took me seriously; that was her style. My ballerina letter cast a magical spell over her. She jumped behind me, let me leave boarding school, and allowed me to take many, many classes a week, never saying, "You're a child, you don't know what you want. You must wait!" Also, Mother selected the very best teachers. If I had been the daughter of someone with less vision, I never could have been a ballerina. Other careers can and do start later, but not an athletic one.

My mother once wrote Trista a note saying she knew she had failed me. It was sad to hear this message relayed to me from my daughter. But the past was over. I could not change it. During the years since Aram's death I had had plenty of time to ponder my life as chief critic. When things had gone wrong over the years, it had been easy for me to blame Mother. I had expected life to pour forth and run like a well-rehearsed ballet: you do the work, and the designated choreography more or less happens. But this was not how it was. Life is unpredictable. The unexpected transpires. The music is often harsh. *Sleeping Beauty* with its glorious finale is not necessarily on the program.

What I regret is that it took so long for me to emerge into a somewhat normal person who could handle everyday life with easy grace. But it did happen. The fears of my childhood traveled with me transmogrified. Pins and needles, mosquitoes, and shrunken heads became stage fright and social withdrawal. My adolescence had lasted a little longer than expected—more than forty years. Two score and four.

On the second trip to visit Mother, I was preparing for a happy celebration. Bob and I had decided to marry.

• • •

While on holiday together after our marriage, Bob and I were invited to a Thanksgiving dinner on a secluded farm in Montgomery, Alabama. Three Priscillas from three generations were present; the oldest painted, the middle one—my friend—danced, and the youngest was in third grade. Two Quentins were there also, a senior and a junior. The younger one told us that there was a twenty-seven-day-old foal on the farm, a filly-to-be, very new to the world.

"I want to see her," I said, thinking in wonder about the miracle of a foal.

Quentin Jr. led us out to the barn, and there, behind a fence, was the little creature with her mother, Alice. She didn't walk; she pranced. Her hoofs went up lightly with a spirited spring. This was her inherent style. She didn't learn to do this; it was just there—always was and ever shall be. Her coloring was light mahogany with a white star on her forehead. I was in love.

Quentin told us that she didn't have a name yet. The middle Priscilla looked at me and said, "How about Allegra?"

All our eyes went to Quentin.

"That's perfect. Allegra it shall be."

I felt honored. Now there were two Allegras, and all together we had six legs—just as many as the three Priscillas. The little creature, an Arabian, cavorted and capered behind her mother, always keeping Alice between us and the fence. The name seemed to suit her. My spirit could race with her for sheer joy under a canopy of apricot clouds. She would always run on her toes. I looked closely. She seemed to be laughing, as Allegras are sometimes compelled to do. My friends told me they would never sell her. This made me happy. No one should ever sell an Allegra. And an Allegra can never be bought.

The classroom is still very important to me. It's a place where the luggage of life can be dropped. Nothing need be held in the hands. It's an improvisational game to play with rhythm and choreography. Class is the inspired input of teacher, pianist, and student, where secret discoveries can be made.

On a recent trip to Rome with Bob, the city was magnificent, but I wasn't. My body suffered from inactivity. So, one day, before the strolling, the museums, or the pasta, I sought a ballet fix.

I found myself in a huge subterranean dance studio. I tested the mirrors, located one that did not distort my proportions, and took a place nearby. While warming up, I watched the other dancers stretching. This group was at the age of elasticity and high extensions, not a rickety split in the room. But from experience I knew that limberness didn't necessarily mean dancing ability.

There had been some confusion about my entrance into this particular class. It was free if you had a contract. The young man at the desk had said, "For professionals with a contract." I didn't have a contract and hadn't even brought my union card with me.

"May I please pay for class?"

"No. It's free if you're a professional with a contract."

"Well, I've been a professional for over forty years."

When the teacher, a Russian, entered the studio, an older man rushed up to him, spoke rapidly in Italian, and then pointed in my direction. This unnerved me. I wondered if I should introduce myself but did nothing. Then class began. The teacher was not a very good dancer, but the combinations he gave were adequate. The pianist, however, was excellent—a gray-haired man with a witty take on the proceedings. Fellini would have liked him. Our instructor was in love with his booming voice. In this room he was commander-in-chief barking out orders. A top banana with power for an hour. I decided not to change any of the steps, just blend in. However, twenty minutes into the barre, when all was going well, I decided to extend one leg just a trifle while doing a port de bras. Immediately, the teacher screamed out, "If you are not professional and can't do the work, get out."

The shock of his shrieking dismissal jolted me. Should I hurl back some insults? How dare he? I was clearly professional. Here I was at the still tender age of fifty-seven being treated as an interloper. Had he detected a small mockery in my musicality—the clown in me playing with sound—or mental insubordination? Well, I was just being my usual anonymous self, but the teacher obviously thought I had insinuated myself into his class.

There was always a touch of Carmelita in me, the Spanish or flamenco dancer's inherent recalcitrant stance. In one dance, Carmelita, dressed in trousers, lifted her knee very high, then with a flick, knocked it down with the heel of her hand in an easy staccato gesture. This was the way to deal with injustice.

The resistance to authority, sometimes subtle, was one of my life's themes, but in this instance I was really behaving myself. A professional does alter steps so that he or she doesn't become injured. This Russian teacher might have detected Balanchine in my batterie, and that may have given him offense. The other dancers present were not that good, finesse was missing. I desired retribution but decided against it. Instead, I finished the barre in meticulous fashion, thought about the lovely star turns I would unveil when I returned to New York, and left.

Dancing well is the best revenge.

Afterword

Much has happened to me in the twelve years since this book was published yet one thing is the same: my life is still formed and framed by my devotion to dance—the art and craft. This passion engages the deepest and most playful parts of me, and so I continue to dance on my carpet at home and practice technique in the classroom while ever striving to learn more, discern more, and as always, listen to the music—its rhythms and mysterious messages.

I am forever grateful to Carmelita Maracci for her intuitive knowledge of where I should continue my studies, which brought my mother and me to the School of American Ballet and led to my professional entrance into the New York City Ballet. This was a rich time. I was exposed to Balanchine's choreographic genius, to music I had never heard before and dancers I had never seen before. I loved being in the corps de ballet, particularly as a monster in Firebird and a Fury in Orpheus, where I could wear Karinska's costumes and listen to Stravinsky's music. While watching and thinking of the future, I discovered structure and story telling in Mr. B's choreography. I also learned discipline—the practice of totally committing to that which is central in one's life.

I longed to become a ballerina and Balanchine helped me achieve that goal. A ballerina—the ultimate artificial feminine presence onstage who lingers in your memory forever. Most often she is seen on pointe in a stylized costume and in flawless makeup. However, Mr. B created roles for me slightly out of that tradition, roles in which I appeared in a white leotard, a transparent kimono, and in black underwear. And he let me commit all the deadly sins onstage—literally and figuratively.

Balanchine nurtured and encouraged me and gave me confidence, praise, and a degree of freedom to interpret his magnificent creations. He will always be etched in my memory. One day, after a rehearsal,

Mr. B told me that the night before he choreographed Divertimento #15, he spoke with Mozart. The ballet was a masterpiece. Mr. B chose me for the original cast, so Mozart could also speak to me. Being in the New York City Ballet in those extraordinary years enabled me to enter Balanchine's world of music and dance and to learn more about myself than I could have anywhere else.

I will always be grateful to my mother and her wandering spirit, her ability to make quick decisions and the phenomenal luck that brought us to the School of American Ballet. I still dream of those great teachers—especially the elegant Felia Dubrovska. Also gratitude to my father, who had a wild imagination and who taught me to see the natural world with wonder. A man of swift appraisals, he once let his children have a four-minute look at the Grand Canyon. I felt that was not enough, so I've extended that moment of watching nature—and later ballet—to over sixty years—with a bit more attention to detail.

I've had many adventures in the great game of ballet. Like all worthy games, it has structure, innovation, and spontaneity. It allows what is unique and individual in the player to flourish. Like a river, it can take surprising turns—it can be unruly and wild, yet contained within limits of form and direction. I love this union of wildness harnessed into clear form. I find this in nature, in dance, and in my children, Trista, Susannah, and Bret, and my lovely granddaughters Miranda and Georgia. Their originality, their keen observations and love of play inspires and delights me. These are the great treasures of my life: together with my sister, Wendy, and brother, Gary, my extended family, and my dear friends.

My fascination with ballet continues; with eager anticipation I watch and discover the continuing flow of great talent in the world of dance.

I toss bouquets on high with all my might to all those who helped me in dance, in writing, and in life.

Index

Allegra Kent was a leading dancer with the New York City Ballet for more than thirty years. She has coached principal roles in the Balanchine repertory with various companies, including Miami City Ballet and Pennsylvania Ballet She has written for Allure, New York Times Magazine, Dance Magazine, and Time Magazine. She is the author of Allegra Kent's Water Beauty Book, The Dancer's Body Book (with James and Constance Camner). A 2009 Dance Magazine honoree, she teaches at Barnard College/Columbia University.